Navy Priest

Navy Priest

The Life of Captain Jake Laboon, SJ

Richard Gribble, CSC

Foreword by Rear Admiral Barry C. Black, USN (Ret.)

The Catholic University of America Press
Washington, D.C.

Copyright © 2015
The Catholic University of America Press
All rights reserved

Design and typesetting by Kachergis Book Design

Library of Congress Cataloging-in-Publication Data
Gribble, Richard.
Navy priest : the life of Captain Jake Laboon, SJ / Richard Gribble, CSC ;
foreword by Rear Admiral Barry C. Black, USN (Ret.).
pages cm
Includes bibliographical references and index.
ISBN 978-0-8132-2725-2 (pbk.)   1. Laboon, Jake, 1921–1988.
2. United States. Navy—Chaplains—Biography.   3. United States. Navy—
Officers—Biography. 4. Military chaplains—United States—Biography.
5. Jesuits—United States—Biography.   6. United States. Navy—Submarine
forces—Biography.   7. Peto (SS-265 : Submarine)   8. Submariners—
United States—Biography.   9. World War, 1939–1945—Pacific Area.
10. Vietnam War, 1961–1975—Chaplains—Biography.   11. Leadership—
United States.   I. Title. II. Title: Life of Captain Jake Laboon, SJ.
VG23.G75 2015   2014038485
271'.5302—dc23
[B]

Dedication

In June 1971, one week after graduating from high school, I passed through Gate 1 at the United States Naval Academy for the first time, beginning an association with an institution and a group of men who have been highly influential in my life. Although I served only the required five years of active duty after graduating from the academy in June 1975, spending my service after initial training on the ballistic submarine USS *Thomas Edison* (SSBN-610 B), my time in the United States Navy continues to influence my life, even after spending twenty-five years as a Roman Catholic priest in the Congregation of Holy Cross. This book would not have been possible had not my life been strongly influenced by the values instilled in me by the naval academy and the friendships and challenges I received from those whom I encountered during my college days. It is appropriate, therefore, that this book be dedicated to the U.S. Naval Academy class of 1975, especially my immediate classmates in First Company with whom I graduated. I am indeed indebted to the positive influence of my alma mater and the fine men with whom I walked that road over forty years ago.

Contents

List of Illustrations	ix
Acknowledgments	xi
Foreword by Rear Admiral Barry C. Black, USN (Ret.)	xiii
List of Abbreviations	xv
Introduction	1
1. The Early Years: 1921–1940	9
2. Formation for Military Service—The U.S. Naval Academy: 1940–1943	36
3. World War II Submariner: 1943–1946	64
4. Formation for the Society of Jesus: 1946–1958	100
5. Fleet Ballistic Missile Submarine Chaplain: 1958–1961	129
6. Circuit Rider, Recruit Chaplain, and Alaska Pastor: 1961–1966	161
7. Return to the Naval Academy: 1966–1969	183
8. War Chaplain—Vietnam: 1969–1970	208
9. Florida, Hawaii, and New London Again: 1970–1976	239
10. Command Climax—Norfolk: 1976–1980	260
11. Jesuit Retreat Master and Pastor: 1981–1988	290
Epilogue: Jake Laboon—The Legacy	318
Bibliography	337
Index	349

Illustrations

Figure 3-1. Launching of USS *Peto*. Courtesy of Laboon family.   77

Figure. 3-2. Western Pacific operational area for U.S. submarines, including USS *Peto*, during World War II. http://www.ibiblio.org/hyperwar/USA/USA-C-WWII/maps/USA-WWII-2.jpg.   78

Figure 3-3. Jake Laboon with the officers of USS *Peto*. Courtesy of Laboon family.   81

Figure 4-1. Woodstock College. Courtesy of Archives of the Archdiocese of Baltimore, Associated Archives at St. Mary's Seminary and University.   109

Figure 4-2. Jake Laboon, ordination. Courtesy of Archives of the Archdiocese of Baltimore, Associated Archives at St. Mary's Seminary and University.   117

Figure 4-3. Jake Laboon with parents, younger brother, and sisters. Courtesy of Laboon family.   117

Figure 5-1. Commissioning of USS *George Washington*. Courtesy of U.S. Navy Submarine Force Museum.   155

Figure 8-1. Jake Laboon in Vietnam. Courtesy of Laboon family.   231

Figure 10-1. Jake Laboon and Admiral Harry Train, retirement ceremony. Courtesy of Laboon family.   285

Figure 10-2. Jake Laboon, retirement. Courtesy of Laboon family.   287

Figure 11-1. Manresa Retreat House. Courtesy of Archives of the Archdiocese of Baltimore, Associated Archives at St. Mary's Seminary and University.   297

Figure 11-2. Jake Laboon, with his brother and sisters at St. Alphonsus parish. Courtesy of Laboon family.   313

Figure E-1. USS *Laboon*. Courtesy of Laboon family.   331

Acknowledgments

Some twenty years ago, as a doctoral student at the Catholic University of America, I was contemplating ideas for a homily to be preached on Pentecost Sunday. The theme that came to my mind was one of commission: the commission that the Christian people were given by the Holy Spirit to go forth and evangelize the world. In thinking about how to introduce my theme, I discovered on the Internet, quite accidentally, the name of a Jesuit priest and Navy chaplain, John Francis Laboon, known to all his friends as Father Jake. I learned that he had been commissioned three times in his life: once to serve his country; a second time to serve his God; and the third time to serve both nation and God. He seemed to be an excellent example to introduce the theme of my homily. Captivated by his life, I conducted some additional research and wrote a short essay for a popular Catholic magazine about him.

Over the ensuing years, while I still periodically used Father Jake as an example when preaching on Pentecost, I never considered any further study about his life. Then one evening, while eating dinner with the priests with whom I live, one older gentleman, knowing that I had just completed a biographical study about a priest in western New York, casually asked, "Rick, what do you want to do next?" I responded saying simply, "I am not really sure." He pushed the issue a little further, challenging me, "Why not write on the Jesuit about whom you have periodically spoken?" I thought to myself, why not? He certainly seems worthy of a biographical study. From these rather distant and mundane roots this book arose. Three years of research on the life of this man of faith and action has led me to several different locations, numerous archives, and the opportunity to speak to dozens of people who knew and were highly influenced by Father Jake. At these places numerous people were extremely helpful in my quest for the information necessary to bring this project to a successful conclusion.

First and foremost, I need to thank the Laboon family. When I began my

Acknowledgments

research Father Jake had four surviving siblings: three sisters, all of whom are religious Sisters of Mercy—Sister deLellis, Sister Rosemary, and Sister Joan; and a younger brother, Joe, who is a retired priest from the Diocese of Pittsburgh. Since my initial meeting with these family members, Sister deLellis has passed to God. My sincere thanks go to them for their hospitality when hosting me and all the information they provided. Numerous archival repositories were searched, and several were of great significance. I wish to acknowledge with gratitude the assistance of John LaMartina, SJ, and Jim Casciotti, SJ, Jesuit priests who as archivist and provincial administrator, respectively, were instrumental in granting me access to Father Jake's Jesuit records. Captain Tierian (Randy) Cash, Chaplain Corps, USN, retired, archivist for the navy chaplain's records at Fort Jackson, South Carolina, assisted me in numerous ways, both during two visits to his facility and answering all sorts of questions via phone and electronic media. John Hodges at the Naval History Museum in Washington, D.C., also assisted in personal visits and by sending me various records electronically. Dr. Jennifer Bryan, archivist at the U.S. Naval Academy, was instrumental in allowing me access to Father Jake's records as a midshipman, as well as numerous other sources within her special collection section of the Nimitz Library. Dr. Tricia Pyne, archivist for the Archdiocese of Baltimore, assisted me with records that dealt with the last eight years of Father Jake's ministry, when he returned to the Society of Jesus at the conclusion of his navy career. Last, I would like to thank Wendy Gulley, archivist for the New London Submarine Base, who provided valuable information about Father Jake's first, and one of the most significant, assignments in his navy career. Additionally, this project could never have been completed without the cooperation of numerous people whom I interviewed, either personally or on the phone. I would like to especially acknowledge the family of Admiral Isaac Kidd and numerous members of the U.S. Naval Academy class of 1968. I wish also to acknowledge those who read my manuscript and made important suggestions for corrections and change: Dr. Christopher Kauffman, professor emeritus from the Catholic University of America; Dr. Jim Kenneally, professor emeritus from Stonehill College; and the aforementioned Randy Cash. I am also deeply grateful to Rev. Barry Black, rear admiral, Chaplain Corps, USN, retired, presently the chaplain of the United States Senate, who volunteered to write the foreword for this book as a labor of love for a man whom he greatly respected.

Foreword

Chaplain Jake Laboon, a servant leader, has blessed my life and ministry. In my early ministry as a navy chaplain, he defined the vision and mission for the U.S. Atlantic Fleet, where I worked. His monthly meetings with the chaplains provided opportunities to be mentored and receive assistance as we wrestled with challenges that threatened to overwhelm us. Jake opened doors in the community for me to preach in pluralistic settings of religious diversity. He gave me my first opportunity to preach in a Roman Catholic church, one of the few times a Seventh-Day Adventist has had that privilege.

Early in my career I received what I thought was an unfair evaluation from my supervisory chaplain. Chaplain Laboon came to my aid. After thoroughly investigating the matter to find the facts, he gave me the option of either telling him what to do or permitting him to handle it his way. I opted for the latter strategy, trusting him to do what was best, and he didn't disappoint me. His efforts not only solved my problem, but helped to catapult my career to splendid heights that I never anticipated.

Jake Laboon is one of the few Americans to have a U.S. Navy ship named in his honor. His passion for God, his commitment to his church, his love for the marginalized, and his visionary leadership create a story that thousands should know. I'm grateful for Richard Gribble's book because those who read it will get to know my friend and a great American, Jake Laboon. He served God's purposes in his generation, providing me with a friendship and model of excellence that enabled me to eventually become the chief of chaplains for the U.S. Navy and the 62nd chaplain of the United States Senate.

Rear Admiral Barry C. Black, USN (Ret),
Chaplain, United States Senate

Abbreviations

AABa	Archives, Archdiocese of Baltimore, Baltimore, Md.
AAM	Archives, Archdiocese of the Military, Washington, D.C.
AANY	Archives, Archdiocese of New York, Yonkers, N.Y.
ACUA	Archives, The Catholic University of America, Washington, D.C.
AGU	Archives, Georgetown University, Washington, D.C.
ASBNL	Archives, Submarine Base New London, New London, Conn.
ASJM	Archives, Maryland Province of Jesuits, Baltimore, Md.
AUSNA	Archives, United States Naval Academy, Annapolis, Md.
GLNSL	Great Lakes Naval Station Library, Great Lakes, Ill.
NAAA	Naval Academy Athletic Association Records
NAM	National Archives, Maryland Branch, College Park, Md.
NCA	Navy Chaplains Archives, Fort Jackson, S.C.
NCWC	National Catholic Welfare Council
NHM	Naval History Museum, Washington, D.C.
NMPR	National Military Personnel Records, St. Louis, Mo.
PPJDA	Personal Papers of J. David Atwater, Chapel Hill, N.C.
PPJL	Personal Papers of Sr. Joan Laboon, RSM, Pittsburgh, Pa.
PPJM	Personal papers of Joe Maloy, Bridgeville, Pa.
PPJoL	Personal papers of Fr. Joseph Laboon, Lakeland, Fla.
PPMW	Personal papers of Michael Walsh, Wilkes-Barre, Pa.
PPNW	Personal papers of Neil Werthmann, Millersville, Md.
PPRL	Personal papers of Sr. Rosemary Laboon, RSM, Pittsburgh, Pa.
PPWC	Personal papers of Walter Chadwick, Hooversville, Pa.
PPWL	Personal papers of William Laboon, Greensburg, Pa.
SACR	St. Alphonsus Rodriguez Church Records, Woodstock, Md.
SFM	U.S. Navy Submarine Force Museum, New London, Conn.

Navy Priest

Introduction

The small town of Woodstock, Maryland, had never seen anything like it. The famous and the prominent from both church and state had come together on a hot but dry August day to bid farewell to a priest, naval officer, mentor, brother, and friend. Together with this cadre of American elites were hundreds of ordinary parishioners at the small church of St. Alphonsus Rodriguez who also came to pay their respects to their pastor. Although not long in their presence, he had nonetheless endeared himself to all because of his great faith, solid example of a positive life, and many expressions of love. It was August 4, 1988, and Father John Francis Laboon Jr., a faithful and proud member of the Society of Jesus, was being honored with a funeral Mass and a humble burial with his fellow Jesuits in a small cemetery adjacent to the site of his theological education. This was totally appropriate based on his simple lifestyle, which always sought the greater glory and honor of God. Father Jake, as he was known to all his friends, died at the age of sixty-seven, relatively young by today's standards, but his multiple and significant accomplishments affected thousands of sailors and marines who were touched by his ministry.

How was it possible that members of Congress, numerous active duty and retired admirals and generals, and other high ranking officers, as well as five Roman Catholic bishops, numerous priests, and hundreds of parishioners gathered in this isolated spot to say goodbye to a 6'5" cigar-smoking priest? The answer to this poignant question is the subject of this work. Jake Laboon, referred to as a "man among men" and a "priest among priests" by many of his contemporaries, had a special gift of authenticity. We are fortunate in life if we encounter an individual whose physical presence, spiritual leadership and guidance, and charismatic personality overpower us in positive ways. This was the experience of those who crossed the path of Father Jake. Physically tall and athletic, he possessed a gentle spirit and disposition.

Jake Laboon: Jesuit and Chaplain

John Francis Laboon Jr. was a rough-and-tumble man who came from Pittsburgh, Pennsylvania, part of America's industrial heartland. Born in 1921, he was raised during the era of the Great Depression in a large family of nine children, of which he was the oldest boy. The Laboons were fortunate, however, that their father had a secure position as director of public works for Allegheny County that kept at bay much of the economic hardship suffered by millions of Americans. Not overly religious as a boy, although, as with his whole family, completely faithful to the church and its traditions, Jake was educated in the local Catholic schools, graduating from Central Catholic High School, where he was a fine student who excelled on the football field.

Jake left Pittsburgh in the summer of 1940 to begin an adventure in the United States Navy that would dominate the rest of his life. The first step was his entrance to the United States Naval Academy as a member of the class of 1944. The almost legendary status that Laboon achieved in life began on the grounds of the academy, known as the Yard, where he built a cadre of friends, especially through his heroics on the football and lacrosse fields. The faith element of his life, which had been planted securely in his youth, was exercised through his participation in the Newman Club and active assistance at St. Mary's Parish in Annapolis. Jake graduated from the naval academy in June 1943, one year earlier than planned, due to the accelerated program necessary during the World War II years at West Point, Annapolis, and the Coast Guard Academy in New London, Connecticut. With his desire to enter the war keen in his mind, Jake shunned his first service selection of aviation, since the training period was long and would delay his entry into the war, choosing submarines instead. Thus after his initial training he was sent west to Pearl Harbor to his one and only World War II assignment, USS *Peto* (SS-265). Laboon completed five war patrols, gaining war-hero status when in late July 1945 he rescued a downed American aviator off the coast of Japan and was awarded the Silver Star for valor.

At the conclusion of the war, Jake Laboon's first commission in the navy was transformed into a new opportunity to serve. Answering a call from God, he resigned his commission in the navy and entered the Society of Jesus, or Jesuits. After a lengthy period of religious formation he was ordained a priest in June 1956. Two years later he combined his duties to country and God by reentering the navy as a chaplain. Beginning in New London, Connecticut, Jake began an illustrious twenty-two-year career as a chaplain by being the first priest to be assigned to the new Fleet Ballistic Missile Submarine (SSBN) program. Jake rose through the ranks, serving several navy and Marine Corps communities across the globe. Along the road he touched the lives of thousands of sailors and marines. While all were equal in his sight, he certainly had great fondness for "white hats," the enlisted men and women who form the backbone of the navy. Jake served the navy well and was recognized for his efforts. One senior reporting officer stated, "When judged by all standards of professional excellence he [wa]s an outstanding chaplain."[1]

The navy was important to Laboon, but principally as a manifestation of his priesthood. The dual commission, to country and to church, was evident in a comment Jake once made: "I would not have become a chaplain if I did not think it was important to the young sailor and marine to remind him of his religious background and beliefs."[2] Those who knew Father Laboon saw him as "outgoing ... very committed to the men and women in uniform. He was fair, but a no-nonsense priest and mentor."[3] During a career that included literally thousands of ministerial experiences, Jake more and more saw the navy as his home. He once told a reporter when stationed in Hawaii, "The Navy gets into your blood. We say at the U.S. Naval Academy they fill you with blue and gold injections."[4] His commissions as naval officer and priest were, for Jake Laboon, wrapped together with the bond of commitment. When serving as a recruit chaplain at the Naval Training Center in Great Lakes, Illinois, he wrote:

---

1. CDR John Laboon, fitness report, May 7, 1968, Laboon file, National Military Personnel Records (hereafter NMPR), St. Louis, Mo.
2. Clipping from the *Navy Chaplain*, July 14, 1995, Laboon file, Archives Maryland Province of Jesuits (hereafter ASJM), Baltimore, Md.
3. Ed Snyder, e-mail to author, December 6, 2010.
4. Clipping, *Honolulu Advertiser*, n.d., Laboon file, Archives United States Naval Academy (hereafter AUSNA), Annapolis, Md.

Introduction

As the needle of the compass is not at rest until it points to the North Pole, so too my conscience is not at rest until it has developed a dedication to the service. This is the secret of the contented soul within the Armed Forces. It is the secret of all who have made great, perhaps heroic, sacrifices for the love of country. On the contrary, where men refuse to surrender themselves to the cause, the winter of their discontent lies cold upon their very personality. There is no complete peace or alloyed happiness.[5]

The dedication that marked the life and ministry of Jake Laboon is wrapped into the legacy he left behind.

Retirement from the navy in 1980 brought Jake back to the Jesuits. Physically far from but always psychologically close to the Society, he had never considered himself an outsider in his religious community. He brought his priesthood, which meant his Jesuit training and life, to his ministry in the navy. Thus after a brief sabbatical he returned to a familiar geographic location, Annapolis, to serve as minister at Manresa-on-Severn, a Jesuit retreat house within sight of the naval academy. Primarily responsible for the physical overhaul of the facility, but assisting with retreats as well, Jake endeared himself to those he served, utilizing the same personality and talents that brought him legendary status in the navy. Jake then moved on to St. Alphonsus Rodriguez, a small rural parish in Woodstock, Maryland, near where he had received his theological training. He served as pastor at St. Alphonsus for almost four years until death claimed him, a victim of esophageal cancer. Shunning the privilege offered him to be buried at the naval academy, he chose instead to lie with his Jesuit brothers near the site of the old Woodstock theologate.

Jake Laboon possessed a certain philosophy of life that characterized his priesthood. Dedication was central to his life; he was never willing to give less than 110 percent to any endeavor. His ability to achieve more than most of his contemporaries was drawn from this basic philosophy. A close friend, Monsignor Robert Ecker, who served with Jake in Vietnam and preached the eulogy at his funeral, described Laboon's philosophy: "If you are going to play the game, you play to win. That is the way he approached the priesthood; that is the way he approached his whole interpretation of life. You play to win. That is why he was so strong."[6] Laboon also realized that life is

---

5. *Great Lakes Bulletin*, September 18, 1964, Great Lakes Naval Station Library (hereafter GLNSL), Great Lakes, Ill.

6. Robert Ecker, interview with author, December 17, 2010.

not a straight and uncluttered journey, but rather is an excursion where we encounter obstacles, detours, and barriers of various kinds that can wound and inflict significant pain. One family friend described how Jake's philosophy aided him in his own journey of life:

> I see him as a cardinal navigational aid to keep us off the rocks and to make sure we do not spend a lot of time feeling sorry for ourselves about the circumstances we happen to be in. In other words, play hurt.[7]

Indeed, Jake Laboon was a pillar of strength, a guiding light for many because of his absolute dedication.

Jake Laboon in History

While in the history of the United States military there have been many prominent and well-appreciated navy chaplains, few have reached the stature and legacy of Jake Laboon. Respected by all he encountered, Jake became an almost iconic figure in the Chaplain Corps. The combination of his naval academy training and World War II experience as a line officer provided him the proper resumé he needed to be accepted by the vast majority of personnel he encountered. He walked in the same shoes of the people to whom he ministered and thus understood many of their feelings and difficulties. His knowledge of the navy system and friendship with many prominent officers, several of whom he knew from the academy, both as a student and a chaplain, gave him entrée where others could not go, allowing him to accomplish more than his contemporaries. This broad experience, when combined with his special gifts for ministry, gregarious personality, and physical stature, molded an individual who was universally acclaimed as special. This "superstar" status within the Chaplain Corps was clearly evidenced by the testimony of many who claimed they knew Jake Laboon even before meeting him; his reputation preceded him. One retired navy chaplain, Rabbi Bruce Kahn, when speaking about the perceived rivalry between Jake and John O'Connor, who was later chief of chaplains and cardinal archbishop of New York, stated, "O'Connor was respected, but Jake was loved."[8]

The iconic status of Jake Laboon and his material legacy mark his life as

---

7. Christopher Kidd, interview with author, August 4, 2010.
8. Bruce Kahn, interview with author, August 3, 2011.

Introduction

significant. His ability to find acceptance in all circles, from white hats (enlisted personnel) to four-star admirals, and his broad experience in various navy venues make his life noteworthy. Moreover, his death did not end his influence; his many friends would not allow his legacy to die. The commissioning in 1995 of USS *Laboon* (DDG-58), only the seventh ship named after a navy chaplain, testifies to his reputation. The opening in 1995 of the Laboon Ministry Center at the naval academy added to his legacy and further demonstrates the importance of his life.

This biography fills a lacuna in historical literature by providing the life story of one of the most prominent navy chaplains of the twentieth century. Scholarly literature, especially biographical studies of United States military chaplains, is limited. The nine-volume *History of the Chaplain Corps*, published by the Navy Department, is the most extensive general history of navy chaplains. Studies of chaplains, especially memoirs, of the Civil War era include John Brinsfield's *Faith in the Fight: Civil War Chaplains* and *The Spirit Divided: Memoirs of Civil War Chaplains: The Union*. Personal accounts of chaplains serving in Vietnam, such as Curt Bowers's *Forward Edge of the Battle Area: A Chaplain's Story* and Cardinal John O'Connor's *A Chaplain Looks at Vietnam*, are also available. *Chaplains with Marines in Vietnam 1962–1971*, by Herbert Bergsma, provides additional information concerning this vexing period of U.S. military history. The sociological and moral aspects of a chaplain's service have been addressed by Harvey Cox in *Military Chaplains: From Religious Military to a Military Religion*, Stephen Mansfield in *The Faith of the American Soldier*, Peter French in *War and Moral Dissonance*, and S. K. Moore in *Military Chaplains as Agents of Peace: Religious Leaders Engagement in Conflict and Post-Conflict Environments*. The limited biographical studies include Stephen Harris, *Duffy's War: Fr. Francis Duffy, Wild Bill Donovan and the Irish Fighting 69th in World War I*. The story of George Fox, Clark Polling, John Washington, and Alexander Goode, the four chaplains lost on one ship, is told in Dan Kurzman's study *No Greater Glory: The Four Immortal Chaplains and the Sinking of the Dorchester in World War II*. William Maher tells the story of Chaplain Emil Kapaun during the Korean War in *A Shepherd in Combat Boots*. The brief life of Maryknoll father Vincent Capodonno, who earned the Congressional Medal of Honor in Vietnam, is told by Daniel Mode in *The Grunt Padre*.

This book was generated through the examination of extensive primary and secondary sources. Primary sources for this work were abundant in variety but limited in scope. Jake's complete navy personnel file, including all of his fitness reports (evaluations) from senior officers in his command, provided an excellent base to understand the various assignments where he served. Additional military records were available at the Navy Chaplain Corps Archives at Fort Jackson, South Carolina, the Naval History Museum at the Washington, D.C. Navy Yard, and the National Archives. These repositories held the war patrol reports of USS *Peto*, as well as invaluable contextual information on the Chaplain Corps and naval commands where Laboon served. It was hoped that records from various chaplains' offices at the bases where he served would be preserved at branch offices of the National Archives geographically closest to the navy facility, but an extensive search found that these records were either purged or, due to the private nature of their content, destroyed. Additionally, it was a disappointment to learn that many records held by the Archdiocese of the Military, transferred from New York to their present location in Washington, D.C., were either lost in the move or were not open to researchers. To document Laboon's Jesuit life the Archives of the Maryland Province of Jesuits and Georgetown University Archives were used. Records and information at St. Alphonsus Rodriguez parish in Woodstock, Maryland, were also consulted. Seventy-five interviews were conducted with numerous people, including members of his family, fellow Jesuits, some significant friends, and former senior navy and Marine Corps officers.

This book seeks to place the life of Jake Laboon within the historical context of church and country. Thus numerous secondary sources were consulted to situate him within the time and the events of his life, which spanned the Great Depression and the end of the Cold War. His birth and early years in Pittsburgh during the Great Depression had a strong influence on his life. Laboon's participation in the submarine war of the Pacific theater marked his future as a chaplain. He lived through the great transition of the Second Vatican Council, which was transformative for Catholics worldwide. Indeed, Laboon witnessed the evolution of American Catholicism from its perception as elitist to the more ecumenical ideas of Vatican II. His tour in Vietnam began in the wake of the 1968 Tet Offensive and ended with America's failed Vietnamization policy. In the process he successfully responded to the moral and social needs of the men caught in the midst of a very unpopular war.

Introduction

When the USS *Laboon* was launched at Bath Iron Works in February 1993, Cardinal John O'Connor, the archbishop of New York, former navy chief chaplain, and a longtime friend of Jake, referred to him as "a man for all seasons." O'Connor unquestionably used this metaphor, drawn from the title of Robert Bolt's famous stage play that depicts the life of St. Thomas More and his bold defense of the Catholic faith against King Henry VIII in sixteenth-century England, to draw a comparison between his friend and a great man of history. Comfortable in every environment and with all manner of people, Jake, during his naval career and priesthood, demonstrated that he truly was a man for all seasons. The challenge for readers is to ask if the qualities manifested by Father Jake Laboon are present in one's own life, as well. The climb to achieve such a goal may be difficult and steep, but it will be worth all of our efforts.

Chapter 1

The Early Years

* 1921–1940

In religion and society relationships flow from the context—physical, social, religious, and familial—in which people are born and raised. The physical environment that influenced the life of John Francis Laboon Jr. was formative in ways that were both obvious and subtle. Pittsburgh, today a bustling metropolitan city of approximately 305,000, the largest urban center in Western Pennsylvania, was the basic physical environment that he experienced in his early years. The city, set on a plateau to the west of the northern reaches of the Appalachian Mountains, is located at the confluence of three great rivers: the Allegheny, Monongahela, and Ohio. This region is divided by ravines formed by warped sedimentary rock that at one time was the home of large beds of bituminous coal. Like most major metropolitan regions throughout the world, the geography of Pittsburgh forms the base upon which the city's reputation and financial livelihood developed. The physical divisions of the area, created by the flow of the rivers, produced an environment that in many ways influenced the history of the region, both secular and sacred. Indeed, historian Timothy Kelly has commented, "This topographical setting has shaped the experiences of the area's residents in powerful ways and no less the Church's experiences."[1] Most urban dwellers find themselves seeking ways to socially separate themselves or identify their ethnicity, common heritage, or religious preference. Pittsburghers,

---

1. Timothy Kelly, "Pittsburgh Catholicism," *U.S. Catholic Historian* 18, no. 4 (Fall 2006): 64, 66.

separated by physical geography, needed to find ways to build bridges, not only physically, but socially among neighborhoods. Despite the physical constraints, they found a way to live in heterogeneous neighborhoods filled with a variety of ethnic and religious groups, all knitted together in island neighborhoods.

The City of Pittsburgh: A Historical Overview

Pittsburgh's geographic location and physical features were important elements in the city's early history. The first Europeans to come to the region were mostly fur trappers and traders. Arriving in the first quarter of the eighteenth century, they found the physical environment helpful both for their livelihood and as a possible place for permanent settlement. The area's vast resources, especially its transportation waterways, made it an ideal central location for trade. Products could be easily transported to areas as far away as New Orleans and several other cities along the paths of the rivers. In 1753, when American colonists became alarmed by French incursions into this region, Major George Washington was sent by the lieutenant governor of Virginia, Robert Dunwiddie, to survey the region of Pittsburgh to possibly use for military defense. In his report to Dunwiddie, Washington stated:

I spent some Time in viewing the Rivers, and the Land in the Fork; which I think extremely well-suited for a Fort, as it has absolute command of both Rivers. The Land at the Point is 20 or 25 Feet above the common surface of the Water; any considerable Bottom or flat, well-timbered Land all around it, [is] very convenient for Building.[2]

One year later, in 1754, Washington's favorable report became the catalyst for the British to build a makeshift structure, Fort King George, at the confluence of the Monongahela and Allegheny rivers. In less than a month, however, the French, with a vastly superior military force, captured the facility. From 1754 to 1758 the French flag flew over Fort Duquesne. In 1758, after regaining control of the region, the British built Fort Pitt at the same confluence point. The Fort was often attacked by native peoples in the region, but was never taken in battle. After the Treaty of Paris ending the Seven Years'

---

2. Quoted in Richard C. Wade, *The Urban Frontier: The Rise of Western Cities, 1790–1830* (Cambridge, Mass.: Harvard University Press, 1959), 8–9.

War (French and Indian War in the United States), was signed in 1763, Colonel John Campbell laid out four square blocks, giving Pittsburgh its first basic physical plan. It was a region that held the rich promise of becoming an industrial center with its rich supply of iron ore and coal and with its rivers providing transportation and water power. Yet Pittsburgh's population growth was rather slow. In 1790 a local census listed only 376 residents; in 1800 the population had risen to 1,565. Still, as early as 1814, the *Niles Register*, in a prophetic comment, reported, "Pittsburgh, sometimes emphatically called the 'Birmingham of America,' will probably become the greatest manufacturing town in the world."[3] When the War of 1812 concluded and the nascent American society could finally grow with little fear of outside intervention, the town was home to 8,000 residents, surpassing the population of Lexington, Kentucky, and making it the largest town in the American West. Indeed, the American historian Richard Wade has commented, "By 1815 Pittsburgh ... was unchallenged in importance."[4] The city, incorporated on March 18, 1816, began to manifest some of its defining characteristics, especially commerce and manufacturing and with it the unpleasant reality of a constant cloud of coal dust. At the outset of the Civil War Pittsburgh had grown to a population of 49,000.

The second half of the nineteenth century was the period when the city became identified as Steel Town U.S.A. One Pittsburgh historian, John Swauger, commented,

In the early 19th century Pittsburgh was a non-industrial town dependent on unmechanized transportation. During the next 50 years the city witnessed remarkable technological progress attended by advancements in transportation and development in industrial residential patterns.[5]

Indeed, by 1870 Pittsburgh had become a heavy-industry metropolis, a total urban industrial landscape. Between 1880 and 1900 Pittsburgh became the largest steel producer in the country; by the turn of the century the city produced 50 percent of the nation's open-hearth steel, 40 percent of all steel, and over 50 percent of coke.[6]

   3. Ibid., 46.
   4. Ibid., 10–11, 43, 48–49.
   5. John Swauger, "Pittsburgh's Residential Pattern in 1815," *Annals of the Association of American Geographers* 68, no. 2 (June 1978): 267.
   6. Sylvester K. Stevens, "The Hearth of the Nation," in *Pittsburgh: The Story of an American City*, edited by Stefan Lorant, 178 (Garden City, N.Y.: Doubleday, 1964).

The Early Years: 1921–1940

The city's ascendancy to a position of an industrial giant helped to solidify its place in the ever-expanding and more complex American economy. Wade accurately expressed this idea. Describing the city's longevity as still youthful, he nonetheless marveled at its potential for manufacturing. He went on to state how Pittsburgh became "an important link in the mercantile chain that bound Eastern cities to the frontier, and yet [simultaneously] became a manufacturing center of increasing importance in the West."[7]

Pittsburgh's rise as an industrial metropolis initiated a demographic shift in the city's population. As with other metropolitan areas, but especially those of the industrial North, Pittsburgh during the Gilded Age and early Progressive Era, approximately 1880 to 1910, experienced a massive influx of immigrants from Southern and Eastern Europe. In what many historians of immigration in the United States have classified as the first great wave of immigration, 1820 to 1860, new arrivals to the country were mostly from Western and Northern Europe. After a twenty-year lull due to the Civil War, during the second wave of immigration, 1880 to 1924, peoples from Eastern and Southern Europe predominated. This demographic shift was manifested in Pittsburgh. For example, in 1880 approximately 25 percent of the population was foreign-born, but only 1 percent were from Eastern or Southern Europe. By 1910, however, 50 percent of the city's immigrant population was from these latter regions.[8]

Pittsburgh's reputation as a steel city was well earned, but its manufacturing base was broader. Indeed, other coal products, especially glass, actually predated steel. The production of kegs and barrels was also important to the city. This tripartite manufacturing agenda became the boom industries in the city, providing jobs for immigrants and giving fuel to the engine that would drive the city's progress forward for nearly the next half century.[9] Immigrant historians John Bodnar, Roger Simon, and Michael Weber succinctly summarized how the city was viewed at the dawn of the twentieth century: "Pittsburgh is the quintessential symbol of the American industrial city."[10]

7. Wade, *Urban Frontier*, 43, 45.
8. June Granatir Alexander, *The Immigrant Church and Community: Pittsburgh's Slovak Catholics and Lutherans, 1880–1915* (Pittsburgh: University of Pittsburgh Press, 1987), xvii–xviii.
9. Kelly, "Pittsburgh Catholicism," 65, 72; Stevens, "Hearth of the Nation," 178.
10. John Bodnar, Roger Simon, and Michael P. Weber, *Lives of Their Own: Blacks, Italians, and Poles in Pittsburgh, 1900–1960* (Urbana: University of Illinois Press, 1982), 13.

The Early Years: 1921–1940

While Pittsburgh experienced its meteoric rise within the nation's industrial complex, the city could in many ways be described by the title of British novelist Charles Dickens's famous work *A Tale of Two Cities*. The significant progress that brought Pittsburgh to a position of prominence within the nation's rapidly increasing industrialized environment created some weighty and undesired consequences. Acknowledging Pittsburgh's positive image as an emerging powerhouse of American industrialism, historian Anthony Penna articulated a growing problem: "Pittsburgh's rapid industrialization and urbanization accentuated its image as a great workshop and minimized the significance of the city's smoky conditions." More directly, quoting the late nineteenth-century author, soldier, and explorer Willard Glazier, who visited Pittsburgh in 1883, Penna writes,

> The smoke sinks and mingling with the moisture in the air, becomes ... a consistency which may almost be felt as well as seen. In truth, Pittsburgh is a smoky, dismal city at her best.[11]

By the early twentieth century many social critics referred to Pittsburgh as a human as well as a physical "inferno."[12] The famous muckraking journalist Lincoln Steffens described the city in a physical sense as "Hell with the lid off."[13] Despite the physical blight of smoke, soot, and fouled air produced by the steel and coke mills, the city still maintained a certain charm. Acknowledging the city's problems, historian Sylvester Stevens painted a more equitable picture:

> Though the city was smoky and dirty and its streets were crooked and poorly paved, it had a beauty of its own. The smokestacks against the red sky, the curving rivers with their steel-girdered bridges conjured a romantic picture. It was the landscape of the workshop, the greatest in the world, a workshop which supplied the railroads with rails, bridges and locomotives, shipyards with steel plates, factories with heavy machinery, telephone, telegraph and electric companies with wires, and which also furnished the tools and implements, the hardware and much of the farm and industrial machinery that went to the growth of the West.[14]

---

11. Anthony N. Penna, "Changing Images of Twentieth-Century Pittsburgh," *Pennsylvania History* 43, no. 1 (January 1976): 50, 49.

12. Roy Lubove, *Twentieth-Century Pittsburgh: Government, Business, and Environmental Change* (New York: Wiley, 1969), 1.

13. Quoted in Gerald W. Johnson, "The Muckraking Era," in Lorant, *Pittsburgh*, 261.

14. Stevens, "Hearth of the Nation," 177.

The Early Years: 1921–1940

The pollution that painted the city with a perpetual charcoal gray glaze and often blocked the sun's normal intensity was accompanied with significant social problems. Anthony Penna suggests that while Pittsburgh, both its political leaders and ordinary citizens, marveled at the city's rise to industrial prominence, other important aspects of daily life were ignored. He writes, "While stressing an image of the city as the workshop, the social well-being of its citizens and the protection of the physical environment was virtually ignored."[15] In the early twentieth century clearly the most prominent issue for the city was its losing battle against Prohibition. The social historian Stefan Lorant has commented, "Prohibition was probably a greater nuisance in Pittsburgh than anywhere else."[16]

Social unrest was closely allied with the general and more widespread battle waged by organized labor. The latter years of the Gilded Age, and especially the succeeding Progressive Era, saw a significant rise in the fortunes and power of organized labor in the United States. Yet, in Pittsburgh and other locations, organized labor's lack of efficacy in its efforts to secure workers' rights was painfully obvious. The infamous Homestead Strike of 1892, where the industrial tycoon Andrew Carnegie managed to smash organized labor, was a constant reminder of how far organized labor still had to go to achieve its ends.[17] However, Pittsburgh's labor leaders began to achieve success. Indeed, Pittsburgh historian Gerald Johnson has written, "By the turn of the century ... public sympathy with labor was becoming generalized and formidable."[18]

Pittsburgh's industrial rise, while driven by the engines of steel and glass mills and with natural resources to feed them, was fueled by the flood of immigrants who poured into the city to work the factories that produced products for which the city had become famous. This influx continued unabated until the immigration and restriction laws of 1921 and 1924 set severe quotas that in effect closed America's golden door to outsiders. In

---

15. Penna, "Changing Images," 53.
16. Lorant, "Between Two Wars," in Lorant, *Pittsburgh*, 333.
17. The Homestead Strike, which began on June 30, 1892, was an action by the Amalgamated Association of Iron and Steel Workers in conflict with Andrew Carnegie and U.S. Steel. On July 6, a battle between strikers and police resulted in several deaths and many injuries. The event was a major defeat for organized labor. The full story of the strike is provided in Arthur G. Burgoyne, *The Homestead Strike of 1892* (Pittsburgh: University of Pittsburgh Press, 1979).
18. Gerald W. Johnson, "Muckraking Era," 270.

Pittsburgh this immigrant influx was largely from Hungary and Slovakia, where a depression in 1870 thwarted an incipient movement toward industrialization. Simultaneously problems arose in the agricultural sector of the nations. Landless peasants and those with little or no work were ripe for emigration, especially to the United States, where markets were expanding and industrialization was booming. Economic conditions were not the only cause for the arrival of workers. Indeed, as the immigrant historian June Alexander has pointed out, seasonal migration was part of the equation. Many who arrived only planned to stay temporarily.[19]

The income for many of these immigrants, despite the availability of work, was low, a situation consistent with the general obstructions to organized labor. The ability of big steel and corporate power to repress workers was strengthened by the support of local police, state troopers, and even hundreds of vigilantes. Declaring themselves 100 percent American, these nativist groups also worried about the rising immigrant population. For the immigrants, surging numbers themselves brought no pathway to a better life. As Pittsburgh historian Frances Couvares, commenting on the future of the rights of immigrants and organized labor, has written:

In a city so dominated by Big Steel, where organized labor and the Democratic Party remained unusually weak until the Great Depression, the path to that future was narrow and less certain than in many other places.[20]

Pittsburgh's industrial rise brought not only many immigrants to the city, but their religious traditions, as well. For Roman Catholicism the immigrant influence was very powerful. The industrial magnet that drew workers to the city shaped Catholicism's presence in the region. In the city as well as in the rest of the country there was a close association of immigration with religion. In a general sense, for Roman Catholics, this desire was manifested in the creation of national parishes. These faith communities, based on ethnic or national origins, isolated themselves in many ways from others of the same generic faith. While Latin, the language of the church, was the norm in all communities, national churches used the vernacular whenever

---

19. Alexander, *Immigrant Church*, 7–8. As one piece of evidence to support her claim, the author points out that at least 19 percent of Slovaks who came to the United States between 1899 and 1910 had been in the country previously.

20. Frances G. Couvares, *The Remaking of Pittsburgh: Class and Culture in an Industrializing City, 1877–1919* (Albany, N.Y.: SUNY Press, 1984), 127, 130.

possible. Clergy native to the particular group were always preferred by the people. Thus it was no surprise that Slovak immigrants to Pittsburgh, who were closely allied with Lithuanians, including the Laboon family, transplanted their faith in the city. On the more spiritual level this meant a strong sense of devotionalism in daily worship and practice.[21] The laity accepted the local bishop's authority, which was the norm in Europe. Concerned that immigrants might lose their faith to the predominant Protestant majority, American bishops labored to keep immigrants within parish and diocesan structures. This practice did not require Slovak Catholics to fundamentally alter their system of religious practice, but rather gave them the structural safety net that allowed them to build their own communities. Thus in an assertive way Slovaks established national churches that acted to mirror their own communities, leading to a greater development of institutional structure. The mother Slovak parish in Pittsburgh was St. Elizabeth, founded in 1895. The general harmony experienced by the Catholic Slovak community in Pittsburgh is described by June Alexander:

> Slovak Catholics wanted to continue practicing their homeland faith and Catholic Church leaders wanted to keep all Catholic immigrants within the established Catholic Church structures. This preservation of faith became an underlying theme in influencing relations between Slovaks and their religious leaders.[22]

Pittsburgh's blend of physical geography and immigrant communities created a rather unusual reality in the city. In many urban settings to which large numbers of varied ethnic immigrant groups arrived, the norm was the creation of separate sectors or corridors within a city for each ethnic or national group. In Pittsburgh, however, a more homogeneous situation was the norm. Although, the physical division of the city by its three rivers and prominent geographic features, most especially its hills, generated separate physical sectors, ethnic groups did not migrate to one particular geographic sector, but rather found themselves populating in all areas of the city. Ethnic groups were found in all sectors and thus created a homogeneous situation where most regions of the city were home to many different immigrant groups. Alexander has explained:

---

21. Timothy Kelly, *The Transformation of American Catholicism: The Pittsburgh Laity and the Second Vatican Council, 1950–1972* (Notre Dame, Ind.: University of Notre Dame Press, 2009), 3.

22. Alexander, *Immigrant Church*, 28.

By 1910 each of the city's immigrant neighborhoods claimed a variety of ethnic organizations, churches and businesses. In essence Pittsburgh's individual immigrant neighborhoods represented aggregations of various immigrant settlement areas.[23]

At the dawn of the twentieth century Pittsburgh thus found itself as a highly successful economic municipality, but a city with some significant difficulties that required attention. One historian synthesized the positive image that Pittsburgh projected to the outside world:

As a center of iron and steel, the city became a powerful prosperous source for uplifting underdeveloped areas of the world. Pittsburgh symbolized the city with a mission of promoting progress around the world.[24]

On the other hand, the physical geography of the region created, as described, a social separation of Pittsburghers. The struggle for the city's citizens was to break down boundaries and to form bridges between communities. Physically this challenge was met. Between 1923 and 1931 alone, Allegheny County constructed ninety-nine bridges to facilitate traffic over the city's rivers and hollows.[25] Still, this physical stratification generated problems in housing, public health, and general social welfare.

The need to investigate and correct social problems in the city prompted action in the early days of the twentieth century. In June 1906 Alice B. Montgomery, chief probation officer of the Allegheny County juvenile court and a local Pittsburgh reform activist, requested that Paul Kellogg, editor of the New York-based publication *Charities and the Commons*, bring together a team to investigate social conditions in Pittsburgh and its environs. Kellogg and Edward T. Devine of the New York Charity Organization Society responded favorably and assembled a team that included some of the most prominent persons in early twentieth-century American social reform: Florence Kelley, John R. Commons, Peter Roberts, and Robert Woods. Financing for this project, which became known as the Pittsburgh Survey, was obtained principally from the Russell Sage Foundation, which appropriated $27,000 for research and another $20,000 for publication of a future re-

---

23. Ibid., 57. The historian Timothy Kelly, commenting on the physical constraints of rivers and hills, stated that Pittsburghers "lived in heterogeneous neighborhoods filled with a variety of ethnic and religious groups and trapped together in island neighborhoods"; see Timothy Kelly, *Transformation of American Catholicism*, 4.
24. Penna, "Changing Images," 52.
25. Timothy Kelly, "Pittsburgh Catholicism," 67.

port.²⁶ The survey was not a product of a widespread demand for social criticism and reform, but rather was the genesis of a small group of business, professional, and welfare leaders in collaboration with the Charities Publication Committee of New York. In 1905 the latter group had undertaken an investigation of social conditions in Washington, D.C. Impressed with the report published by the committee, the Pittsburgh Survey was endorsed by such prominent people as Mayor George Guthrie, H. D. W. English, president of the Chamber of Commerce, and Joseph Buffington, a judge in the U.S. Circuit Court, Third Circuit. The survey team began its work in the fall of 1907 and completed it in the spring of 1908. Findings of the survey were published in three successive issues of *Charities and the Commons* beginning in January 1909.²⁷

The survey's published report critiqued the city's major industries for exploitation of workers. This led to the appointment of a civic commission that engaged famous city planner Frederick Law Olmstead Jr. to make recommendations for changes. Olmstead suggested widening streets and construction of a civic center, among other improvements. Yet social scientists Maurine Greenwald and Margo Anderson have concluded, "The survey failed to arouse Pittsburghers—either influential citizens or the middle-class—to improve everyday life for workers in Pittsburgh, solve environmental problems of the area, or meet the immediate 'needs of the poor' at the time."²⁸ Still, the results of the survey and the subsequent work of Olmstead brought about the formation of a citizens' committee expressly to promote "the Pittsburgh Plan," which was championed through *Progress*, which was issued irregularly from 1921 to 1941.²⁹

The Pittsburgh Survey, a unique experiment in American social and community analysis, proved to be helpful beyond the city. The visible social decay present in many urban centers led to a national drive to improve living conditions for the majority of city dwellers. Critics who decried the survey as a "deadly diatribe by outside do-gooders" were more than offset by those who saw it as "a model for other cities."³⁰

26. Maurine W. Greenwald and Margo Anderson, eds., *Pittsburgh Surveyed: Social Science and Social Reform in the Early Twentieth Century* (Pittsburgh: University of Pittsburgh Press, 1996), 7, 1.
27. Lubove, *Twentieth-Century Pittsburgh: Government, Business, and Environmental Change*, 6–7.
28. Greenwald and Anderson, eds., *Pittsburgh Surveyed*, 9.
29. Penna, "Changing Images," 55.
30. Ibid.; Greenwald and Anderson, eds., *Pittsburgh Surveyed*, 6.

With the Pittsburgh Survey as a background, the city entered the twentieth century as a typical urban center with potential for greatness but plagued by problems. The historian Roy Lubove described the city at the turn of the century:

Pittsburgh was a symbol as well as the city. It was synonymous with the spectacular advance of American industry, and the byproducts: labor unrest, poverty, assimilation of a heterogeneous immigrant working force, and disruption of community cohesion. Pittsburgh was also the symbol for a broader metropolitan and regional complex whose one unifying force was business enterprise.[31]

Indeed, by 1910 Pittsburgh was the nation's chief industrial center due in large measure to the tripartite business tycoons Andrew Carnegie, head of U.S. Steel, George Westinghouse, who created Westinghouse Electric and Manufacturing Company, and Andrew Mellon, founder of the Aluminum Corporation of America (ALCOA) and Gulf Oil.[32] The city, which in 1910 boasted a population of 533,000 and had experienced great triumphs, was also plagued by significant problems. Political corruption, especially in the mayor's office, was rampant at the time, creating "one of the most shameful chapters in the city's history."[33] Big business added insult to injury as, without any significant countervailing forces, its leadership was free to shape the life of the region. By the early days of the twentieth century this meant pollution of the physical environment and failure to restore decent housing, health, and social welfare.[34]

Pittsburgh's local problems coexisted with a general euphoria that characterized America in the post–World War I era. Stefan Lorant has described the epoch:

As the '20s began, they promised to be years of prosperity, a promise more than fulfilled. They were years of crazy living and crazy spending, years of the flappers, short skirts and bobbed hair, years of pole sitters, six-day racers, goldfish swallowers, marathon dancers, years of the homemade whiskey, bootleggers and gangsters. It was "The Jazz Age," in which the restless search for pleasure seemed to be the paramount aim of life. It was the era of Edna St. Vincent Millay, Scott Fitzgerald,

---

31. Lubove, *Twentieth-Century Pittsburgh: Government, Business, and Environmental Change*, 2.
32. Kenneth J. Heineman, *A Catholic New Deal: Religion and Reform in Depression Pittsburgh* (University Park: Pennsylvania State University Press, 1999), 2.
33. Gerald W. Johnson, "Muckraking Era," 266; Joe T. Darden, "The Effect of World War I on Black Occupational and Residential Segregation: The Case of Pittsburgh," *Journal of Black Studies* 18, no. 3 (March 1988): 302.
34. Lubove, *Twentieth-Century Pittsburgh: Government, Business, and Environmental Change*, 6.

Sinclair Lewis—an era which burnt its candles at both ends, the era of *The Great Gatsby* and of *Babbit*.[35]

Pittsburgh sought to capitalize on this general euphoria, but, unfortunately, the era began badly in the city when the international flu pandemic of 1918 killed 2,052 people in the city, 525 more than claimed by World War I. Strikes by transportation and mine workers one year later threatened to stall the city's forward progress. Pittsburgh in 1920, with a population of slightly over 588,000 and commercially successful, was still not a beautiful place to live. Buildings constructed with little planning, congested streets, and polluted rivers, as well as smoke and smog that blackened the sky, created an uninviting environment.[36]

The city's negative image prompted the creation of plans for significant improvements. In 1926 the reform-minded Pittsburgh Chamber of Commerce launched a program, "Pittsburgh Forward," which became the biggest community awakening in Pittsburgh's entire history." Its stated purpose was "[to] sell Pittsburgh to Pittsburghers." Plans for new playgrounds, streets, parks, waterways, and railroads were described and promoted in the publication *Progress*. The magazine's stated purpose was "the preparation and adoption of a thorough business-like program of rebuilding for Pittsburgh."[37] Still, no unified plan for renewal of the physical environment was adopted; the city's rather negative image continued.

Pittsburgh Catholicism in the Early Twentieth Century

Christianity first arrived in a formal way in what is today Western Pennsylvania during the first days of the nineteenth century. In 1802 the Western Mission Society organized for the "purpose of diffusing the knowledge of the gospel among the inhabitants of the new settlements, the Indian tribes, and if need be among some of the interior inhabitants." A similar organization, the Pittsburgh Bible Society, founded in 1815, was dedicated to the dissemination of the "word of God among the poor and destitute."[38] In the

---

35. Lorant, "Between Two Wars," 333. 36. Ibid., 327–28.
37. Penna, "Changing Images," 55.
38. Leland D. Baldwin, *Pittsburgh: The Story of a City* (Pittsburgh: University of Pittsburgh Press, 1937), 158–59.

first decade of the nineteenth century Pittsburgh boasted two Presbyterian congregations; in 1805 an Episcopalian parish was organized. The Methodist faith established its first congregation in 1810, but a more permanent church was erected in 1818.[39]

Although Fort Duquesne had a chapel dedicated to the Assumption of the Blessed Virgin Mary of the Beautiful River and a Mass was celebrated there in 1754, not until 1808 was a Roman Catholic congregation organized in the region. The first church in the area was St. Patrick's, built around 1810 by Father William Francis X. O'Brien. The church was dedicated one year later by Bishop Michael Egan of Philadelphia.[40]

Formal organization of the church in Pittsburgh came in the midnineteenth century. Construction of a cathedral church, St. Paul the Apostle, began in 1827, but the edifice was not dedicated until May 4, 1834. Bishop Michael O'Connor took up residence in 1841, but the Diocese of Pittsburgh was not formally erected until August 7, 1843. This first cathedral church was destroyed by fire, but a new and grander structure was consecrated on June 24, 1855, by Francis Kenrick, the archbishop of Baltimore. The present cathedral was consecrated on October 24, 1906, by the apostolic delegate to the United States, Archbishop Diomede Falconio.[41]

The massive influx of Eastern European immigrants, many of whom were Catholic, to work Pittsburgh's steel mills precipitated significant growth in the diocese. By 1890 there were 70,410 Catholics in Pittsburgh, comprising nearly 24 percent of the city's population. In 1906, however, the population had more than doubled to 150,545. Slightly fewer than 50 percent of the parishes had a Catholic school.[42] The influence of the immigrant population upon the Pittsburgh church was described by the historian Timothy Kelly:

---

39. Ibid., 157–58.

40. Ibid., 158; Edward Joyce, "The Roots of the Diocese," in *Catholic Pittsburgh's One Hundred Years*, by the Catholic Historical Society of Western Pennsylvania, 93–95 (Chicago: Loyola University Press, 1943).

41. Joyce, "Roots of the Diocese," 94–95.

42. Alexander, *Immigrant Church*, 29; Joseph Cascino, "From Sanctuary to Involvement: A History of the Catholic Parish in the Northeast," in *The American Catholic Parish: A History from 1850 to the Present*, edited by Jay P. Dolan, 24 (New York: Paulist Press, 1987). In 1940 the Diocese of Pittsburgh was the seventh-largest in the country with 366 parishes; see Heineman, *Catholic New Deal*, 3.

The Early Years: 1921–1940

The diocese came of age during the waves of immigration from Eastern and Southern Europe and had to accommodate a range of relatively distinct Catholic traditions. Though they varied in many particulars, these immigrant Catholics brought a heavy devotional sensibility to the region that flavored Catholic practice until the middle of the twentieth century.[43]

This new wave of immigration allowed Pittsburgh to host the largest Croatian and Slovak populations outside Europe. Slovak fraternal organizations such as the First Catholic Slovak Union and the Slovak Catholic Federation arose to assist the people with their daily needs.[44]

While Eastern European Catholics were a significant element to the growth of the church in Pittsburgh, the city, like most metropolitan regions in the nation, had a strong Irish influence. This was especially seen in the hierarchy. For example, from 1889 to 1904 the diocese was under the direction of an Irishman, Bishop Richard Phelan. His successor, John Canevin, an Irish American, served until 1921.

Geography as well as the immigrant population had a huge effect on the development of the church in the Pittsburgh area. The aforementioned creation of heterogeneous sectors in the city, crafted as a result of the physical barriers of rivers and mountains, forced residents within each separate neighborhood to devise mechanisms for living in the small world imposed upon them. The result for Pittsburgh Catholicism was a proliferation of churches with small numbers of parishioners within single neighborhoods. The church in Milwaukee was similar, possessing a high number of relatively small ethnic parishes.[45]

Besides the physical confines of the city, Pittsburgh also found itself to be culturally alone. It did not associate with East Coast cities, and it was too far east itself to be called Midwest. The historian Timothy Kelly has described the situation:

The sense of cultural isolation afforded Pittsburghers the space to develop a colloquial religious style or culture. It is not clear, however, that local Catholics took full advantage of this freedom.[46]

---

43. Timothy Kelly, "Pittsburgh Catholicism," 65.
44. Alexander, *Immigrant Church*, 30–31.
45. Timothy Kelly, *Transformation of American Catholicism*, 4; Timothy Kelly, "Pittsburgh Catholicism," 71.
46. Timothy Kelly, "Pittsburgh Catholicism," 71–72.

This cultural isolation, together with the physical separation of sectors in the city, actually worked together to create a diocese more homogeneous than many of its day. Indeed, Kelly commented, "Pittsburgh Catholics mastered the skill of negotiating a multitude of social boundaries within a constrained physical space."[47]

The general condition of the church in Pittsburgh is best illustrated by some analysis of the administrations of its local ordinaries. Bishop John Canevin, who headed the diocese from 1904 to 1921, was skillful in his ability to promote the church and to articulate its relationship to the state during a time when anti-Catholicism continued to raise its venomous head. Quoting John Ireland, archbishop of St. Paul, Canevin stated,

Should the particular case arise where it is plain that you are set aside solely because you are Catholic, then in the name of Americanism protest so loudly that never again will similar insult be offered to your American citizenship.[48]

He met attacks of bigotry calmly and in a spirit of Christian charity; he defeated intolerance with his equanimity in patience. Fighting against the perception that Catholics could not be loyal Americans, he encouraged his flock to get involved with public affairs. When the United States entered World War I, he forcefully spoke on the need for all citizens, Catholics and non-Catholics, to answer the call:

When the government of the nation has declared that the state of war exists, war becomes the law of the land, and the law of the land demands obedience and loyalty of every subject. It is the duty of every citizen to defend his country's rights, maintain honor, protect from wrong, and aid it in securing a just and lasting peace.[49]

Canevin also made significant contributions to the diocese in the areas of education and lay retreats, the latter a rather new idea in the early twentieth century. Following the directive issued from the Third Plenary Council of Baltimore in 1884, which ordered all parishes to have a school within two years, Canevin encouraged his pastors, as much as possible, to construct schools if one did not already exist in their parish. In 1918 the bishop conducted a financial drive to assist the Passionists at St. Paul's Monastery in

---

47. Ibid., 68.
48. Quoted in Francis A. Glenn, *Shepherds of the Faith, 1843–1993: A Brief History of the Bishops of the Catholic Diocese of Pittsburgh* (Pittsburgh: Catholic Diocese of Pittsburgh, 1993), 131.
49. Ibid., 133.

the diocese with their ministry of year-round weekend retreats for laymen, a novelty at the time and a ministry in which Jake Laboon would participate later in his life.[50]

Hugh Boyle, the sixth bishop of Pittsburgh, another Irish American, replaced Canevin in 1921. At the time there were 700,000 Catholics in the diocese of Pittsburgh, making it the second-largest (excluding archdioceses) in the country. Boyle's appointment brought much joy to the faithful in Pittsburgh, for he was a popular man who had distinguished himself in previous ministries, including his care and support for strikers in 1919 and most especially his leadership in Catholic education as superintendent of Catholic schools. As bishop he became integrally involved with the National Catholic Welfare Conference (NCWC), the national governing body of the American Catholic hierarchy, which was established in a permanent way in 1919. He served as a member of the administrative committee and at various times as chairman of the Education, Press, and Legal departments. Like his predecessor, he also supported the nascent lay retreat movement.[51]

Boyle's work with the NCWC was important for the American church, but his role in education was critical for the Pittsburgh church. He was encouraged that many Catholic children in Pittsburgh were receiving a Catholic education, but some 54,000 (40 percent of the total) were not. Thus he challenged Pittsburgh Catholics to raise the necessary funds (his goal was $3 million) so that more schools, especially high schools, could be built. His campaign was conducted between March 29 and April 7, 1924. Contributions and pledges exceeded the goal, amounting to $5 million. Boyle was also responsible for the promotion of teacher training. This was accomplished through the foundation of the Knights of Columbus Normal School

---

50. Ibid., 131–32.

51. James Reeves, "The Diocese under Bishop Boyle," in Catholic Historical Society of Western Pennsylvania, *Catholic Pittsburgh's One Hundred Years*, 77, 83. His work as chairman of the Department of Education was important in the 1920s as a significant drive seeking to federalize public education was advancing through Congress. As the Catholic lobby and voice in Washington, the role of the National Catholic Welfare Conference (NCWC) to counter this initiative was indeed significant. Reeves has stated concerning Boyle's effort, "His judgment, many say, was valuable during the struggle." For more detailed information about the effort to federalize education, see Douglas Slawson, *The Department Of Education Battle, 1918–1932: Public Schools, Catholic Schools and Social Order* (Notre Dame, Ind.: University of Notre Dame Press, 2005); see also Slawson, *The Foundation and First Decade of the National Catholic Welfare Council* (Washington, D.C.: The Catholic University of America Press, 1995), especially 85–88.

in 1921. Additionally, in 1932 he designated Duquesne, Mount Mercy (today Carlow University), and Seton Hill as approved teacher training centers for Catholic schools in the diocese.[52] The historian James Reeves commented about Boyle:

During the depression decade his skills as a trustee and as a master in finance were obvious. He grappled with circumstances, fashioned occasion, and made decisions in the interests of his flock.[53]

Another significant aspect of the administration of Bishop Boyle was his promotion of public Catholicism. Prior to World War II, as Pittsburgh historian Timothy Kelly has shown, church devotions were generally performed within the Catholic community. They served to bind the community to values and traditions that sustained the faithful in the midst of an often hostile environment. Such practices helped to bolster the walls of the cultural ghetto and keep outside forces at arm's length.[54] Boyle, on the other hand, advocated a more public display of Catholicism. This actually began during the period 1910 to 1912 when the Holy Name Society, with the approval of Bishop Canevin, sponsored outdoor processions and benedictions for three consecutive years. Boyle organized Eucharistic rallies in outdoor stadiums that drew large crowds. He nurtured a spirit of Catholic social activism through his assistance in the composition of "The Present Crisis," the NCWC statement of 1933 that strongly condemned greed and called for the faithful to heed the lessons of Pope Pius XI's encyclical, *Quadragesimo Anno*, published on the fortieth anniversary of the church's first and landmark statement on social welfare, *Rerum Novarum*.[55] Boyle sought to confront industrial exploitation of workers through the development of a strong Catholic voice for social justice.

The most significant manifestation of this voice was through the church's

---

52. Glenn, *Shepherds of the Faith*, 146–49; Reeves, "Diocese Under Bishop Boyle," 78–79.

53. Reeves, "Diocese Under Bishop Boyle," 83.

54. Timothy Kelly, "Suburbanization and the Decline of Catholic Public Ritual in Pittsburgh," *Journal of Social History* 28, no. 2 (Winter 1994): 312–13.

55. Ibid., 312–13, 318; Timothy Kelly, "Pittsburgh Catholicism," 65; Heineman, *Catholic New Deal*, 373–74. *Rerum Novarum*, written by Pope Leo XIII and published in 1891, was a landmark document for social Catholicism. Among other things, the encyclical promoted the concepts of a living wage, adequate rest from labors, and the right of workers to organize. *Quadragesimo Anno* reiterated much of what the earlier document had stated, with an update to the present need and situation in the world.

support of labor priests. The era of the Great Depression saw the emergence of the labor priest in the United States. Catholic labor historian Neil Betten has written:

> Although labor priests were a phenomenon among European social reformers earlier, and occasionally an American cleric had worked closely with the labor movement, during the Depression American Catholic clergy chose a far more extensive involvement in the labor movement than at any other time.[56]

Three priests who were prominent national figures in support of organized labor were John Ryan, as head of the Social Action Department of the NCWC, Francis Haas, who served the Roosevelt administration on the National Labor Board, and Peter Dietz, who founded the Militia for Christ. The general response of Catholic clergy in their support of organized labor is well described by the New Deal historian Kenneth Heineman:

> Without God, the Catholic reformers believed man lost all inhibitions, for he was no longer accountable to a supreme being. Consequently, the realization of social justice required the creation of a God-informed economic system. In this way Catholic labor activists were theologically anti-capitalist, anti-Communist and anti-Nazi without being in a political contradiction.[57]

Boyle was supportive of the efforts of labor priests in Pittsburgh. This was manifested most directly through his promotion of the Catholic Radical Alliance, founded 1936 "for the purpose of DOING something about the present social and economic mess"[58] George Barry O'Toole and Carl Hensler were the alliance's theoretical planners, while Charles Owen Rice, a famous labor priest, was the group's spokesman and chief activist. In describing the work of the alliance, Rice stated, "We stood for unions, we stood for freedom of workers to join associations, we called for modification of the social and economic systems and we were strongly pro-peace."[59] The alliance, in turn, was a strong supporter of the Congress of Industrial Organizations (CIO), an umbrella organization for unions established by John L. Lewis in 1938. Rice, who became a CIO organizer, and Philip Murray, a dedicated Catholic layman, were instrumental in forming the Association of Catholic Trade Unionists (ACTU), in

---

56. Neil Betten, "Charles Owen Rice: Pittsburgh Labor Priest, 1936–1940," *Pennsylvania Magazine of History and Biography* 94, no. 4 (October 1970): 519.
57. Heineman, *Catholic New Deal*, 392.
58. Ibid., 377, emphasis original.
59. Glenn, *Shepherds of the Faith*, 153; Betton, "Charles Owen Rice," 526.

1937. The group's inaugural national meeting was held in Pittsburgh in 1941.[60]

Public Catholicism was also seen in Pittsburgh through political action, especially the church's stance against Communism. In his seminal work on this topic, the historian Richard Gid Powers has referred to Catholicism as the "backbone" of the anti-Communist movement.[61] In Pittsburgh the church obtained a position of influence within the Democratic Party, allowing Catholics to fight Communist unionists in an attempt to build a more just and moral society. Catholic opposition to Communism was strong, but social justice activists were equally concerned about how an exploitative capitalist economy was abusing local citizens.[62]

Jake Laboon: Youth and Family

John Francis Laboon Jr., the third child of nine and first son of John F. Laboon and Catherine Reilly, was born in Pittsburgh on April 11, 1921. He was baptized at the family parish, Church of the Resurrection, in the Brookline district of the city two weeks later, on April 24, with his aunt and uncle, John and Margaret Reilly, serving as godparents.[63] The family, six girls, Mary Jane, Patrice (later Sister deLellis), Katherine (Kay), Claire, Rosemary (later Sister Rosemary), and Joan, (later Sister Joan), and three boys, John (later Father Jake), Tom, and Joe (later Father Joe) resided on Bay Ridge Road.[64]

Jake Laboon's ancestral heritage mirrored the aforementioned waves of immigrants who came to this country. His maternal grandparents came from County Mayo on the west side of Ireland. His mother, Catherine, one of five children, was the daughter of John Reilly and Honora Brady. The Laboons had immigrated to the United States two generations earlier from Lithuania. Jake's grandfather, who worked as a tailor, was the father of thirteen children, the eldest of whom was John. Catherine and John were married on January 29, 1917, at St. Agnes Church.[65]

---

60. Heineman, *Catholic New Deal*, 383; Betton, "Charles Owen Rice,"526–29.

61. Richard Gid Powers, *Not Without Honor: The History of American Anticommunism* (New York: Free Press, 1995), 51.

62. Heineman, "A Catholic New Deal: Religion and Labor in 1930s Pittsburgh," *Pennsylvania Magazine of History and Biography* 118, no. 4 (October 1994): 368.

63. Certificate of baptism (copy), May 18, 1946, John Laboon papers, ASJM. The priest who baptized Laboon was J. L. Quinn.

64. Rosemary, deLellis, and Joan Laboon, interview with the author, August 4, 2010.

65. Certificate of matrimony (copy), n.d., Laboon papers, ASJM; Kenneth White to author,

The Early Years: 1921–1940

Jake was a typical lad in a large Catholic family in pre-Depression America. He enjoyed playing with his siblings and many children in his neighborhood. It was clear that he would be tall, as his physical prowess dominated from his earliest days. He suffered through many of the typical childhood diseases, including mumps and whooping cough, as well as a tonsillectomy.[66] He started school at the Church of the Resurrection, but when the family moved to a new home on Bower Hill Road in Mt. Lebanon, a middle- to upper-class section of Pittsburgh,[67] he was enrolled at St. Bernard, which opened under the direction of the Sisters of St. Joseph in 1926.[68]

St. Bernard was the only parish in the Mt. Lebanon section of the city; this apparent dearth in places of worship was contrary to a significant rise in numbers of church institutions that was consistent with the city's general population growth. In 1900 there were 195 parishes in the diocese, 46 of them considered national churches, and 109 elementary schools. In 1920 the number of parishes with resident pastors was 329; by 1930 there were 366 parishes and 237 elementary schools. Between 1919 and 1930 the Catholic population of the diocese more than doubled, from 280,000 to 581,327.[69]

St. Bernard, which became the Laboon family parish, grew in population and significance during Jake's years as a youth. In 1919 a small group of Catholics from the Dormont region of Pittsburgh went to Bishop Canevin requesting that another parish be established in the area. The petitioners suggested it was too far for people to attend Mass in Brookline or Beechview. After reviewing a study of the region that he ordered as an initial response, Canevin, on July 20, 1919, ordered the establishment of a new parish to embrace most of Dormont and Mt. Lebanon, as well as parts of Banksville, Greentree, Beadling, and Scott Township.[70]

As with most new parishes, St. Bernard's early years were characterized

---

October 18, 2012. The witnesses for their wedding were Edward Laboon and Mary Reilly, brother and sister of the groom and bride. The priest celebrant was D. H. Hagarty.

66. Report of physical examination, September 19, 1946, John Laboon file, NMPR.
67. Dr. Robert Blume, interview with the author, January 19, 2011.
68. Rosemary, deLellis, and Joan Laboon, interview with the author, August 4, 2010.
69. Joseph Cascino, "From Sanctuary to Involvement," 38. As a comparison with other dioceses in Pennsylvania, Pittsburgh's percentage of parishes with schools was 65 percent, Philadelphia 74 percent, and Harrisburg 67 percent; see also Reeves, "Diocese under Bishop Boyle," 81.
70. "The 'Cathedral' in the South Hills," St. Bernard Parish History, n.d. [1969], 9. Dr. Robert Blume, a Laboon family friend and fellow member of St. Bernard Parish, claims that anti-Catholic sentiments in the neighborhood of Dormont would not allow a Catholic Church to be built in its environs. Thus St. Bernard was constructed on the border of Dormont, but physically in Mt. Lebanon.

by constant change and the need for flexibility. The first Mass was celebrated by the new pastor, Father Thomas H. Bryson, on August 31, 1919, in a carriage house that served as a temporary church structure. Bryson held the position of pastor at St. John's in Baden, near Ambridge, while also serving as chaplain at Mt. Gallitzin Academy, which was administered by the Sisters of St. Joseph. The initial census of St. Bernard parish revealed 160 families. When the Laboon family moved into Mt. Lebanon, the parish census was approximately 500 families. Temporary churches were used for many years; only in 1947 was a fifth and permanent church actually constructed.[71]

His family remembers Jake as an excellent student and athlete. However, in these early days there was no hint of his future vocation to the priesthood. His sisters commented, "He was no more religious than any other boy of his age."[72] Taking the name of Francis, Jake was confirmed on May 16, 1934, at St. Bernard by Pittsburgh's local ordinary, Bishop Hugh Boyle.[73] He graduated from St. Bernard's one year later.

Laboon's youth was both typical and extraordinary. As will be described later, the family, due to the father's position, was upper-middle-class and did not suffer significantly from the disastrous Great Depression that dominated the American scene from 1929 until America's entrance into World War II. On the other hand, the day-to-day existence of Jake, his siblings, and parents was quite typical. Much later in life, Jake Laboon commented on his childhood:

I came from a large family. It was a disciplined family with a lot of respect for authority, both in the family and at the schools I attended. There was no question who was boss at home—my father and mother.[74]

Jake's maternal grandmother lived with the family in an upstairs bedroom known lovingly as "Grandma's Room." The family regularly gathered in the evening to pray the rosary, a custom ingrained in Irish tradition. In addition to regular Sunday attendance, the Laboon family tradition was to attend Mass each Friday together. During the seasons of Advent and Lent daily attendance was the norm.[75]

71. Ibid., 9–17.
72. Rosemary, deLellis, and Joan Laboon, interview with the author, August 4, 2010.
73. Certificate of confirmation (copy), May 18, 1946, Laboon papers, ASJM.
74. News clipping, n.d. [1980], personal papers of Joe Maloy (hereafter PPJM), Bridgeville, Pa.
75. Sr. Joan Laboon, RSM, interview with the author, September 9, 2012; Rosemary, deLellis, and Joan Laboon, interview with the author, August 4, 2010.

The Early Years: 1921–1940

Jake Laboon's youth in Pittsburgh was lived to a large extent in the context of the Great Depression. On Black Tuesday, October 29, 1929, the bottom fell out of the New York Stock Exchange, generating a market crash that became synonymous with an era of economic misery in the United States. General structural weaknesses in the economic system, overinvestment, underconsumption, and malfeasance by some bankers and industrialists created an economic bubble that burst. The perfect storm for economic disaster descended upon the American people. Commenting on the extent of the disaster, the famous economist John Kenneth Galbraith, writing in *The Great Crash*, stated, "The striking thing about the stock market speculation of 1929 was not the massiveness of the participation. Rather it was the way it became central to the culture."[76] National income in the United States during the era toppled in a cascade effect from $81 billion in 1929 to $68 billion in 1930 and eventually to $41 billion in 1932. Unemployment rates during the same period rose to greater than 25 percent; labor income dropped 42.3 percent between 1929 and 1933. During the same four-year span, the Gross National Product, or GNP, fell by 35 percent.[77]

The Great Depression struck Pittsburgh, but the full impact did not hit until 1931. The Pittsburgh historians John Bauman and Edward Muller commented:

Mercifully the full impact of the Great Depression arrived somewhat belatedly in Pittsburgh, not until 1931. Sustained by the lingering effects of Pittsburgh's vital 1920s steel making economy, and by the region's impressive home-building boom as well as by the surprising resilience of the city's retail and wholesale sectors, Pittsburgh's economy sputtered rather than plunged into the Stygian void of the Great Depression.[78]

However, when the effects did strike the city, they hit with the fury of a sledgehammer. Indeed the historian Stefan Lorant writes,

The Depression ... hit Pittsburgh harder than other areas where industries were less predominant. The factories of the city quickly cut back production; workers were dismissed overnight.[79]

---

76. Quoted in Lorant, "Between Two Wars," 336.
77. David A. Shannon, *Between the Wars: America 1919–1941* (Boston: Houghton Mifflin, 1965), 109.
78. John F. Bauman and Edward K. Muller, *Before Renaissance: Planning in Pittsburgh, 1889–1943* (Pittsburgh: University of Pittsburgh Press, 2006), 195.
79. Lorant, "Between Two Wars," 343.

The demise of the steel industry was the bellwether of the disaster. At the Depression's low ebb, steel production was one-tenth of its capacity; 40 percent of Pittsburgh steelworkers lost their jobs. On September 3, 1929, U.S. Steel stock sold for $262 per share; in 1932 it sold for $22 per share. Unemployment grew as high as 32 percent in the city and as high as 56 percent in the steel mills.[80]

The pain inflicted by the Depression was great, but Pittsburgh and its citizens, led by private relief agencies and public corporations, responded to stem the tide of misery. In February 1932 Howard Hines teamed with Richard Beatty Mellon to assemble a group of seventy-five businessmen to seek a solution to the Depression's unemployment situation. The group drafted the "Pittsburgh Plan to Stabilize Employment." The plan called for corporations and individuals to make contributions to be used for payment of wages to previously unemployed workers who would engage in municipal improvements that otherwise would not have been undertaken due to lack of financial resources. Funds were administered through an organization, the Allegheny County Emergency Association, or ACEA. Projects were initiated in 1931. By May 1932 more than $2.3 million had been used in these projects.[81] The Pittsburgh Plan foreshadowed the Works Progress Administration (WPA) of the New Deal, yet both programs were inadequate to secure a recovery for Pittsburgh workers.

Another major source of support, both physically and spiritually, was the church. Direct assistance through parishes and various social service agencies was effective, but the most significant and enduring aspect of church involvement was its support for organized labor. On a national level Bernard Sheil, auxiliary bishop of Chicago, John Duffey, bishop of Buffalo, and Archbishop Robert Lucey of San Antonio were notable advocates for workers' rights and unions. In Pittsburgh Father James Cox, the youthful pastor of the Cathedral of St. Paul, was prominent. He gained the name lo-

---

80. Ibid., 340–43; Heineman, *Catholic New Deal*, 5. The historian Bruce Stave has noted a significant difference in unemployment rates between various groups in the city. In 1933 15.7 percent of white Pittsburghers were unemployed; at the same time 43.4 percent of African Americans were out of work; see Bruce M. Stave, *The New Deal and the Last Hurrah: Pittsburgh Machine Politics* (Pittsburgh: University of Pittsburgh Press, 1970), 33.

81. Stave, *New Deal*, 110; Bauman and Muller, *Before Renaissance*, 196. Stave points out that, as in many other communities, it was the Pittsburgh and Allegheny County private relief groups that shouldered the economic burden at the outset of the Great Depression. With time, as the 1930s progressed, politicians and government got much more heavily involved.

cally as "Mayor of Shantytown" in his ministry to the growing ranks of the unemployed who resided in the largest "Hooverville" in the city, located in the city's Strip District, adjacent to St. Patrick Church.[82] Besides his work in the city, Cox gained national attention in January 1932 by organizing a hunger march to Washington, D.C., vainly attempting to convince the Hoover administration to extend federal aid to the jobless.

Pittsburgh, like the nation as a whole, reeled from the misery wrought by the Great Depression, but the city was also forced to endure the wrath of Mother Nature. On St. Patrick's Day 1936, Pittsburgh suffered a terrible flood that inundated the downtown triangle where the Monongahela and Allegheny rivers combined to form the Ohio. Physical death and injury to over 3,000, plus the loss of some 100,000 homes, added to the already significant economic burden of the city. By March 23 the flood waters had receded sufficiently so that cleanup could begin, but the damage had been done.[83]

As Americans and Pittsburghers the Laboon family felt the pain of their nation and city, but their suffering was mitigated through the fortunate position of the father. In 1923 Joseph Armstrong became chairman of the Allegheny County Commission. In January of the next year he revamped the county government, creating the Department of Public Works, a self-contained organization with the technical and administrative personnel necessary to design roads and bridges and to supervise their construction without the need to engage expensive outside consultants. John Laboon, a graduate of Carnegie Institute of Technology and a member of its board of trustees, was appointed as director of public works. As a prominent member of Pittsburgh's city administration, Laboon was fortunate to retain his position in the dark days and immediate years after Black Tuesday, thus keeping the family financially secure throughout the economic downturn.[84]

In 1935 additional good fortune came to the Laboon family through the ascendancy of the Democratic Party under Franklin Roosevelt. As an adjunct to his position with the Department of Public Works, the senior Laboon also became the local administrator for the WPA. While some reports at the time accused Laboon of favoritism toward Roosevelt and New Deal

---

82. Bauman and Muller, *Before Renaissance*, 195.

83. Lorant, "Between Two Wars," 355.

84. Clipping, *Pittsburgh Catholic*, December 13, 1985, Personal papers of Sr. Joan Laboon, RSM (hereafter PPJL), Pittsburgh; John Laboon to CDR W. L. Larson, USN, June 28, 1939, John F. Laboon, Midshipman personnel file, John Laboon Jr. file, AUSNA.

supporters in his distribution of WPA funds, he nonetheless carried a large portion of the local face of Washington's solution to the Depression.[85] At the end of 1935 Laboon left his position with the WPA while retaining his position as director of public works. He also accepted a new station as superintendent of highways for the new county commissioner.[86]

The fortune of the Laboon family to escape many of the trials of the Great Depression was highly advantageous for Jake, especially with respect to his Catholic education. We have already seen how his elementary education was provided by his home parish of St. Bernard. The next step in his education was found at Central Catholic High School, administered by the Christian Brothers. Central Catholic was constructed as a result of Bishop Boyle's 1924 effort to raise funds for the construction of schools. Located in the Oakland section of Pittsburgh, the school was dedicated on September 11, 1927. The next day, 488 boys from forty-two different parishes registered in grade nine.[87]

Jake matriculated to Central Catholic in the fall of 1935. During his tenure classes for freshmen and sophomores were programmed, consisting of religion, history, Latin, English, and plane geometry. He was an excellent student, achieving "high scholastic achievements in the regular class work." His lowest mark, an 87, was in U.S. history. At Central Catholic he took four years of English and two years of Latin, plus algebra, geometry, trigonometry, U.S. and European history, physics, biology, general science, and German.[88]

The school provided students with numerous and broad activities. They were introduced to various cultural events such as symphony and band concerts, plays, and noted speakers. During his time as a student, Laboon contributed articles to the school's newly inaugurated newspaper, "The Viking," which "was successful from the start because of the perseverance of the staff." Jake was active in the German Club and was a staff member for *The Tower*, the school's annual.[89]

---

85. Stave. *New Deal*, 117, 143, 146. Laboon was accused by some of playing favorites in his administration of WPA funds. While he acknowledged inefficiencies in the system, he rejected any notion that his decisions were based on party politics.

86. Ibid., 147.

87. Central Catholic High School, History page, http://www.centralcatholichs.com/history.aspx.

88. *The Tower*, Central Catholic High School Annual, 1939; Central Catholic High School transcript, n.d. [1939], Laboon file, certificate form, n.d. [1939], AUSNA.

89. *The Tower*, Central Catholic High School Annual, 1939.

The Early Years: 1921–1940

Jake's size and excellent physical condition made him a natural athlete. At Central Catholic he played varsity football and basketball, but the former was his forte and the sport for which he would later be recruited to the naval academy. As a sophomore he saw limited duty as a substitute, but in his latter two years he was one of the stars of the team, playing quarterback and serving as the team's punter. In the fall of 1938, Jake's senior year, Central Catholic was nearly unstoppable, winning its first seven games. Losing only to Donora 19–0, the Golden Avalanche of Central Catholic finished strong, winning their final game of the season. Speaking of Jake's exploits on the field, the school's annual reported, "His passing and running produced many scores, leading the team to an 8–1 record."[90] Jake's heroics on the gridiron and on the basketball hardwood led to his eventual induction into the Central Catholic Hall of Fame.

Outside the classroom and athletic field, Jake Laboon matured into a gregarious young man who was much admired by family and friends. He was remembered by his family as "a good big brother" and by friends as "a great guy." He was respected as a "guy's guy." One neighborhood friend, writing to Jake's sister several years after his death, commented, "Remember as kids how we always looked up to him." Despite his imposing frame, he always had a genuine smile and manifested a caring way for all he met.[91] He was popular and was described by his sisters as a "regular ladies' man." As a teenager Jake took responsibility seriously. As soon as he was old enough to drive he took a job delivering Western Union telegrams. As one member of his family said, "He always had a job. He was not afraid of work."[92] Jake clearly reciprocated the love and care others showed for him. Speaking at Jake's funeral on August 4, 1988, fellow Jesuit priest William Graham commented, "Pittsburgh and family were [for Jake] the ones who made the various times memorable, happy, and full."[93] His sisters recalled how Jake at times, scraping together 21 cents for a gallon of gas, took his sisters on rides in the rumble seat of his Model T Ford.

For Jake Laboon, like all people, youthful times pass, and, with the expe-

---

90. Ibid.
91. Rosemary, deLellis, and Joan Laboon, interview with the author, August 4, 2010; Robert Ecker, interview with the author, December 19, 2010; Helen to Joan Laboon, RSM, n.d. [1992], Personal papers of Sr. Joan Laboon, RSM (hereafter PPJL), Pittsburgh.
92. Rosemary, deLellis, and Joan Laboon, interview with the author, August 4, 2010.
93. Jake Laboon funeral audio tape, PPJL.

riences gained, the need to move to a new chapter in life arrives. This transition began for Jake on June 14, 1939, when he graduated second in his class of 112 at Central Catholic.[94] It was a time to acknowledge accomplishments of the past, but to look forward to the many possibilities of the future.

Conclusion

Pittsburgh was the seedbed of the life of John Francis Laboon as a naval officer and priest. The city's diverse regions, formed because of physical geography, and its tight-knit Catholic parish communities, combined with a strong family background, created the base from which Laboon would launch a career that positively influenced the lives of thousands of people, military and civilian. This rock-solid base was not only the proper environment to allow God's will to be done in Jake's life, but also nurtured his vocation by demonstrating his ability to adapt as needs would arise. His core values and ideas, formed as a youth, would carry him far in the service of God's people.

94. Certificate form, n.d. [1939], Laboon file, AUSNA.

Chapter 2

Formation for Military Service—The U.S. Naval Academy

★ 1940–1943

The seed for the life and ministry of Jake Laboon had been planted in the city of Pittsburgh, but in order for it to mature and blossom he needed to leave the tranquility of his home and venture into the world. For Jake Laboon the initial challenge was military service, made more acute especially after the September 1, 1939, German blitzkrieg into Poland, which led eventually to American participation in World War II. It was time for him to go forth into a new arena of life—to take up the challenge, morally, physically, and intellectually, at the U.S. Naval Academy. Unaware at the time of the distinction that would be his, Jake was nonetheless ready and willing to meet the unknown future with the spirit of openness to the possibilities that might come his way. He brought with him all the tools he needed for future success—sufficient intellectual acumen, physical prowess, a strong work ethic, the determination to succeed, and a strong faith in God to guide him in all his endeavors.

An Academic and Life Interim

After graduating from Central Catholic, Jake Laboon opened a new chapter in his life. He explained to a reporter many years later:

Formation for Military Service—The U.S. Naval Academy: 1940–1943

When I was in high school in Pittsburgh, I saw the film "Brother Rat," which was about Virginia Military Institute. I became fascinated with the service academies. I wanted to go to West Point but I couldn't get an appointment.[1]

Since West Point was not an option, Jake set his sight toward the naval academy. Edgar E. "Rip" Miller, one of the "Seven Mules" who played with the legendary "Four Horsemen" of Notre Dame in the mid-1920s, was serving at the time as an assistant football coach at Navy. After graduating in 1925, Miller spent one year as an assistant at Indiana before coming to the naval academy. He was greatly interested in Laboon and began to recruit him as early as March 1939.[2]

In the late 1930s there were two ways to gain admission to the naval academy. First, candidates for the service academies were required to obtain an appointment from their local congressional representative, U.S. Senator, or, in select cases, from the vice president. Enlisted candidates already in the service could compete for positions through a series of competitive examinations. Once a nomination had been secured, candidates normally were required to pass a rigorous entrance exam. Jake Laboon was nominated to the U.S. Naval Academy by Congressman Joseph McArdle of Pennsylvania's 33rd Congressional District.[3] However, he failed the qualification exam and was thus forced to seek an alternative method, the college certificate, which necessitated the completion of specific classes with satisfactory marks to satisfy deficiencies from the substantiating exam.

Laboon's father immediately began to lobby for Jake's admission the following year. The senior Laboon first informed Commander W. J. Larson, secretary of the USNA Academic Board, that Rip Miller had recruited him to play football at Navy. He went on to say, "It is my intention to have him

---

1. Clipping, *Honolulu Advertiser*, n.d. Laboon file, AUSNA. Extant data, including interviews with his family, does not provide any additional answer as to why Jake sought entrance to a service academy. However, it is likely that the strong influence of his father, through his work in government, contributed to his decision.

2. Lars Anderson, *The All Americans* (New York: St. Martin's Press, 2004), 29–31; Rip Miller to Dick Heise, March 7, 1939; Rip Miller, memorandum for W. J. Larson, March 9, 1939, Laboon file, AUSNA. Miller developed a very sophisticated recruiting operation for his players. Called the birddog system, Miller relied on academy graduates, former sailors, and his friends to act as his eyes in places all over the nation. Thus Miller had scouts everywhere. Anderson writes, "If there was a good high school player in the area who had the grades to get into the Academy, Miller knew about him"; see Anderson, *All Americans*, 30.

3. Representative Joseph A. McArdle (1903–67), a Republican, represented Pennsylvania's 33rd Congressional district from 1939 to 1942 during the 66th and 67th Congresses.

attend Carnegie Institute of Technology for the next year." He sought advice on subjects he should take, not only to qualify for the academy, but to be of advantage to him in the future.[4] Larson told Laboon that Jake must take at least six credits of English and six credits of math, emphasizing, "These are the two mandatory courses in the college certificate and will also serve to offset his failure therein in our substantiating examination." Larson then provided an overall plan:

On the assumption that he [Jake] received final year grades meeting our requirements, I may say that it will be entirely possible for him to undertake a schedule of courses at the Carnegie Institute of Technology during the ensuing year that will serve to offset his failure in the substantiating examination and will at the same time qualify him for admission by the college certificate method. I feel quite safe in saying that this standard freshman year schedule for engineering students will answer this purpose very nicely, provided your son can complete each semester's work in each subject with the final grade meeting our requirements.[5]

Larson also told the senior Laboon that once Jake was registered at Carnegie, his course schedule, along with his senior grades from Central Catholic, should be forwarded to the academy. Once these were in place, he concluded, "We will be in a position to give a definite opinion concerning the outlook for acceptance of his high school and college certificate."[6]

In September 1939 Jake Laboon matriculated at Carnegie Tech, his father's alma mater, as a first-year student. His student life was under the watchful eyes of his father, Rip Miller, and others in the athletic department at the academy. Miller was assured in a memorandum in late November that Laboon was on a satisfactory course for entrance in the summer of 1940:

The schedule of freshman year courses which he is undertaking at Carnegie Institute of Technology during the present school year is an entirely acceptable one for the purpose of offsetting his failure in the substantiating examination last year and to establish sufficient credits to warrant his admission by the college method and without mental entrance examination. As a matter of fact his schedule at Carnegie is a very good one and as the boy's high school record indicated him to be an above average student, I am quite sure if he applies himself properly during the remainder of the school year he will have no difficulty in meeting the requirements.[7]

---

4. John Laboon to CDR W. L. [sic] Larson, USN, June 28, 1939, Laboon file, AUSNA.
5. CDR W. J. Larson to John Laboon Sr., July 10, 1939, Laboon file, AUSNA.
6. Ibid.
7. Memorandum to Rip Miller, November 20, 1939, Laboon file, AUSNA.

The memorandum concluded,

> In view of his statement that he has a principal appointment for the class entering in 1940, it would appear that his prospects are decidedly "rosy" and he has only to meet the grade requirements specified above in order to meet the mental entrance requirements.[8]

At Carnegie Jake in many ways lived the life of the typical college student. The opportunity to have another year at home allowed him access to family and friends. Frequent parties at the Laboon home, where friends gathered for fun and conversation, were hosted by Jake and his sister Kay. On campus, he joined a fraternity and played freshman football and basketball.[9] Unfortunately, Jake's academic progress did not keep pace with his other activities. It was reported to Miller that Laboon had an unsatisfactory mark in English at the mid-semester grades. The report continued, "If he must sacrifice his standing in another subject in order to give more time to English, I suggest he lighten up on his work in the course in social relations."[10] By the end of the semester, Laboon, while not achieving good marks, did manage the minimum grade of "C" in both English and math.[11]

Jake's tenuous academic performance at Carnegie continued in the spring semester, raising concern from academy officials. Curious as to how his first semester at Carnegie would affect his chances for entrance, Jake was advised to take courses similar to those from the previous fall semester. The key, however, was to achieve a satisfactory mark of "C" or better.[12] Commenting on Laboon's rather languid fall academic performance, one academy official stated in February 1940, "These are the lowest acceptable grades and he should certainly make every effort to maintain at least that standard during the second semester."[13] As late as April, concern was still apparent. Commander Larson of the academy's academic board wrote to Jake, telling him that if he could not complete all of his courses at Carnegie satisfactorily,

---

8. Ibid.
9. Rosemary, deLellis, and Joan Laboon, interview with author, August 4, 2010; "Biography of John Francis Laboon, Jr.," PPJL.
10. Dick Heise to E. E. Miller, December 14, 1939, Laboon file, AUSNA.
11. Form K "Certificate of Accredited College, University or Technological School," n.d. [1940], Laboon file, AUSNA. Laboon's marks in total were: Chemistry—C; Math—C; English—C; Drawing and Descriptive Geometry—D; Social Relations—C; Physical Education—A.
12. Certificate for accreditation, Laboon file, AUSNA.
13. Dick Heise to Mrs. Muth (memorandum), February, 1940, Laboon file, AUSNA.

"at least complete English and Analytic Geometry with satisfactory grades." He also told him that the grade of "C" or better in these two subjects, together with his high school and other college credits, will be acceptable for admission without the mental entrance examination.[14]

Jake eventually managed to qualify for the naval academy. His academy academic record reads, "Mr. Laboon qualified for admission to the Naval Academy by presenting 16 acceptable units of credit from Central Catholic High School, Pittsburgh, Pennsylvania, and on the basis of college credits indicated herein." While his marks were not stellar, Jake entered the academy with twenty-four college credits, sufficient to gain admission through the college certificate method.[15]

Naval Academy Days

From the days of John Paul Jones, considered the father of the U.S. Navy, responsible far-sighted people have seen the need for a systematic and intensive education for young naval officers. Education of midshipmen in the early nineteenth century was highly inconsistent. Naval regulations issued by President Thomas Jefferson in 1802 directed that the chaplain aboard ship should "perform the duty of the schoolmaster" and "instruct the midshipmen and volunteers in writing, arithmetic, and navigation, and in whatsoever may contribute to render them proficient."[16] By the mid-nineteenth century this obvious neglect to provide formal training for naval officers drew the attention of officials in Washington. Indeed, Abel P. Upshur, secretary of the navy between October 1841 and July 1843, during the administration of President John Tyler, wrote in an 1842 report ideas that were shared by many:

Little or no attention has hitherto been paid to the proper education of Naval officers. Through a long course of years, the young midshipmen were left to educate themselves and one another ... their schools are kept in receiving ships and cruising vessels, in the midst of a thousand interruptions and impediments, which render the whole system of little or no value.[17]

---

14. CDR W. J. Larson to John Laboon Jr., April 13, 1940, Laboon file, AUSNA.
15. John F. Laboon Jr., U.S. Naval Academy (hereafter USNA) transcript; John F. Laboon midshipman information sheet, Laboon file, AUSNA.
16. "A History of the U.S. Naval Academy, 1845–1958," p. 2, USNA Command History, 1966, Naval History Museum (hereafter NHM), Washington, D.C.
17. Ibid., 1.

Beyond the directive of Jefferson, the first attempts for the education of naval officers were rather informal. Three schools, in Norfolk, New York, and Boston, were started in the 1820s. The format was informal, and attendance was voluntary.

Beginning in 1842 a series of events combined to bring about the formal foundation of what became the naval academy. That year the *Somers* affair scandalized the navy. Midshipman Philip Spencer was convicted of mutiny and hanged from the yardarm of the *Somers*. The incident confirmed that something had to be done to elevate the standards of the navy—especially in regard to the training of young officer candidates. At the same time the introduction of steam propulsion brought the navy into a technological age that necessitated knowledge of engineering. Additionally, establishment of a fourth naval school in Philadelphia in 1839, which flourished under the guidance of Professor William Chauvenet, demonstrated the feasibility of a naval school ashore.[18]

The appointment on March 11, 1845, of the noted historian and educator George Bancroft as secretary of the navy was a significant catalyst. Bancroft immediately set to work to establish a naval school. In August he accomplished the transfer of Fort Severn from the army to the navy; the transfer resulted in nine buildings being provided for the school. He also managed to have four professors transferred from the highly successful Philadelphia Naval School as seed faculty for the new Annapolis location. On August 7, 1845, Bancroft appointed Commander Franklin Buchanan as superintendent and directed him to draw up a plan of operation. Buchanan took charge of Fort Severn on August 15.[19]

Buchanan wasted no time in carrying out the directive of Secretary Bancroft to establish a new naval school. He set standards for candidates for the new school. Men were to be between the ages of thirteen and sixteen inclusive, of good moral character, and free from any defects that "would not disqualify him [from] performing the active arduous duties of a sea life." Most importantly, he established rigorous academic requirements for the midshipmen. His first order to the academic board, issued October 4, 1845, read in part:

18. Ibid., 2–3.
19. Ibid., 2–4.

The course of instruction will be comprised under the following heads—Mathematics, Natural Philosophy, Chemistry, Gunnery, the use of steam, Geography, English Grammar, Arithmetic, History, the French and Spanish languages and such other branches desirable to the accomplishment of a Naval officer as your judgment may dictate.[20]

In 1850 the school was placed under the direction of the chief of the Bureau of Ordnance and Hydrography and renamed the Naval Academy.

During the Civil War fear that Maryland would join the Confederacy forced a move of the academy from Annapolis to Newport, Rhode Island. In September 1865, with the cessation of hostilities, the midshipmen and their training vessel returned to Annapolis. The academy's first post-war superintendent, Rear Admiral David Porter, who served from September 1865 to November 1869, was tasked with the rehabilitation and expansion of the buildings and grounds, which were in poor condition from four years of neglect. Under Porter not only were the original buildings refurbished, but new ones were constructed to meet the needs of the burgeoning midshipmen population, which gradually increased over the years. In 1895 the academy's board of visitors recommended the construction of new buildings to replace those refurbished and erected during the administration of Porter. An appropriation of $10 million from Congress made this development possible. Many of the prominent buildings still utilized, including Bancroft Hall, Dahlgren Hall, MacDonough Hall, the chapel, Isherwood Hall, and the superintendent's residence, all date from this era. The short duration of the Spanish-American War of 1898 had little impact on the academy. However, the war did create the first of three periods when training was accelerated to expedite the delivery of new officers to the fleet.[21]

At the academy the first three decades of the twentieth century were a time of academic achievement, modernization, and professionalism. Following a second accelerated schedule due to World War I, the school returned to a normal four-year academic program. Modernization of curriculum and training, needed to keep pace with the rapid advancement in naval technol-

20. Ibid., 6, 17. The tradition of training midshipmen at sea began with the USS *Preble* in 1851. In 1904 the coast squadron of the Atlantic Fleet embarked midshipmen, setting a pattern for the standard midshipman cruise in ships of the fleet. These began in earnest in 1912.

21. Ibid., 9–14. This first truncated program found thirty-nine members of the class of 1898 graduating two months early on April 2. Members of the class of 1899 were ordered to sea at their own request one month later, followed in June 1898 by forty-six men of the class of 1900 and twenty-nine from the class of 1901.

ogy, was essential and led to the academy's accreditation by the Association of American Universities on October 25, 1930. More than two years later, on May 25, 1933, Congress authorized the superintendent to confer the bachelor of science degree on all graduates, backdated from the date of accreditation. By the time Jake Laboon entered, the academy had grown to an enrollment of 3,100 midshipmen.[22]

The storied history of the academy was certainly known at least in brief by Laboon when he received orders to proceed there for a physical exam on July 15, 1940. Two days later he and 980 other members of the class of 1944, the largest in academy history to date, strode through Gate 1 into the Yard to begin their plebe summer training. One reason for the large class was a law passed by Congress in early 1940 that allowed men who were Congressional appointee alternates, as well as the principal nominee, to gain entrance to the academy if otherwise qualified.[23] The class was greeted by the superintendent, Rear Admiral Wilson Brown, and the commandant of midshipmen, Captain Milo Draemal.[24]

Induction day most assuredly was a whirlwind experience. With their first-class (1/C—senior) mentors barking orders, the new plebes were shuttled from place to place, receiving their uniforms and other necessary gear, being measured for class and formal uniforms, receiving a regulation haircut, and eventually being assigned to a room. Initially Jake was a member of Third Company, whose members resided in the fourth wing and first deck of Bancroft Hall, the common dormitory for all midshipmen. His roommate that summer was Walter Chadwick, another Pennsylvanian from Johnstown. The room was rather Spartan, a rough wooden table with a reading lamp, two unpainted wooden chairs, two single iron beds, radiator, washbasin, and two lockers.[25]

22. Ibid., 14–15.
23. Robert Harvey, interview with author, July 5, 2011. Harvey himself gained entrance to the academy through this alternative method.
24. Chester Nimitz to John Laboon Jr., June 26, 1940, Laboon file, AUSNA; Admiral Randy King, interview with author, April 7, 2011; Anderson, *All Americans*, 31–34; Annual Register, U.S. Naval Academy, 1939–1940; Executive Department USNA notice, July 17, 1940, PPJM. All members of the class of 1944 were required to present a $350 deposit for clothes and books. If desired, $250 of the $350 could be taken from the midshipman's pay over time. On another note, Jake soon learned that he was not the only member of his class to have a somewhat torturous experience in the entrance process. For example, his future football teammate Bill Busik had attended Meade, a prep school in California to ready himself academically for the academy.
25. Anderson, *All Americans*, 41; Capt. Walter Chadwick, USN, interview with author, July 1, 2012.

Formation for Military Service—The U.S. Naval Academy: 1940–1943

The Bancroft Hall accommodations might have been standard, but in the spring of 1941 the normal academy four-year academic program, as during the Spanish-American War and World War I, was accelerated to expedite the delivery of qualified junior officers to the fleet. In March 1941 President Franklin Roosevelt approved a fast-tracked training program at the three service academies: West Point, Coast Guard, and Annapolis. In early March 1941, Rear Admiral Chester Nimitz, chief of the Bureau of Navigation, announced to the Senate Appropriations Committee the dimensions of the program. The class of 1941 graduated in February; the class of 1942 would graduate in February 1942 and the class of 1943 in June 1942. Each succeeding class's training would be three years; the program would be in place for "two, three or four years, depending on the duration of the emergency."[26]

The accelerated training program for the class of 1944 required several modifications from the norm. Midshipmen took classes during the summer as well as fall and spring semesters. Thus certain at-sea training experience was sacrificed. The second class, or junior year, was eliminated; midshipmen advanced from fourth class (plebe) to third class (youngster) to first class. Thus the last two years were accomplished in one by cutting out drills and other nonessential military exercises and by attending the aforementioned summer classes. The class received no Christmas leave in 1940. However, even after the surprise attack on Pearl Harbor on December 7, 1941, Christmas leave was granted to all midshipmen. Later, one of Jake's classmates, Admiral Randy King, commented on the unexpected leave period: "Everyone got charged up."[27]

The fast-tracked training program was only one aspect of a changing face to the academy. In 1941 a physical expansion of the Yard was made with the reclamation of twenty-two acres from the Severn at the foot of the naval hospital. Additionally, the academy purchased 7.5 acres on the southeast corner of the Yard for the construction of Halsey Field House. A major addition was also made to Bancroft Hall through the construction of wings one and two at a cost of $1,786,000. The project, done to accommodate an

---

26. *Annapolis Evening Capital,* March 8, 1941.
27. Admiral Randy King, interview with the author, April 7, 2011; Clement O'Brien, interview with the author, January 27, 2011.

additional five hundred midshipmen, made the building into its now final block "H" construction.[28]

The physical changes at the academy were accompanied by concerns raised due to America's entry into the war. The Japanese attack on Pearl Harbor prompted new and immediate security procedures. Free access to the academy by civilians ended. Those seeking access to midshipmen or other personnel in the Yard were required to have proper identification and present themselves at the main gate. More significantly, even prior to Pearl Harbor, representatives George Padcock (R-Illinois) and S. M. Young (D-Ohio) suggested to the secretary of the navy that a second naval academy be established on the shores of Lake Erie in Ohio. The idea was rejected by the Navy Department and the president. The House Naval Committee, investigating the proposal, reported that such legislation "would be most injurious to the spirit of unity existing, and to the uniformity of training naval personnel." It went on to say, "The recent additions to the Naval Academy at Annapolis will provide all the regular officers required by the expanded Navy as now planned."[29]

The generally hot and humid Maryland summer provided the environmental background to the intense initial training received by Jake and his classmates. Historian Larry Berman has described the nature of the experience: "Plebe summer is designed to lay the foundation of life of a naval officer."[30] During the summer months, while upperclassman were engaged in at-sea training (and some assuredly in academic classes due to the accelerated program), the class of 1944 was involved with intense initial training in marching, sailing, marksmanship, and a battery of physical fitness tests, including swimming. Upperclassman showed no mercy toward plebes. Verbal abuse and physical punishment (hazing) were meted out, especially when

---

28. "History of the U.S. Naval Academy, 1845–1958," 15; *Annapolis Evening Capital*, October 24, 1940; Walter Chadwick, interview with author, July 1, 2012.

29. *Annapolis Evening Capital*, March 8, 1941, October 4, 1941, December 2, 1941. Secretary of the Navy Frank Knox, in responding to the proposal, stated, "The establishment of a second Naval Academy and an additional air training base at this time is not merely unnecessary but would be detrimental to the national defense because of the expenditure involved and because it would require the services of a number of regular officers who are urgently needed for combatant duties with the fleet."

30. Larry Berman, *Zumwalt: The Life and Times of Admiral Elmo Russell "Bud" Zumwalt, Jr.* (New York: HarperCollins, 2012), 43.

new arrivals did not know the programmed responses to various questions published in the academy student handbook, "Reef Points."[31] Plebes were often posed "professional questions" about military science that required research to answer. Responses were required by the time of the next meal if another time was not specifically stated. The writer Lars Anderson described the overall purpose of plebe indoctrination:

> It is the duty of the upperclassmen to impress upon the plebe that there is nothing that walks or crawls on earth that is lower than he.... He learns that as a plebe, he has no name, that he is "mister" to the members of every class but his own, and that "Sir" is the word he will use most frequently. After a while, he becomes used to it and learns one of the most valuable lessons—that to be able to command, one must know how to obey.[32]

With time the academy's demanding routine and long tradition became ingrained in Jake and his classmates. Plebes were up at 6:30 a.m. reveille and were occupied the entire day. Taps and lights out came at 10:05 p.m. Besides memorizing "Reef Points," other traditions abounded, including never traveling on any curved walkways in the Yard, "chopping" (light jog) and squaring all corners when traveling through Bancroft Hall, and most especially meal etiquette, which included "square meals" while being constantly badgered with questions from upperclassmen.[33] Plebes also quickly learned about the significance of the bronze replica of Tecumseh, Indian chief at the Battle of Tippecanoe, whose likeness once served as the figurehead of the USS *Delaware*. Located at the head of the courtyard fronting on Bancroft Hall, Tecumseh was known by midshipmen as the "God of 2.0" or the God of "C," the minimum grade average required at the academy. Midshipmen cast pennies before him and paid him tribute with left-hand salutes on the

---

31. One typical response to be memorized by plebes is illustrative. To the question "Why don't you understand?" a plebe was required to respond, "Sir, my cranium, consisting of Vermont marble, volcanic lava, and African ivory, covered with a thick layer of case hardened steel, forms an impenetrable barrier to all that seeks to impress itself upon the ashen tissues of my brain, hence the effulgent and ostensibly effervescent phrases just directed and reiterated for my comprehension have failed to permeate the somniferous forces of my atrocious intelligence, sir."

32. Anderson, *All Americans*, 41. Although Anderson published his book in 2004, the ideas were valid during Jake Laboon's time as a midshipman and before.

33. Plebes ate their meals with a straight back not touching the chair, chins "braced up" and eyes "in the boat" (straight ahead) unless they were addressed by an upperclassman. The term "square meal" comes from the motion of one's arm with a utensil taking food from one's plate, eating, and returning the utensil to the plate. The motion outlined a square.

way to exams. When battling archrival Army in sports, Tecumseh was always adorned in war paint.[34]

The academy and its tradition placed Jake in an uncomfortable position, but this was complemented by his time on the football field, a place where he was in his element. The *Annapolis Evening Capital* reported that two hundred men sought tryouts for the plebe team. Because he was recruited, however, Jake had an inside track, although he was not specifically mentioned as one of the "most promising yearlings." The paper suggested, "There are a number of sturdy kids in the squad, but the plebes have not half the heft that last year's team possessed."[35] Jake's attitude toward sport was premised on rivalry. One family friend years later recalled Jake saying, "Competition amongst men makes all men better."[36]

The academy plebe team of 1940, coached by John W. Wilson, played a five-game schedule, including contests against freshman teams from Georgetown and the University of North Carolina, Belmont Abbey College, and two prominent prep schools. Before the scheduled first game against Georgetown on September 28, Jake broke his left hand in practice.[37] Extant data is not clear on Jake's participation on the team that fall. Apparently his broken hand healed rather rapidly, for he was listed as a probable first-team starter at the position of end for the game against Admiral Farragut Academy on October 12. He also played as a substitute end in the team's 31–0 victory over Belmont Abbey College.[38] Despite the lackluster assessment of the team's potential by the local newspaper, the Navy Plebes finished the season 5–0.[39]

The camaraderie that Jake felt as a member of the plebe team provided immediate joy and, more importantly, inaugurated a friendship that would last the rest of his life. The plebe squad at times found itself practicing with

---

34. Anderson, *All Americans*, 42–43; Berman, *Zumwalt*, 41.
35. *Annapolis Evening Capital*, September 5, 1940.
36. Christopher Kidd, interview with author, October 4, 2010.
37. Medical history form, September 8, 1940, Laboon file, NMPR.
38. *Annapolis Evening Capital*, September 5, 1940, October 11, 1940, November 4, 1940. The original plebe schedule for 1940 was: September 28—Georgetown Freshmen; October 12—Admiral Farragut Academy; October 19—University of North Carolina Freshmen; October 26—Bullis School of Washington; November 2—Belmont Abbey College; November 16—Hun School, New Jersey. The final scheduled game was not played.
39. Besides the varsity and plebe teams, Navy also sported a varsity "B Squad" that had a four-game season, finishing 3–1; see *Annapolis Evening Capital*, November 16, 1940.

the varsity, allowing Jake to meet Isaac Kidd Jr., two years ahead of Jake and the center on the team. Kidd's father, Admiral Isaac Kidd, died on the battleship *Arizona* at Pearl Harbor only days before his namesake's graduation.[40] Jake's association with Isaac Kidd, who eventually rose to the rank of admiral, was extremely fortuitous, for it aided him significantly in his future career as a chaplain. While the two men served together only at the end of their careers, their enduring friendship and the contacts that Kidd provided for Jake were invaluable.[41]

Jake's love of sports and his general congenial personality allowed him to flourish. He was very popular among his fellow midshipmen. He was described by one classmate as one who "made his presence felt. He was a man who was extremely comfortable in his own skin. He enjoyed the respect, admiration, and affection of his classmates, regardless of their religious affiliation." In another context he was described as "genuine. There was nothing artificial or contrived about Jake." Another midshipman described him as "a really nice guy; everyone liked Jake." Many saw him as a man of great humor and "one of the most pleasant people that we had."[42] The sports historian, Lars Anderson, described Laboon:

There was a sweetness in his character that endeared him to admirals, midshipmen, and janitors alike. He talked to everybody about everything; no subjects were off limits.... His teammates quickly came to regard him as the biggest talker on the team.[43]

The 1943 "Lucky Bag" annual, which sported a photo of Jake as a 1/C "3-Striper" (midshipman lieutenant), provided a summary of his academy experience and his relationship with peers:

Big Jack was big! One of the tallest men in the regiment, "Boon" starred as an end on the football field and as [a] defenseman on the lacrosse team. Even though he is seriously minded, Jack has an ever-ready grin which is as infectious as it is long. Academically, "Boon" was not to worry, yet his conscience kept him working with the result that he was always "in the velvet." Returning the good jibes of "organ grind-

---

40. Chaplain Thomas Kirkpatrick, the first chaplain to die in World War II, was also on the *Arizona* on December 7, 1941.

41. *Baltimore Sun,* August 5, 1988; Christopher Kidd, interview with author, October 4, 2010.

42. Robert Harvey, interview with author, July 5, 2012; Charles Cooper, interview with author, February 15, 2011; Admiral Randy King, interview with author, April 7, 2011; Clement O'Brien, interview with author, January 27, 2011.

43. Anderson, *All Americans,* 93.

ers" and "peddle pounders" with his incomparable smiles, he played the organ at his church. Hoping that he can squeeze himself into a cockpit, Jack plans to enter the Air Corps.[44]

Jake fully participated in the life of the academy and the various activities provided for midshipmen. "Graduating" from the life of a lowly plebe, Jake and his immediate company classmates started their 3/C (youngster/ sophomore) year as members of 12th company. Admiral Elmo Zumwalt, the youngest man in navy history to be appointed chief of naval operations, who was one year ahead of Laboon, described his transition to 3/C status:

I must admit that Youngster year is 100 percent more fun than Plebe year. Plebe year … means no imperfection—the plebe is the lowest form of life.… Youngster year regain[s] self-respect, partake[s] in all pranks known—water fights, hosing, etc.[45]

Jake took his turn as the one who could mete out punishment upon plebes. Years later Rear Admiral Doniphan Shelton, class of 1945, spoke of an encounter when Laboon, a youngster, whacked Shelton with a broom as part of a hazing ritual. Shelton commented, "I didn't see the rationale for that, and it did hurt."[46]

While there were many new aspects to Jake Laboon's life as a midshipman, his rock foundation of faith became his "sanctuary" to which he could escape. Several of his classmates and fellow midshipmen noticed and commented on this aspect of his life. One classmate referred to Jake's faith as "strong and abiding." He went on, "If a class could have a spiritual leader, an Ayatollah, Jake was it." Another classmate remembered how Jake often visited George Schlichte, a member of the class of 1943, who was considered by other midshipmen as "the religious type." Years later Schlichte became the first rector of Pope John XXIII Seminary in Boston.[47] One of his lacrosse teammates said that, whenever possible, Jake crossed the railroad bridge over the Severn to visit Manresa, a Jesuit retreat house where he would later serve after his retirement from the navy.[48]

---

44. "Lucky Bag," 1943, U.S. Naval Academy Library.
45. Berman, *Zumwalt*, 56.
46. Reminiscences of RADM Doniphan B. Shelton, transcribed, AUSNA.
47. Pope John XXIII Seminary in Boston was founded and still functions as a house of religious formation for men in second careers. George Schlichte was known for his discipline when serving as rector at the seminary.
48. Gordon Ochenrider, interview with author, April 14, 2012.

Laboon's faith was also manifested in very tangible ways, both in the Yard and in the city of Annapolis. During Laboon's time at the academy, the chaplain's office was served by Commander (later Captain) William Thomas and Lieutenant Paul W. J. Dickman.[49] Shortly after his arrival Jake joined the Newman Club at the academy and later served as both vice president and president of the organization. On Sunday mornings he led the Catholic church party in its weekly trek to St. Mary's Church, located on Duke of Gloucester Street in Annapolis. Jake was not merely an attendee; he played the organ at Mass.[50]

Besides his faith, Jake's large and very supportive family was another anchor that steadied him during his academy days. He could not have been more proud when he observed three of his siblings enter the Sisters of Mercy in Pittsburgh. Patrice, who took the religious name deLellis, entered in 1937. She taught home economics for many years at Mercy College (today Carlow University). Rosemary entered in 1940 and taught in Catholic elementary schools for forty years; Joan, the youngest girl in the family, entered in 1945, teaching school and serving as a high school principal in Puerto Rico for many years.[51] Besides the entrance of three members of the family into the convent, the war years also brought a major change in the life of Jake's father. In January 1943, John Laboon left his position with Allegheny County and volunteered to serve as a military governor in Europe. His decision generated some financial concerns for the family, since his salary from the federal government was less than half what he received from the county, but Jake was proud that his father was willing to serve, trusting that his mother could adequately hold the family together during his absence. After he completed a training session in Charlottesville, Virginia, the senior Laboon was sent to the Province of Livorno in Italy. There he served until the end of the war. In March 1946, when he returned to Pittsburgh, he was appointed as chief engineer to a new group, the Allegheny County Sanitary Authority, created by the secretary of the Commonwealth of Pennsylvania.[52]

---

49. Jennifer Bryan, Ph.D., e-mail to author, July 2, 2013.

50. John F. Laboon, midshipman personnel record, AUSNA; Anderson, *All Americans*, 93, 232; Joseph Laboon, interview with author, August 19, 2010.

51. *Catholic News Service*, December 25, 2009; Rosemary, deLellis, and Joan Laboon, interview with author, August 4, 2010.

52. John F. Laboon, "The Diary of a Military Governor in World War II," n.d., personal papers of Joseph Laboon (hereafter PPJoL), Lakeland, Fla.; Joel A. Tarr, ed., *Devastation and Rule: An Envi-*

Activities and family concerns, while certainly of great importance to Jake, would always have to take second place to his academic pursuits. During Jake's tenure at the academy midshipmen took a standard academic program with few variations. Only later, when he returned to the academy as a senior navy chaplain, were majors and elective programs in place. During his plebe year the program was highly technical, concentrating in mathematics and chemistry, but including literature, composition, and Spanish. His grades were mediocre; his lowest grade was 2.76 in composition, his highest 3.31 in spherical trigonometry. These marks placed him in the lower 20 percent of his class in most subjects, save mathematics. During his sophomore year a strong emphasis on mathematics continued, but this was complemented with several "professional" subjects such as seamanship, engineering materials, mechanisms of naval machinery, and naval history. He continued to study Spanish as well as taking a course in U.S. foreign policy. His 1/C year of study concentrated on science and engineering, with a continuation of the necessary navy professional courses as well as classes in modern European history, U.S. government, and Spanish. His final-year grades ranged from 2.82 to 3.41, placing him again in the lower 25 percent of his class.[53]

As one might expect from his rather mediocre classroom performance, Jake Laboon's naval academy legacy is not found in his academic achievements, but in his athletic prowess. Recruited to play football and with his plebe year under his belt, Jake advanced to the varsity during the 1941 season. Navy was coached that year by Emery "Swede" Larson, a member of the class of 1922 who started coaching at Navy in 1939. He had played football as a midshipman, captaining the team in 1920. That year and in 1921 he was selected as a second-team All American. Larson also played lacrosse at the academy, receiving first-team All-American status in 1922. After graduation he took a commission in the Marine Corps and in 1939 was assigned as commanding officer of the marine attachment at the academy. Lars Anderson described Larson: "He had a presence, and air that you could feel when he

---

ronmental History of Pittsburgh and Its Region (Pittsburgh: University of Pittsburgh Press, 2003), 81; William Dawson, SJ, interview with author, October 28, 2010. Due to his service Mr. Laboon was appointed a Knight of Saint Gregory by Pope Pius XII and was awarded the Cross of the Cavalier of the Crown of Italy by the Italian government.

53. John F. Laboon Jr. USNA academic transcript; John Laboon midshipman personnel file, AUSNA; annals registers, USNA, 1941–42 and 1942–43, USNA Library.

walked into a room.... Though he did not have a booming voice or a heavy-set build, Larson commanded attention with his magnetizing persona."[54]

Larson headed a five-man coaching staff that included Rip Miller as line coach and Commander J. E. Whelchel as one of two backfield coaches. Larson's philosophy and formula for a winning team was based on hard work. In the fall of 1939, having assumed the head coaching position the previous spring, Larson spoke to the plebe team about what it would take to achieve greatness:

> You are the future of the varsity team; you are the guys who will someday lead this program to greatness. It will be a lot of work. I am not going to lie to you. In fact, you are going to work harder than you have ever worked before. But that is why, when it really matters, we'll be victorious. It all starts out there on the practice field. That is where we'll win games. Now let us get to work and do this together.[55]

Prospects for the 1941 navy varsity were high. In mid-September the *Annapolis Evening Capital* reported, "Navy after a fine year in 1940 expects to have one of its greatest years in the campaign just ahead." One week later an equally bold prediction was published:

> A winning Naval Academy team can materially aid the morale of the entire naval service as well as build up added favorable public sentiment for the service. Fortunately, the midshipmen seem to possess the will, the ability and the manpower to accomplish this essential objective, despite the stiff opposition they will encounter week after week between now and the closing days of November.[56]

The team had twenty-nine returning letterman; only twelve were lost from the previous year's team. Viewing high prospects himself, Larson told his players before their first game,

> We have a chance to be one of the best Navy teams in the history of Navy football. But at this point, it is just a chance. We have to work hard and stay focused now until the season is over.[57]

The 1941 navy team was a combination of the old and the new. As in the past and like most high school, college, and professional teams, Navy used the

---

54. Anderson, *All Americans*, 44–46.

55. Quoted in Ibid., 47. The entire varsity coaching staff for 1941 season was: Major Emery Larson, head coach; Edgar "Rip" Miller, line coach; Raymond Swartz, assistant line coach; CDR J. E. Whelchel, backfield coach; Keith Molesworth, backfield coach; see *Annapolis Evening Capital*, September 3, 1941.

56. *Annapolis Evening Capital*, September 16, 1941, September 24, 1941.

57. Quoted in Anderson, *All Americans*, 75.

single-wing offense, which had been the concept of Glenn (Pop) Warner, the legendary coach at Carlisle, beginning in 1906. The 1941 season saw some innovations that were common to all teams. First, the concept of single-platoon football ended and free-player substitutions began. Second, a player numbering system went into effect: numbers 10–49 would be used by backs; numbers 50–89 would be used by lineman.[58] Larson kept eighty-eight players on the squad. The star of the team was tailback Bill Busik, a triple threat to run, pass, or punt; the captain of the team was Bob Froude. The *Annapolis Evening Capital* listed three players from the 1940 plebe team as "promising candidates": Carl Siegfried, Melvin Montgomery, and Casey Plozay. Jake Laboon was not shown on the preseason depth chart for first or second string.[59]

As the principal line coach, Rip Miller worked with Jake, who as an end wore number 87. From his days at Notre Dame, Miller understood the role of a lineman and taught it to his players. He often donned pads and mixed it up with them. He was quoted in the November 1926 issue of the *Athletic Journal:*

> The main objective of the offensive lineman is to obtain quick contact and above all things to keep that contact. Whether a lineman uses a shoulder charge to drive a man out of the way of a play, or whether he reverts to a body block to prevent the drifting defensive opponent from slicing into a play, or whether he runs interference in the open field, the thing uppermost in his mind at all times is—to keep contact. Too many offensive linemen give up early.[60]

Working with great coaches like Miller, Laboon and his teammates prepared themselves for the 1941 season, one of the most storied in the academy's history.

The season began in fine fashion as Navy rolled to three consecutive lopsided victories, surrendering only two points to Lafayette in the process. Sporting new uniforms, the Midshipmen opened the season on September 27 against William and Mary, the thirteenth consecutive time the teams had met in an opening game. The game was played in the naval academy yard at Thompson Stadium, with a capacity of 21,660 fans. Larson was most concerned that his players had examinations just prior to the game. However, with the team's star tailback, Bill Busik, leading the way, Navy crushed its opponent 34–0. Jake saw action as a substitute end. Navy was equally dominat-

---

58. Ibid., 75–76, 79.
59. *Annapolis Evening Capital*, September 3, 1941, September 24, 1941.
60. Quoted in Anderson, *All Americans*, 77.

Formation for Military Service—The U.S. Naval Academy: 1940–1943

ing in its second contest, playing on the road and rolling over West Virginia 40–0. The *Annapolis Evening Capital* commented, "The two crushing defeats [victories over William and Mary and West Virginia] by the Navy powerhouse have placed the Middies in the forefront of Eastern teams—but the testing is still to come." Again, Jake saw action at end.[61] The same scenario was repeated on October 11, playing at home with a 41–2 defeat of Lafayette.

Although Jake was not a starter, he nevertheless received significant support from his family. Generally his parents and some siblings made the long drive from Pittsburgh to Annapolis to watch games. Such events were a joy for all, providing opportunities to swap stories and rekindle the familial ties that were so important to Jake.[62]

With three lopsided victories under their belt, the Navy eleven entered into the most challenging part of their season. Trumpeting the team's early success, the local paper commented:

Navy as a team is big, streamlined, and powerful. Substitutes when made usually are in team units. Despite the power available Navy's present-day offense includes complex reverses and considerable deception.... Navy is exceptionally well-balanced in precision playing for this time of the year.[63]

On October 18, with the entire brigade of midshipmen, some 3,110, in attendance, Navy defeated Cornell 14–0 at Baltimore Stadium. At midseason, with a record of 4–0, Navy was rated number five in the country.[64] On the following Saturday Navy traveled to Boston to take on the Harvard Crimson. While the midshipmen statistically outplayed their opponents, sloppy execution, including four lost fumbles and several critical penalties, resulted in a frustrating 0–0 tie.[65]

Needing to regroup after their worst performance of the season, Navy found itself on center stage on November 1 playing the University of Pennsylvania before 73,000 fans in Philadelphia's historic Franklin Field. Two

61. *Annapolis Evening Capital*, October 6, 1941.
62. Joseph Laboon, interview with the author, August 19, 2010; Sr. Joan Laboon, RSM, interview with the author, September 9, 2012.
63. *Annapolis Evening Capital*, October 16, 1941.
64. At this midseason point the teams rated above Navy were Minnesota, Texas, Michigan, and Duke. The sports historian Lars Anderson claims that at this high point for 1941 Navy football, the team received a bid to play in the 1942 Rose Bowl. The claim could not be verified by this author; see Anderson, *All Americans*, 90.
65. *Annapolis Evening Capital*, October 27, 1941.

battalions of midshipmen, together with the seventy-five-member Navy band, traveled to the game. In a driving rainstorm the Midshipmen defeated the Quakers 13–6, placing Navy back on course for a stellar season. Navy dominated the game offensively, traveling inside Penn's ten-yard line six times, but only scoring on two occasions. The game was memorable and became legendary for Jake Laboon in a much different way. Not having played against Cornell or Harvard, Jake was eager to see action. With Navy ahead 13–0, Bill Busik was knocked cold by a "cheap shot" from a Penn player after a play had ended. While the officials apparently did not see the incident, Rip Miller did and would not let the episode go without retribution. Miller called Laboon and asked him if he had seen what happened. When Jake acknowledged he had, Miller proceeded to tell him, "Get in there and I do not want that end [the Penn player who committed the foul] to be in the game much longer." Jake understood his mission. On the very next play Laboon lined up against the Penn player. As the ball was snapped he grabbed a fistful of mud from the field and flung it into the player's face. The play from scrimmage drifted away from these two, allowing them to stand together, and Jake struck the player with all his might in the face. The Penn player suffered a broken nose; Jake was ejected from the game. Miller told Jake, "I did not tell you to take him out in front of everybody.... I meant for you to be a little more subtle about it." Nevertheless, Miller approved and was proud that Laboon protected his own.[66]

The 1941 season closed with games against Notre Dame and Princeton, followed by the traditional contest against archrival Army. The entire brigade of midshipmen was transported to Baltimore for the November 8 game against Notre Dame. While Navy outgained and in many ways outplayed the Fighting Irish, Notre Dame's sensational quarterback, Angelo Bertelli, who led the nation in passing in 1941 and won the Heisman Trophy in 1943, played a stellar game, and Notre Dame outlasted Navy 20–13. The next week, however, Navy bounced back and defeated Princeton 23–0 be-

66. *Annapolis Evening Capital*, October 31, 1941; Anderson, *All Americans*, 91–93; William Dawson, SJ, interview with the author, October 20, 2010. The *Annapolis Evening Capital* reported, "Busik was badly shaken up and lost one of his front teeth"; the *Washington Post* reported, "Busik was helped from the field not to return"; see *Annapolis Evening Capital*, November 4, 1941 and *Washington Post*, November 2, 1941. Anderson claims that Laboon felt disturbed about what had happened; he writes, "One of the most popular Midshipmen at the Naval Academy, Laboon had a clear idea of the line between right and wrong, and he felt he had crossed it."

fore 42,000 fans at Palmer Stadium in New Jersey. Navy's potent offense gained 507 yards, while the defense limited Princeton to 85 total yards.[67]

Navy's final game of the 1941 season, the traditional rivalry against Army, was "Swede" Larson's last, as he was reassigned to the fleet. Army was coached by Earl "Red" Blaik. Like Larson, who had played for Navy, Blaik, although undersized, played for the Cadets and was a third-team All American. During his tenure he transformed Army's football program, including coaching the great World War II teams anchored by Glenn Davis and Felix "Doc" Blanchard. Traditionally played on the Saturday after Thanksgiving in Philadelphia, the game was attended by the First Lady, Eleanor Roosevelt, and Ilo Wallace, wife of Vice President Henry Wallace, as well as the secretary of war and other dignitaries. Although Jake did not play and therefore did not earn the coveted N* indicative of participation in a victory over Army, Navy won the game 14–6.[68]

The 1941 season gained the Navy team several accolades. In the final college ratings the Midshipmen garnered tenth position, with Minnesota at the top spot and Notre Dame at number three. Navy won the Lambert Cup, symbolic of the Eastern United States grid championship. The *Annapolis Evening Capital* succinctly summed up the year: "Annapolis had a brilliant team this year."[69]

On December 7 the superintendent hosted the team at his residence in the Yard to celebrate a great season and a victory over Army. Jake, his teammates, and some of the team's "drags" were enjoying themselves at the party when the superintendent received a call informing him of the attack on Pearl Harbor. The superintendent told the players, "We are now at war, gentlemen. Return to quarters and await further orders."[70]

The 1942 team, with big shoes to fill, presented a very different look from the previous year. First, the coaching staff was different. Commander John Whelchel, who had served as a backfield coach under Larson, was

---

67. *Annapolis Evening Capital*, November 7, 1941, November 10, 1941, November 24, 1941.

68. Anderson, *All Americans*, 106, 109, 117–18, 57–60; *Annapolis Evening Capital*, November 28, 1941, November 29, 1941, December 1, 1941. The N* is an award, worn on a sweater, that indicates the individual has earned a letter, with the * signifying a victory over Army in his sport. An ironic and tragic twist of history was present in the 1941 Army-Navy football program; on page 180 there was a photo of the USS *Arizona* plowing through a huge ocean swell. The caption read, "It is significant that, despite the claims of air enthusiasts, no battleship has yet been sunk by bombs." The Japanese attack on Pearl Harbor would come only one week later.

69. *Annapolis Evening Capital*, December 1, 1941, December 2, 1941.

70. Anderson, *All Americans*, 147. The term "drags" is academy jargon for a date. Thus players and some of their girlfriends were present at the reception.

named head coach. Rip Miller, Keith Molesworth, and Ray Swartz were holdovers, as well. Two new men, R. C. Scaffe and Lieutenant C. R. Shea, joined the coaching staff. Another important change was that Navy (and Army) could use freshman on the varsity as long as their accelerated three-year academic program was in place, thus rescinding an NCAA rule first adopted in 1922.[71] Alan Cameron, a veteran halfback from the 1941 squad, was elected team captain. Jake Laboon, described as a "star blocker" who "moved through opposing players like machete through a wheat field," was listed on the initial depth chart as a first-string end along with Bob Wilcoe.[72] He was expected to handle things on the weak side flank of the line.[73]

Unfortunately, the misfortune that greeted him on the preseason practice field as a plebe rose again now in his final year. On September 17 the team participated in a two-hour scrimmage with the Chicago Bears. The practice was designed to show the Navy squad how the innovative "T" offense operated and to provide the Bears, in route to a game in Boston with the Eastern Army All Stars, a bit of exercise. During the scrimmage Jake was knocked cold when tackling a ball carrier. He remained unconscious for fifteen minutes and later had no recollection of events immediately prior to the incident. He was hospitalized for a few days, prompting him to request and receive permission to take some required examinations in the hospital.[74] While Jake returned to practice approximately one week later, the injury set him back considerably for the entire season.[75]

71. "Summary of Freshmen Eligibility," NCAA, attachment to e-mail from Ellen Summers to Richard Gribble, April 1, 2013. Special consideration was given to the naval academy and West Point in 1942 for freshmen eligibility due to their specialized three-year academic program. In 1944 the freshmen ineligibility for all schools was rescinded for the war years. In 1947 the prewar non-eligibility rules for freshmen resumed. The freshmen eligibility restriction was eliminated in 1972.

72. Anderson, *All Americans*, 230; *Annapolis Evening Capital*, September 8, 1942.

73. *Annapolis Evening Capital*, September 24 1942.

74. *Annapolis Evening Capital*, September 18, 1942; medical history record, September 17, 1942, Laboon file, NMPR; John Laboon to Superintendent USNA, September 18, 1942; Superintendent USNA to John Laboon, September 21, 1942, Laboon file, AUSNA. Years later Laboon told Dr. Joseph DeSantis that during the scrimmage he was playing the linebacker position instead of his normal end. On one particular play he was smashed by an offensive guard and then "run over" by the fullback, causing his concussion. The incident later prompted his teammates to give Jake the nickname "Sleepy Laboon," a takeoff on Sleepy Lagoon, a popular song at the time; see Jack Clary, "Ballfield to Battlefield," *Naval History* 18, no. 5 (October 2004): 37, clipping, John Laboon biographical file, U.S. Navy Submarine Force Museum (hereafter ASBNL), New London, Conn.

75. *Annapolis Evening Capital*, September 30, 1942; the paper reported that he was replaced by George Brown.

Navy's 1942 season, especially in comparison with a previous year, was one of mediocrity. The team opened, as it had the past thirteen years, with William and Mary. Decimated by injuries that included those of team captain Alan Cameron and Laboon and not showing "the finesse, precision, and timing of a smooth working outfit," Navy lost 3–0 before fewer than 15,000 fans at Thompson Stadium. Navy won the statistics, more than doubling the offensive output of William and Mary, but it could not capitalize, even though the offense crossed the fifty-yard line seven times during the game. The next week Navy cruised past Virginia 35–0; one week later the team lost to Princeton 10–0 before 25,000 fans in a game played at Yankee Stadium. Having recovered sufficiently, Jake was used as a substitute end in both games. The up-and-down season and Jake's substitute role continued the next week on October 17 as the Midshipmen defeated Yale 13–6 at Baltimore Stadium. Half the brigade traveled to Baltimore via the Steamer *Bay Belle* and witnessed an impressive offensive performance.[76]

The remainder of the season continued the seesaw course of the first half, although the team did finish with a flourish. On October 24 Navy was shut out 21–0 by Georgia Tech at Thompson Stadium. The numerous injuries to starters gave Jake the opportunity to play left tackle in the game. However, some undisclosed injury did not allow him to play the next week when the team traveled to Cleveland to play Notre Dame. Navy played the Irish tough, but again the brilliant play of Angelo Bertelli proved the difference as the men from South Bend won the contest 9–0. Despite two consecutive losses and numerous injuries to key players, Navy pulled a major upset by defeating Penn on November 7 in Philadelphia. The Quakers won the statistics, but Navy, cheered on by over 800 1/C midshipmen among the 74,000 in attendance, managed a 7–0 victory in a low-scoring contest. One week later Navy defeated Columbia 13–9 in Baltimore. Once again Navy was outplayed in the statistics, but a touchdown pass with a little over one minute to play proved the difference. In both these contests Jake returned to substitute duty, this time as a tackle.[77]

Navy closed out its 1942 campaign against Army on November 28.

---

76. Ibid., September 25, 1942, September 28, 1942, October 2, 1942, October 5, 1942, October 8, 1942, October 12, 1942, October 15, 1942, October 19, 1942. The midshipmen traveled to Baltimore via steamer because the Office of Defense Transportation had scuttled all unnecessary military transportation by train.

77. Ibid., November 9, 1942, November 14, 1942, November 16, 1942.

Formation for Military Service—The U.S. Naval Academy: 1940–1943

Due to wartime travel restrictions, the game was played at Thompson Stadium for the first time since 1893. Only 11,700 people attended what was described by one observer as one of the most aggressive games ever played between the two rivals. Army was favored to win, but the Midshipmen prevailed 14–0. The *Annapolis Evening Capital* commented, "The Navy team—playing even better than it did when it humbled the Penn powerhouse—nearly drove the cadets off the field."[78] Jake earned his N* by virtue of his participation in the game, but it was not without some conflict. Jake was once again, as in the Penn contest of November 1, 1941, sent into the game to "take care of business." In this case Army's tough defensive tackle, Robin Olds, who would later rise to the rank of general, was playing havoc with Navy's halfbacks. Jake initiated the confrontation by throwing dirt into Olds's face, prompting the latter to swing a punch at Laboon. While he missed, Jake in response knocked out one of Olds's two front teeth.[79]

Jake Laboon was recruited to play football and played during his three years at the academy. However, it was the game of lacrosse, which Jake had never played, that actually brought him to the apex of his athletic prominence. William H. "Dinty" Moore, Navy's legendary lacrosse coach, some of his football teammates, and a classmate, Bob Booze, recruited Jake to play. In the early 1940s spring football practice did not exist, and Moore was on the hunt for good athletes to play lacrosse. The game was foreign to Jake, but because of his great athleticism, he was a natural. The extant record on Jake's participation in lacrosse is not clear. He earned the block "44" (his class year) for the 1940–41 season, his plebe year, yet he earned no accolade for the sport during his youngster year. Yet the "Lucky Bag" photo of the lacrosse team in 1942, while having no caption with names, shows Laboon on the team.[80]

Navy's 1942 team posted a 7–2 record, including key wins over Dartmouth, Cornell, and Rutgers, but suffering a loss to the Black Knights of the

---

78. Ibid., October 29, 1942, October 23, 1942, November 27, 1942, November 30, 1942; Anderson, *All Americans*, 182.

79. Jack Johnson, interview with author, January 27, 2011; Admiral Charles Heid, interview with author, July 31, 2011.

80. Gordon Ochenrider, interview with the author, April 14, 2012; Joseph Laboon, interview with the author, August 19, 2010; Stephen Phillips, interview with the author, August 13, 2010; John Laboon Jr., USNA academic transcript, Laboon file, AUSNA; Donald T. Fritz, "The Original All-American Hero," September 1990, clipping, PPJL. Ochenrider remembers practicing with Jake during their common youngster year.

Hudson. Once again, extant data does not provide a clear record of Jake's participation during this year. His teammate, Gordon Ochenrider, who played offense, scrimmaged against Laboon, who was a defenseman. He described Jake as "tough and determined." The only extant official record, the *Annapolis Evening Capital*, never mentions Laboon as a starter or substitute throughout the season.[81]

Any uncertainty concerning Jake Laboon's presence on the lacrosse field was put to rest in 1943 as he and his teammates, under Moore's direction, produced a championship team. The 1943 "Lucky Bag" accurately predicted how the season would go: "With behemoths like Sieggy [Clyde Siegfried], Big [George] Montgomery, Laboon and Anania guarding [Ray] Strassle in the net, goals are going to be as scarce as Nazis in Libya."[82] In the early season Navy mowed down its opponents in dramatic fashion. Jake was the starter at "point," a defensive position. The team's one blemish was a 7–6 loss to Princeton on May 1. The season culminated with a 12–5 thrashing of Army in a game played in the Yard on Farragut Field.[83] The contest earned Jake his second N* for a victory over Army. During the game, Jake's father, who had left his position with Allegheny County Pittsburgh to become a military governor in Italy, sat on the Navy bench. He described the scene in his diary: "I sat on the Navy players' bench in my Army uniform as the Army officers across the field eyed me wondering who the traitor was."[84]

The victory over Army was not Jake's last lacrosse contest, as he and five of his teammates were selected to play on the South squad in the annual North-South All Star game, played at Homewood Field at Johns Hopkins University in Baltimore. Starting the game at defensive point, Jake completely shut out Princeton's two-time All-American forward, Bud Palmer. The South squad won the game 9–5 before 4,500 fans.[85]

---

81. The *Annapolis Evening Capital* has box scores for most all the games of the 1942 season. Laboon is never listed as a player. This lack of evidence combined with his transcript record, which gives no indication that he earned a naval academy letter ("NA") for his participation in the 1942 team, leads one to believe that for reasons that are unclear he did not play that year. Yet his teammate Gordon Ochenrider remembers competing against him on the practice field.

82. "Lucky Bag," 1943, U.S. Naval Academy Library.

83. Navy lacrosse record, Naval Academy Athletic Association records (hereafter NAAA), Annapolis, Md.; "Lucky Bag, 1944," U.S. Naval Academy Library.

84. John F. Laboon, "Diary of a Military Governor," n.d. [1943–1945], PPJoL.

85. *Annapolis Evening Capital*, May 31, 1943, June 5, 1943; John F. Laboon, "Diary of a Military Governor," n.d. [1943–1945], PPJoL. The six Navy players who played on the South team were Ray Strassle, John Laboon, Clyde Siegfried, Gordon Ochenrider, Bob Booze, and George Montgomery.

Navy's stellar season brought awards to the team and many of its players. Despite the one loss to Princeton, Navy was voted the U.S. Intercollegiate Lacrosse Association National Champion. Several members of the team earned the coveted title All American. First-team selections went to Bob Booze and Gordon "Bud" Ochenrider; Jake Laboon, Clyde Siegfried, and Ray Strassle earned second-team All-American status. "Monty" Montgomery was a third-team selection.[86]

Unquestionably, sports were an integral part of Jake Laboon's naval academy experience, but the reality was that the United States was fighting a two-front war and the immediate need for more qualified officers in the Atlantic and Pacific theaters could not be delayed. In January 1943 Jake took his precommissioning physical examination. While his concussion on the football practice field was usually considered a "disqualifying" scenario for certain service-selection assignments, the report issued by the medical team did not consider the injury sufficient grounds to bar him from any possibilities. It read, "[He] is physically qualified for duty involving actual control of aircraft." Clearly Jake had considered naval aviation, but he chose another route. Many years later he explained his decision: "I wanted to become a naval aviator. I wanted to get into action right away. But I felt the war would be over by the time I got to be an aviator." At another time he explained further, "I volunteered for submarine duty because I wanted to get into combat as soon as I could."[87]

With his service selection made and the national championship lacrosse season ended, Jake was ready for graduation and commissioning. June (Graduation) Week 1943 ran from Saturday, June 5, to Wednesday, June 9. Jake's family attended many of the events.[88] Festivities included two brigade parades, a chapel service with the sermon preached to the graduating class

---

86. List, 1943 Men's All-Americans Lacrosse; see http://www.usila.org/AllAmericanPDFs/1943_AA.pdf.

87. Physical examination for flying, January 12, 1943, Laboon file, NMPR; *Honolulu Advertiser*, n.d., Laboon file, AUSNA; clipping, personal papers of William Laboon (hereafter PPWL), Greensburg, Pa. Apparently many midshipmen volunteered for submarine duty, but there were insufficient billets. Thus those who volunteered were put in a pool and from that, one hundred were selected, including Laboon and his plebe summer roommate Walter Chadwick; see Walter Chadwick, interview with author, July 1, 2012.

88. Prior to the shift in the timing of academic semesters that led to graduation in May, the tradition at the naval academy was to celebrate "June Week," a celebration of approximately five days culminating in graduation. Today, since graduation is in May, the term "Graduation Week" is used.

by the senior chaplain, Captain William Thomas, and the superintendent's reception. On Saturday, June 5, athletic awards were presented in Tecumseh Court. At the ceremony 160 athletes, including Jake, received the coveted N* for victories over Army.[89]

Graduation for the class of 1944 was held in Dahlgren Hall on June 9, 1943. Jake, who graduated 568 of 766 (the largest graduating class to date), and 728 of his classmates were commissioned ensigns in the U.S. Navy.[90] The graduation speaker was Secretary of the Navy Frank Knox. Speaking to the assembled midshipmen, their families, and friends, Knox challenged his audience "to answer the call to leadership in the nation's hour of greatest need." He suggested an open mind was a requisite quality: "An attitude that 'I learned it all at Annapolis,' will help neither you nor the Navy. There will never be a time in your life when you will not have much to know." He also acknowledged the challenges of the accelerated program necessitated by the demands of war: "The fact that you are being commissioned a year earlier than pre-war classes places a responsibility upon you for further individual study and self-improvement. You are leaving your classrooms, but I hope you do not feel you are leaving the path of learning. From today forward through your naval careers your continued education will be governed by your own initiative and by your own desires." Knox spoke of the present generation's "loftier mission." He stated, "Your generation is destined to pioneer the new age that lies ahead of us—the age which tyranny sought to rule in which you and your fellows will win for all free men." The secretary spoke of the privilege given these young officers to serve the brightest and best trained enlisted in navy history. He concluded his address, "The men who guide your country will not let you down. You must not let them down."[91] The ceremony ended with the traditional cry: "Three cheers for those who leave us and three cheers for those we leave behind." The caps of over seven hundred midshipmen were sent skyward; it was their time to do the duty for which they had been trained.

89. Joseph Laboon, interview with author, August 19, 2010; *Annapolis Evening Capital*, June 4, 1943, June 5, 1943.

90. John F. Laboon Jr., midshipmen personnel File, AUSNA; *Annapolis Evening Capital*, June 9, 1943. Twenty-five members of the class were commissioned second lieutenants in the Marine Corps. A few were not commissioned; a few others had their commission status pending their time of graduation.

91. *Annapolis Evening Capital*, June 9, 1943.

Conclusion

At the age of twenty-three Jake Laboon had already demonstrated many of the fine qualities that would characterize his life in service to God and country. His "never say die attitude" was manifested in his difficult but successful path to the naval academy. Once he arrived, however, there was no looking back, for he was constantly poised to push forward to achieve personal goals, but never at the expense of others. From his earliest days he endeared himself to his navy classmates, both through his athletic success and by his strongly demonstrated faith in God and nation. His desire to utilize his training as productively and rapidly as possible led him to choose submarines, the most dangerous of all possible service-selection choices. It was time for him to leave the relative serenity and familiarity of Annapolis, his family, and classmates and venture forth, during a time of war, to meet the challenges his commission as a naval officer would bring.

Chapter 3

World War II Submariner
★ 1943–1946

The naval academy class of 1944 graduated at a time when the United States was once again embroiled in a world war, fighting a two-front conflict against the Axis powers in Europe and the Pacific. The war had already affected the Laboon family when John Laboon Sr. left the comfort of his position with Allegheny County to serve as a military governor in Italy. The war would come home even more graphically through the service of its eldest son, who was in harm's way for the last eighteen months of the conflict. Volunteering in submarines, Jake Laboon held a strong desire to be an active player in the war. With this in the forefront of his mind, Jake took up arms seeking to do his part to bring the world back to stability and peace. His service was noteworthy, not only because of the distinction he would bring upon himself through an act of heroism, but more importantly because of how it would color the remainder of his life. With self-confidence, personal flair, and strong faith, Laboon proved to be an inspiration to his peers in the submarine force while providing the base for a highly significant military career that would touch thousands.

Preliminary Duties and Training

With the festive nature of June Week concluded, it was time for the newly minted Ensign, U.S. Navy, Jake Laboon, to take his place in the fleet. Approximately half of the class of 1944 was granted leave until June 27. The other half, including Jake, was ordered to report on or before 12 noon on June 13, 1943, to the chief of Naval Air Operational Training at the Naval Air Station, Jacksonville, Florida, "for temporary duty involving flying as a technical observer."[1] Many of his classmates who were also bound for submarine duty were sent to Jacksonville for temporary active duty until space was available in the training school at New London. During his three months in Florida Jake was trained as a backseat passenger in planes, with much time spent in the classroom on the recognition of enemy planes and ships.[2] Compared to his recent experience at the academy, Jake and his classmates enjoyed their free time. In recalling their common experience, Admiral Robert Long spoke of Jake: "There were times in Florida when he was as wild as you can imagine. But you always had the feeling that here was a person that would help you if you needed help. He was a friend."[3] Jake spent the last week of his brief Florida tour at the Naval Air Station, Daytona Beach, where his commanding officer noted, "His performance of duty was in all respects satisfactory." It was noted in his fitness report that his short tenure in Florida did not allow for full observation of his officer qualities, but concluded that his "duty as a technical observer has been satisfactory."[4]

Jake detached from Daytona Beach on August 21 and reported to the submarine school in New London, Connecticut, on September 27 "for temporary duty under instruction in submarines."[5] During the interim he took his post-academy one-month leave, which was delayed due to his orders to report immediately to Florida after graduation. Returning home to Pittsburgh, he spent some time with his family discussing his immediate future.

After his leave Jake reported to the Naval Submarine School at New London, which was first established in December 1915. The faculty and extent of training for both officers and enlisted personnel expanded with time, but on July 1, 1940, in order to meet anticipated need, the training program for officers was actually shortened from six months to thirteen weeks. Enlisted personnel continued their six-week program. This change allowed for two additional officer classes each year. In 1942, with practice training acutely

1. Chief of Naval Training to Ensign John Laboon, May 25, 1943, Laboon file, AUSNA.
2. Walter Chadwick, interview with author, July 1, 2012.
3. Reminiscences of Admiral Robert Long, transcribed, AUSNA.
4. Ensign John Laboon, fitness report, August 14–21, 1943, August 21, 1943; fitness report, n.d. [August 1943], Laboon file, NMPR.
5. Chief of Naval Training to Ensign John Laboon, May 25, 1943, Laboon file, AUSNA.

needing two submarines, the *Cachalot* and *Cuttlefish* were sent to New London specifically for use by the school.[6]

The intense training at sub school was tempered by a very inviting environment. Jake and his fellow officer trainees received instruction both in class and at sea. Technical subjects included torpedo and deck-gun firing procedures and diving procedures, plus a thorough study of diesel electric engines. An advanced tactical course for maneuvering submarines was also part of the curriculum. A course in advanced first aid was required, as submarines never carried a medical doctor. Students were also tested on the "Monsen Lung," ascending a training tower from water depths of twelve, eighteen, thirty, and one hundred feet.[7] Sea training was held on the recently arrived *Cachalot* and *Cuttlefish*. This strict schedule was made quite palatable through the somewhat idyllic environment where many of the officer trainees resided. Nonmarried students were placed in the bachelors' officers' quarters, which provided much greater freedom than the routine of the academy. Many of the married students rented cottages near the beach and commuted to New London. Walter Chadwick, Jake's plebe summer roommate, commented, "It was an idyllic honeymoon with visions of beautiful bliss and bountiful families."[8]

Laboon completed his sub school training on December 22, 1943. Consistent with his class standing at the academy, he was listed as number 225 of a graduating class of 258, leading to a performance evaluation that rated him as average among his peers.[9] In a graduation speech, Commander Elijah Bacon, officer in charge of the submarine school, told his audience that their training at New London must be accompanied by good thinking and

6. "Seamen of the Deep: Training for Sub Duty Speeded," *Newsweek* 18 (October 6, 1941): 30; "History of Commander Submarine Force US Atlantic Fleet," Enclosure to COMSUBLANT to CNO, October 16, 1959, SUBFORCLANT, NHM.

7. Ibid.; "Submarine School Trains Been for Toughest Service," *Life* 12 (March 30, 1942): 95, 98. The Monsen Lung was a device that was invented to allow one to ascend from the depths of the ocean to the surface quickly without incurring decompression sickness, commonly known as "the bends." In theory the Monsen Lung could be utilized to bring sailors to the surface if a submarine sank in waters where rescue was possible.

8. Walter Chadwick, "Wedding Bells and Dreams," personal reflection, n.d, personal papers of Walter Chadwick (hereafter PPWC), Hooversville, Pa.

9. Ensign John Laboon, fitness report, n.d. [December 1943], Laboon file, NMPR. This report states that Laboon graduated 236 of 250, yet a list of officers in the September–December 1943 submarine school class lists him as 225 of 258; see Submarine School U.S. Sub Base, New London, September–December 1943 class list, submarine school records, ASBNL.

proper analysis of situations. Personal safety, he suggested, must be subordinated to the need to defeat the enemy. He concluded his talk with a very positive exhortation:

> Judging from the efficient and enthusiastic manner in which each of you has performed your duties here, I am confident that you will meet your new responsibilities in submarines with the same fine spirit.[10]

Jake left New London, enjoying leave until January 15, 1944. With four other members of his sub school class, he was ordered to proceed to San Francisco for transportation to Commander Submarine Force Pacific Fleet.

Submarine Duty in the Pacific Theater

Prior to the December 7, 1941, attack on Pearl Harbor, the United States' strategy for a possible war with Japan was called Plan Orange. The blueprint called for the U.S. Army garrison in the Philippines to fight a holding action against the Japanese while U.S. warships from the Pacific and East coasts would, after a layover in Pearl Harbor and Guam to refuel and resupply, assemble at the Philippines for one battle to defeat the Japanese fleet in one blow. According to the plan, submarines were to be used as scouts and combat auxiliaries to the surface fleet. No one could imagine Japan's strategy, which was designed to knock out American attack forces before the United States could respond.[11]

The Pearl Harbor attack generated an immediate response from Admiral Harold Stark, chief of naval operations. Within hours of the assault, Stark issued the following order: "Execute unrestricted air and submarine warfare against Japan."[12] Prior to World War II, submarine captains were repeatedly told that only combat vessels could be attacked in war. Stark's order was a direct contradiction to this policy, which had been generated as a result of the Washington Conference of 1922, which stipulated that merchant ships could be attacked only if they refused to submit to a search and

---

10. CDR Elijah Bacon, "Graduation Lecture," n.d. [December 1943], submarine school records, ASBNL.
11. Keith Wheeler, *War under the Pacific* (Chicago: Time-Life, 1980), 22–24.
12. Dan Van der Vat, *Stealth at Sea: The History of the Submarine* (London: Weidenfeld and Nicolson, 1994), 277; Michael Sturma, "Atrocities, Conscience, and Unrestricted Warfare: U.S. Submarines during the Second World War," *War in History* 16, no. 4 (2009): 449; Norman Polmar, *The American Submarine* (Annapolis, Md.: Nautical and Aviation, 1983), 57–59.

must not be destroyed unless the safety of crew and passengers were ensured. Historian Michael Sturma commented, "As with the bombing of cities, unrestricted submarine warfare reflected the exigencies of total war—that is, war against an entire society."[13] The CNO's directive also violated the 1930 London Naval Treaty, which in part read:

The following are accepted as established rules of International Law:

1. In their action with regard to merchant ships, submarines must conform to the rules of International Law to which surface vessels are subject.

2. In particular, except in the case of persistent refusal to stop on being duly summoned, or of active resistance to visit or search, a warship, whether surface vessel or submarine, may not sink or render incapable of navigation a merchant vessel without having first placed passengers, crew and ship's papers in a place of safety. For this purpose the ship's boats are not regarded as a place of safety unless the safety of the passengers and crew is assured, in the existing sea and weather conditions, by the proximity of land, or the presence of another vessel which is in a position to take them on board.[14]

Stark's order was a change of policy, but it was not without practical reasons. Since the time of the *Lusitania* was sunk by a German U-boat in 1915, the United States had supported strict protocols for submarine warfare but, as Sturma points out, "the Japanese attack on Pearl Harbor elicited an immediate change in both American policy and mindset toward submarine warfare."[15] In a pragmatic sense the new policy went far beyond the concept of revenge. Japan's attack on Pearl Harbor had not touched submarines; to risk a submarine when inquiring if a Japanese vessel was carrying weapons was impractical. Additionally, to stop a Japanese merchant and inquire about its status would welcome a whole host of planes, placing the boat in danger. Considering Japan's dependence on outside sources for oil and many raw materials, Sturma has suggested that the sinking of a merchant ship "appeared [to be] a sound strategy."[16]

---

13. Sturma, "Atrocities," 449, 464. The relevant article of the 1922 Washington Conference reads, "A merchant vessel must be ordered to submit to visit and search to determine its character before it can be seized. A merchant vessel must not be attacked unless it refuses to submit to visit and search after warning, or to proceed as directed after seizure. A merchant vessel must not be destroyed unless the crew and passengers have been first placed in safety"; see E. O. Goldman, *Sunken Treaties: Naval Arms Control between the Wars* (University Park: Pennsylvania State University Press, 1994), 293–94.

14. Goldman, *Sunken Treaties*, 317.   15. Sturma, "Atrocities," 449.

16. Ibid., 456.

World War II Submariner: 1943–1946

The fact that submarines were not lost at Pearl Harbor allowed them to be used in a ferocious assault on the Japanese. The nature of the attack and the freedom to operate that Stark's directive provided gave boat skippers a license to operate that they used liberally. Indeed, Sturma wrote, "Few American submarine commanders or crews seem to have had any qualms about sinking Japanese merchant ships on sight."[17] Submarines were the first to go on attack against the Japanese, and, with the exception of one or two defensive deployments in aid of the surface fleet, they remained on the offensive for the duration of the Pacific war.

The unrestricted warfare policy ordered by Stark was not specifically addressed in a moral sense by the church in the United States, but it was clear that the bishops and generally all Catholics supported the war effort. Shortly after the attack on Pearl Harbor, Archbishop Edward Mooney, chairman of the National Catholic Welfare Conference Executive Board, wrote to President Roosevelt. Referencing the words of the Third Plenary Council of Baltimore (1884), he expressed contemporary support for the war effort:

> The historic position of the Catholic Church in the United States gives us a tradition of devoted attachment to the ideals and institutions of government we are called upon to defend.... Today in the force of peril ... we reaffirm their [the council's] sacred words.[18]

Approximately one year later the U.S. bishops collectively issued a statement of support. In part it read:

> While war is the last means to which a nation should resort, circumstances arise where it is impossible to avoid it. At times it is the positive duty of the nation to wage war in the defense of life and right. Our country now finds itself in such circumstances.[19]

Similar support was found from leading Catholic theologians and the media. The French theologian Jacques Maritain professed that the Allies were "waging a just war." The American Catholic weekly *Commonweal* characterized the war as a conflict between those who would enslave the world and

---

17. Ibid., 450; Van der Vat, *Stealth at Sea*, 245.
18. "Letter of Most Reverence Edward Mooney, NCWC, to Franklin Roosevelt, December 22, 1941," in *Our Bishops Speak*, by Raphael Huber (Milwaukee: Bruce, 1952), 351.
19. "Statement of Archbishops and Bishops of the United States on Victory and Peace," November 14, 1942, in Huber, *Bishops Speak*, 110.

those who maintain a world embodying human freedom. One editorial concluded, "Between such opposing forces no compromise is possible. In this case the war is a positive duty."[20]

The strategic use of submarines in the Pacific theater was premised on the basic functions of sea power and the navy. First, in its most general understanding, the function of sea power is to maintain command of the ocean; the purpose of the navy is to make the sea a barrier for the enemy, but a highway for one's own forces. In order to achieve these goals a nation needs the physical armament to achieve command and create a highway while keeping enemy forces at a distance. Since U.S. surface forces, save its aircraft carriers, had been so severely crippled at Pearl Harbor, it was necessary for the remaining forces—namely, submarines—to initiate a forceful response.[21]

As the forward vanguard to push back the Japanese onslaught, submarines were the primary vessel. In the European theater the idea of "taking the war to Germany" was manifested through an intense bombing campaign. The solo raid by Jimmy Doolittle and his squadron of sixteen B-25 bombers that struck Tokyo on April 18, 1942, demonstrated that Japan was not entirely beyond the reach of U.S. aircraft, but, especially at this early stage of the war, such raids were not feasible as ordinary tactics. Therefore, submarines needed to take an offensive position. Sturma has accurately captured the situation, comparing the European and Pacific theaters: "In an analogous way, unrestricted submarine warfare allowed the United States to take the war to the enemy in the wake of Pearl Harbor."[22]

At the outset of the war there were fifty-five American submarines in the Pacific: twenty-eight at Cavite, Philippines, and twenty-seven at Pearl Harbor. Of these, however, twelve were S-class vessels, relics of the 1920s; eleven others were not available for combat duty.[23] Despite the small num-

20. Jacques Maritain, "Just War: Criteria for a Just War as They Apply to the Present Conflict," *Commonweal* 31 (October 22, 1939): 200; "Bishops' Statement on the War," *Commonweal* 37 (November 27, 1942): 131.
21. Bernard Brodie, "New Tactics in Naval Warfare," *Foreign Affairs* 24, no. 2 (January 1946): 210; Brodie, "War at Sea: Changing Techniques and Unchanging Fundamentals," *Virginia Quarterly Review* 19, no. 1 (January 1943): 7.
22. Sturma, "Atrocities," 464.
23. Wheeler, *War under the Pacific*, 22; Karl Lautenschlager, "The Submarine in Naval Warfare, 1901–2001," *International Security* 11, no. 3 (Winter 1986–87): 119. One journalist says that in December 1941 there were a total of 111 U.S. submarines in service in the Atlantic and Pacific, with

bers, U.S. submarines were able to operate deep in enemy waters from the first days of hostilities, even when, at the same time, Allied surface and land forces were losing engagements and being forced to retreat. While Japan controlled the Western Pacific for the first two years of the war, American submarines were able to maintain pressure on Japanese merchant shipping, increasing their rate of sinkings with time. Submarine commanders used a combination of stealth, tactical reconnaissance, and an unconventional strategy that differed from classical Anglo-American concepts of naval warfare to achieve success.[24] All subs conducted supply runs, spying, and rescue missions in forms of special operation, but their main purpose throughout the conflict was to be the chief offensive weapon of the naval war in the Pacific.

Japan, especially due to its geographic location as an island nation and its need for massive amounts of imports to maintain its war footing, became especially vulnerable to submarine attacks. Indeed, 75 percent of the nation's requirements for seventeen basic raw materials and significant percentages of other raw materials and food stuffs were imported. Japanese merchant vessels were working to full capacity prior to the war, so any loss to that fleet would be significant. Japan had some 1,600 ships totaling six million tons at the outset of the war, but with open attacks by submarines and with the nation's limited capability for shipbuilding, ship losses directly affected the nation's ability to continue the war.[25] The first confirmed submarine kill happened on December 16, 1941, when USS *Swordfish* (SS-193) torpedoed and sank a 8,662-ton Japanese freighter off the coast of Indochina.[26]

U.S. submarine strategy was, of course, part of a larger picture for victory in the Pacific theater. The approach to defeat Japan was actually a compromise between two different plans. General Douglas MacArthur, head of all Allied army forces in the Western Pacific, operating from Australia after his narrow escape from the Philippines, suggested all American, Australian, and New Zealand forces must advance on Japan from the south—the New

---

an additional seventy-three under construction; see Walton L. Robinson, "Down-Under Ships of the Navy: Submarine Force of Unprecedented Striking Power," *Scientific American* 167 (November 1942): 196.

24. Lautenschlager, "Submarine in Naval Warfare," 119–22. Conventional warfare was basically to battle head to head, but submarines were more for stealth and thus somewhat unconventional.
25. Ibid., 119.
26. Polmar, *American Submarine*, 59.

Guinea-Mindanao axis. The navy strategy, developed by admirals Ernest King, Chester Nimitz, and William "Bull" Halsey, generally agreed with MacArthur, but was opposed to placing all forces in one package, preferring a north route through the Marianas, Marshall, Gilbert, and Caroline islands. Thus the U.S. schema was a compromise between MacArthur and the navy plan that advanced using parallel movements.

The first major triumph in this compromise policy was at Midway, June 4–7, 1942. Under Nimitz's command American naval forces managed to sink or fatally damage four Japanese aircraft carriers, crippling the enemy's ability to launch at-sea air attacks. The significance of the Midway victory was explained by retired Admiral Samuel Morison:

> Midway was the most decisive battle of the war. Had the Japanese won it, they would have turned Midway Island into an air base from which they would have rendered Pearl Harbor untenable.... After our miraculous victory of Midway ... the Japanese fleet was thrown on the defensive, an unwelcome role for which they were ill-prepared.[27]

This victory and the psychological boost it gave to U.S. forces, as well as the offensive potential of submarines and the building capacity of American factories, signaled a major change in the direction of the war.

At the outset of the war, however, especially after the Japanese attack on the Philippines, the U.S. Asiatic fleet was forced to relocate, settling initially in Fremantle on the southwestern coast of Australia by March 1942. One month later the United States took possession of New Farm Wharf in Brisbane. The facility became known as U.S. Navy Repair Unit 134. With various sub tenders onsite at different times, the base became the center for submarine operations of the U.S. Asiatic fleet. By May 1942, twenty-seven patrols had been conducted from Brisbane.[28]

The dearth of submarines in the Pacific theater and their new role as the vanguard for an offensive attack against Japan prompted a massive building program to get boats to the war front as soon as possible. During the war

---

27. Samuel E. Morison, "American Strategy in the Pacific Ocean," *Oregon Historical Quarterly* 62, no. 1 (March 1961): 30.

28. Larry Kimmett and Margaret Regis, *U.S. Submarines in World War II: An Illustrated History* (Seattle: Navigator, 1996), 34; Wheeler, *War under the Pacific*, 63; "U.S. Navy Submarine Operations and Maintenance Base World War Two," personal papers of Michael Walsh (hereafter PPMW), Wilkes-Barre, Pa. At different times the tenders present at Brisbane were USS *Griffin*, USS *Fulton*, and USS *Sperry*.

years the United States built 203 submarines. By January 1944 there were 100 subs operating in the Pacific; one year later in January 1945 there were 156, thus tripling the number of boats present in the region from the time of Pearl Harbor.[29]

The surprise attack by the Japanese prompted a major wake-up call for the U.S. military in general, including submarines and their commanding officers, both of which were generally ill-prepared for war. The U.S. historian Arthur Neal has written:

> The trauma of the Japanese attack on Pearl Harbor was intensified by the fact that the United States had been caught unprepared. As a nation we had failed to develop an adequate awareness of the importance of the wars in Europe and Asia for our own national security. The lack of military preparation now contributed to a collective sense of vulnerability.[30]

The interwar peace generated a virtual amnesia in developing tactics and strategy concerning the ways submarines operated. Indeed, by the time the war in the Pacific was only one year old, forty commanding officers, representing nearly 30 percent of the total in the growing submarine force, had been relieved of command, mostly as a result of unproductive patrols.[31] At the outset of the war American submarines in the Pacific carried no radar. By mid-1942, however, starting with the surface search and then adding an air-search capability, radars were back-fitted onto existing platforms and added to new construction.[32]

The most glaring problem that faced American submarines at the outset of the Pacific war was inferior and malfunctioning torpedoes. At the beginning of the war submarines were using the Mark X torpedo, a relic of World War I. The "fish" carried a 500-pound warhead with the capability of reaching a target at 3,500 yards at a speed of 36 knots. Subs were quickly outfitted with Mark XIV torpedoes that carried a 640-pound warhead with a range of 4,500 yards at 36 knots (9,000 yards at 31 knots).[33] Problems with the

---

29. Polmar, *American Submarine*, 57; Lautenschlager, "Submarine in Naval Warfare," 119; Sturma, "Atrocities," 451; Wheeler, *War under the Pacific*, 166; David M. Kennedy, ed., *World War II Companion* (New York: Simon and Schuster, 2007), 202–3.

30. Arthur Neal, *National Trauma and Collective Memory: Extraordinary Events in the American Century* (Armonk, N.Y.: M. E. Sharpe, 1998), 59.

31. Wheeler, *War under the Pacific*, 26–29.

32. Ibid., 26–27; Polmar, *American Submarine*, 63.

33. Van der Vat, *Stealth at Sea*, 247.

Mark XIVs (which had been designed in 1931) arose almost immediately. Submarines on patrol that fired Mark XIVs often missed their Japanese targets. Charles Lockwood, who in May 1942 was commander of Submarines Southwest Pacific in Fremantle, Australia, petitioned Washington to find a solution. In late June 1942, Lockwood, frustrated with inaction, ordered a test to be run in Frenchman's Bay near Fremantle. Mark XIVs fired at a fishnet were found to run fifteen feet deeper than their set depth. In addition, many submariners believed that the magnetic exploder on the weapon was defective. Still, Washington balked until the CNO lit a fire under the Bureau of Ordnance to correct the defects.[34] The problems were ultimately corrected, but an unpublished "Submarine Operational History of the U.S. Navy in the Second World War" stated, "Undoubtedly torpedo inferiority added months to the war and thus cost the U.S. thousands of lives and billions of dollars of treasure."[35]

Fixing the problems with personnel and ordnance allowed the American submarine fleet in 1943 to forcefully exert itself. Indeed, U.S. subs ranged far and wide and began to achieve significant results, sinking both Japanese warships and merchants. After June 1943, the primary torpedo of choice was the Mark XVIII. This was an electrically propelled weapon, a significant advance from the previous weapons where steam oxygen bubbles created a wake, alerting enemy vessels. Targets could be engaged at greater ranges, which provided a significant advantage in tactics and greater safety for the submarine in avoiding reprisal attacks.[36]

Fortunately for Jake Laboon, the general problems of personnel and weaponry that plagued the submarine force at the outset of the war had been corrected by the time he arrived at Pearl Harbor in January 1944. Laboon had been assigned to USS *Peto*, which was on patrol from its home base at Brisbane at the time of his arrival. Therefore, he was given temporary duty with Commander Submarine Division (CSD) 142 under the ultimate command of Commander Submarine Force Pacific Fleet (COMSUBPAC), now headed by Admiral Charles Lockwood. CSD-142 used the USS *Bushnell* (AS-15), a sub-

---

34. Clay Blair Jr., *Silent Victory: The U.S. Submarine War against Japan* (Annapolis, Md.: Naval Institute Press, 1975), 169–70, 275–76, 278. Magnetic exploders were preferable to contact, as contact would not allow the weapon to penetrate the vessel, thus requiring more torpedoes to disable enemy shipping.

35. Quoted in Van der Vat, *Stealth at Sea*, 262.

36. Polmar, *American Submarine*, 49–51; Wheeler, *War under the Pacific*, 69–71.

marine tender, as its flagship.³⁷ *Bushnell*, a Fulton class tender, was launched on September 14, 1942, at Mare Island Navy Yard and commissioned on April 10, 1943. Under the command of Commander Carroll T. Bonney, she arrived at Pearl Harbor on July 3, 1943. When Laboon arrived the ship had just returned from a run to Midway Island to deliver provisions and structural materials for American personnel there.³⁸

Jake was assigned duties with relief crews that serviced submarines during their refit periods between patrols. He was described by his division commander as possessing a "pleasing manner" yet forceful when necessary. He was considered "industrious and eager to learn in respect to certain phases of submarine training," yet "exhibited little interest in others." He performed his assigned duties in a satisfactory manner. His April 1944 fitness report stated, "This officer needs experience at sea to determine his whole capabilities."³⁹

Duties Aboard USS *Peto* (SS-265)

Peto, Jake Laboon's duty station for the remainder of the war, was a "fleet boat" that became the war horse for the Pacific theater. These boats, first launched with USS *Porpoise* (SS-172) were a significant advancement over the World War I vintage S-class. Fleet boats were approximately 300 feet in length and were powered by four diesels and four battery-powered electric motors. *Peto*, a GATO-class submarine, was 311 feet long and 27 feet at the beam; her draft was 17 feet. The boat could operate at 21 knots on the surface and 9 knots submerged; test depth was 300 feet. Displacing 1,525 tons on the surface and 2,424 tons submerged, she was launched on April 30, 1942, and commissioned on November 21, 1942.⁴⁰ *Peto*, placed under the command of Lieutenant Commander William Nelson, was the first of twenty-eight submarines built and side-launched in the Great Lakes by the Manitowoc Shipbuilding Company of Wisconsin.⁴¹ Thus she was the first submarine ever

---

37. Abstract of service, n.d.; Ensign John Laboon, fitness report, n.d. [April 1944], Laboon file, NMPR.

38. NAVSOURCE Photo Archives, http://www.navsource.org/archives. *Bushnell* was 530 feet long with a 73-foot beam and a draft of 25.5 feet.

39. Ensign John Laboon, fitness report, n.d. [April 1944], Laboon file, NMPR.

40. Polmar, *American Submarine*, 47–48; "History of USS *Peto*," n.d., PPJM.

41. The norm is for ships or submarines to be launched—that is, to enter the water for the first time—by slipping stern, then bow into the water. *Peto* and some other submarines were side-launched—that is starboard and then port (or vice versa) into the water.

constructed in inland waters. The boat was tested to operational depth in Lake Michigan and then towed to Lockport, Illinois, placed on a floating dry dock, and transported down the Mississippi River to New Orleans. From New Orleans *Peto* sailed to Panama, transited the canal, and on March 14, 1943, arrived at New Farm Wharf, Brisbane, Australia as part of Submarine Squadron Four.[42]

After her arrival in Australia she went through nine days of refit and then a training period of seven additional days, which included firing two exercise torpedoes, before she was released to the USS *Fulton* on March 30 for her final load out of stores. *Peto*, under Nelson's command, sailed from Brisbane on its first three patrols. Her first patrol was conducted between April 2 and May 20, 1943.[43] The boat patrolled in the Rabaul shipping lanes, being on station for thirty-four days. The patrol netted only five contacts, all of whom spotted *Peto*, forcing her to take evasive action. The patrol report stated, "The patrol again emphasized the fact that Japanese antisubmarine technique has greatly improved. Every known precaution for prevention and detection, particularly in the final phase of approach, must be exercised."[44] *Peto's* second patrol, also conducted in the Rabaul shipping lanes between June 10 and August 4, 1943, gave the boat its first kill, a small, 2,000-ton hydrographic-meteorological vessel. A 10,000-ton Japanese oiler was attacked on July 7, causing slight damage.[45] After a short refit, *Peto* set out on her third patrol, September 1 to October 21, 1943, assigned this time to the Caroline Islands. After two rather frustrating initial patrols, this run was more fruitful. On October 1 *Peto* spotted three medium-sized Japanese freighters. Torpedoes were launched at all three, with the first two as confirmed kills; the third vessel was damaged but did not sink.[46]

Peto's fourth patrol was conducted in union with three other submarines.

---

42. "History of USS *Peto*," PPJM; Polmar, *American Submarine*, 53. *Peto's* wartime complement was ten officers and approximately seventy enlisted. She carried twenty-four torpedoes, but was capable of carrying mines, to a maximum of forty, as well; see John D. Alden, *The Fleet Submarine in the U.S. Navy* (Annapolis, Md.: Naval Institute Press, 1979), 101.

43. USS *Peto* war patrol, May 20, 1943, National Archives Maryland Branch (hereafter NAM), Silver Spring, Md.

44. USS *Peto* war patrol, second endorsement, May 22, 1943, NAM.

45. "History of USS *Peto*," PPJM; Blair, *Silent Victory,* 934; John D. Alden and Craig R. McDonald, *United States and Allied Submarine Successes in the Pacific and Far East During World War II* (Jefferson, N.C.: McFarland, 2009), 86, 89.

46. USS *Peto* war patrol, December 15, 1943, NAM; "History of USS *Peto*," PPJM; Alden and McDonald, *Allied Submarine Successes*, 103.

World War II Submariner: 1943–1946

Figure 3-1. Launching of USS *Peto* in the Great Lakes

Following a more extensive refit and short overhaul at the Submarine Repair Facility Brisbane,[47] she set sail on November 14, 1943, with orders to patrol between the Caroline Islands and New Guinea. The patrol of fifty-five days, including forty in the target area, was conducted in a cooperative with three other American submarines: *Gato, Raton,* and *Ray*. The cooperative was sent to find and destroy a Japanese convoy. *Peto* was sent south in the patrol area and on December 1 encountered a small convoy. The lead ship was attacked and sunk. Exiting the area, *Peto* was depth-charged, but escaped unharmed. One week later before dawn on December 9, while cruising on the surface, a lookout cited a darkened ship. *Peto* submerged, approached, and fired six torpedoes, but the ship saw the weapons in the water and immediately turned toward the boat, narrowing the angle of attack, leading to a miss. *Peto* was forced to dive deep and was once again depth-charged but escaped any serious damage.[48] After these two close encounters, *Peto* conducted a spe-

---

47. USS *Peto* war patrol, June 7, 1944, NAM. Major repair jobs on *Peto* included overhaul of the number 1 and number 4 main engines, replacement of an auxiliary engine, and installation of a 20 mm gun mount.
48. Blair, *Silent Victory,* 482; Alden and McDonald, *Allied Submarine Successes,* 117; USS *Peto* war patrol, June 7, 1944, NAM.

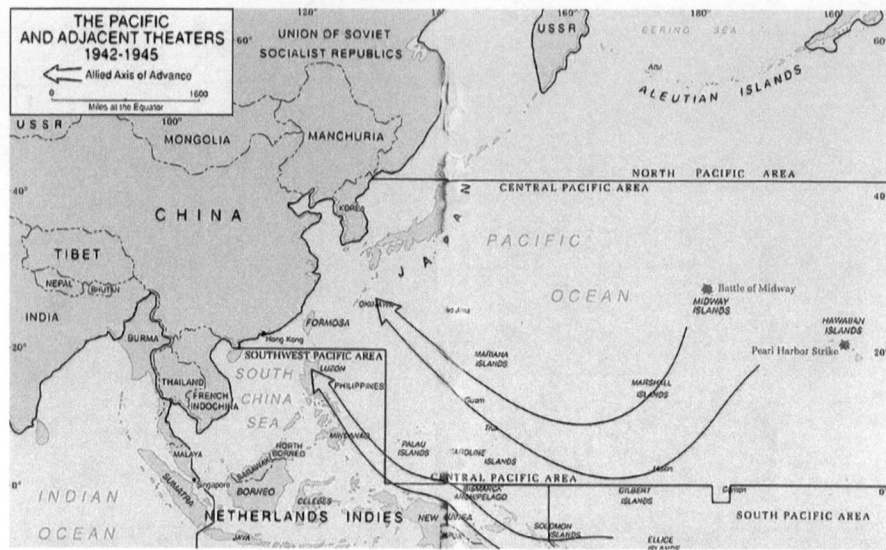

Figure 3-2. Western Pacific Operational Area for U.S. submarines, including USS *Peto*, during World War II

cial mission for Commander Task Force 31 between December 25, 1943, and January 2, 1944; she returned to Brisbane five days later.[49] The cooperative "experiment" using four submarines in one area was deemed a success. The officer in charge at Brisbane, Captain James Fife, was pleased that the majority of the targeted convoy was destroyed. Years after the events, the World War II submarine historian Clay Blair commented, "Although they did not operate as a formal wolf pack, the effectiveness of their combined firepower pointed the way to more cooperative efforts."[50]

Peto's initial four patrols, while not greatly successful from the perspective of tonnage sunk, did, especially in its latter run, point toward future success. Blair has described the submarine's "new life" beginning in 1944:

In one sense it could be said that the U.S. Submarine war against Japan did not truly begin until the opening days of 1944. What had come before had been a learning period, a time of testing, of weeding out, of fixing defects and weapons, strategy, and tactics, of waiting for sufficient numbers of submarines and workable torpedoes.[51]

49. USS *Peto* war patrol, June 7, 1944, NAM. The nature of the "special mission" is not given in the patrol report.
50. Blair, *Silent Victory*, 482.   51. Ibid., 554.

As a comparison, for the first two years of the Pacific war, American submarines sunk 335 vessels with a total tonnage of 1.5 million. However, during the first half of 1944 submarines were sinking an average of 200,000 tons per month.[52] Clearly, as the Pacific war began to turn decidedly in favor of the United States, the role of the submarine, including USS *Peto*, became that much more significant, pushing Japanese forces back and reclaiming the Western Pacific.

Peto prepared for her fifth and final patrol from Brisbane with a new look. During the boat's refit period a significant overhaul was conducted of the number 2 main and auxiliary engines as well as installation of new electronic equipment, especially Identification Friend or Foe (IFF), a specialized radar system that allowed submarines to differentiate Allied from Japanese planes, and a new radio system. Most importantly, on January 22, 1944, Lieutenant Commander Paul van Leunen relieved Commander Nelson as commanding officer of *Peto*.[53]

Under the command of her new skipper, *Peto* set out on her fifth war patrol on February 2, 1944. Lasting sixty days, almost half of the patrol was spent transiting from Brisbane to the boat's new home port at Pearl Harbor. For the first portion of the boat's thirty-two days on station, *Peto* operated with USS *Cero*. On February 18 a group of Japanese ships was sighted and attacked. One of *Peto's* torpedoes struck a Japanese freighter, crippling but not sinking the vessel. *Peto* surfaced to view the damage and observed another Japanese ship depth-charging *Cero*. Firing its gun, *Peto* managed to distract the Japanese vessel sufficiently, allowing *Cero* to escape.[54] *Peto* continued east, unsuccessfully attacking Japanese forces on March 3, but sinking a cargo ship on March 4. The boat was depth-charged after the successful attack, but managed to escape and continue east. After a brief stop in Midway on March 25, *Peto* arrived at her new home port of Pearl Harbor on March 29.[55]

Peto's mechanical condition at the end of five patrols was such that her first Pearl Harbor refit was extended. The patrol report commented, "The material condition of the *Peto* indicates that she will require Navy yard over-

---

52. Wheeler, *War under the Pacific*, 81; Sturma, "Atrocities," 451.
53. "History of USS *Peto*," PPJM; USS *Peto* war patrol report, March 29, 1944, NAM.
54. Ibid.
55. Ibid.

haul at the end of her next patrol.[56] Equally, if not more, important was the belief that torpedo problems had led to failures in attacking Japanese shipping. The report stated, "These torpedoes were the poorest ever received on board ... which indicated laxity in the overhaul activity."[57]

Peto's arrival in her new home port allowed Jake Laboon to report finally to his first (and only) submarine command on April 10, 1944. He was initially assigned as communicator. Jake had chosen submarine duty because it would expedite his movement to the fleet and participation in the war. His attitude toward serving at a time of war was expressed many years later while serving as a chaplain at Great Lakes Naval Training Center:

> I am prepared to always choose what is the more perfect thing in great or small matters, even to the following of my leaders in complete detachment from the goods and honors of this life, to the actual surrender of my life in time of war or necessity.[58]

In a similar light, a Jesuit classmate stated, "Jake was fearless. He did not know what fear was."[59]

Peto conducted an extended eighteen-day refit made necessary by to the wear and tear of five war patrols. She conducted sea trials between April 18 and April 27. After a final load out of stores she left on April 28 in route to her patrol area, accompanied by USS *Perch*. After a brief one-day stop in Midway, the two subs and USS *Picuda* transited west to their patrol area south of Formosa. *Peto* stayed in the patrol area only eighteen days, being "forced to leave the area due to expenditure of fuel." During this brief period the boat held six ship and twelve aircraft contacts. However, *Peto* stayed at a distance, failing to engage any contact; not one torpedo was fired during the patrol.[60] The boat also encountered problems with sampans, which were considered "a considerable annoyance," especially concerning the possibility of becoming entangled with fishing nets.[61]

After completing one war patrol it was clear that the crew's perception

---

56. USS *Peto* war patrol report, first endorsement, April 1, 1944, NAM.
57. USS *Peto* war patrol report, March 29, 1944, NAM.
58. *Great Lakes Bulletin*, September 18, 1964, GLNSL.
59. William Dawson, SJ, interview with the author, October 28, 2010.
60. The *Peto's* war patrol report provides no specific reason for not engaging the Japanese. One may presume the target aspect on the vessels encountered was poor. As will be noted, however, navy officials were not pleased with *Peto*'s performance, leading directly to a change in command.
61. USS *Peto*, war patrol report, June 19, 1944; USS *Peto*, war patrol report, first endorsement, June 20, 1944, NAM.

Figure 3-3. Jake Laboon (back row, center) with the officers of USS *Peto*

of Laboon and his impression of the boat were mutually good and strong. Michael Walsh, a radioman who served under Laboon, remembered Jake as timid, laid-back, and friendly. He commented, "Being an Annapolis graduate I was surprised he was friendly toward the enlisted men." Frank Sciosa, another member of the ship's crew, stated, "Mr. Laboon was a different guy. He made you feel like he was one of the gang."[62] Laboon's impression of his *Peto* experience was recorded years later:

She was not the hottest boat in the force, but she was a good submarine, had a good crew and we always did our job. The most ships we sank on a run was six up in the Yellow Sea during my first patrol. That was nothing spectacular.[63]

During the patrol Jake was "under instruction" as junior officer of the watch and a member of the coding board (a group of officers assigned to decode

62. Michael Walsh and Frank Sciosa, interview with the author, September 15, 2010.
63. News clipping, n.d. [1962], PPWL. It was actually Laboon's second patrol, the boat's seventh, that produced these kills. The official totals were four sunk and one damaged.

classified radio messages). His superiors noted his desire to learn, reporting that "He has performed all ... duties assigned in an efficient manner."[64]

Peto's return to Pearl Harbor on June 19 was not greeted with great fanfare. Captain W. M. Downes, Commander Submarine Squadron Eight (COMSUBSQUAD 8) was rather harsh in his evaluation of the performance of *Peto*'s commanding officer, van Leunen. Labeling the patrol as "unsuccessful," Downes wrote, "It is also felt that the Commanding Officer erred in not endeavoring to intercept the *Picuda* contact on 20 May, and also in not pressing home the attack on June 2nd." Confusion in orders from Commander Task Group 17.14, interpreted by *Peto* one way and *Perch* in a second, was another problem.[65]

Peto did not stay long in Pearl Harbor, leaving only two days after her arrival on June 21, for a scheduled overhaul in San Francisco, arriving there on June 28. The overhaul was conducted at Hunters Point by the submarine division of Bethlehem Steel Company. Major alterations included modification of the conning tower, installation of a five-inch gun, movement of number 1 periscope to the conning tower, conversion of number 4 main ballast tank to a fuel tank, addition of two berths to officers country, and more berthing in the forward torpedo room. Most probably because of the scathing criticism received from Commander Submarine Squadron 8 concerning *Peto*'s failure to engage the enemy during its sixth patrol, Commander Hugh Caldwell replaced van Leunen as the boat's commanding officer.[66]

The West Coast visit of *Peto* gave the crew some time for rest and relaxation as well as needed medical examinations. On his promotion to lieutenant junior grade, Jake was examined at the submarine dispensary. The examination revealed that he had the onset of cellulitis, necessitating his hospitalization at Treasure Island between September 24 and September 27. He was eventually given a clean bill of health and returned to duty as the boat prepared to return to Pearl Harbor.[67]

Peto left San Francisco on September 29, arriving at Pearl Harbor on October 7. After the boat conducted four days of sea trails, eight days of

64. Ensign John Laboon, fitness report, September 27, 1950. It is not clear why this fitness report is dated 1950, but it does clearly speak of his time between April 1 and June 19, 1944.
65. USS *Peto* war patrol report, second endorsement, June 20, 1944, NAM.
66. USS *Peto* war patrol report, December 6, 1944, NAM.
67. Physical examination statement, September 7, 1944; medical history, n.d. [1944]; statement of temporary appointment, September 1, 1944, Laboon file, NMPR.

training, and two days of load out, she sailed west on October 23, arriving at Midway on October 27 to top off fuel.[68] Later that same day *Peto*, along with USS *Spadefish* and USS *Sunfish*, collectively Attack Task Group 17.13 under the command of *Spadefish*, proceeded to their patrol area in the Yellow Sea.[69] When the task group arrived on station, they found the area almost saturated with mines. Commenting on this situation, the patrol report stated:

> It is incredible that six submarines [reference to Task Group 17.13 and another group of three submarines] could be all over these mine infested waters for three weeks without striking one, so it seems reasonable to assume that at least in a great many cases they were duds. In any event they were a nuisance and a general tenseness prevailed whenever they were sighted.[70]

Attack Task Group 17.13's operational tactic, reminiscent of the German wolf-pack strategy of World War I, was initially conceived in the spring of 1943. At that time Captain James Fife Jr., Commander Submarines, Asiatic Fleet, with information on Japanese convoy routes, devised the strategy of placing as many submarines in the area as possible, using them to attack in groups. Clay Blair has written, "This was the crude beginnings of wolf-packing by the Pacific Submarine Force."[71] The official name for this new tactic was "Coordinated Submarine Attack Group." Usually three boats worked together, with the commanding officer of one vessel acting as overall commander of the unit. The first official "pack" of the Coordinated Submarine Attack Group was in December 1943 with USS *Shad*, USS *Cero*, and USS *Grayling*.[72]

The need to coordinate the efforts of three submarines necessitated special tactics. First, skippers were told not to use radio communication unless absolutely necessary to minimize the possibility of detection by Japanese anti-submarine units. Second, the three boats in the "pack" would never at-

---

68. An interesting twist, uniting Jake's time at the naval academy and his present position on *Peto*, occurred during the short transit between Pearl Harbor and Midway. During the war Notre Dame's football coach, Frank Leahy, was serving as an officer in the army. It was the task of *Peto* to ferry Leahy to Midway. Laboon, who had encountered Leahy two years earlier on the football field, now found himself in a much different position. Leahy was sick the entire transit between Pearl Harbor and Midway. Notre Dame had won the game in 1942, 9–0, but in this case Navy was victorious over Leahy; see *Valley Independent*, news clipping, May 25, 1966, PPWL.
69. "History of USS *Peto*," PPJM; USS *Peto*, war patrol report, December 6, 1944, NAM.
70. USS *Peto* war patrol report, December 6, 1944, NAM.
71. Blair, *Silent Victory*, 387.
72. Van der Vat, *Stealthy at Sea*, 271.

tack simultaneously, lest one boat accidentally attack another. Third, the basic strategy was for one boat to attack and then drop back behind the convoy as a trailer and reload; the other two stationed themselves on the starboard and port flanks of the convoy, attacking alternately with the hope that one attack would turn the convoy toward the other. The special tactics and increased danger of the operation led most submarine captains to argue against wolf-packing. Blair explains,

> Generally the skippers objected to wolf-packing, especially to having a senior division commander on board making the decisions and trying to coordinate the tactics. All lived in dread that wolf-packing might sooner or later result in the sinking of one friendly submarine by another.[73]

Peto's seventh war patrol would prove to be its proudest moment. Jake continued to serve as communicator and as a member of the coding board, but now in addition to his administrative duties he was standing deck watches. *Peto* operated with *Spadefish* and *Sunfish* in an attack group under the command of Commander G. W. Underwood, skipper of *Spadefish*. Just after midnight on November 12, *Peto* received a report from USS *Barb* of two Japanese convoys of nine ships each, located twenty miles to the north of *Peto*. Additionally, it was learned that an American plane had ditched in the same general area. *Peto* was ordered by *Spadefish* "to attack at discretion and search for [the] plane."[74] Shortly after 6 a.m. Caldwell ordered *Peto*'s crew to battle stations. During the next thirty minutes the boat was involved in a firefight with a Japanese convoy. During the ensuing battle, *Peto* fired a total of ten torpedoes from the bow and stern tubes. In the first salvo of four torpedoes, hits were gained on the first and third; the target slowed but did not stop. A second salvo of six torpedoes struck the lead and middle ships in the convoy, sinking the first and enveloping the second in smoke. Immediately thereafter *Peto* received depth charges and thus exited the area at flank speed.[75]

Two days later, on November 14, *Peto* received information of new Japanese contacts in the area and made a flank speed run to the specified location. The next day, at 7:45 p.m., *Peto* "started another busy night chas-

---

73. Blair, *Silent Victory*, 551.
74. USS *Peto*, war patrol report, December 6, 1944, NAM.
75. Ibid. When *Peto* communicated with *Barb* at 6:00 p.m., the latter claimed five kills and one damaged vessel.

ing contacts at four engine speed." Two days later, on November 17, again just prior to 8 p.m., *Peto* sighted eight Japanese ships, including one escort carrier at 12,000 yards. However, any possible attack was frustrated by an alert radar-equipped escort, which forced the *Peto* to escape to the northwest while under attack from depth charges and possibly torpedoes. Ninety minutes later *Peto* acquired a convoy at 20,000 yards. Caldwell moved his boat into the area. The war patrol reads, "After an hour and a half of trying to slip in on the bow quarter and flank, I [Caldwell] decided to attack from directly ahead, and this failing, to shift flanks. A last resort would be an attack at radar depth." After several maneuvers Caldwell decided on the latter tactic, yet before an attack could commence, one of the Japanese ships was hit, prompting an escort to run toward *Peto*, forcing her to pull away.[76]

A few hours later, at 1:30 a.m. on November 18, *Peto* once again regained contact with the Japanese convoy and commenced an approach. Writing in the war patrol report, Caldwell stated, "He [the Japanese vessel] is apparently lost and has no escort. This is what I have been looking for all along." At 2:31 a.m. *Peto* was ready to attack. The target was described as "very long and low, with engines out, three masts located symmetrically with a cruiser stern and flush deck." *Peto* fired three torpedoes at an oiler, leaving the vessel burning and sinking. The war patrol report states, "She was lighted up beautifully and we could see her clearly—must be a new type." Just after 4:30 a.m. *Peto* acquired another contact at 18,000 yards and commenced tracking. At 5:34 a.m. she attacked, firing three torpedoes, one of which struck the target, which "sank in four minutes."[77] The day closed when *Peto* received word from *Queenfish* that she was attacked by Japanese patrol vessels and cautioned the former to "watch out." Caldwell commented, "I guess the Nips are plenty mad. Ships were blowing up all over the Yellow Sea last night."[78]

Compared with the flurry of action during the first half of November, the remainder of *Peto*'s patrol was unexciting, but possibilities for more action were present. Between November 19 and 23, the boat's radar detected numerous contacts, both sea vessels and planes, but the former were small

---

76. Ibid. The report hypothesized that *Sunfish* attacked the convoy just prior to *Peto's* planned assault.

77. Ibid.

78. Ibid.; see also Alden and McDonald, *Allied Submarine Successes*, 237–38. All the ships that *Peto* sank in its November 1944 barrage were cargo or freighter vessels of some type.

and not worth a torpedo. During the next five days, additional contacts were received, and the bodies of two Japanese sailors were found floating in the water. The war patrol report concluded, "These men were undoubtedly lost on the night of 17–18 November."[79] On November 29 *Peto* held a radar contact at 15,000 yards. The boat closed and between 3 a.m. and 6:45 a.m. was involved in three different attacks, firing all her remaining eight torpedoes at the target, which maintained course and speed. The report noted,

> Never have I seen a more perfect setup.... I cannot understand how it was possible to miss. All other attacks with much worse dope have been successful. Needless to say everyone is disappointed to have an otherwise gratifying patrol end with a flop. The 56 percent torpedo score has been reduced to 37.5 percent.

Caldwell concluded that the torpedoes must have been defective. Even with the final disappointment, Underwood's task group, nicknamed "the urchins," collectively sank heavy tonnage on the patrol.[80] With no more weapons on board, *Peto* sailed for Guam, arriving on December 6.

Analysis of *Peto*'s seventh patrol was very laudatory. The boat was credited with four ships sunk, three cargo vessels and one oiler, totaling 29,000 tons. A fourth ship at 7,500 tons was damaged. The boat's new skipper, Commander Caldwell, praised the performance of his vessel and the crew:

> The Commanding Officer, who has not quite gotten the sand out of his shoes from his years in the S-boat Navy, is most gratified with the performance of the *Peto* and with all hands who performed their duties in an exemplary manner.[81]

Caldwell himself received high accolades from Captain G. L. Russell, Commander Submarine Squadron 10: "The performance of *Peto* on this patrol reflects the aggressiveness and sound judgment of her new commanding officer, who obtained excellent results on his first run."[82] Rear Admiral J. H. Brown Jr., Commander Naval Submarine Training Command, was equally complementary in his review and analysis of the patrol:

> This patrol [*Peto* number 7] was a well-planned aggressive and alert performance throughout. Full advantage was taken of exchange of information amongst the submarines of the group, and numerous contacts resulted. Seven aggressive attacks

---

79. USS *Peto*, war patrol report, December 6, 1944, NAM.
80. Theodore Roscoe, *United States Submarine Operations in World War II* (Annapolis, Md.: U.S. Naval Institute Press, 1954), 401–2.
81. USS *Peto*, war patrol report, December 6, 1944, NAM.
82. USS *Peto*, war patrol report, first endorsement, December 9, 1944, NAM.

were made and severe damage inflicted upon the enemy.... The Commander Submarine Force Pacific Fleet congratulates the commanding officer, officers, and crew of the *Peto* for their aggressive and highly successful patrol.[83]

The completion of such a successful patrol was followed by a much-deserved period of rest and relaxation for the men of the *Peto*. During a typical refit, the boat was turned over to a relief crew for repairs while the regular crew took a needed rest. The importance of refit personnel was acknowledged by Rear Admiral Charles Lockwood, COMSUBPAC, who referred to the relief crews as "the heart and soul of all submarine squadrons."[84] During a typical refit it was the responsibility of the relief crew to check machinery, conduct repairs, and do all necessary cleaning and specialized testing for new equipment and those items repaired. Generally a refit period was three to four weeks; the first two during which major repairs were conducted, and the latter portion for sea trials, load out, and other last-minute preparations for the next patrol.

While the relief crew performed its important task of repair and restoration of the boat, the submarine's normal company enjoyed a short period of rest and relaxation. A government publication commented, "During this two-week period the regular crew had no official duties to perform other than to rest and relax and divorce their minds from all the thoughts of war and combat." This break was considered essential for the mental health of the crew. The government publication continued,

War patrols, normally lasting from 45 to 60 days, introduced a protracted mental tension unknown to other types of warfare. Without the rest periods to ease tension, the personnel would have soon cracked up under the strain.[85]

It was common as well for sailors who completed four war patrols to be sent for one patrol period to a relief crew as a secondary way to relieve the tensions and anxiety from sea duty.[86]

Peto's crew spent its post-patrol refit in Guam during December 1944 at Camp Dealy, the rest area for submariners. Charles Cooper, a naval academy classmate of Jake Laboon and at the time attached to USS *Spikefish*,

---

83. USS *Peto*, war patrol report, second endorsement, December 23, 1944, NAM.
84. Wheeler, *War under the Pacific*, 156.
85. *U.S. Submarine Losses in World War II* (Washington, D.C.: U.S. Government Printing Office, 1946), 2.
86. Michael Walsh and Frank Sciosa, interview with the author, September 15, 2010.

was in refit on Guam at the same time as *Peto*'s crew. The crew was housed in Quonset huts. Days were spent playing sports, going to the beach, or simply resting and relaxing in various ways. Cooper remembered how sailors would "horse around" by dropping coconuts on the metal roofs of the quonset huts and yell "Depth Charge." Michael Walsh and Frank Sciosa, shipmates of Laboon, remembered how Jake organized transportation via jeep for officers and sailors to attend Mass on Sunday.[87]

Peto's Guam refit period was extended slightly due to a casualty incurred during repairs. On December 18 the refit crew, while making repairs, accidentally flooded the forward engine room to the upper deck plates. Pumping the water from the boat and then thoroughly removing the various byproducts of sea water caused a slight delay in the boat's return to Pearl Harbor. The flooding necessitated replacement of major components, a function that could only be performed at Pearl Harbor. Thus, on December 21, *Peto* sailed east and arrived in Hawaii on January 2, 1945. There, the number 1 and number 2 main generators were replaced and other pieces of equipment damaged from the flood were repaired or replaced as necessary.[88]

Peto, in company with *Thresher*, *Shad*, and *Tilefish*, sailed from Pearl Harbor on January 31, 1945, commencing the boat's eighth war patrol. The group was under the command of Commander J. R. Middleton Jr., the skipper of *Thresher*. The boats stopped at Saipan on February 12 to top off fuel and then continued west to the patrol area of the Luzon Strait and South China Sea between Hainan Island and Pratas Reef, arriving on February 15.

Jake Laboon, with two patrols under his belt, including the harrowing experience of *Peto's* seventh war run, was still the least experienced officer on the boat. During this eighth patrol he was trained to be torpedo and gunnery officer. It is clear that he was highly respected by all ship's company, officers and enlisted alike. His fitness report during this period read, "This officer is well-rounded in training and is considered qualified for any duty of his rank."[89]

The patrol was interrupted on February 19 when a crew member, Electrician's Mate Third Class E. A. Bettencourt, was diagnosed with an acute

---

87. Charles Cooper, interview with the author, February 25, 2011; Michael Walsh and Frank Sciosa, interview with the author, September 15, 2010.

88. USS *Peto*, war patrol report, April 9, 1945, NAM.

89. USS *Peto*, war patrol report, April 9, 1945, NAM; LTJG John Laboon, fitness report, February 28, 1945, Laboon file, NMPR.

appendicitis. The patrol report states, "All symptoms indicate sick man's appendix has ruptured." COMSUBPAC provided instructions on how to treat the man, prompting *Peto*'s commanding officer, Commander Caldwell, to comment, "Was surprised to receive no plans for transferring him. I considered [the] man critically ill and this looked like a good time for a little reverse lifeguard service by aviators." Finally, on February 22, four days after the initial report of his illness, Petty Officer Bettencourt was transferred to *Burrfish* in an operation that due to high seas took two-and-a-half hours. *Peto* then "headed back to join the pack."[90]

The second half of *Peto*'s patrol was as lackluster as the first. Some excitement was generated on March 5, when the boat was attacked by a plane. Three bombs that exploded near *Peto* disabled the hydraulic system for some time. During the next seven days she and *Thresher* held contacts and pursued, but no attacks were made. On March 8 *Peto* went to battle stations but "never got close enough to cite targets in low visibility." On March 12 the two boats began tracking a large Japanese freighter of the Tatuwa class that was accompanied by two escorts. *Shad* had joined the chase, but the target eluded all three submarines. Three days later, on March 15, *Peto* and *Shad* were given orders to commence lifeguard duties southeast of Hong Kong. *Peto* thus "set course for new station."[91]

The concept of lifeguard duty, the largest special operation for submarines during the war, was originally designed for the Gilbert and Marshall Islands campaign, which began in November 1943. Rear Admiral Charles Pownall, commander of Aircraft Carrier Task Group 50.1, planned a series of preliminary raids on Gilbert outposts, including Marcus and Wake Islands, areas patrolled by American submarines. Pownall suggested the possibility of using submarines to rescue aviators should planes be shot down. He stated, "Just the knowledge that it [possible rescue] was there would boost the morale of the aviators." Although somewhat hesitant at the outset for fear that such an operation would expose subs to air attacks, in the end Rear Admiral Charles Lockwood, COMSUBPAC, gave full approval for the program.[92] The first lifeguard operation involved *Snook*, *Skate*, and *Steel-*

---

90. USS *Peto*, war patrol report, April 9, 1945, NAM.
91. "History of USS *Peto*," PPJM; USS *Peto*, war patrol report, April 9, 1945, NAM.
92. Wheeler, *War under the Pacific*, 135; Roscoe, *United States Submarine Operations*, 465. Admiral Chester Nimitz, commander of U.S. naval forces in the Pacific, also approved the operation.

head. On October 7 *Skate* rescued six aviators off Wake Island.[93] During the life of the program 504 aviators were rescued, the majority, 380, in 1945.[94]

Peto's lifeguard duty did little to invigorate the boat's lackluster patrol. Caldwell even petitioned COMSUBPAC to allow his boat to patrol an extra week in a more productive area. He wrote, "We are getting a little discouraged with little hope of contacting anything but planes and junks." Caldwell's request was granted, and the three submarines were extended for five days. In the end, however, on March 28, *Peto* set sail for Saipan with a full complement of torpedoes; she arrived on April 2. After topping off fuel, she proceeded west to Midway in the company of *Blazers*, *Tratta*, and *Flasher* and a couple of escorts. The group arrived one week later on April 9.[95]

Peto's eighth patrol was unremarkable, but COMSUBPAC officials did not consider the dry run to be in any way the fault of the boat's leadership. Frequent aircraft contacts forced *Peto* to dive frequently to avoid bombs. Only two ship contacts were made, but neither was strong, and a planned attack could not be made. Caldwell summarized his frustration, yet as always praised his crew:

To have this dry run follow a really juicy one and knowing full well that "someone has to do these things" is no consolation. In spite of the above [lack of action] the morale of the *Peto* remains high and she is ready to make the next one successful.[96]

After a two-week refit and training exercises at Midway, conducted under *Peto's* new command, Submarine Squadron 32, the boat made ready for her ninth war patrol. She set sail on May 4 and transited to the Marcus

---

93. Kimmett and Regis, *U.S. Submarines in World War II*, 94; Roscoe, *United States Submarine Operations*, 465.

94. Wheeler, *War under the Pacific*, 139–40; Kimmett and Regis, *U.S. Submarines in World War II*, 94; Roscoe, *United States Submarine Operations*, 474, 468–69. Aviators rescued through the Lifeguard program were 7 in 1943, 117 in 1944, and 380 in 1945. A total of 86 submarines rescued at least one aviator. In April 1944 USS *Tang* rescued 22 aviators on one mission. Roscoe commented on *Tang*'s rescue mission: "*Tang*'s remarkably successful lifeguard mission did more than obtain the desired fire cover. It created a wide immediate demand for submarine lifeguard service." Downed aviators could not give exact coordinates of their location, as this would invite enemy strafing fire and danger for the lifeguard submarine. Thus a system called "Reference Point" was developed. On each raid the pilot was given a reference point that was coded using comic book characters. If necessary, a pilot would signal distance and bearing from the reference point. For example, if Wake Island was the reference point a pilot could report 12 Dagwood 200. Dagwood was a popular comic strip character of the 1940s. Thus, the pilot was located 12 miles from Wake Island on a bearing of 200 degrees.

95. USS *Peto*, war patrol report, April 9, 1945, NAM.

96. Ibid.

Island patrol area. During the first phase the patrol *Peto* was assigned lifeguard duty, replacing USS *Jallao* in the patrol area. In addition to standing ready to rescue aviators, *Peto* was also instrumental in guiding American pilots to their targets.[97] The boat saw little action, leading the crew to a sense of monotony and frustration. The patrol report commented, "The least they [U.S. pilots] could do would be to say 'hello.' I guess the only time we get attention from these boys is when they get into trouble. We certainly hope that none of these people get into trouble, but the monotony is weighing us down."[98] On May 22 *Peto* was ordered to Saipan to replenish fuel. Before she left the area, however, she closed in on the coast of Marcus Island and took pictures of enemy installations.[99]

The boat arrived in Saipan on May 26, but left the next day for the second half of her patrol. Nevertheless, the one-day reprieve was noted in the patrol report: "All hands enjoy[ed] beer and festivities." On May 30, after a few days of submerged operations on patrol, *Peto* was ordered "to proceed at best speed to lifeguard station and report ETA [Estimated Time of Arrival]."[100] On May 31 and June 1 the boat searched for aviators, but other subs had arrived first. One week later, on June 9, *Peto* sighted the parachute of a P-51 pilot who had bailed out. Eventually the chute sank, but the man was sighted about 1,000 yards away. However, when *Peto* arrived the pilot had disappeared. The incident was noted in the patrol report: "This was a terrible tragedy for all hands. To have seen the pilot float down and to be almost at him when he hit, only to lose him, was heartbreaking."[101] Three days later a downed pilot was transferred from USS *Tratta* to *Peto*, which on June 15 set course for Guam, arriving four days later.[102]

Despite her lack of action, *Peto* was complimented following its relatively short forty-four-day patrol. The patrol report endorsement read in part:

The alert, aggressive and efficient performance of all types of duty throughout this patrol by the *Peto* was deserving of more concrete success than circumstances permitted. Her valuable reconnaissance of Marcus Island and effective coaching of planes into attack position, however, were no small accomplishments.[103]

97. USS *Peto* (SS265), information sheet, n.d. PPJL.
98. USS *Peto*, war patrol report, June 19, 1945, NAM.
99. Ibid.
100. USS *Peto*, war patrol report, June 19, 1945, NAM.
101. Ibid.   102. Ibid.
103. USS *Peto*, war patrol report, third endorsement, July 1, 1945, NAM.

Peto's difficulties in locating downed aviators prompted her skipper to call for better procedures for planes and submarines in locating men in the water. He wrote, "Some valuable aviators are probably lost due to this deficiency and its correction should be given high priority."[104]

The tenth and final war patrol for *Peto*, one that would be filled with action and be transformative in the life of Jake Laboon, began on July 14, 1945. After completing its typical refit in Guam alongside the submarine tender *Proteus* and now assigned to Submarine Squadron 20, the boat journeyed northwest to take up station on lifeguard duty, as it had done during its last two patrols. *Peto* remained on station beginning on July 18, save for a few hours in the evening of August 1, when the boat picked up a Japanese vessel zigzagging every three minutes. *Peto* pursued the contact for several hours, but the tactical situation never allowed an attack.

July 24, 1945, was a memorable day for *Peto* and Jake Laboon. Shortly before noon the boat received word of two downed pilots, both from USS *Lexington*, close aboard off the Hamamatsu coast. The first, who was easily rescued, informed Caldwell that his wing man had bailed out closer to land. The patrol report reads, "It is apparent that the pilot is very close in and we will probably draw gunfire. Secured all topside personnel except CO [Commanding Officer] and OOD [Officer of the Deck] and crossed our fingers."[105] Caldwell was hesitant to proceed due to mines in the water and fire from shore batteries. Nonetheless, he ordered *Peto* toward the pilot's location, maneuvering within five hundred yards of him. He asked for a volunteer to go with a tow line to rescue the aviator. Jake Laboon stepped forward to answer the call. Caldwell told him that if shells from shore batteries got too close to the boat, it would be necessary to leave the area and dive, thus abandoning Laboon and the pilot. The patrol report relates what happened:

Made lightning rescue of Ensign W. F. Donnelly, USN, VBF 94, as three shells whined overhead, landing 1,000 yards over. We are in 35 fathoms, 4 miles from land where people can be seen on the beach, and a passenger train, stopped on a trestle, had a ringside seat. But we were not there to sightsee and so commenced retiring at flank speed. Ltjg Laboon did [a] heroic job by jumping in with line attached to grab the exhausted pilot and dragged him in before all the way [forward movement] was off the boat. Our Hellcats now wagged their wings and departed leaving us bare-

---

104. USS *Peto*, war patrol report, June 19, 1945, NAM.
105. USS *Peto*, war patrol report, August 30, 1945, NAM.

faced but they were shortly replaced by two Corsairs. No more potshots were taken at us although we must have been within range for another fifteen minutes.[106]

With the two pilots now on board, *Peto* cleared the area at flank speed.[107]

The next day *Peto* sighted and began to close in on a Japanese sampan. At 3,000 yards *Peto* fired upon the vessel with its 20 and 40 mm guns. The boat closed to within one hundred yards of the sampan and fired fifty additional rounds of 40 mm and one hundred fifty rounds of 20 mm at the target. The patrol report stated, "Sampan in shambles and sinking by the stern—ceased firing and proceeded to lifeguard station, no survivors." After this brief incident *Peto* returned to lifeguard duty, circling on station ten miles south of Hamamatsu.[108]

Peto's encounter with the sampan illustrates an ongoing moral dilemma of the Pacific war. In the early days of the war American attacks on small craft were few. There was no apparent resistance to the idea of sinking Japanese tankers or freighters, as the aforementioned immediate order from the chief of naval operations, Admiral Harold Stark, to initiate unrestricted warfare, allowed such action. However, more ambivalence was present with respect to smaller craft such as schooners, sampans, junks, and fishing trawlers. In the Pacific there was no general rule as to how to operate; individual commanders were given great latitude in their decisions. Submarine attacks on small Japanese craft were generally rationalized with the belief that such vessels could be serving as pickets, conveying information of Allied movements to Japanese Navy forces. The historian Michael Sturma speaks of a less altruistic rationale: "At times ... it appears that attacks mounted on small craft were mainly inspired by boredom, frustration, or an attempt to raise morale."[109]

---

106. Ibid.

107. Laboon's rescue of the pilot was both heroic and ironic. The man Jake rescued, W. F. Donnelly, was a Pittsburgher who had been the Laboon family paperboy and had one day taken the family car "for a joy ride"; see Anderson, *All Americans*, 233, and Joseph DeSantis, interview with the author, March 31, 2011.

108. USS *Peto*, war patrol report, August 30, 1945, NAM.

109. Sturma, "Atrocities," 455, 464–68. In his article, Sturma, while critiquing the actions of American forces in the Pacific, places much greater blame on decisions made in the European theater. He suggests that the carpet bombing of some Axis cities was ordered from the top. In the Pacific war, however, since no general directive was given, it was the prerogative of submarine commanders to decide how they would handle specific situations. In his mind, therefore, problems in Europe were much worse than the Pacific.

Due to the lack of extant data, it is impossible to gage what Jake Laboon believed about the morality of attacking small craft or even noncombatant vessels. But under the circumstances of the war and the fact that, while a practicing Catholic, Laboon at this point in his life had no formal training in moral theology, he probably had no reason to question the morality of attacking these vessels. Additionally, he would have been trained at the academy to follow lawful orders first and to consider the morality of actions later.[110]

The lifeguard mission of *Peto* sprang into high gear on July 30. Shortly after noon an American PBY aircraft landed in *Peto*'s general patrol area to pick up an aviator who had been in the water approximately four hours. However, while landing, the aircraft was damaged, thus generating the need to rescue a total of nine: the downed aviator and the crew of the PBY. As *Peto* moved to the site another U.S. plane dropped a life raft. *Peto* entered the area with great caution, as mines were present. Eventually all nine were brought aboard. Later that same day all eleven rescued by *Peto* during the previous forty-eight hours were transferred to USS *Gabilan* (SS-252).[111]

The last full month of World War II found *Peto* back on lifeguard duty. Having rescued eleven American aviators from the sea, the boat and her crew narrowly escaped death on August 9. Shortly after 4 p.m. *Peto* received a message that included the position of two "yellow jackets." Caldwell directed the boat to the location at full speed. While in route *Peto* was spotted by a Japanese plane. The patrol report describes the scene:

JapJill [Japanese plane] appeared out of [the] mist and made run on us, dropping a large bomb from about 400 feet that exploded 200 feet on the port beam. He then passed over our bow at 100 feet, banked left for a suicide dive, but was intercepted by four Corsairs, one of whom shot him down in flames 300 yards away.... It was very spectacular and fine work by our cover, but we would feel more secure if they had gotten him before he made [a] run on us.[112]

---

110. The author's own experience as an academy graduate who, after graduation, served on a fleet ballistic missile (FBM) submarine in the Pacific theater is relevant. As a member of the team responsible to possibly launch nuclear weapons during the period of the Cold War, it was incumbent on me to follow orders. Like Laboon, I practiced my Catholicism faithfully while in the navy, but did not give serious consideration to the morality of nuclear weapons, either as deterrence or use. While the time difference between Laboon and the author is approximately thirty years, certain basic parameters of military life and order do not change.

111. USS *Peto*, war patrol report, August 30, 1945, NAM; "History of USS *Peto*," PPJM.

112. USS *Peto*, war patrol report, August 30, 1945, NAM.

Following the close call, *Peto* proceeded toward the location of the possible survivors, but did not find anyone. The next day, however, *Peto* received instructions from COMSUBPAC to search for a pilot from the British aircraft carrier HMS *Formidable* in an area adjacent to the location reconnoitered the previous day. Fortune was with *Peto* and the pilot, who was rescued and described "in excellent condition and spirits."[113]

On August 15, as she continued to patrol her lifeguard station, *Peto* received the joyous news that the war was over. Immediately the boat began blowing her whistle, after which the crew began to celebrate. Medical brandy was brought to the wardroom, and a toast was given by all officers. The next day *Peto* received instructions to rendezvous with *Balao* and *Tigrone* and proceed to Guam. The boat arrived on August 20 and moored alongside the tender *Sperry* in Apra Harbor. Topped off with fuel and supplies, *Peto* left the next day in the company of *Toro* and *Perch* for Pearl Harbor, arriving on August 30.[114]

Peto's final war patrol was considered a success on all fronts. Her lifeguard rescues of twelve aviators, including Laboon's dramatic action in the face of enemy fire, were favorably noted. The success of *Peto*'s final run, described as "a splendid heads-up patrol," was made possible through the hard work of captain and crew. Squadron and division endorsements to *Peto*'s patrol report were very laudatory:

The Commander Submarine Squadron 10 takes pleasure in congratulating the Commanding Officer, officers, and crew of the USS *Peto* upon the daring and efficient rescue of 12 aviators during this 10th and last patrol.[115]

Jake Laboon was commended by his commanding officer for his service as torpedo and gunnery officer. Describing him as a "splendid submariner,"[116] Caldwell wrote, "This officer has performed all his duties in a highly satisfactory manner and is fully qualified for and recommended for promotion."[117]

---

113. Ibid.; "Derek Morton Story," n.d., PPJL. The pilot rescued by *Peto* was SubLT Derek Morton, who lived in New Zealand. He remained aboard the boat through VJ Day, enjoying the hospitality of the boat and being a formidable force in games of poker.
114. "History of USS *Peto*," PPJM; USS *Peto*, war patrol report, August 30, 1945, NAM; "Derek Morton Story," PPJL.
115. USS *Peto*, war patrol report, second endorsement, September 2, 1945, NAM.
116. LTJG John Laboon, fitness report, August 31, 1945.
117. LTJG John Laboon, fitness report, August 7, 1945.

World War II Submariner: 1943–1946

What was the overall role and efficacy of the submarine in bringing victory to the United States in the Pacific war? Contemporary and subsequent analyses both conclude that submarines were by far the most effective vehicle for destruction of the Japanese fleet. While surface ships were also highly efficacious against Japanese shipping, it was the ability of submarines to operate for long periods in enemy waters that gave them great power. Submarines were never more than 2 percent of U.S. naval strength in the Pacific, yet they accounted for more than half of all Japanese tonnage sunk during the war.[118] The potential for submarines had been predicted back in 1912 when then Lieutenant Chester Nimitz forecast:

> The steady improvement of the torpedo together with the gradual improvement in the size, motive power and speed of submarine craft of the near future will result in a most dangerous offensive weapon, and one which will have a large part in deciding fleet actions.[119]

Writing in *Foreign Affairs* in 1943, the political scientist George F. Eliot stated, "In our operations against Japan, the submarine is a most important weapon, if indeed, it is not the most important one in our armory."[120] Commenting at the same time and speaking of the action of American submarines in the war, the historian Bernard Brodie wrote, "The Japanese have felt its bite in the Western Pacific."[121] Immediately after the war, the naval historian Rear Admiral Ernest Eller opined, "The submarine service ... played a giant role indeed in transforming disaster into victory."[122] More than twenty-five years later, the scholar Karl Lautenschlager stated, "Submarines were by far the most important factor in the destruction of the Japanese merchant marine."[123]

The losses incurred by Japan at the hands of American submarines were indeed significant. Statistics vary, but at least two hundred Japanese warships were sunk by submarines during the war.[124] Merchant shipping, how-

---

118. J. T. McDaniel, "Fire in the Torpedo Room," *Naval History* 25, no. 4 (August 2011): 47.
119. *U.S. Submarine Losses in World War II*, http://www.history.navy.mil.
120. George F. Eliot, "The Submarine War," *Foreign Affairs* 21 (April 1943): 385.
121. Brodie, "War at Sea," 11.
122. *U.S. Submarine Losses in World War II*, iii.
123. Lautenschlager, "Submarine in Naval Warfare," 120.
124. Wheeler, *War under the Pacific*, 23; Polmar, *American Submarine*, 63. Wheeler says 201 Japanese warships were claimed by submarines; Polmar says the number was 214, including 1 battleship, 4 fleet carriers, 4 escort carriers, 12 cruisers, 42 destroyers, and 23 submarines.

ever, was where submarines were most deadly. Some 1,178 Japanese merchants of over five hundred tons gross were sunk by American submarines. The significance of this loss was noted by naval historian Norman Polmar: "These merchant losses literally starved Japan out of the war."[125] Submarines were sinking merchants at a much higher rate than Japan's ability to replace them. U.S. subs were also highly effective against their counterparts from Japan. Twenty submarines, 15 percent of the Imperial Navy's submarine losses, came at the hands of American boats.[126] Even Japanese General Hideki Tojo credited aggressive U.S. submarine operations against Japan as one of the three major factors leading to his nation's defeat.[127]

The great success of the American submarine fleet in the Pacific must be weighed against the losses incurred by U.S. boats during the war. In total the United States lost 52 submarines, 48 in the Pacific, which represented 15.4 percent of the boats that sortied. This was the highest attrition rate of any branch of the various services. In comparison, Japan lost 129 of 190 subs, many the victims of warships. Japanese submarines sank 184 merchants totaling 907,000 tons, plus two aircraft carriers, two cruisers, ten destroyers, and several smaller vessels, including submarines.[128]

Transition to Peace

Following a short period of R and R for the crew in Pearl Harbor, *Peto* sailed east for her eventual decommissioning. The boat passed through the Panama Canal and then, after a stopover in New Orleans, proceeded to the Philadelphia Navy Yard, arriving in November 1945. In June 1946 she was placed in the reserve fleet. *Peto* was struck from the naval register in August 1960.[129]

The end of the war brought a significant award for Jake Laboon. Jake's

---

125. Polmar, *American Submarine*, 61.
126. Lautenschlager, "Submarine in Naval Warfare," 122, 109. Lautenschlager provided some statistics: At the outset of the war Japan merchant tonnage was 6 million. During the war years 3.3 million tons were constructed and 0.8 million tons were captured, for a total of 10.1 million tons. Japanese losses during the war were 7.8 million tons, almost 79 percent.
127. Morison, "American Strategy," 35. The other two factors were (1) U.S. leapfrogging strategy in the various island groups and (2) bold threats by fast carrier forces.
128. *U.S. Submarine Losses in World War II*, 1; Lautenschlager, "The Submarine in Naval Warfare," 122; Van der Vat, *Stealth at Sea*, 257. American submarine personnel losses were 374 officers and 3,131 enlisted.
129. Michael Walsh and Frank Sciosa, interview with the author, September 15, 2010; "Biography of John Francis Laboon, Jr.," PPJL.

heroic effort to save Lieutenant Donnelly was recognized by the navy as he was awarded the Silver Star, the third-highest medal for valor. The award was conferred on Laboon on November 20, 1945, by Rear Admiral Milo Draemal, commandant of the Fourth Naval District at Philadelphia, who coincidentally was the commandant of midshipmen when Laboon was at the academy. The citation read:

> For conspicuous gallantry and intrepidity in action while in charge of a two-man rescue party of the USS *Peto* during the war patrol of that vessel. His skill and prompt action, while under fire of enemy shore batteries and under conditions too hazardous to permit more than one man on deck to assist him, resulted in the rescue of a survivor from a U.S. Navy aircraft. He jumped into the water before the submarine had come to a full stop and pulled the exhausted pilot aboard, allowing the ship to retire quickly from a dangerous position close to the enemy shore. His conduct throughout was an inspiration to the officers and men in his ship, and in keeping with the highest traditions of the United States Naval Service.[130]

The transition from war to peace, as seen in the decommissioning of *Peto*, as well as in the general stand-down of American forces after the war, was experienced as well by Jake Laboon. On April 1, 1946, he received a promotion to lieutenant. Two months later, in June, he was appointed commanding officer of LSM-25, a small support vessel that was only commissioned on May 9, 1944.[131]

Jake's time in command was very short-lived, however, as on July 23 he submitted a letter resigning his commission in the U.S. Navy. Possibly influenced to some degree by the scheduled departure of LSM-25 to a forward area outside the continental limits of the United States, but more especially because of his desire to enter the seminary, Jake's letter to the secretary of the navy held a sense of urgency. He wrote,

> In order to avoid waiting for a full year outside of the Society [of Jesus], I am very anxious to be released from the Navy in September 1946. It is also important that I enter the Society of Jesus Seminary this year, 1946, while I still have a vocation. I am now twenty-five (25) years of age, and time is an important factor.[132]

---

130. Silver Star citation (copy), March 17, 1947, Laboon file, NMPR. CDR Hugh Caldwell, commanding officer of the *Peto*, was also awarded the Silver Star; the enlisted torpedoman who hauled in Laboon and Donnelly was awarded the Bronze Star.

131. LT John Laboon to secretary of the navy, July 23, 1946, Laboon file, NMPR.

132. Ibid. Laboon further explained that the seminary began with a formal retreat on October 1, 1946. It was imperative, therefore, that he be released prior to this date.

Laboon's resignation, dated November 20, 1946, was accepted. He was granted sixty days' terminal leave on September 20, 1946.[133]

Conclusion

Although World War I had been fought as the "war to end all wars," the United States, after the Japanese attack on Pearl Harbor on December 7, 1941, found itself embroiled in a two-front war in the European and Pacific theaters. After graduating from the naval academy in June 1943, Jake Laboon, seeking to enter the fray as soon as possible, passed up aviation and volunteered for submarines. After his initial training was completed at New London he was sent west to Hawaii, joining the crew of the USS *Peto* (SS-265). Built during the war at the Manitowoc shipbuilding facility in Wisconsin, *Peto* had already completed five war patrols by the time Laboon reported for duty in April 1944. During the next sixteen months, during which Laboon completed five war patrols, *Peto* contributed to the American victory by sinking six auxiliary vessels, including merchant ships and oilers. It was Laboon's heroism, however, in August 1945, rescuing a downed American pilot in hostile Japanese waters, that earned him the Silver Star for gallantry, for which he would always be remembered. Henceforth, Jake Laboon was seen as a war hero who met the enemy and was triumphant. Yet, feeling a call to a higher order, with the U.S. Navy and the nation in stand-down after the war, Laboon resigned his commission to enter religious formation in the Society of Jesus. He went forward stridently, as he always did, to conquer new adventures and vistas.

133. Secretary of the navy to LT John Laboon, August 7, 1946, Laboon file, NMPR.

Chapter 4

Formation for the Society of Jesus
★ 1946–1958

While the United States' victory in the Spanish-American War of 1898 had thrust the country onto the world scene as a major player, there is no doubt that it was the Second World War that caused America to emerge as leader of the free world. The euphoria of winning the war and the nation's new status as a world power gave the American people a sense of confidence on a level they had never previously enjoyed. For the average citizen the immediate postwar period was a time when families began to grow and prosper and individual initiatives in education and the work environment began to thrive. The movement of families to the suburbs, the birth of the Baby Boom generation, and a growing sense of confidence were manifestations of the successful achievements of what the prominent journalist Tom Brokaw described as "the Greatest Generation."[1]

American Catholics participated fully in this era of prosperity. Although there were exceptions, the veil of anti-Catholicism that had been so prominent for generations began to tear away.[2] The election of President John F. Kennedy, the only Catholic to capture the White House, was the event that symbolized the distance his coreligionists had achieved. With the assistance of the GI Bill Catholic veterans flocked to colleges and universities, leading to the es-

---

1. Tom Brokaw, *The Greatest Generation* (New York: Random House, 1998). Brokaw sees the generation that lived its youth in the Great Depression, its early adulthood during World War II, and its adult and retirement years in the postwar U.S. boom as "the greatest generation."

2. For example, anti-Catholic rhetoric, such as that of Paul Blanshard in his *American Freedom and Catholic Power* (Boston: Beacon Press, 1949), which argued that Roman Catholics could not be good U.S. citizens due to their loyalty to the pope, continued to be published.

tablishment of numerous Catholic institutions of higher learning. If numbers are any marker of success, then clearly the postwar years marked the entry of American Catholics into the middle class. Seminaries and convents were full, and children were educated in Catholic elementary and high schools. Catholics celebrated the sacraments regularly and attended weekly Sunday Mass.

The faith that allowed Catholic veterans to return to a more routine and normal life was manifested for many in their desire to enter religious life or the priesthood. While there seems to be little evidence that Jake Laboon was overtly interested in the priesthood during his early days in Pittsburgh, the seeds for his vocation had been planted in his youth, and they were nurtured by his experiences of war.

Entry to the Society of Jesus

Jake Laboon spent the years 1940 to 1946 as a navy midshipman and submarine officer, but having resigned his commission to enter the priesthood, he was clearly choosing another direction in life. What was the source of his religious vocation? In an article published shortly after his arrival at New London, his first permanent duty station as a chaplain, Jake stated, "It [religious vocation] had been in the back of my mind even at Annapolis, but my plans for the future had to wait for a war."[3] His roommate, Bill Leahy, remembered how Jake always had said, "I really like helping others. I just need to figure out what is the best way to do that."[4] In an interview in the early 1970s, Laboon explained further:

Much of it was family influence.[5] I was brought up in a strong Catholic family and of nine children, three of my sisters are nuns and another brother is a priest. That is five in religion out of nine. What really convinced me was the war.[6]

---

3. "Navy's Only Padre Who Wears Dolphins," unpublished essay, April 13, 1959, Religious Services file, ASBNL. On another occasion Jake was quoted, "I had been thinking about the seminary before I went to the Naval Academy, but I was not sure it was what I wanted"; see news clipping, n.d [1980], PPJM.

4. Quoted in Anderson, *All Americans*, 93.

5. An interesting aspect of the possible family influence in the religious vocation of Jake Laboon was articulated by his father. During the latter's time as military governor in Livorno, Italy, he made several visits to (now) St. Padre Pio. In his military diary Laboon Sr. writes, "I visited Padre Pio several times and on one occasion asked him if there was any possibility of Jack [Laboon family name for Jake] becoming a priest. He replied immediately in the affirmative and when I asked him how soon, he said the War must come to an end. Jack would have to get out of the service and study, and find it was God's will"; see John Laboon, "The Diary of a Military Governor in World War II," 56, PPJoL.

6. *Honolulu Advertiser*, clipping, n.d., Laboon file, AUSNA. Interestingly, in an interview his

As he indicated, the horrors of war, as experienced firsthand from five patrols on USS *Peto*, also had a major impact on Jake's thinking and his movement toward the priesthood. He once stated, "I was always interested in the church, and I figured that I had seen enough of the world. I decided if I came out of the war alive I would become a priest."[7] On another occasion he provided further insight into his vocation: "The war pressured me into a decision. I found many young people in the Navy were groping for direction and I felt that if I became a priest I could help them find it."[8]

It is clear that Laboon's vocation to the priesthood was strengthened during his active duty service. His shipmates have verified his comments. Burt Findley, a member of *Peto*'s wardroom (officers), stated that he was not surprised at all when Jake told him of his decision to resign his commission and enter the seminary. Findley stated, "We had [spoken] many long hours on religion. He was a Catholic and I was a Baptist. Except for my mother, he had the most supreme faith of anyone I ever met."[9] While members of the crew might not have known about his inclination toward a religious vocation, they nonetheless often came to him with their problems. He was seen as their "acting chaplain." Both the crew and his fellow officers "admired his faith" and brought their concerns and problems to him, confident that he could help.[10] The captive environment of a submarine and the strain of combat produced the need for someone to listen, and Jake proved an able, willing, and worthy ear. He explained:

Aboard a sub, you live so close with others, it is like being in a prisoner-of-war camp. You're closed up with 100 people for a long time. As the trust level increases, everybody talks. I learned many of them [the crew] were groping, looking for help. These were the topics—religion, politics, sex. You'd get around to all three if you're with a person long enough.[11]

---

three female siblings, all religious Sisters of Mercy, claimed that their presence in the convent was not a strong influence on him; see Rosemary, deLellis, and Joan Laboon, interview with the author, August 4, 2010.

7. "Navy Names Destroyer after Priest," clipping, n.d [1993], Laboon papers, ASJM; "Navy's Only Padre Who Wears Dolphins," April 13, 1959, ASBNL.

8. News clipping, n.d. [1980], PPJM.

9. Quoted in Michael Walsh, e-mail to the author, August 22, 2010.

10. "Navy's Only Padre Who Wears Dolphins," unpublished essay, April 13, 1959; Joseph A. Owens, "Parish under the Sea," *Columbia* (November 1960): 7.

11. *Honolulu Advertiser*, clipping, n.d. Laboon file, AUSNA.

Jake claimed that the call to the priesthood was indeed strong. He admitted, "It bugged me so much I had to give it a try." Yet he also claimed that his call was not crystal-clear, stating, "Even to the day I entered the seminary I was not sure."[12]

Jake's return to the United States and his proximity to home with *Peto* docked at the Philadelphia Navy Yard gave him the opportunity to visit various religious communities, indicating that, at least immediately after the war, his specific direction was not clear. Accompanied by his father, who wanted to make certain that Jake was doing the "right thing," Jake visited the Benedictine community at St. Vincent's in Latrobe, Pennsylvania, as well as the Jesuits at Wernersville.[13] Eventually, Jake, taking the advice of a friend, made his choice, explaining, "I decided on the Jesuits for two reasons. I wanted to become a teacher and I never wanted any money of my own."[14]

In February 1946, having made his decision, Laboon spoke with the local navy chaplain, Father Francis Ballinger, who in turn spoke with a Jesuit friend, Father D. B. Chetwood. The latter contacted his provincial, Father David Nugent, who was willing to see Laboon. Nugent was informed that Jake was a naval officer with war experience and a graduate of Annapolis. Chetwood continued, "He was brought to me by a Navy Chaplain, an old friend who recommends the boy in the highest terms. I was with him over an hour and was very favorably impressed." The letter closed by telling the provincial that Laboon was stationed at the Philadelphia Navy Yard and expects to be discharged in September.[15]

As with any candidate who seeks admission to religious life, a process was set up to review Jake's application. First he met with the provincial in Baltimore on February 16. The interview went well, and Jake was asked to

---

12. Ibid.; *Great Lakes Bulletin*, March 19, 1965, GLNSL.

13. Rosemary, deLellis, and Joan Laboon, interview with the author, August 4, 2010. John Donlon, a close friend of Laboon during his days as a navy chaplain, claims that Art Rooney, the owner of the Pittsburgh Steelers and a friend of Jake's father, wanted the younger Laboon to play professional football.

14. *Honolulu Advertiser*, clipping, n.d., Laboon file, AUSNA; news clipping, n.d. [1980], PPWL. Laboon's motivation for choosing the Jesuits is not clear from extant data. In interviews his surviving siblings could not recall any overt reason he provided for his choice. Thus, based on the data, it seems that the Jesuits' association with education was a great draw.

15. D. B. Chetwood, SJ, to "Father Provincial" [David Nugent, SJ], February 6, 1946, Laboon file, ASJM.

submit a letter of recommendation from his home pastor. The letter was very positive, highlighting his family background: "He [Laboon] comes from an excellent family. Three of the sisters have entered the Sisters of Mercy in Pittsburgh; one of them [has] already [been] admitted to final profession."[16] There was some concern about Jake's association with the death of noncombatants during the war. While acknowledging that Jake was a "fine fellow," one evaluation read, "Directed torpedo towards ammunition ships. Blew them up. May be an impediment."[17] In the end Jake was accepted as a candidate for the Society of Jesus. He was told to submit a letter from a chaplain who knew him at the naval academy and to inform the Jesuits of a firm date for his discharge from the navy.[18]

The Jesuit Novitiate and Juniorate

During the mid-1920s the Jesuits in the Eastern United States enjoyed a minor explosion in the number of vocations to the Society. By 1927 this situation led to the creation of the New England province, separate from the New York and Maryland province. The novitiate of St. Andrew-on-Hudson in Poughkeepsie, New York, was inadequate to accommodate the numerous vocations. Thus it was decided that a separate facility for the Maryland portion of the province was necessary. Fortunately, at this same time, Nicholas and Genevieve Brady, wealthy New York Catholics, ceded land to the Society near Wernersville, Pennsylvania. The couple included a substantial gift to construct a novitiate. The house, a huge facility of 160,000 square feet and built in the English Renaissance style, cost $2 million. Started in 1928, the building was completed in May 1930 and dedicated on May 31 by Cardinal Denis Dougherty, archbishop of Philadelphia. The facility, under the leadership of the rector, Joseph Didusch, SJ, and the master of novices, J. Harding Fisher, SJ, and named for Saint Isaac Jogues, welcomed its first group of novices, who came from the New York novitiate, Saint Andrew, on

---

16. Jerome Hannah to Reverend Provincial, February 19, 1946, Laboon file, ASJM.

17. *Informatio de Candidato Scholastico*, May 27, 1946, Laboon file, ASJM. The extant source does not reveal who specifically voiced this concern, but it was clearly a Jesuit who had some role in the evaluation of candidates who applied to enter the Society. As stated previously, Laboon's duty as a naval officer necessitated his obedience to lawful orders. At the time the morality of targeting noncombatants would not have been part of Jake's thinking.

18. Anonymous to John Laboon, n.d. [February 1946], Laboon file, ASJM.

June 2. Within sixteen months there were 131 members of the Wernersville community, including scholastics, brothers, and priests.[19]

Jake Laboon entered the Society of Jesus at Wernersville on October 31, 1946, one of a class of sixty-three novices.[20] His parents, proud that another one of the children had chosen religious life, drove Jake to his new home.[21] Due, however, to a slight delay in being discharged from the navy, Jake did not participate in the month-long Spiritual Exercises of St. Ignatius that novices typically make after their entrance into the Society. Instead he made them a year later, with the entering class of 1947.[22] When Jake arrived the rector at the novitiate was Father William E. Welsh, SJ; the director of novices was Father John McEvoy, SJ. The novice master's influence was significant. The historian of the novitiate, Kathy Scogna, writes, "John V. McEvoy, SJ was a well-liked Novice Master, a spiritual guide who influenced a generation of Jesuits by the example of his own life." He stressed the importance of athletics for those pursuing a spiritual life. He was an avid hockey player and often competed with the novices.[23]

Many of those who entered at Wernersville with Jake Laboon were, like him, veterans of the war, but he was the only officer. A classmate and fellow veteran, William Dawson, SJ, stated that several younger members referred to the veterans as "roughnecks." Being older and coming from a military environment was difficult for many in the class, both older and younger, but from different perspectives. Again, Dawson comments, "The psychological gap between us and the men right out of high school was somewhat of a problem."[24] Laboon's classmates said he rarely spoke about his military service; few knew of his heroic efforts during the war.

Novitiate year was a highly structured period of prayer and reflection

---

19. Kathy Miller Scogna, *A House of Bread: The Jesuits Celebrate 70 Years in Wernersville, Pennsylvania* (Wernersville, Pa.: Kathy Miller Scogna, 2000), 14–29, 63, 67.

20. Catalog, Maryland Province of Jesuits, Woodstock papers, Archives Georgetown University (hereafter AGU), Washington, D.C. The total number of novices was 107, including those in their second year. Jesuit formation for priesthood requires a two-year novitiate: the canonical year required of all religious and a second year that can be used for study.

21. Joseph Laboon, interview with the author, August 19, 2010.

22. Neil McLaughlin, SJ, interview with the author, January 20, 2011. McLaughlin, a novitiate classmate with Laboon, remembered that Jake arrived after the others had finished their thirty-day retreat. The "Long Retreat" was the nickname given to the "Spiritual Exercises" of Saint Ignatius Loyola. All Jesuits are required to conduct the Spiritual Exercises at the outset of the novitiate.

23. Scogna, *House of Bread*, 76–77.

24. William Dawson, SJ, interview with the author, August 28, 2010.

for all religious in preparation for profession of the vows of poverty, chastity, and obedience. From rising at 5:30 a.m. to retiring at 9:30 p.m., every day was scheduled to include prayer and meditation, Mass, rosary recitation, spiritual reading, classes, and conferences, as well as meals, indoor and outdoor recreation periods, and limited free time. Novices were responsible to serve tables, wash dishes, clean the house, and work on the grounds of the property, including planting trees, creating walking paths, and tending acres of lawn. During outdoor recreation periods they walked in groups of three. Visitors were welcomed only on Sundays. In order to prepare for their future celebration of the sacraments, novices spoke only Latin in the house.[25] This was a significant struggle for Jake, as his knowledge of the language was limited to his Central Catholic High School education many years earlier.

Athletic exercises and events were a significant part of the recreational novitiate experience, especially under John McEvoy. A Jesuit classmate remembered how competitive Jake was in any athletic endeavor, describing him as "a very aggressive player." Robert Blume, M.D., who entered the novitiate a couple of years after Jake, heard legendary stories, even though Laboon had only moved on one or two years earlier. He recalled, "The name Laboon came up when speaking of his athletic discipline. He was well known as a tough competitor. He was a rugged male persona." Athletics, which had been integral to Jake from his days at Central Catholic, would remain an important element of his life, including his future days as a navy chaplain.[26]

Although not a strongly emphasized part of the year, novices did take classes in Latin and Greek in preparation for their future studies. Rather atypically from his past and future academic endeavors, Jake achieved highly satisfactory marks during his novitiate experience. He achieved grades of "B" in Latin composition and elementary Greek during his first year and marks of "A" in Advanced Latin Composition and Intermediate Greek during his second year.[27]

The end of the canonical novitiate year required Jake Laboon to make a serious decision about his future. Convinced that he was following God's plan

25. Ibid.; Neil McLaughlin, SJ, interview with the author, January 20, 2011; Scogna, *House of Bread*, 74.

26. Neil McLaughlin, SJ, interview with the author, January 20, 2011; Dr. Robert Blume, interview with the author, January 19, 2011.

27. Academic record (copy), John F. Laboon, College of Saint Isaac Jogues, September 2, 1956, NMPR.

Formation for the Society of Jesus: 1946–1958

and was walking the proper path, he petitioned his superiors to pronounce his devotional vows on November 13, 1947, the Feast of Saint Stanislaus Kostka, a Polish Jesuit novice of the sixteenth-century Counter-Reformation who died at the tender age of seventeen. Receiving permission, Jake Laboon professed his vows with his proud family and a few friends in attendance.[28]

Now, as an official member of the Jesuit community, Jake moved on to the juniorate, also located at Wernersville. Traditionally, the juniorate was a period of two years of classical study equivalent to the first two years of one's undergraduate education. Because Jake had a college degree and was older than most of his peers, his religious formation was adapted for his specific needs. His courses, beginning in January 1948, centered in areas where *lacunae* existed in his previous education. Jake spent three semesters in formal study. Again, pointing toward his future theological education, his classes featured study of Latin and Greek, including Greek drama, poetry and prose of classical Greek literature, and readings of Roman poets and historians. His marks were mediocre, ranging from C+ to B.[29]

Besides his intense study of Latin and Greek, the juniorate was also a time of soul-searching for Jake Laboon. While he was still in the early stages of his formation toward the priesthood, Jake was considering his options after ordination. After completing almost two semesters of intense study, Laboon shared his feelings with his provincial. After much prayer and reflection he told the provincial that he wished to volunteer to go to a newly established mission in Jamshedpur, India. He was convinced that God was directing him toward this ministry. Jake hesitated to commit this belief in writing because he did not want to leave his parents before his ordination. However, convinced of the validity of his call, he finally decided to do so:

> If I am sent today or tomorrow, I know it will be God's will, and therefore I did not want anyone or anything to interfere with my complete oblation to the Master. Since now I have my vows, I am ready to do what God deems best for me, and now I volunteer whol-heartedly [*sic*] for the missions.

---

28. John Laboon, NSJ, to David Nugent, SJ, November 2, 1947; Nugent to Laboon, November 5, 1947, Laboon file, ASJM. Normally Jesuits profess vows at the end of their second year at the novitiate. Although there is no extant data, presumably due to his age, Jake petitioned to take vows after only one year. He then began his juniorate.

29. Academic record (copy), John F. Laboon, College of Saint Isaac Jogues, September 2, 1956, NMPR.

He also informed the provincial that during World War II he had spent significant time on Midway, Guam, and Saipan and therefore was accustomed to a tropical climate. He concluded, "This is merely by way of information that you know that I can stand a climate such as India's."[30] The provincial, in response, was noncommittal, but nonetheless he encouraged his young scholastic: "As you yourself have written, all our life is directly in the hands of God. He will see to it that what is best for you and also for your good parents, is done."[31]

Philosophy, Regency, Theology, and Ordination

In 1860 Jesuit officials decided that a theological house of study was necessary for scholastics of the Maryland and Missouri provinces. Although it took some time, on January 24, 1866, 139 acres of an old farm near Woodstock, Maryland, was purchased by the Society for this purpose. On April 13 an additional 110 acres were acquired. A little over a year later, on March 7, 1867, the Maryland state legislature granted a charter to "The Woodstock College Baltimore County." On September 23, 1869, inaugural ceremonies were held, and classes began four days later on September 27. Father Angelo Paresce, SJ, who had served as master of novices and provincial, was selected as director. He was joined by a faculty of eleven Jesuits, mostly from Europe, and sixteen Jesuit brothers, who were responsible for the day-to-day maintenance of the facility. There were forty-nine scholastics in the inaugural class. On June 13, 1873, the college was dedicated to the Sacred Heart.[32]

During the next hundred years Woodstock College became the theological training ground for thousands of Jesuits. Besides the standard facilities of any seminary, Woodstock had some additional features. First, the college had an extensive language laboratory to help students in training for ministry in non-English–speaking lands. It also had a specialized library of over 130,000 volumes, one of the best theological facilities of its kind in the country. Additionally, the seminary had a shortwave radio station and a twenty-man volunteer fire department. Laboon served on that fire brigade.[33]

---

30. John Laboon, SJ, to David Nugent, SJ, December 6, 1948, Laboon file, ASJM.
31. David Nugent, SJ, to John Laboon, December 11, 1948, ASJM.
32. "Woodstock College of the Sacred Heart," Diamond Jubilee booklet, 1944, 2–5; Woodstock College of the Sacred Heart, Catalog, 1960–63; John LaMartina, SJ, "The Founding of Woodstock College," unpublished essay, ASJM.
33. *Baltimore Sun*, December 27, 1959, Woodstock College papers, clippings, 1944–66, AGU.

Formation for the Society of Jesus: 1946–1958

Figure 4-1. Woodstock College

The Jesuit educational philosophy that greeted Jake Laboon in 1949 had a very long tradition. The description of religious formation in the Woodstock catalog stated:

The Society of Jesus pursues its religious and apostolic purposes in the broad field of education: scholarly, pastoral, and missionary activity at home and abroad.... Besides the careful spiritual formation of her members, which is the Society's first concern, her subjects must have a broad liberal intellectual training, equipping them for a rich personal life and effective social leadership and a precise professional preparation, enabling them to excel in the works they are called upon to achieve.[34]

Woodstock was a major theological center for the Jesuits in the United States until the early 1970s. In February 1968 it was announced that Woodstock would move to share facilities with Union Theological and Jewish Theological Seminaries in New York City. This was scheduled for September 1969 and was to be the first educational complex in the United States with major Catholic, Protestant, and Jewish seminaries. Complications, however, voided the effort. In January 1973 it was decided by the provincials of the ten U.S. Jesuit provinces to consolidate theological training for future Jesuits, leaving seminarians in Berkeley, California, Chicago, Illinois, and Cambridge, Massachusetts. The decision was made, therefore, to close Woodstock. The decision was approved by the Jesuit Superior General Pedro Arrupe, SJ; see *New York Times*, February 20, 1968, Woodstock College papers, clippings, 1967–69; Religious News Service, January 8, 1973, Woodstock College papers, Archives Archdiocese of Baltimore (hereafter AABa), Baltimore, Md.

34. Woodstock College of Sacred Theology, catalog, 1960–63, 14, ASJM.

Formation for the Society of Jesus: 1946–1958

The Jesuit system of education sought as a universal theme to provide theological formation necessary for future activity as a Jesuit priest. More concretely, students were to acquire a *corps doctrinae* (core doctrine) to be derived from study of the theological sciences. These goals sought to make theology an influential part of a student's life, impart skills for priestly ministry, and provide the opportunity and stimulus for scholarly work.[35]

Jesuit education was on two different tracks, commonly known as long and short courses. The major difference between the two programs was found in the types of courses offered and the direction each track took. As one might conclude, the long course was more extensive, involved more difficult courses, and was structured for those more oriented toward the study of philosophy and theology, many of whom would find future ministry in one of the Jesuit educational institutions, especially on the college or university level. On the level of rigor the programs were very similar. Both tracks required demanding oral examinations in philosophical or theological subjects at the end of the year.[36]

In June 1949, after completing his approximately eighteen months in the juniorate, which included intensive study of Greek and Latin, Jake left Wernersville and came to Woodstock to begin his philosophical studies. While not as regimented as the novitiate, the routine at Woodstock for scholastics, under the leadership of Fr. Ferdinand C. Wheeler, SJ, who served as rector, was strenuous. Scholastics rose at 5:30 a.m. for "first visit," followed by meditation and daily Mass.[37] After breakfast the day was filled with classes, study, and some free time for recreation, which during good weather included football and golf, as the grounds were sufficiently large for a few holes.[38]

---

35. Ibid., 15–16.
36. Ibid., 23. Most Jesuit scholastics began their philosophy training in the major program. However, some chose the short program and others, after completing a couple of semesters and not achieving sufficiently high marks or failing to pass a philosophy exam administered in Latin, were placed into the short program. The emphasis was on direction of one's ministry more than native intelligence. It would be incorrect to assume that a scholastic engaged in the short program was any less intellectually gifted than others, although this possibly could be the case. It is more correct to say the individual had difficulty with Latin and/or philosophical principles.
37. When scholastics awoke they were asked to make a brief visit to the chapel, after which they would prepare themselves for their day and return at 6 a.m. for meditation and celebration of Mass.
38. Catalog, Maryland Province, Society of Jesus, 1950, Woodstock papers, AGU; William Dawson, SJ, interview with the author, October 28, 2010.

Formation for the Society of Jesus: 1946–1958

During his first year of philosophy Jake's academic performance was adequate but, as during his time at the naval academy, not stellar. During the fall semester 1949 Jake took courses in scholastic philosophy, advanced logic, epistemology, and statistics; the ensuing spring semester of courses included ontology, educational psychology, advanced calculus, and "interpretation." His grades for these classes ranged from C+ to B.[39] His classmate William Dawson commented on the struggle Laboon experienced in the classroom: "He had a brilliant mind, but it was not into that pattern." He asked many questions in philosophy classes that in the mind of Dawson were "*non-sequiturs*"; they had nothing to do with the topic of the lecture.[40]

The next two years of philosophy were equally difficult for Jake. During the summer months of 1950 he took courses in "Religion in Secondary Schools" and "Bibliography, Research and Methodology," which he completed quite satisfactorily. However, during the regular academic year his mediocre performance continued. His course load included Cosmology, History of Greek Medieval Philosophy, Introduction to the Theory of Equations, Psychology, and Advanced Mathematics. His grades ranged from C to A, but the higher marks were in mathematics, an area that required a different type of thinking as compared to philosophy. Once again, in the summer of 1951, Jake took classes in General Methods in Secondary Education and History-Philosophy of Education. His exceptional marks in these two courses were, unfortunately, followed by another mediocre academic year. Continuing his combination of courses in philosophy and mathematics, he made no improvement in the former courses but continued his high marks in the latter.[41]

After completing his rather rocky road of philosophy, Jake was ready for the next step of his Jesuit formation, a period of regency in active ministry. Jesuit scholastics are sent for some period of time to work in active ministry between the completion of philosophy and the start of theological study "so they can come back and prove their worth in work as well as spiritual life."[42] Jake Laboon was sent to Saint Joseph's Preparatory in Philadelphia to teach for one year. As with all the places where he would ultimately minister, Jake was influential to many at St. Joe's.

39. Academic record (copy), John F. Laboon, Woodstock College, September 7, 1956, NMPR.
40. William Dawson, SJ, interview with the author, October 28, 2010.
41. Academic record (copy), John F. Laboon, Woodstock College, September 7, 1956, NMPR.
42. Joseph Currie, interview with the author, September 21, 2012.

Jake Laboon spent academic year 1952–53 teaching physics, math, and religion and coaching football and basketball at the school. His former students commented very favorably on his lively personality and expertise in pedagogy. His patience with students and ability to explain difficult concepts to them were qualities that all admired. One former student explained, "He was well regarded and well respected by the students—to say the least."[43] As a well-respected teacher, Jake demonstrated personal care for each student, but he always maintained high standards, especially with respect to discipline. One former student commented, "There was no tomfoolery in his classroom, not so much because he was 6′5″ and 215 pounds, but there was an aura about him which gave the students the idea they should be respectful of him."[44] Jake's interest in students prompted him to go out of his way to help them. Former students remember him coming to the classroom on Saturdays to work with them on difficult concepts in physics, especially assisting students who had failed a test. One story illustrates his outreach to students in need. It seems that one student, a classic underachiever, was being "raked over the coals" by every teacher on a particular day. When this student arrived in Jake's physics class, the students asked their teacher, "Are you going to pick on Morgan today?" Laboon responded, "I think Bernie's been worked over enough today. We'll just let him go and see what he will do tomorrow."[45]

Jake Laboon's love of sports was also manifested during his regency year at Saint Joe's Prep. His extensive experience at the naval academy as a two-sport athlete, including three seasons on the gridiron, made him a natural as an assistant football coach. Working with linemen, especially ends, the position he had played at Annapolis, Jake assisted head coach Andy Gordon, who was new to the school as well. Gordon was a Saint Joe's alumnus and had played at the school as well as Villanova. Jake's experience as a division officer aboard *Peto*, handling various personnel issues, helped him mentor his young players. Speaking about Jake, one player commented, "Laboon was the most sane and calm of the coaches."[46] When football sea-

---

43. Jack Johnson, interview with the author, January 27, 2011; see also Joseph Ryan, interview with the author, March 2, 2011, and Bernard Kueny, interview with the author, February 8, 2011; John P. McNicholas, e-mail to the author, January 16, 2012.
44. Jack Johnson, interview with the author, January 27, 2011.
45. Bernard Kueny, interview with the author, February 8, 2011.
46. Ibid; Joseph DeSantis, interview with the author, March 31, 2011; Joseph Currie, SJ, interview with the author, September 21, 2012.

son ended, Jake quite naturally became the junior varsity basketball coach. Although he had not played in college (save one year at Carnegie Tech), his physical height, general athleticism, and knowledge of sports provided him with more than sufficient tools to coach a high school basketball team.[47]

Beyond the classroom and the athletic field, Jake assisted with various student projects, making himself available to others. In the spring of 1953 Jake and another Jesuit regent, Paul Brennan, organized a charter bus trip to visit the naval academy. If students did not have the money for the trip, Jake found a way to finance it, including using his own stipend. Jake was also involved in the lives of his students, often visiting their homes and getting to know their parents. One former student related how he told Laboon about a personal problem that needed resolution. The very next day Jake was at his door ready to assist. Years later the student commented, "He [Laboon] was someone you could always count on."[48]

The impact and influence Jake Laboon left on the students of St. Joe Prep during his one-year regency were, indeed, significant. His former pupils spoke of how he was "universally admired by the students." He was described as a "Terrific guy—big, robust." He was not seen as a great scholar, but rather a great human being who knew how to deal with people. His reputation from the naval academy, and especially his heroic efforts in World War II, preceded him and helped him to command respect. He was "warm and friendly" and willing to do anything to assist students.[49] One former student stated, "Father Jake Laboon had an impact on my life that goes far beyond that of a normal high school science teacher. Outside the classroom he became a hero to me and a number of my classmates."[50]

Jake Laboon was a model for many of the high school students he encountered during his regency year. A few students, influenced by Jake's background and experience, entered the naval academy; this included Frank Delano, who became captain of the 1960 Navy basketball team. Jake

---

47. Joseph Currie, SJ, interview with the author, September 21, 2012; Donald McBride, interview with the author, February 25, 2011.

48. Joseph Ryan, interview with the author, March 2, 2011; Joseph DeSantis, interview with the author, March 31, 2011; "Navy Names Destroyer after Priest," clipping, n.d. [1993], Laboon file, ASJM.

49. Donald McBride, interview with the author, February 25, 2011; Jack Johnson, interview with the author, January 27, 2011.

50. John P. McNicholas, e-mail to the author, January 16, 2012.

was considered a likable, very down-to-earth person; he was seen as the "ultimate guy," "a man's man," yet always humble; "he never spoke about himself."[51] For some, Jake served as a father figure through his constant encouragement and kindness. Some suggested that while Laboon realized that he had a certain presence that attracted others to him, this was never to boost his ego; rather it enabled him to help other people.[52] His humility was infectious. One person testified that from their first meeting, "There was something about the man that we all liked and it never changed."[53]

Having completed his regency year at St. Joe Prep, Jake returned to Woodstock to begin his formal theological studies, the last major step in his formation for priesthood. During the summer of 1952 Laboon took summer school classes at Fordham to prepare himself for the fall semester at Woodstock.[54] Arriving at the seminary, then under the leadership of Father Joseph Murray, SJ, Jake started his theological study in the long program, a continuation of his three years of philosophy. The long course emphasized theology as a discipline for the formation of students in the field, so that in time one could become a master of it and its method. This track was primarily academic; the short course was more professionally and pastorally oriented. All students in long and short courses were required to take classes in the instruction and practice of sacred eloquence, ecclesiastical rites, and liturgical music to prepare students for sacramental ministry. Additionally, attendance at a weekly moral theology conference was mandated. These courses and others were taught by some of the most prominent American scholars of their day, including well-published theologians John Courtney Murray and Gustave Weigel.[55]

As in the past, Jake struggled through his theological studies. During his first year his courses included Fundamental Theology, Moral Theology, Ecclesiastical Law, Ecclesiastical History, Patrology, and Biblical Greek. The principal area of study was Fundamental Theology, with students taking

51. Joseph Ryan, interview with the author, March 2, 2011; Donald McBride, interview with the author, February 25, 2011; Jack Johnson, interview with the author, January 27, 2011; Joseph DeSantis, interview with the author, March 31, 2011.
52. Jack Johnson, interview with the author, January 27, 2011.
53. Joseph Ryan, interview with the author, March 2, 2011.
54. John Laboon to "Dear Sir," July 12, 1952, Laboon alumni file, AUSNA.
55. Catalog, Maryland Province of Jesuits, 1954, Woodstock papers, GUA; Catalog, Woodstock College of Sacred Theology, 1960–63, 21–23, ASJM.

twenty semester hours, generally equivalent to seven classes. Jake managed a grade of C+ in this general topic; his grades in all the others were B, with one B+. His second year was also mediocre. Course topics included Dogmatic Theology, Moral Theology, Biblical Exegesis, Ecclesiastical Law, Oriental Questions (Liturgy), and Biblical Hebrew. In the area of Dogmatic Theology, the principal subject for the second year, Jake received a grade of C. His other marks ranged from C+ to B+. His grades in the area of Fundamental and Dogmatic Theology were the minimum for passing, and after two years it was decided that he would be shifted to the short course.[56]

During his last two years of theology Laboon followed the short course. Many of the subjects in the short course were the same as the long course, but were taught by different professors. However, students in the short course were not required to take courses in Biblical Greek, Biblical Hebrew, Oriental Theology, and special disciplines such as Psychology of Religion and Pastoral Psychology and Patrology. In keeping with the nature of the short course, in place of these subjects, instruction in catechetical and pastoral methods was substituted. In place of research seminars, academic circle exercises in the application of theology to ministry were substituted. This allowed the student to learn what theology has to offer and to be able to communicate that information adequately to all classes of men and women through various ministries within the Society. Instruction and study emphasized this practical end. Scholastics who completed the short course with a four-year average of at least 7 (C+) in the fields of Fundamental and Dogmatic Theology and a grade of at least 6 (C) in all other subjects, plus a satisfactory forty-five minute oral examination, were granted the baccalaureate in sacred theology (STB) degree.[57]

During his latter two years of theology, following the minor course, Jake

56. Catalog, Woodstock College of Sacred Theology, 1960–63, 24, ASJM; Catalog, Maryland Province of Jesuits, Woodstock papers, GUA; John Laboon, academic record, 1952–54, Woodstock College administrative records, ASJM; academic record (copy), John F. Laboon. Woodstock College, September 2, 1956, NMPR. The Jesuit academic system was set up on a numbers basis:

Long Course	1–4	5	6	7	8	9	10
	F	C	C+	B	B+	A	A+

Short Course	1–5	6	7	8	9	10
	F	C	C+	B	B+	A

Although not extant, Laboon must have failed his Latin philosophy exam, which also moved him to the short course.

57. Catalog, Woodstock College of Sacred Theology, 1960–63, 21–23, ASJM.

took classes in Dogmatic Theology, Biblical Exegesis, Ecclesiastical History, and Liturgy or Oriental Questions. Dogmatic Theology and Biblical Exegesis were the predominant areas, with twenty-nine and seventeen semester hours of study required, respectively. While not "lighting the world on fire" with his academic acumen, Jake nonetheless had prepared himself intellectually and pastorally for his future ministry as a priest.

The culmination of ten years of religious formation for Jake Laboon reached its apex on June 17, 1956. He, along with sixteen classmates, were ordained to the priesthood in the chapel at Woodstock College by Francis P. Keough, the archbishop of Baltimore.[58] Jake celebrated his first Mass at his home parish, St. Bernard, in Mt. Lebanon, Pittsburgh, on June 24, 1956. He was joined by several Jesuits serving in various roles in the liturgical celebrations of the pre-Vatican II church. The Mass was attended by his family and many friends, including a contingent of former students from St. Joe Prep, who made the pilgrimage to Pittsburgh for the event.[59]

Jake Laboon had reached a milestone with his ordination, but his future was unclear concerning his ministry options. He was asked by the Society to present three options, but Jake only offered two: teaching or returning to the military. Laboon would have time to reflect and dialogue with his religious superior over his decision during the next two years, which he needed to finish his theology and participate in his tertianship.[60]

American Catholicism in the 1950s

Jake Laboon was baptized a Roman Catholic shortly after birth, but the church into which he was born and the American Catholic experience he found upon his ordination to the priesthood were, indeed, very different. The physical growth and more importantly the broader acceptance of Catholicism in American society from the 1920s to the mid-1950s was trans-

---

58. Publicity release, Laboon file, AUSNA; Dismissorial letter, Francis P. Keough, Laboon file, NMPR; *Jesuit*, Maryland Province, June 1956, PPJL.

59. "Rev. John F. Laboon, Jr.," Laboon alumni file, AUSNA; Joseph Ryan, interview with the author, March 2, 2011. Jesuits and others who joined Jake for his first Mass were: Fr. James Donahue of Loyola High School (Baltimore), who served as deacon; Raymond J. Doherty of the Diocese of Pittsburgh, who served as archpriest; and Joseph A. Cawley, president of St. Joseph's Prep, who preached the sermon.

60. Rosemary, deLellis, and Joan Laboon, interview with the author, August 4, 2010; *Honolulu Advertiser*, n.d. [1971–72], Laboon file, AUSNA.

Figure 4-2. Jake Laboon (far right) and classmates, ordination, June 17, 1956

Figure 4-3. Jake Laboon with his parents and younger brother, Father Joe, and Sisters deLellis, Rosemary, and Joan

formative for the church. In order to understand the environment in which Father Laboon would now minister, some background knowledge concerning Catholicism's place in American society in the 1950s is essential.

The general religious environment in the United States in the mid-1950s was described by the Jewish intellectual and scholar Will Herberg in his seminal work, *Protestant, Catholic, Jew*. While noting positive signs, Herberg also saw a rising tension between a secularist tendency and religious revival:

> Whether we judge by religious identification, church membership, or church attendance, whether we go by the best-seller lists, the mass media, or the writings of intellectuals, the conclusion is the same: there is every sign of a notable "turn to religion" among the American people today.

He continued, "The secularism dominating the American consciousness is not an overt philosophy; it is an underlying often unconscious orientation of life and thought."[61] In short, Herberg was articulating what he saw as a paradox between American religion and society, a situation where Americans think, feel, and act in terms quite obviously secularist, but at the same time exhibit every sign of a widespread religious revival. For Herberg, the environment was both the problem and a challenge.[62]

American Catholics were certainly aware of and possibly practiced the general trends described by Herberg. The mid-1950s was for them a time to deal with other issues. Catholics rejoiced over their continual growth throughout the first half of the twentieth century. In 1957 there were slightly over 36 million Roman Catholics in the United States, comprising 21 percent of the population, living in 111 dioceses and 27 archdioceses. The number of priests in the country increased through the decade, growing from 42,970 in 1952 to 48,349 in 1956, although the ratio of the number of Catholics per priest actually rose from 642 to 690 during the same time period.[63] Despite

---

61. Will Herberg, *Protestant—Catholic—Jew: An Essay in American Religious Sociology* (Garden City, N.Y.: Doubleday, 1955), 1.

62. Ibid., 3. In another place (page 2), Herberg wrote, "This is at least part of the picture presented by religion in contemporary America: Christians flocking to church, yet forgetting all about Christ when it comes to naming the most significant events in history; men and women valuing the Bible as Revelation, purchasing and distributing it by the millions, yet apparently seldom reading it themselves. Every aspect of contemporary religious life reflects the paradox—pervasive secularism amid mounting religiosity, 'the strengthening of the religious structure in spite of increasing secularization.'"

63. Ibid., 153; Francis X. Curran, "Vocations Keep Climbing," *America* 96 (February 9, 1957): 521–22.

advances, a lingering sense of inadequacy remained in the American Catholic psyche. In this light, speaking of the minority status theory first articulated by the historian Fr. Thomas McAvoy, CSC, the Jesuit scholar Walter Ong described his understanding of American Catholicism in the 1950s: "It is out of this defense mentality that the American Catholic consciousness as a whole has drawn its notion of its position in history."[64]

Anti-Catholicism, which had been part of the American scene from the Colonial era, continued to color the Catholic environment into the 1950s. Paulist Father John Sheerin took on publicly the longstanding argument held by many Protestants that Catholics did not believe in the constitutional guarantee of religious liberty; rather, bishops sought the union of church and state, the elimination of Protestantism, and the creation of a "Catholic nation."[65] Commenting on the anti-Catholic rhetoric of Paul Blanshard in his 1949 book *American Freedom and Catholic Power*, the Catholic sociologist and noted pacifist Gordon Zahn wrote:

> Even if Catholics abandon all of their *unnecessary* "separatist" attitudes and behavior patterns, sources of anti-Catholic tension would remain in the mere fact that they [Catholics] continued to adhere to beliefs and practices that are demanded by their faith. This is a fact that must be faced.[66]

Persistent tensions between Protestants and Catholics, based on lingering animosity from the sixteenth-century Reformation and the belief that Catholics, through their loyalty to the pope, could not simultaneously be loyal to American government officials, were part of the 1950s religious environment.

One important issue directly related to anti-Catholicism was the contemporary relationship between Catholics and Protestants. Sheerin, editor of *The Catholic World*, worried that tensions between Catholics and Protestants might "explode at any time into open hostilities." He suggested that there

---

64. Walter Ong, *Frontiers in American Catholicism: Essays on Ideology and Culture* (New York: MacMillan, 1957), 3. Thomas T. McAvoy's theme of the Catholic minority permeates all his writings, whether historical, educational, or popular. The reader may see the following articles written by McAvoy for more clarification: "American Catholics and the Second World War," *Review of Politics* 6 (April 1944): 131–50; "American Catholic Tradition," *Ave Maria* 66 (July 12, 1947): 46–49; "Catholics and the American Way," *Ave Maria* 53 (May 3, 1941): 551–53; and "The Philosophers and American Catholic Education," *Catholic Historical Review* 48 (November 1949): 579–85.

65. John B. Sheerin, "American Bishops and Protestant Fears: How Soon a Catholic America?" *Catholic World* 187 (August 1958): 321–22.

66. Gordon C. Zahn, "Catholic Separatism and Anti-Catholic Tensions," *America* (October 27, 1956): 96 (emphasis original).

were numerous misconceptions on each side that needed to be quickly discarded. He wrote, "The quicker we Catholics and Protestants consign our stereotypes of each other to the trash-barrel, the sooner we can get on with the building of a happy America."[67] Sheerin suggested that the Protestant fear of a rising Catholic population was a paper tiger, as Catholics still had little significant influence in American society. He offered a solution to dampen the hostilities between the two principal Christian groups in the United States:

> It seems to me that we can help to dissipate this prejudice by making the church in America as American as possible.... We should not become super patriots, building up a national church, but we should vest that part of the church that is visible in America in garments appropriate to the tastes and customs of the American people.[68]

The Jesuit Gustave Weigel believed tensions had subsided because Protestants had accepted Catholics on equal footing. He wrote,

> Catholics have a "growing sense of security," and are "no longer afraid of the American Protestant." ... Ancient bogies and the ghosts of former times have been destroyed. The Catholic is now perfectly ready to associate with the Protestant with affection and trust.[69]

The longstanding negative view toward the church held by many Americans prompted some prominent Catholics to suggest ways to reverse such attitudes. Francis Spellman, the cardinal archbishop of New York, presented a very positive view of Catholicism through his unflinching patriotism, which Blanshard had questioned only a few years earlier. Spellman expressed this belief through his collateral duty as head of the military ordinariate, which Jake Laboon would soon enter, and his strong anti-Communist stance. McAvoy called for a stronger national organization of the church, one that would be consistent with the remarkable national conformity in faith and practice of American Catholics. Father John Murphy, studying at the time at the Gregorian University in Rome, suggested that American Catholics needed to find their own expression of faith, to move out of the shadows of past decades, using the spirit and the resources of the day.[70]

---

67. Sheerin, "American Bishops," 323.
68. Sheerin, "Protestant-Catholic Cold War," *Catholic World* 182 (December 1955): 164.
69. Gustave Weigel, quoted in "Era of Good Feeling?" summary of address, *Time* 71 (June 2, 1958): 66.
70. Gerald P. Fogarty, "Public Patriotism and Private Politics: The Tradition of American

As mentioned earlier, the 1950s was a decade when Catholicism began to move more into the mainstream of American life. The Catholic sociologist Father Joseph Fichter, SJ, referred to a "notable class realignment" that moved many Catholics into middle-class America.[71] The 1950s also saw several leading intellectuals of the period converted to Catholicism, including conservatives L. Brent Bozell, Russell Kirk, Jeffrey Hart, and Joseph Sobran. The American Catholic historian Patrick Allitt has commented, "They saw in it [the church] a natural conservative institution which was better able to contain the political and intellectual challenges of the day than any other organization in the free world."[72] Catholic historian Theodore Maynard also offered a more positive outlook. He wrote, "Good will toward us [Catholics] is now normal, even if we are still considered a strange people and regarded with some suspicion." He even suggested that for many Americans Catholics were becoming their equals. Yet his comments were tempered by a dose of reality: "Around our neck ... dangles a necklace of millstones, put there by unlucky social and historical circumstances. It will be a long time before we shall be able to shake it completely off."[73]

Greater acceptance of Roman Catholics in the United States during the decade of the 1950s could not erase significant disagreements within the Catholic community itself. Historically, a divide between liberals and conservatives has been present in American Catholicism since the time of John Carroll, the first Catholic bishop in the United States. As the nineteenth century progressed, his "Enlightened Catholicism," expressed by greater openness to society at large and the Protestant majority specifically, was challenged by some of his successors to the See of Baltimore and by other prelates, such as Michael Corrigan of New York and Bernard McQuaid of Rochester. This theological divide was most significant during the Americanist crisis between 1884 and 1899. While not affecting the ordinary "Catholic in the pew," nonetheless powerful bishops battled for control of the

---

Catholicism," *U.S. Catholic Historian* 4, no. 1 (1984): 47; John L. Murphy, "The American Catholic," *Catholic World* 182 (February 1956): 335; McAvoy, "The Catholic Church in the United States," in *The Catholic Church in World Affairs*, edited by Waldemar Gurian and M. A. Fitzsimmons, 360–61 (Notre Dame, Ind.: University of Notre Dame Press, 1954).

71. "U.S. Catholics Climb Economic Scale," *Christian Century* 75 (July 2, 1955): 773.

72. Patrick Allitt, "American Catholics and the New Conservatism of the 1950s," *U.S. Catholic Historian* 7, no. 1 (Winter 1988): 20–21.

73. Theodore Maynard, "Lurking Suspicion of Catholicism," *Catholic World* 180 (February 1955): 331, 327, 329.

future direction of the American church through various issues that arose during the last decade-and-a-half of the nineteenth century. The debate was only somewhat squelched in January 1899 when Pope Leo XIII issued *Testem Benevolentiae*, a personal letter to Cardinal James Gibbons of Baltimore that condemned Americanism (a more liberal approach to American Catholicism), stating that any accommodation of the faith to a local environment (such as the United States) would be within the purview of the pope, not any local individual or group of bishops.[74]

This liberal-conservative debate in American Catholicism was also waged in the 1950s. The debate was synthesized by John Moody, a priest professor of the period: "For some 'liberal Catholic' is likely to arouse the picture of one who is betraying the cause; while for others 'conservative' will have the implication of an enemy of the faithful and the good."[75] He went on to write,

The value of the liberal-conservative dialogue can be lost by the absence of light, as well as the abundance of heat. The moat in the conservative's vision is his inadequate sense of history. He is apt to insist on the abiding necessity of some factor which was introduced as a response to a particular historical need.... But the liberal has his own hazard: he has no criteria beyond his own fallible judgment, to distinguish permanent advances in knowledge from passing fashions.[76]

Providing a possible resolution to the division, Father John Murphy suggested a middle path:

The American Church must take a more active part in the work of adapting the Church to modern life. American Catholicism has come of age, and it must take its proper place in the intellectual, the social and liturgical life of the universal Church.[77]

---

74. The historical period of Americanism, 1885–1899, has been addressed by numerous scholars through various articles and books. The only complete monograph on the topic of Americanism is dated; see McAvoy, *The Great Crisis in American Catholic History, 1895–1900* (Chicago: Henry Regnery, 1957). There are numerous essays and sections of books on the topic. A representative selection includes: William J. Portier, "Inculturation as Transformation: The Case of Americanism Revisited, *U.S. Catholic Historian* 11 (Summer 1993): 107–24; Fogarty, "The Catholic Hierarchy in the United States Between the Third Plenary Council and the Condemnation of Americanism," *U.S. Catholic Historian* 11 (Summer 1993): 19–36; Philip Gleason, "The New Americanism in Catholic Historiography," *U.S. Catholic Historian* 11 (Summer 1993): 1–18; Portier, "Isaac Hecker and Americanism," *Ecumenist* 19 (November–December 1980): 9–12; Michael Baxter, "The Unsettling of Americanism," *Communio* 27 (Spring 2000): 161–70.

75. John N. Moody, "Catholic Liberal—Conservative Debate: With Editorial Comment," *Commonweal* 67 (February 14, 1958): 504.

76. Ibid., 506.

77. Murphy, "American Catholic," 333.

Another significant debate internal to the American church was the dearth of Catholic intellectual life. The issue was brought to the forefront in 1955 through the seminal article "American Catholics and the Intellectual Life," by Monsignor John Tracy Ellis, a professor of church history at the Catholic University of America. Ellis stridently critiqued American Catholics for their failures in intellectual pursuit:

> Admittedly the weakest aspect of the Church in this country lies in its failure to produce national leaders and to exercise commanding influence in intellectual circles, and this at a time when the number of Catholics in the United States is exceeded only by those of Brazil and Italy and their material resources are incomparably superior to those of any other branch of the universal Church.[78]

Ellis provided reasons that, in his opinion, this situation existed. First, he spoke of the persistent anti-Catholicism present in the country. He also said that the character and background of the vast majority of American Catholics—namely, their immigrant status, which often resulted in poverty and even illiteracy—hindered them from achieving any significant intellectual heights.[79] He further suggested that a "Catholic mentality" at universities that was more interested in enforcing orthodoxy than intellectual-risk-taking, which was essential in scholarship, was the main reason Catholics, despite a broad-based education system, had failed to produce many quality scholars.[80]

Ellis's essay generated a firestorm of reaction within the American Catholic intellectual community. Many agreed with the general premise and tenor of Ellis's comments. Speaking at the 1956 annual conference of the National Catholic Education Association, one religious sister blasted the American church for its lack of intellectual vigor on all levels:

> The chief obstacle to the development of Catholic intellectualism in our colleges is, I believe, the absence of an intellectual tradition in our American Catholic population. This is true not only for the rank-and-file of Catholics; it is also true of our bishops and religious superiors, both men and women, who are responsible for the education and training of religious teachers and for the selection of lay teachers for all levels of our Catholic educational system.[81]

---

78. John Tracy Ellis, "American Catholics and the Intellectual Life," *Thought* 30, no. 118 (Autumn 1955): 353.

79. Ibid., 353–56.

80. Allitt, "American Catholics," 26; Ellis, "American Catholics," 353–54.

81. Quoted in Thomas F. O'Dea, *American Catholic Dilemma* (New York: Sheed and Ward, 1958), 10.

Equally harsh was the sociologist of religion, Harvard professor Thomas O'Dea, who stated, "Catholics have not even done what might reasonably have been expected of them to foster letters, speculation, and the arts."[82] The Jesuit priest John Courtney Murray, who specialized in the area of church-state relations, suggested that the church, in trying to uphold the tradition, was actually losing a major aspect of it:

> In a day when anti-intellectualism hangs like smog over the American scene, the Catholic intelligence has another job. Firm confrontation of error is the traditional church duty. But anti-intellectualism is in itself an error. It is altogether alien to the tradition wrought by Saint Augustine's injunction, "Love intelligence greatly." It has been said that love of intelligence still stands too far down the list of American Catholic loves; the list needs to be revised.[83]

The Catholic journalist John Cogley concentrated his critique on the lack of theological innovation. In February 1958 he wrote:

> American Catholic theology seems to be committed to a holding action. Our theological journals are clerical home organs, either so specialized as to have the musty flavor of a Ph.D. thesis, so confession-oriented as to have the clinical flavor of a medical manual, or so concerned with rubrical niceties as to have the frivolous flavor of Emily Post's masterpiece.[84]

While the preponderance of response to Ellis's challenge was supportive, there were less critical voices. While acknowledging the "malaise" of American Catholicism's intellectual life, the Jesuit historian and philosopher Walter Ong saw the situation as full of potential. The present environment gave every indication that Catholics could and would make positive strides in theology and other academic disciplines.[85] Bishop (later Cardinal) John Wright of Worcester, Massachusetts, highlighted the historical aspect of Catholicism's support for education, building schools as quickly as we build homes and altars. He suggested that the authentic Catholic attitude toward the intellectual life rejects the idea that the church itself or even most of its members are at any time suspicious of intellectual pursuit or indifferent to or unsympathetic with scholarship. He did acknowledge,

---

82. Ibid.
83. John Courtney Murray, "Special Catholic Challenges," *Life* 39–40 (December 26, 1955): 145–46.
84. John Cogley, "Anyone Listening?" *Commonweal* 67 (February 7, 1958): 185.
85. Ong, *Frontiers*, 9.

however, that the dangers of intellectual stagnation are real. He concluded, "The wrath of the stupid has laid waste the world quite as often as the craft of the bright."[86]

Quite obviously American Catholicism could not avoid the reality of the Cold War and throughout the 1950s demonstrated its loyalty to the nation by its strong anti-Communist stand. Indeed, the historian Timothy Kelly has written, "The clearest, most menacing materialist crisis to threaten American Catholics—and the entire world—was communism."[87] Almost from the time of the Bolshevik Revolution, American Catholics had stood against the Red menace. Catholic support for the efforts of Senator Joseph McCarthy (R-Wisconsin) to root out Communists from the federal government was generally strong. Indeed, some, such as L. Brent Bozell and William Buckley, connected the new conservatism found in Catholic America with McCarthyism.[88]

American Catholicism's staunch rejection of Communism served as a building block to foster the advance of Catholics in the public sector. While Catholics were challenged to be more careful in demonstrating livelier respect for Democratic processes, on both large and small questions the nation as a whole was given warning that politically Catholics had come to maturity and were willing to apply for the nation's highest office.[89] Clearly the greatest manifestation of the rise of Catholics in the public sector was the drive of Senator John F. Kennedy, a Catholic from Massachusetts, to be a serious candidate for president. While several specific fears of a Kennedy presidency were raised, one writer claimed, "There will be little doubt in the minds of most . . . that Catholicism has ceased to be a serious handicap for a Democratic Presidential candidate and may even be a major asset."[90]

---

86. John J. Wright, "Catholics and Anti-Intellectualism," *Commonweal* 63 (December 16, 1955): 275, 277.

87. Timothy Kelly, *Transformation of American Catholicism*, 10.

88. Allitt, *American Catholics*, 20–23.

89. "Catholics in Public Life: Discussion," *Commonweal* 65 (January 4, 1957): 349.

90. Lawrence H. Fuchs, "A Catholic as President?" *America* 99 (September 13, 1958): 622–23. Fuchs also presented four major categories of reasons that a Catholic like Kennedy would not be acceptable to the American people: (1) liberal intellectual fears—based on perceived value conflicts; (2) anti-Catholicism—obvious reality from the past; (3) Catholic fear—some Catholics themselves fear a Catholic president would reignite anti-Catholic sentiments. Catholics would be blamed for every mistake Kennedy would make; (4) Catholic pride—fears on the part of Protestants that Catholics are ready to "rock the boat."

The fears possessed by some concerning the rise to prominence of a Catholic in the public sector was symptomatic of the more general issue of the role of the laity in the church. Before the Second Vatican Council took up this issue in a formal sense, the 1950s saw the advancement of the laity, including women, coming to the forefront. John Sheerin expressed the conviction, "We are coming into the era of the layman."[91] A better educated laity sought greater participation in the church. The journalist Richard Menges acknowledged the new role the laity could play: "Men and women often will look to the clergy for ultimate answers to ... problems. But informed laymen too have some answers to give, and there are signs they are beginning to give."[92] This new lay activity was not simply to be exercised in the church, but rather with business and other secular activities. Again, Menges advised readers,

> The ideal—sadly under achieved—would seem to be that Catholics carry their zeal not only into the activities of their parish organizations, but into every facet of their business, professional lives. Initiative guided by Faith—this is the foundation stone of Catholic lay leadership.[93]

In an eerie foreshadowing of what the church would say in an official capacity through Vatican II, Cardinal Emmanuel Suhard, who died in 1949, once stated with respect to the need for greater lay participation in the church, "The principle of adaptation itself is time honored in the Church. Both in theory and in practice, we find that the Church always tries to adjust itself to various circumstances of time and place."[94]

Tertianship

Knowledge of the status of American Catholicism in the 1950s is helpful to understand the environment that Jake Laboon encountered in the time immediately after his ordination. Following his first Mass in Pittsburgh, Jake was granted some time with his family before returning to Woodstock for his final year of theology. He completed the short course in the summer of 1957 and then proceeded to his tertianship, which he served at the shrine of the North American Martyrs in Auriesville, New York.

91. "Layman's Role" (editorial), *Commonweal* 66 (June 28, 1957): 316.
92. Richard M. Menges, "Lay Leaders: A Problem," *Catholic World* 185 (July 1957): 282.
93. Ibid., 283.
94. Murphy, "American Catholic," 331.

The shrine at Auriesville had an interesting history. In 1884 General John S. Clark, using research data he had gathered, was able to convince people, including the famous American church historian John Gilmary Shea, that the site of the martyrdom of the Jesuit missionary St. Isaac Jogues was at Auriesville. That year a hundred-acre plot of land at the site was purchased by the Jesuits; in July 1885 the first small chapel was erected—the Shrine of Our Lady of Martyrs. Construction of the tertianship of the North American Martyrs Shrine began in the spring of 1938. The cornerstone was blessed by Bishop Edmund Gibbons of Albany on September 25, 1938; the building was ready for occupation in March of the next year. It was described as "a modest permanent residence, with cheerful simplicity as the dominant note of the building." The first tertians, from St. Andrews-on-Hudson, arrived on April 4, 1939.[95]

Jake arrived at the shrine on September 1, 1957, ready to participate in ministry that centered on youth. He described the tertianship as "the long retreat on ascetical theology ... the last trial before the Society places its stamp of approval on you."[96] Laboon gave retreats to youth and participated in various activities with the Boy Scouts and students at Cardinal Farley Military Academy. He reported to his provincial about his experience:

I found this type of work especially gratifying, as I enjoy working with young men, talking to them, and trying to inspire them to better lives as Catholics. Some of Ours, as well as Externs who have watched me in action with young men, tell me that I have a special knack for this type of work and would do well to continue in such work whenever possible.

Besides his work with youth, this period of tertianship provided him with the opportunity to study the constitutions and instructions of the Society and to read extensively. Additionally, he was very happy about his spiritual development.[97]

After his year at Auriesville it was once again time for Jake to transition, only this time into fulltime active ministry. Two years earlier, at the time of his ordination, he expressed interest in returning to the navy or teach-

---

95. "The Shrine of the North American Martyrs," Woodstock letters, 58:105, 113; 68:171, 175, ASJM.

96. John Laboon, SJ, to William Maloney, SJ, April 4, 1958, Laboon file, ASJM; *Catholic Review*, July 17, 1981, AABa.

97. John Laboon, SJ, to William Maloney, SJ, April 21, 1958, Laboon file, ASJM.

ing high school students. His time as a tertian had demonstrated his skill in working with youth and provided him with more experience for his desire to teach. Yet he was uncertain as to which path he should follow. He wrote to his provincial,

> My preferences for the future are quite confusing, because I am at present torn between high school work—teaching mathematics, or any work associated with our high schools—and the work of a chaplain in the United States Navy. Because of my background in the Navy, I am sure that I would be able to do much good with both the enlisted personnel and the officers. This conflict of interest exists, and I do not want to solve the difficulty or make a choice for myself, I am placing high school work and the work as a chaplain *ex aequo*. My talents and interests cover both types of work.[98]

Obedient to his peers, Jake, while expressing his views, offered himself for the needs of the Society:

> I submit my talents and interests to you, Reverend Father Provincial, so that you may know that I am completely indifferent to whatever work you assign me. I mentioned my interests and talents but at the same time, the work of the Province is first in my mind. If you feel that you have any work which you would like me to do in the immediate future, I humbly submit willingly to your judgment.[99]

His only request was that if the decision was made for him to return to the military, the Navy Department would appreciate one month's notice to complete the necessary paperwork.[100]

Conclusion

Through his training at the naval academy and his distinguished and heroic service aboard the USS *Peto* during World War II, Jake Laboon had been commissioned to and successfully served his nation. However, the war cemented in him a calling from God, first heard in his earlier life, to follow Jesus Christ through the priesthood. Resigning his commission in 1946, Laboon entered the Jesuit novitiate at Wernerville, Pennsylvania, in November, initiating a long road that culminated in June 1956 with his ordination to the priesthood. While not a great student, he did successfully complete his preparations and, after finishing his final step of formation through his tertianship in Auriesville, New York, stood ready to begin a new career.

98. Ibid.
99. Ibid.
100. Ibid.

Chapter 5

Fleet Ballistic Missile Submarine Chaplain
★ 1958–1961

Commissioned to serve his nation as an officer in the U.S. Navy, Jake answered a longstanding, but recently stronger call from God by entering the Society of Jesus. Ordained a Jesuit priest in 1956, he decided, with the approval of his religious superiors, to combine his two former commissions, one to the nation and a second to God into service of God and country as a chaplain in the U.S. Navy. Serving the church as a navy chaplain was a natural fit for one who loved God, country, and the U.S. Navy. The fact that he was the only navy chaplain who wore the gold dolphins of a qualified submariner, coupled with his standing as an academy graduate, gave Jake Laboon instant recognition by his peers and those he served. His unique combination of fleet experience and respect gave him the tools to better serve officers and sailors alike.

Return to the Navy

Jake Laboon's movement into full-time active ministry became his preoccupation as his tertianship drew to a close. He showed openness to the needs of the province and the will of the provincial, but toyed with the idea of returning to the navy for many years. Evidence exists that as early as November 1953 Jake had been in communication with navy officials about the possibility of returning as a chaplain.[1] On July 1, 1956, he received an appointment to the rank of Lieutenant Junior Grade in the Chaplain Corps, U.S. Navy Reserve. Eight months later, on February 1, 1957, he received his commission.[2] Approximately ten years later, describing his reentry into the navy, Jake commented, "My religious superiors asked me if I wanted to return to the Navy and I said yes. I guess the Navy's in my blood."[3] Between February 1957 and August 1958 Laboon was listed as an "inactive chaplain."[4] It is also apparent that the chief of chaplains for the navy, Rear Admiral Edward Harp Jr., believed Jake's desire to reenter the navy would be most welcome due to his experience. One letter to Harp read, "This priest is a Naval Academy graduate with quite a submarine warfare record."[5] Jake reported to his provincial concerning his Navy status:

The Navy Department understands that I am not available for active duty until after I finish my Tertianship in June 1958. At that time, the Navy also understands that my appointment or my release to active duty will depend entirely upon my superiors.[6]

As a reserve officer Jake served at the discretion of the navy's need. He was called to active duty in September 1958.[7]

Jake's motivation to reenter the navy was based primarily on his desire to minister to young sailors and marines, but his strong dedication to the military life was also a factor. He once stated, "I wouldn't have become a chaplain if I didn't think it was important to the young sailor and marine to remind him of his religious background and beliefs."[8] Jake saw the military as a choice, but one that required total dedication. He described his motivation:

---

1. Statement of service, n.d.; Statement of purpose, n.d., Laboon file, NMPR. These documents say Laboon's "Pay Entry Base Date" was November 22, 1953; his "Active-Duty Base Date" was April 10, 1955. This information makes it clear that Jake had every intention of reentering the navy immediately after his ordination and he was free to enter active ministry.

2. Commission appointment, February 11, 1957; chief of naval personnel to John Laboon Jr., February 28, 1957, Laboon file, NMPR. Various documents provide different dates for Laboon's commission in the chaplain corps: some suggest February 11, 1957; others suggest February 17. Sources do agree on his date of rank—July 1, 1956; see Clifford Drury, *The History of the Chaplain Corps, United States Navy*, vol. 3, *Biographies* (Washington, D.C.: Bureau of Naval Personnel, 1984), 93.

3. *Great Lakes Bulletin*, March 19, 1965, GLNSL.

4. General information sheet, Laboon file, NMPR.

5. Thomas McCarthy to RADM Edward Harp Jr., October 16, 1956, Laboon file, NMPR.

6. John Laboon, SJ, to William Maloney, SJ, March 19, 1957, Laboon file, ASJM.

7. "U.S.S. Laboon Commissioning Booklet," n.d. [1995], PPJL.

8. Ibid.

For those of us who are members of some branch of the service, it should not merely be a question of dedication to that particular outfit, but rather a matter of degree of dedication. To be dedicated to the Navy or the Marine Corps for us is taken for granted. We would not wear the uniform unless there was some consecration of ourselves to our country. This is not enough. So ask yourself the question, "To what degree am I dedicated to the Navy or to the Marine Corps?"[9]

He saw the military as an opportunity for one who worked hard to achieve significant rewards. He once wrote,

The greatest thing about the military is the opportunity it offers. When I got to the Naval Academy, I knew no one. You go in, take your civilian clothes off, and stand there and you're all like. You begin your career the day you enter the Naval Academy. The same is true of an enlisted person. He can go as high as his desires and abilities will take him.[10]

The Navy Chaplain Corps

Those who served in the early years of the U.S. Navy Chaplain Corps were tasked to possess charismatic personalities as much as knowledge of religious practice. The corps was formally established on November 28, 1775. The second article of navy regulations read:

The Commanders of the ships of the 13 United Colonies are to take care that divine services be performed twice a day on board, and a sermon preached on Sundays, unless bad weather or extraordinary accidents prevent.[11]

The father of the U.S. Navy, John Paul Jones, during his time as commanding officer of *Ranger* and *Bonhomme Richard*, described the qualities he sought in a ship's chaplain:

[I desire] a man of reading and of letters whose sanctity of manners and happy principles would diffuse unanimity and cheerfulness thro' the ship. Such a man would necessarily be worthy [of] the highest confidence, and might, therefore, assure himself of my esteem and friendship, and always have a place at my table.[12]

On October 30, 1778, William Balch became the first chaplain to receive a commission in the U.S. Navy, reporting aboard the frigate *Boston*.

9. *Great Lakes Bulletin*, September 18, 1964, GLNSL.
10. Clipping, n.d., PPWL.
11. CDR Robert Warren, "The Naval Chaplaincy," essay, n.d., p. 55, folder 5750/11, historical articles, box 29, Navy Chaplains Archives, Fort Jackson, S.C. (hereafter NCA).
12. Ibid.

As the early days of the nineteenth century progressed, the duties of navy chaplains became more specific and defined. In January 1802 President Thomas Jefferson issued a new addition to naval regulations that included references to the duties of a chaplain. He was to read prayers at stated times, perform all funerals, and serve as a schoolmaster instructing the midshipmen and volunteers in writing, arithmetic, navigation, and other disciplines that would help them become proficient in their naval service. The chaplain was to work under the direction of the commanding officer. By 1813, however, a separation had taken place between the billets of chaplain and schoolmaster. By an act of Congress, passed on January 2, 1815, all new ships of the line were to carry a chaplain and schoolmaster.[13] Proper attire for chaplains was also mandated by a directive of the secretary of the navy, published on January 20, 1844:

Chaplains shall wear Black Coat, with a black velvet collar, and the navy button now in use (they need not, however, provide themselves with new coats until those they have are worn out). While performing religious services on the Sabbath, or on other occasions, on board vessels of war or at yards and shore stations, they shall wear the Black Silk Gown usually worn by clergymen.[14]

In short order, however, the order was modified to allow chaplains discretion on their clerical garb.

Growth of the chaplain corps in the nineteenth century was slow, both in general and particularly for Catholics. In 1841 there was still only a quota of twenty-four navy chaplains for the entire fleet. Consistent with the general attitude of many Americans toward Catholics in the first half of the nineteenth century, it took some time before a priest was assigned as a chaplain. The first Roman Catholic priest to serve on a navy ship was Adam Marshall, who in December 1824 was listed as the "schoolmaster" aboard the *North Carolina*. The first official Catholic priest chaplain, Charles Parks from the Archdiocese of New York, was commissioned in 1888. The first priest chaplain to be killed in action was a Jesuit, Father Anthony Rey, who died under the command of General Zachary Taylor in the Mexican War of 1846.[15]

13. William F. R. Gilroy and Timothy J. Demy, *A Brief Chronology of the Chaplain Corps of the United States Navy* (Washington, D.C.: Bureau of Naval Personnel, 1983), 1–4, 6, 9.

14. Ibid., 16.

15. Ibid., 13; Daniel L. Mode, *The Grunt Padre: The Service and Sacrifice of Father Vincent Robert Capodanno, Vietnam, 1966–1967* (Oak Lawn, Ill.: C.M.J. Marin, 2000), 61.

World War I became the catalyst for a significant increase in the chaplain corps. As late as 1913 the number of chaplains was the same as in 1842; in 1917, the year of the United States' entry into the war, it was still only forty. However, by the time of the armistice in 1918 there were 203 navy chaplains. This huge increase created a need for administrative control and supervision, leading to the appointment of the first navy chief of chaplains, a Southern Methodist minister, John Brown Frazier.[16] In order to prepare chaplains for service, Frazier developed and published *The Navy Chaplain's Manual*. The postwar era also saw the chaplain corps operate on denominational and confessional lines for the first time.[17]

Greater numbers of Catholic clergy in the chaplain corps generated a need for organization on the denominational level. On November 24, 1917, Pope Benedict XV organized the military ordinariate and appointed auxiliary bishop Patrick J. Hayes of New York as the first military ordinary of the United States. Hayes was extremely effective in recruiting priest chaplains for the war effort; the total in all branches of the service by November 19, 1918, was 1,523, governed by five geographical vicariates.[18] In 1939 the vicariate for the military was formed and placed under supervision of Archbishop Francis Spellman of New York.[19]

America's participation in World War II created an even greater need for chaplains. George Rixey, the executive officer to the army chief of chaplains, spoke in general of the duties of the chaplain: "To the chaplain comes the extraordinary privilege of interpreting to those potential saviors of our nation how the high qualities of citizenship and social morality may be transmitted into military virtue and effective military action." Rixey made a clear connection between the work of the chaplain and patriotism.[20] The

---

16. It should be noted that between 1880 and 1920 the U.S. Navy Chaplain Corps began to take formal shape. Many issues, such as accession of chaplains, administration, and organization of chaplain ministries, were being discussed prior to the actual appointment of a chief of chaplains. The idea of appointing a chief of chaplains had been discussed during this same period.

17. Warren, "The Naval Chaplaincy," essay, n.d., p. 55, folder 5750/11, historical articles, box 29; chapter in Chaplain History (1967), 5750, box 217, NCA; Drury, *History of the Chaplain Corps*, 1:172.

18. Mode, *Grunt Padre*, 61–62. The discrepancy between army and navy chaplains was significant, as the navy had fewer than fifty chaplains prior to World War I.

19. In 1985 Pope John Paul II created the Archdiocese for Military Services and Appointed Joseph Ryan as its first archbishop; see Mode, *Grunt Padre*, 62.

20. Chaplain George F. Rixey, "The Chaplain's Ministry," January–February 1942, military

debt owed to the churches and their ministers was acknowledged by Fleet Admiral Chester Nimitz:

> Throughout my many years of service in the Navy and particularly during World War II, I have become increasingly aware of the Navy's debt to the church, which, through its chaplains, has applied spiritual vision and guidance to the man in the service.[21]

World War II also produced the first navy chaplain, Father Joseph O'Callahan, SJ, to be awarded the Congressional Medal of Honor.

The decade of the 1950s was a time of significant effort in the recruitment of new navy chaplains. After the conclusion of the Korean War, military enrollments remained rather high, and the need of chaplains was great, yet many Catholic chaplain billets remained open. A clarion call was raised for priests from various dioceses and religious communities to consider service in the armed forces.[22] The need for Catholic chaplains prompted a new and somewhat controversial program to recruit Catholic seminarians to be chaplains in a reserve status. A Defense Department statement read, "Qualified theological students will be recruited for appointment as ensigns in the Naval Reserve for inactive duty."[23] The navy had authorized such recruitment, but James Griffiths, auxiliary bishop and chancellor of the military ordinariate, voiced caution:

> The most solemn assurances are given that such seminarians would not be called but I pointed out that in spite of this, we do not permit those who are already ordained as Catholic priests to apply for the military chaplaincy unless they are at least three years ordained.[24]

---

affairs chief of chaplains, box 115, Office of the General Secretary, NCWC, Archives The Catholic University of America (hereafter ACUA), Washington, D.C.

21. Chester W. Nimitz to Francis Spellman, October 8, 1947, military affairs 1944–55, box 57, Office of the General Secretary, NCWC, ACUA.

22. "The Armed Forces," enclosure, Harold Prudell to Msgr. Paul Tanner, January 26, 1954, box 57, military affairs chaplains, 1951–54, Office of the General Secretary, NCWC, ACUA. This essay claims that only 18 percent of Catholics in the military attended Mass on Sundays, thus the apparent lack of chaplains.

23. Department of Defense Office of Public Information press release, March 18, 1952, box 57, military affairs chaplains, 1951–54, Office of the General Secretary NCWC, ACUA. The directive said that young men between the ages of nineteen and twenty-nine who were attending or had been accepted for entry into an approved theological seminary were eligible for appointments as ensigns.

24. James Griffiths to Howard Carroll, March 24, 1952, box 57, military affairs chaplains, 1951–54, Office of the General Secretary, NCWC, ACUA.

Clearly, Jake, due to his experience, did not follow this general rule in his own reentry into the navy.

The church organization that governed military chaplains became more formalized at the time of Laboon's return to the navy. In a decree published on September 8, 1957, the Holy See established a new military vicariate for the United States, effectively raising the military ordinariate to the status of a diocese. Consistent with the original foundation in 1939, the presiding archbishop of New York would also have the title of military vicar. In part the decree read, "Military chaplains will thus provide for the welfare of the souls entrusted to them, with the rights and duties of pastors."[25]

The duties and responsibilities of chaplains like Jake Laboon were multiple and broad. The basic mission was articulated by George C. Marshall in a 1951 secretary of defense memorandum: "It is the national interest that personnel in the Armed Forces be protected in the realization and development of moral, spiritual and religious values consistent with the religious beliefs of the individual concerned."[26] The specific navy chaplain vocation was quite similar: "The mission of the Navy Chaplain Corps is to protect, encourage, and train personnel of the Navy establishment in the realization and development of moral and spiritual values consistent with the religious beliefs of the individual concerned."[27] Navy chaplains were to provide the opportunity for worship, but more was required. One navy directive of 1951 instructed chaplains, "Take a personal interest in the off-duty activities of personnel and ensure the availability of a well-rounded program of religious, educational and recreational activities."[28] Jake Laboon fulfilled this directive in every command where he served.

The personal qualities required of a chaplain were not foreign but rather quite natural to Jake Laboon. Above all, a chaplain must be a man of God who serves as friend, counselor, and guide to all members of a command. The intangible quality of presence was essential. One chaplain explained,

25. NCWC News Service release, September 9, 1957, box 57, military affairs chaplains, 1951–54, Office of the General Secretary, NCWC, ACUA.

26. Memorandum—secretary of defense, May 26, 1951, box 57, military affairs chaplains, 1951–54, Office of the General Secretary, NCWC, ACUA.

27. Fact sheet concerning U.S. Navy chaplains, n.d. [1951–54], box 57, military affairs chaplains, 1951–54, Office of the General Secretary, NCWC, ACUA.

28. Navy directive, "Protection of Moral Standards," October 24, 1951, box 57, military affairs chaplains, 1951–54, Office of the General Secretary NCWC, ACUA.

"Just the mere presence of such a chaplain brings comfort, consolation, and steadfastness to an organization. To know he is in camp or on the battlefield is alike an inspiration and benediction to the soldiers."[29] Retired Navy Chaplain Father Joseph O'Donnell, CSC, articulated three important qualities for any military chaplain: (1) the ability to listen with both heart and soul; (2) the need to be credible; and (3) the capacity to understand the nature of confidentiality and the rule of privilege.[30]

Many of the duties of the navy chaplain were those common to any pastor. As Father O'Donnell expressed, "Being a chaplain in the military is not all about war, blood and guts. Much of the chaplain's work is the same as that of any parish priest."[31] Conducting services, celebrating sacraments, educating youth, ministering to the sick and dying, performing funeral services, and engaging in extensive pastoral counseling are all part and parcel of the ministry. One chaplain succinctly summarized his work: "In short, he [the chaplain] should be the shepherd of the flock entrusted to him, so far as his own religious convictions and those of the men whom he serves will permit."[32]

The chaplain is primarily a pastoral minister, but he is also an officer in the U.S. Armed Forces. For some this dual function of the military chaplain compromises one's ability to minister to conscientious objectors or others who may for moral reasons disagree with directives or orders that violate one's conscience. Others suggest that the military life, which promotes violence, is completely inconsistent with religious practice, especially Christianity. This issue arose during Laboon's time in Vietnam and continued after his death when a U.S. naval vessel was named for him. Those desiring to be chaplains, therefore, had to understand: "The chaplain is a soldier as well as a priest and should be proud of both aspects of his personality."[33]

The ecumenical nature of the military chaplaincy is another foundational premise. It was essential that chaplains realize that, no matter how firm their own convictions and approach to God is, these cannot be the final word in one's ministerial outreach. The chaplain is responsible to meet

---

29. Rixey, "Chaplain's Ministry."

30. Joseph F. O'Donnell, "Clergy in the Military—Vietnam and After: One Chaplain's Reflection," in *The Sword of the Lord: Military Chaplains from the First to the Twenty-First Century*, edited by Doris L. Bergen (Notre Dame, Ind.: University of Notre Dame Press, 2004), 221–22.

31. Ibid., 221.

32. Rixey, "Chaplain's Ministry."

33. Robert T. Reilly, "Priests in Uniform," July 21, 1962, box 57, military affairs chaplains, 1951–54, Office of the General Secretary, NCWC, ACUA.

the religious needs of all men and women within the scope of the command. One former chaplain described this necessity:

> Their commission is to provide or coordinate spiritual and religious support for soldiers and their families without regard to one's religious affiliation or lack thereof. In other words the role of a military chaplain, in most cases, is an institutional one rather than an ecclesiastical one.[34]

Jake Laboon expressed similar ideas by describing the variety of services accessible to those in the military: "Religion is awfully important. Perhaps we do not do as much as we could, but if a man wants to take care of his religious and spiritual needs, he has the tools available to him."[35]

Chaplain School

The navy chaplain corps was founded in the late eighteenth century, but not until World War II was a system in place for unified training, both from a religious and most importantly military perspective. The navy chaplain school, located at Norfolk and affiliated with the College of William and Mary in Williamsburg, opened on February 20, 1942. However, with the rapid demobilization after the war, the facility closed on November 15, 1945. For the next four years local naval districts supervised chaplain training. Between 1949 and 1951 training was once again centralized, this time in Washington, D.C., under the direction of Chaplain Thomas Mullins, who worked in the office of the chief of chaplains. In February 1951, due to the outbreak of hostilities in Korea and the consequent need for an expanded chaplain corps, a chaplain training program was opened at Newport, Rhode Island, with Chaplain Daniel F. Mechan as officer in charge. Mechan and two others, Orlando Involdstad Jr. and Richard W. Ricker, comprised the original faculty. Far from perfect, the new training center was, nonetheless, a major step in the right direction. One commentator at the time wrote:

> Less dramatic than the wartime chaplain indoctrination program, this scheme was considered a distinct improvement over the haphazard training chaplains had received in earlier periods.[36]

---

34. Claude D. Newby, *It Took Heroes: One Chaplain's Story and Tribute to Combat Veterans and Those Who Waited for Them* (Bountiful, Utah: Tribute Enterprises, 2000), viii.
35. Clipping, n.d. [1980], PPWL.
36. "The Chaplain School," folder 1521/11, box 127, NCA; Gilroy and Demy, *Brief Chronology*, 33; "Chapter in Chaplain History" (1967), box 217, NCA.

The initial class of twenty-three recruit chaplains was given an eight-week training and indoctrination course; a four-week refresher course was given for reserve chaplains recalled to active duty.[37]

After completing a physical examination that found him qualified to serve, Jake Laboon reported to the Commanding Officer Naval Schools Command, Naval Station, Newport, on September 22, 1958. When he arrived he was welcomed by the officer in charge, Commander Merle N. Young, and his assistant, Lieutenant Commander Paul Reigner. Jake's class comprised ten of the thirty-two students in the chaplain school, representing eighteen different denominations.[38] The school's stated purpose concentrated on military training: "Chaplains' School is in no sense a theological seminary. Its sole aim is to train already qualified clergyman how best to 'bring Navy men to God and God to Navy men.'"[39]

The eight-week training program had two major components. The first four weeks, concentrating on naval orientation, was supervised by navy line officers. Using training films, lectures, and particularly visits to many active-duty sites, chaplains began to understand what it meant to be an officer in the U.S. Navy. Field trips to Quonset Point Naval Air Station in Rhode Island, the submarine base at New London, and the U.S. Coast Guard Academy, plus a day at the Charlestown Naval Shipyard in Massachusetts, were parts of the training program. Jake's class also visited the naval academy. Marvin Snyder, one of Laboon's classmates, commented, "We were given a gala welcome because Jake was a graduate."[40] The chaplain trainees were also given a brief course at the firefighting and damage control schools. The second major section of the program was associated with training chaplains to carry out their duties and responsibilities, both ashore and afloat. Three subunits of the section were included: a character guidance program; history of the naval chaplaincy; and first aid. Chaplains were introduced to the specifics of other religious traditions in order to carry out the motto "Cooperation without Compromise." This ecumenical feature of the training was, for many, the most difficult, but it was essential to the mission to minister to all, regardless of the chaplain's religious tradition. Chaplains were given a brief introduc-

---

37. Ibid.
38. His classmates were John Dozier, Arlo Dahm, Norman Engebretson, Marcian Kandrac, Robert J. Young, Marvin E, Snyder Jr., Francis McGovern, James Vaughan, and John Brock.
39. "The Chaplain School," folder 1521/11, box 127, NCA.
40. Marvin E. Snyder, interview with the author, May 16, 2011.

tion to the Code of Conduct and the Uniform Code of Military Justice. Last, this section assisted chaplains to see that military and religious duties were not in conflict, but rather complementary to each other.[41]

The group bonded during their two months together. Living together in the bachelor's officers' quarters allowed for numerous informal discussions about all sorts of topics, including those covered in classes. Having Roman Catholic priests, Jewish rabbis, and Protestant ministers all sharing a common educational experience, with a common purpose, created a sense of dedication to the cause of strengthening the moral and spiritual welfare of all naval personnel.[42]

Jake Laboon made a very clear and strong impression on his fellow classmates as well as his instructors. One of his classmates commented, "He was one of the outstanding members, especially with his [previous] history with submarines." During recreation periods he took the lead in sports contests.[43] Ross Trower, an instructor at the Officers Candidate School at Newport and occasionally an instructor in Pastoral Counseling at the chaplain school, stated, "I immediately liked him very much." Trower would later serve with Jake in Hawaii, and from that command was promoted to rear admiral to serve as the navy chief of chaplains. Speaking of Laboon as a student, Trower opined, "He was certainly an outstanding character in his class. He knew the Navy well. He was a heroic man; the other chaplains looked up to him."[44]

Jake's performance evaluation at chaplain school was indicative of the positive impression he made. He was described as "conscientious in pursuing his studies," "dedicated as a clergyman and ... show[s] great interest in the total welfare of all personnel in the command he serves." His fitness report concluded:

A graduate of the U.S. Naval Academy and with experience and knowledge gained as a line officer, he has the distinct advantage of possessing a fine personality, a manly appearance, and a personal bearing that inspires confidence.... He gives every indication of becoming an outstanding Chaplain of great value to the Naval Service.[45]

---

41. "The Chaplain School Today," *Navy Chaplain Bulletin* (Fall 1957): 11–12; "The Chaplain School," folder 1521/11, box 127, Navy Chaplain School, NCA.
42. "The Chaplain School," folder 1521/11, box 127, Navy Chaplain School, NCA.
43. Marvin E. Snyder, interview with the author, May 16, 2011.
44. Ross Trower, interview with the author, May 14, 2011.
45. LTJG John Laboon, fitness report, November 13, 1958, Laboon file, NMPR. The reader

Fleet Ballistic Missile Submarine Chaplain: 1958–1961

First Duty Station—Patuxent River Naval Air Station

The exceptional impression that Jake Laboon gave to both classmates and teachers at chaplain school was acknowledged through the Hollywood format of television just prior to his official return to the navy. In November 1957, shortly after commencing his tertianship at Auriesville, Thomas Dykers, executive producer of Twin Dolphins Productions, wrote to Laboon about producing an episode of the television show *The Silent Service* chronicling the last war patrol of USS *Peto*, when Jake earned the Silver Star. Dykers sought Laboon's technical assistance with the program. He wrote, "I am very anxious to center a good bit of the story around you as a young Ensign [*sic;* Laboon's rank was lieutenant junior grade] precipitated into combat in a submarine."[46] In response Jake sent a tape recording that detailed his actions in the rescue of Lieutenant Donnelly. In return Dykers told Laboon:

> I feel sure that we can make a very exciting story around the *Peto*'s exploits, and particularly around those of a very fine young officer named Laboon. I was very much inspired with what you accomplished, and although this comes some 13 years late, I want to congratulate you on a very heroic and humane performance.[47]

Because Jake was still in the midst of his tertianship, he wrote to his provincial, William Maloney, asking for permission to go to New York in order to be interviewed for the show. Extant data do not give the provincial's response, but the *Silent Service* episode, titled "*Peto* Plucks Some Chickens," aired on April 25, 1958, the eighth episode of the series' second season.[48]

Jake Laboon's second "Hollywood adventure" happened slightly over one year later while he was stationed at the submarine base at New London. In the late 1950s television producers were seeking personable heroes for positions on game shows. For example, John Glenn, the first American astronaut to circle the earth, was a game show contestant during his pre-

---

should be aware that, in general, fitness reports (periodic performance evaluations) on officers are "inflated." Language that exalts the individual under evaluation is not uncommon. A mediocre or poor fitness report can seriously jeopardize an officer's ability to advance in rank. This reality does not, however, negate the good work that Laboon accomplished. The consistency of remarks made by his superiors over the course of his career testifies to the significant accomplishments of his ministry.

46. Thomas M. Dykers to John Laboon, SJ, November 21, 1957, Laboon file, ASJM.
47. Thomas M. Dykers to John labbon, SJ, December 31, 1957, Labbon file, ASJM.
48. John Laboon, SJ, to William Maloney, SJ, January 21, 1958, Laboon file, ASJM. The episode was directed by Jean Yarbrough and starred Anthony Eisley and Gil Lasky.

astronaut days as a jet plane test pilot. John Harvey, the second, ill-fated commanding officer of USS *Thresher*, was a contestant on the NBC game show *Concentration*.[49]

In early 1959 Jake was interviewed for the popular game show *To Tell the Truth*. He appeared on the program on April 21. Wearing the khaki-colored uniform of a navy lieutenant, chaplain corps, Jake was correctly identified by two of the panelists, the celebrities Ralph Bellamy and Polly Bergen; Kitty Carlisle and Tom Poston both chose one of the two imposters, one of whom was dressed in navy blues and the other in a clerical collar.[50]

In some ways Jake Laboon's celebrity status followed him everywhere, but as he reported to his first assignment following chaplain school, his reality as a servant to others was foremost in his mind. Sporting the rank of lieutenant, Laboon arrived at Patuxent Naval Air Station (NAS) in Maryland to serve in temporary duty for a chaplain who was ill and incapacitated. Jake was assigned to the Naval Air Test and Facilities for Fleet Unit under the direction of Rear Admiral T. B. Clark; NAS Patuxent River was commanded by Captain W. P. Woods.[51]

Laboon entered his new duties with great fervor by learning the lay of the land and getting to know the people he was to serve. Jake served as the Catholic chaplain at the station and was complimented by his commanding officer for his "already demonstrated outstanding abilities." He carried out his duties with "intelligence, enthusiasm, initiative, and tact." It did not take long for Jake's presence to be felt by those he served. Church attendance increased dramatically, "to such an extent that the Chapel is always overcrowded during his services."[52] Jake's contribution to the Catholic worshiping community at Patuxent was only one aspect of his ministry. Capitalizing upon his experi-

---

49. Norman Polmar, *The Death of the USS Thresher: The Story behind History's Deadliest Submarine Disaster* (Guilford, Conn.: Lyons Press, 2004), 28–29. *Thresher* was the first U.S. nuclear submarine to be lost at sea, April 10, 1963.

50. *To Tell the Truth*, http://www.imdb.com; Walter Chadwick, interview with the author, July 1, 2012; Jack Johnson, interview with the author, January 27, 2011; videotape, *To Tell the Truth*, April 21, 1959. Johnson, one of Jake's students at St. Joe Prep during his regency year, relates a story of when the episode was aired on television. The program was actually tape-recorded in the afternoon. When the program aired in the evening, Johnson and Laboon watched the show together in a New York bar. Jake complained to Johnson about how terrible he looked on camera.

51. Acceptance and oath of office, LT John Laboon, January 5, 1959; LTJG Laboon, fitness report, December 22, 1958, Laboon file, NMPR; CO, U.S. Naval Air Station, Patuxent River to CNO, October 16, 1959, Patuxent River NAS folder, NHM.

52. LT John Laboon, fitness report, February 24, 1959, Laboon file, NMPR.

ence at Auriesville, Jake undertook, shortly after reporting, sponsorship of the station's Teenage Club, including reorganizing the group and rewriting its by-laws. In short order the club, which had been somewhat stagnant, was once again vibrant and thriving. Jake was also an active participant in navy relief, assisting families with specific or special needs. On the command level he was effective in working with sailors with previous discipline problems. His fitness report read in part, "Those chronic offenders referred to him for guidance have ceased to appear at Captain's Mast."[53]

When Jake Laboon's three-month temporary duty at Patuxent River concluded, his senior officers and the people were all sorry to see him leave. Many people, officers, enlisted, and members of the civilian community of all faiths, asked how his tour of duty could be extended. Jake's capacity for original and constructive work in all facets of his ministry was noted. His commanding officer commented, "In all problems and assignments given him he has grasped the situation immediately and provided the correct solution. His handling of men and youths of the station and the results he obtained are indicative of outstanding leadership"[54] His magnetism was also favorably noted:

> He conducts himself with dignity and poise, yet generates in those about him a feeling of assurance and confidence. Men of all faiths voluntarily bring their problems to him.[55]

His commanding officer noted that while he was a chaplain in the naval reserve, as distinguished from the regular navy, his promotion should nonetheless be rapid:

> LT Laboon is the most outstanding Chaplain of his grade ever observed. Although attached to this command a relatively short period of time he has gained the admiration and respect of all hands. Through his individual efforts our community relations have been greatly enhanced.[56]

Having completed his temporary assignment at Patuxent River, Jake was scheduled to be sent to the Marine Corps Air Station at Cherry Point,

---

53. Ibid. The Uniform Code of Military Justice (UCMJ) has four levels of action that can be taken against a suspected offender of the law. Captain's mast is the least severe, allowing the commanding officer to adjudicate cases for relatively minor offenses. Summary, special, and general courts-martial are reserved for more egregious offenses.
54. Ibid. 55. Ibid.
56. Ibid.

North Carolina. However, prior to his release from Maryland, his orders were changed and he was sent north to New London, a place he knew well from his post-academy days in submarine school. He was assigned as chaplain for the new and emerging fleet of ballistic missile submarines that would soon become the navy's primary weapon in the Cold War battle of nuclear deterrence, often referred to as Mutually Assured Destruction (MAD).[57]

Fleet Ballistic Missile Submarine (SSBN) Chaplain

The submarine base to which Jake Laboon returned in the spring of 1959 was a facility with a short but proud history. On April 11, 1868, the city of New London and the state of Connecticut gave the navy a one-mile tract of land on the Thames River. Originally the land was used for small craft. In 1872 two brick buildings and a pier were constructed; six years later a third building was added. The area was basically abandoned between 1907 and 1915, but in October 1915 four submarines, the G-1, G-2, G-3, and G-4, and the USS *Ozark*, acting as a tender, arrived. In July 1916 the submarine school at New London was opened. The New London submarine base, an expansion from the school, was officially authorized on March 4, 1917, with an appropriation of $1.25 million for buildings, shops, and other necessities for the maintenance and upkeep of submarines. The first base commanding officer was Captain Yates Sterling Jr.[58]

World War II, the event as described earlier that propelled the United States into a massive building program for submarines, was also the catalyst that brought great growth to the submarine base at New London. On February 1, 1941, in anticipation of possible hostilities, the type command, Commander Submarine Force Atlantic (COMSUBLANT), was established with Rear Admiral R. S. Edwards in charge. By the end of 1958 there were seven submarine squadrons stationed at New London, including seventy submarines (three of which were nuclear—*Nautilus*, *Seawolf*, and *Skate*) and eleven auxiliary ships. When Jake Laboon arrived in the spring of 1959 the submarine base, now the largest in the world, comprising 547 acres of land

---

57. John Laboon, SJ, to William Maloney, SJ, October 31, 1958; John Laboon, SJ, to John Daly, SJ, August 19, 1959, Laboon file, ASJM; roster of chaplains, USN—USNR, February 2, 1959, 1301, box 7, NCA.

58. New London sub base command history 1959, report, August 27, 1959, NHM.

and over three hundred buildings, was under the command of Captain Philip Garnett; COMSUBLANT was Rear Admiral F. B. Warder.[59]

The submarine world that Jake Laboon reentered in the late 1950s was vastly different from that of World War II less than fifteen years earlier. The major transition was the movement from conventional to nuclear power in the propulsion systems of submarines. In 1946 then Captain Hyman G. Rickover, naval academy class of 1922, was placed in charge of a group at Oak Ridge, Tennessee, to research a useful way to harness the power of the atom. Deciding that submarines would be the most effective vehicle, Rickover in 1947 came to Washington and organized a joint agency with the Atomic Energy Commission and the Naval Reactors Branch of the navy to develop a reactor. Westinghouse was given the contract, and on May 21, 1953, the first prototype reactor began to generate power in an isolated site west of Idaho Falls, Idaho.[60] The successful generation of nuclear energy led directly to the commissioning of USS *Nautilus* (SSN-571) in September 1954. Four months later, on January 17, 1955, under the command of Commander Eugene Wilkinson, *Nautilus* went to sea for the first time; Wilkinson broadcast to the world, "Underway on nuclear power."[61]

The successful deployment of *Nautilus* prompted the construction of many other nuclear submarines and served as the vanguard for an all-nuclear submarine force. By the time of Jake Laboon's arrival in New London the United States had a handful of nuclear boats, and plans were underway for a series of others. The USS *Seawolf* (SSN-575), like *Nautilus* in its design, was commissioned in March 1957. The USS *Skate* (SSN-578), the first of a class of nuclear submarines that included the *Swordfish, Sargo,* and *Seadragon,* was commissioned in December 1957. This was followed by a more streamlined, faster, and deeper diving class of six boats named after the lead vessel, USS *Skipjack* (SSN-585), commissioned on April 15, 1959. In addition several "experimental" nuclear submarines were constructed to determine the feasibility of various propulsion systems. Two of the most prominent in this category were USS

59. History of Commander Submarine Force U.S. Atlantic Fleet—enclosure, COMSUBLANT to CNO, October 16, 1959, SUBFORLANT; New London Submarine Base 1960–61, report, December 8, 1960; New London sub base command history, 1959, report August 27, 1959, NHM.

60. E. E. Kintner, "Admiral Rickover's Gamble," *Atlantic* 203 (January 1959): 31.

61. Sherman Naymark, "'Underway on Nuclear Power': The Development of the Nautilus," *U.S. Naval Institute Proceedings* 96, no. 4 (April 1970): 56. Wilkinson's words became a battle cry for the promotion of nuclear propulsion in the navy.

Triton (SSRN-586) and USS *Tullibee* (SSN-597). *Triton*, commissioned in 1959, was the first nuclear submarine to circumnavigate the world submerged; it was the only American boat ever powered by two nuclear reactors. *Tullibee*, commissioned in November 1960 and the smallest American nuclear submarine ever built, was constructed with a reactor that used natural circulation in its operating system.[62]

The transition to nuclear propulsion was quite obviously a significant advancement from the diesel-submarine navy that Jake Laboon and his contemporaries knew, but there was an equally significant simultaneous addition to the submarine force that was prompted by the Cold War and the concept of nuclear deterrence. By August 1958 the United States had several submarines, *Tunny, Barbero, Grayback, Growler,* and *Halibut*, which were designed to launch nuclear-armed Regulus missiles from the surface. However, in order to remain undetected and thus less vulnerable to attack, it was necessary to create a weapon that could be launched from below the surface.[63] This strategic need led directly to the inauguration of the Polaris missile and submarine program, first authorized in January 1957. The initial goal was to have two missile submarines, *George Washington* and *Patrick Henry*, ready for deployment by the end of 1963.[64]

The chief of naval operations, Admiral Arleigh Burke, chose Rear Admiral William Francis "Red" Raborn to head up the Polaris program. Given an initial sum of $37 million for development, Raborn assembled a team of forty-five to meet the navy's goal.[65] In a speech to the Navy League, Raborn described the challenge set before himself and his team:

What many people do not realize, however, is that in the Polaris program we are talking not only of the missile ... or "bird" as it is commonly called, but of a wholly new concept of weaponry, the dispatching of this "bird" from beneath the surface of the sea.[66]

62. For more information on the development of the U.S. Navy's nuclear submarine fleet, see F. W. Lipscomb, *Historic Submarines* (New York: Praeger, 1970); Paul Beaver, *Nuclear Powered Submarines* (London and New York: Arms and Armour Press, 1986); Yogi Kaufman, *Sharks of Steel* (Annapolis, Md.: Naval Institute Press, 1993); and Robert Hutchinson, ed., *Jane's Submarines: War beneath the Waves from 1776 to the Present Day* (London: HarperCollins, 2001).
63. History of Commander Submarine Force US Atlantic Fleet—enclosure, COMSUBLANT to CNO, October 16, 1959, SUBFORLANT, NHM.
64. Edward H. Kulcum, "First Polaris Launched from Submarine," *Aviation Week and Space Technology* 73 (July 25, 1960): 32; "New Weapons System," *Time* 71 (March 3, 1958): 15.
65. "New Weapon System," *Time* 71 (March 3, 1958): 15.
66. William F. Raborn, "Polaris Submarine," *Vital Speeches* 24 (May 1, 1958): 429.

The missile had to be designed within the limitations of space and weight on a submarine; the propellant fuel had to be solid, not liquid. Additionally, it was necessary to design storage, handling, launching, and fire control equipment that would permit submarines to be used as a launching platform for the missile.[67] Still, while acknowledging that complete development of the weapon system was some time off, a *Newsweek* editorial concluded that Polaris "could be one of the most formidable [weapons] in the U.S. arsenal."[68]

The Polaris program received a boost in urgency from an unexpected source when in October 1957 the Soviet Union launched Sputnik, the first satellite, into space. This event prompted the decision to speed the development of a submarine platform from which Polaris could be launched. Officials ordered two of the Skipjack-class attack submarines under construction to be cut in half and a 130-foot missile compartment added to the boat.[69] The sense of urgency was also picked up by the media. One journalist, seeing the Polaris program as a front line of national defense, called for separate funding for the Polaris program, thus eliminating economic wrangling within the Department of Defense over how monies would be allocated.[70]

The deterrent capability of the Polaris program, as the primary weapon and as a complement to bombers and land-based missiles, was possibly the most important rationale to speed development, both of the weapon and the submarine platform.[71] Admiral Rickover, the father of the nuclear program, spoke to this reality:

> Armed with this missile, the nuclear-powered submarine will become an underwater satellite. It will be large enough to store, maintain, and fire intermediate range ballistic missiles, and it will be able to move anywhere at any time, completely submerged.

He went on to say, "The nuclear powered submarine, ... with nuclear warheads could make our Navy an ever more effective deterrent force."[72] One

---

67. Ibid.
68. "Polaris: The Big Undersea Deterrent," *Newsweek* 51 (April 4, 1958): 35.
69. Jules Bergman, "William Raborn's Multi-Billion-Dollar Gamble," *Reader's Digest* 78 (February 1961): 184.
70. W. H. Hessler, "Navy's Submersible Missile-Launching Base: Polaris," *Reporter* 18 (June 12, 1958): 15–16.
71. The *New York Times* journalist Hansen W. Baldwin believed that in theory the Polaris program would replace long-range bombers and land-based missiles"; see Baldwin, "New Battleship: The A-Submarine," *New York Times Magazine* (March 16, 1958): 13.
72. Hyman G. Rickover, "Another Kind of Satellite: U.S. Missile Firing Submarines," *U.S. News and World Report* 43 (October 25, 1957): 62.

journalist referred to Polaris as "the most dependable means of retaliation available to us in the near future."[73] Others commented on how Polaris would have a direct impact on the Soviet Union. The retired Admiral Samuel Morison wrote:

> Survivability is the strategic boon offered to us by floating Polaris bases. Polaris promises the communist nations that they will get hit, and badly hit, even if their first flight of ICBMs neutralize our land bases in the United States and flatten some of our leading cities.[74]

An editorial in *America* read:

> The fleet of missile subs would be the undersea analog of a constant airborne alert of our Strategic Air Command. It would ring the Soviet heartland with a nuclear threat as widely dispersed and endlessly mobile, yet almost undetectable by present techniques and thus indestructible after a sneak attack on the United States.[75]

Admiral Raborn, who saw Polaris as the weapon to complete "the chain of deterrence needed to enforce all-out peace,"[76] provided from his insider position the best overall synthesis of how the new missile system would serve as an effective deterrent:

> Polaris will bring within range of direct attack from the sea virtually all important military targets in the Communist controlled heartland. It can reach these targets in some 15 minutes from the instant of firing.... With their world-wide cruising radius, nuclear powered submarines can patrol for months at a stretch, move submerged at high speeds for thousands of miles. They will be almost impossible to locate or trace by even the most advanced methods of surveillance. The very knowledge that they are there, within range and ready to launch their missiles within minutes, would exert a strong and constant deterrent influence on any leadership, no matter how reckless or power crazy.[77]

The transition to nuclear propulsion and the development of the Polaris missile and its submarine platform were in progress when Jake Laboon ar-

---

73. Hessler, "Navy's Submersible Missile-Launching Base," 15.
74. Morison, "American Strategy," 48.
75. "Polaris: New Star of Peace?" *America* 103 (August 13, 1960): 531.
76. Raborn, "Polaris Submarine," 431.
77. Ibid., 431. In another part of the same speech, Raborn commented further: "This weapon [Polaris] is primarily a deterrent to aggression, for if it is actually fired the chips will be down, and the all-out general war will have become a tragic reality. As a deterrent, however, the Polaris weapon system will fill a needed and entirely unique position on our 'team' of capabilities to retaliate instantly, unpreventably [*sic*], and with annihilating fire power"; see Raborn, "Polaris Submarine," 430.

rived in March 1959. He was assigned to the staff of Deputy Commander Submarine Force Atlantic Fleet and to the position of chaplain for Submarine Squadron 14, the first fleet ballistic missile submarine squadron.[78] Due to its unique character, Laboon's assignment was initially described in general terms:

> Lieutenant Laboon, a Catholic chaplain, serving on the staff of Commander Submarine Force, U.S. Atlantic Fleet, has been assigned to assist the Force Commander in the religious, morale, and personal welfare problems associated with the Navy's new Fleet Ballistic Missile Submarine Program.[79]

It did not take long before the impact of Jake's presence was felt. Indeed, wherever he went his athletic nature, naval academy education, past heroics, and general positive demeanor went ahead of him. Rear Admiral Ross Trower commented, "His name became known around the Navy early on."[80]

The specialized ministry to which Jake Laboon was assigned, unique in the history of the chaplain corps, was strongly influenced by the sixty-day submerged voyage of USS *Seawolf*. Between August 7 and October 6, 1958, *Seawolf*, under the command of Commander Richard Lanning, cruised for a record sixty days continually submerged, traveling almost 14,000 miles in the process. The cruise, the longest submerged period of any submarine to date, was conducted to test how men would endure long periods at sea under water.[81] Referencing *Seawolf's* endurance cruise, Laboon commented:

> The 60-day patrol of the atomic sub *Seawolf* indicated a need for religious coverage. We have crews away from port for extended periods, weeks on end of living with an atomic reactor and soon ballistic missiles as well. These patrols are almost the equivalent of war in the minds of all who were involved in them and morale must be kept high.[82]

---

78. Ralph Blair, interview with the author, August 17, 2012; Harry Train, interview with the author, January 19, 2011; *Virginia Pilot*, clipping, March 18, 1995, personal papers of Rosemary Laboon (hereafter PPRL), Pittsburgh, Pa. One source claims that Isaac Kidd, who had met Jake while playing football at the naval academy, recommended Laboon to the CNO, Admiral Arleigh Burke, for his position with Squadron 14.

79. "Navy's Only Padre Who Wears Dolphins," April 13, 1959, religious services file, ASBNL.

80. Ross Trower, interview with the author, May 14, 2011.

81. "Sixty Days," *Newsweek* 52 (October 13, 1958): 30–31; clipping, n.d. [October 1958], photo albums, vol. 2, ASBNL; J. Robert Moskin, "Sixty Days Out of This World," *Look* 22 (December 23, 1958): 23; History of Commander Submarine Force US Atlantic Fleet—enclosure to COMSUBLANT to CNO, October 16, 1958, SUBFORLANT, NHM.

82. *New York Times*, clipping, May 4, 1959, Laboon alumni file, AUSNA.

As the only active-duty chaplain who also wore the "Golden Dolphins," indicative of his qualification in submarines, Jake was a natural selection to serve the nascent Fleet Ballistic Missile Submarine (SSBN) program. His September 1959 fitness report acknowledged his suitability for his position: "Chaplain Laboon is a natural for the Submarine Force inasmuch as he is an Annapolis graduate and formally executive officer on USS *Peto*."[83] Unlike chaplains in the past who had been assigned to submarine bases or to squadrons, Laboon was appointed to active duty aboard submarines on patrol.[84] One writer concluded, "Father Laboon was obviously the man to chart the spiritual course for the [submarine] Navy."[85] Jake was joined on this assignment by Lieutenant Guy Leonard, a Southern Baptist chaplain. Laboon commented to his provincial, "He and I get along well."[86]

Jake wasted no time preparing himself for his new ministry. He immediately began to work with the crew of the USS *George Washington* (SSBN-598), the first fleet ballistic missile submarine, scheduled to be launched on June 9. A crew for the USS *Patrick Henry* (SSBN-599), the second boat in this class, would soon arrive. In order to know more of the technical aspects of the new missile technology, Jake was sent to Dam Neck, Virginia, to take a course, "FBM Weapon System Orientation."[87]

Jake was excited about his assignment to the submarine force. Based on his World War II experience, he viewed it as a return home and an opportunity to build a navy community with which he was very familiar. Shortly after arriving in New London, he stated, "I like submarines very much. It is a big happy family with a high [intelligence] type of personnel. Neurotics don't last long."[88] He looked forward to working with both the submarine crews and their families. Once again he stated, "I hope to have a large parish before long. At sea I'll care for the men; on the base I'll look out for their families.[89] Excit-

---

83. LT John Laboon, fitness report, September 10, 1959, Laboon file, NMPR. The fitness report was in error in its details, as Laboon was never executive officer of *Peto*.
84. Owens, "Parish under the Sea," 4.
85. Ibid., 6.
86. John Laboon, SJ, to John Daly, SJ, August 19, 1959, Laboon file, ASJM.
87. Ibid., April 20, 1959; OIC, U.S. Naval Guided Missile School, Dam Neck, Va., to Commander U.S. Naval Submarine Base, New London, February 2, 1960, NMPR. The course was designed to introduce students to all aspects of the FBM weapon system, but stressing the missiles, launcher system, submarine navigation, and fire-control systems.
88. *New York Times*, April 20, 1959.
89. Ibid., May 4, 1959.

edly, Jake wrote to his provincial about his new assignment. He described his ministry as "very interesting" and hoped that he would be at this duty station long enough to see the program become successful. He also informed his superiors of the great need for chaplains, suggesting, it seems, that more Jesuits might want to follow in his footsteps: "Some time I would like to talk over with you the great need for Catholic priests in the Armed Forces. One of the problems is the great workload which those priests now in the service carry."[90] Happy to speak with Laboon, the provincial was not very encouraging, concluding, "Manpower is the great need for all our endeavors. It will be for years to come."[91]

Jake's enthusiasm and good work were apparent to his military superiors, as well. In his first fitness report after reporting to New London he was described as "a highly gifted officer who is endowed with outstanding qualities of mind and body." He was applauded for his knowledge concerning the organization of the submarine force and his technical understanding of the boats themselves, information quite obviously gained from his previous experience. In a highly laudatory tone, his reporting senior officer wrote:

[He] has taken a keen interest in the spiritual and moral well-being of the submariners, not only in the FBM Program, but in other submarines home ported at New London.... He takes advantage of any opportunity to mingle with the men and assist them in any of their problems.[92]

The establishment of the Polaris Family Center, designed to assist family members of deployed SSBN officers and men, was the first and primary activity for Laboon and his chaplain partner, Guy Leonard. The two junior chaplains, aided by some volunteers and paid staff, set up their office aboard *APL*-43, a floating personnel barge, located five miles from the sub base.[93] Laboon described the environment:

At present there are about 200 men from the two submarines [*George Washington* and *Patrick Henry*] with me on the barge. My work consists in many things, but the chief one is to keep the morale of the men connected with this program high.[94]

---

90. John Laboon, SJ, to John Daly, SJ, August 19, 1959, Laboon file, ASJM.
91. John Daly, SJ, to John Laboon, SJ, August 21, 1959, Laboon file, ASJM.
92. LT John Laboon, fitness report, September 10, 1959, Laboon file, NMPR.
93. Guy Leonard, "Submarine Chaplain," *Navy Chaplain Bulletin* (Spring 1960): 4.
94. John Laboon, SJ, to John Daly, SJ, August 19, 1959, Laboon file, ASJM.

Contemporaries who benefited from the program related that while religious services and some education programs were provided, counseling was the central work of both chaplains. This was true for the submariners, but also for their families, all of whom were beginning to experience a new and to this point unique situation. Long periods (generally two months) with no communication placed a great strain on families. Laboon described the situation:

> There are two ends to the line. It's a tremendous strain for the families. These people need all the systems they can get. The officers and enlisted men attached to the nuclear subs say as one voice to me, "Father, you can best serve us by caring for our families. It's wonderful to have a priest with us, but it is even better to know you are looking after our loved ones."[95]

The center provided numerous services beyond counseling, including transportation, advice on finances, and for wives new to the navy system, assistance navigating the military way of life.[96]

Operational observation of the stresses experienced by FBM crews was considered crucial to understand better and thereby minister more completely to the submarine community. Jake wrote to his provincial, "When the FBM subs begin operating, we will go to sea with the submarines. In addition, I am going to sea on the nuclear powered submarines, to get the tone of life aboard the[m]."[97] Anticipating what he might find, Jake further commented:

> On our missions [submarines] the men have plenty of time to think. There are few distractions down below. At first I will do a lot of observing to find out how the chaplains can best serve these men. Because the idea is new, we will be feeling our way along.[98]

Thus, in an effort to study the living conditions and needs of sailors living underwater for long periods of time in the proximity of a nuclear reactor and nuclear weapons, Laboon rode several subs, including *Triton*, *Skate*, *Swordfish*, *George Washington*, and *Patrick Henry*.[99]

---

 95. Owens, "Parish under the Sea," 7.
 96. John Donlon, interview with the author, September 9, 2011.
 97. John Laboon, SJ, to John Daly, SJ, August 19, 1959, Laboon file, ASJM.
 98. *Catholic Transcript*, May 14, 1959, biographical file—Laboon, ASBNL.
 99. Owens, "Parish under the Sea," 6. Jake did not ride *George Washington* or *Patrick Henry* for complete patrols, but nonetheless spent significant time on these vessels and others. His partner in the Polaris Family Center, Chaplain Guy Leonard, did make one complete patrol. James Hogan,

His time at sea taught Jake many lessons with respect to the psychological as well as the spiritual needs of the crew. The mental pressure of constant readiness in an enclosed and atypical environment to normal human life was Laboon's first concern. His observations led him to believe that deterrent patrols were, in the minds of officers and crew, equivalent to war and thus morale must be kept high.[100] The spiritual needs of the crew were varied and had to be addressed in multiple ways. Jake commented,

> Some men prefer their religion in private while at sea, if a chaplain isn't around. It is perfectly O.K. for a fellow to go off by himself and say his prayers. But some want and probably need a more formal type of service.[101]

Some of the things that Jake suggested for Catholics were a rosary service and taped sermons by Bishop Fulton Sheen, Father Robert Gannon, SJ, and Father Ignatius Smith, OP, which he carried with him. To this collection Jake added tapes of his own sermons on the "Life of Christ," "The Ten Commandments," and "The Sacraments." He provided Bibles, missals, and other literature, as well.[102]

Jake Laboon's efforts and the work of the Polaris Family Center were highly efficacious. He was praised by his reporting senior as "one of our most outstanding chaplains. He is a wholly dedicated officer." His past experience at the naval academy and his teaching experience provided a perfect fit for his duties. Additionally, his positive personality was recognized as being highly advantageous: "He [Laboon] has a dynamic personality and enthusiastically participates in all naval duties, naval recreation attempts and normal military routines."[103] His professional knowledge and specific work with this new mission to FBM crews and their families were also noted. He was commended for "a professional knowledge which far exceeds that of his contemporaries." Understanding and appreciating problems, he provided seasoned and solid advice and offered mature judgments for all,

---

a Catholic chaplain, rode *Theodore Roosevelt* (SSBN-602) for a patrol; see Chaplain Newsletter, n.d [1977], biographical file—Laboon, ASBNL; James J. Hogan, "Another Look at FBM Subs," *Navy Chaplain Bulletin* (Winter 1962–63): 7–10, 13.

100. *New York Times,* May 4, 1959.
101. Owens, "Parish under the Sea," 6.
102. Ibid.
103. LT John Laboon, fitness reports, January 13, 1960 and September 12, 1960, Laboon file, NMPR.

regardless of rank. He was described as "a man of action and assisting each man to find a solution."[104] Laboon's ability to minister to different groups under various environments, including outreach to civic groups and even being a good neighbor, was also well appreciated and applauded. One report read, "His efforts are not limited to the pulpit but reach out to the human relations field."[105] His military and pastoral abilities were summarized:

This is a willing "can-do" chaplain who works well with all civilian or military, seniors and juniors alike.... He is the type of leader who says "follow me" and the lad will have to keep a full head of steam to keep up.[106]

Several ideas proposed by Laboon to meet the ministerial needs of sailors and families became a practical guide for the missile submarine on deployment.[107]

Jake's leadership qualities, honed through his past naval experience and most recent religious formation, were also noted. He was described as "a born leader who inspires those working with him." He was further labeled "a keen student of human nature and an officer who consistently inspires confidence under the most difficult circumstances." Noting his past experience, which significantly aided his decision-making ability, his fitness report stated:

He is a most effective leader and takes over on the ball field or at the conference table. He commands respect because of his do-as-I-do attitude as he leads his men instead of driving them. It is refreshing to watch him have his men rally round to a simple viewpoint with his persuasive techniques.[108]

His leadership skills generated improved relationships within the ranks of the noncommissioned sailors with whom he had contact.[109]

The launching and subsequent commissioning of USS *George Washington*, the first fleet ballistic missile submarine, placed in context the ministry of Jake Laboon during his second sojourn at New London. Speaking in April 1958, Rear Admiral William Raborn, director of the Polaris program, stated that three ballistic missile submarines had been authorized and two more were to be included in the 1959 fiscal year budget supplement.[110]

104. LT John Laboon, fitness report, January 13, 1960, Laboon file, NMPR.
105. LT John Laboon, fitness report, September 12, 1960, Laboon file, NMPR.
106. LT John Laboon, fitness report, January 13, 1960, Laboon file, NMPR.
107. Ibid.
108. LT John Laboon, fitness report, September 12, 1960, Laboon file, NMPR.
109. LT John Laboon, fitness report, January 13, 1960, Laboon file, NMPR.
110. Raborn, "Polaris Submarine," 430.

Fleet Ballistic Missile Submarine Chaplain: 1958–1961

George Washington, originally built as a 260-foot skipjack-class fast attack, was modified with the addition of a 130-foot missile compartment, making it the world's largest submarine. Her first commanding officer was Commander James Osborne, naval academy class of 1941.[111] *George Washington* was launched on June 9, 1959, and commissioned on December 30. Jake gave the invocation and benediction at both ceremonies.[112] The significance of the event was not lost on Laboon. Writing to his provincial, he pleaded:

> Please keep me and this program in your Masses. This is most important since all concerned say the USS *George Washington* (SSBN-598) is the most important ship the United States has ever built. It has to be a huge success.[113]

The hopes and dreams of the American military establishment were fulfilled in a significant way in midsummer 1960. On July 20 the *Washington* successfully fired two Polaris test missiles, striking targets 1,200 miles from the launch site. Raborn was elated about the successful launch, especially coming approximately three years earlier than the original project finish date:

> This new star of peace hoisted a trail of smoke from saltwater to space, as a signal of a bright new addition to sea power, a new strategic use of the world's oceans which will be felt around the world and across the iron and bamboo curtains.[114]

Following a second successful missile launch in August, the boat went to Charleston, South Carolina, for a final load out of sixteen missiles and then in November left for her first deterrent submerged patrol, returning to New London after sixty-six days on January 21, 1961. Eventually, *George Washington* was forward deployed out of Holy Loch, Scotland.[115]

George Washington's success was the catalyst to the full deployment of the FBM program. As with *Washington,* Jake Laboon was present at the launching and commissioning of USS *Patrick Henry* (SSBN-599) and gave the invocation at the commissioning of USS *Robert E. Lee* (SSBN-601). He

---

111. "Deep Deterrence," *Time* 73 (June 15, 1959): 28; Richard F. Denopewolff, "Our New Missile-Firing Submarines," *Science Digest* 47 (April 1960): 35–39.

112. USS *George Washington* (SSBN-598), launching program, June 9, 1959; commissioning program, December 30, 1959, photo album, vol. 1, ASBNL.

113. John Laboon, SJ to John Daly, SJ, August 19, 1959, Laboon file, ASJM.

114. Quoted in "Euphoria Polaris," *Nation* 191 (August 6, 1960): 63.

115. "Polaris Goes to Work," *Time* 76 (November 20, 1960): 21; Sub Base, New London, report 1960–61, December 12, 1961, NHM.

Fleet Ballistic Missile Submarine Chaplain: 1958–1961

Figure 5-1. Commissioning of USS *George Washington*, December 30, 1959

was also present at the launching of the USS *Ethan Allen* (SSBN-608), the first of a new FBM class constructed from the outset as fleet ballistic missile submarines.[116] Eventually forty-one FBMs were constructed. The last, USS *Will Rogers* (SSBN-659), was commissioned on April 1, 1967.[117]

The introduction of the FBM fleet into the American defense arsenal raises the question of the morality of nuclear deterrence. Pope John XXIII in his 1963 encyclical letter *Pacem in Terris* suggested that it was wrong for

---

116. USS *Patrick Henry* commissioning program, n.d. [April 9, 1960], USS *Patrick Henry* photo album, vol. 1; "Robert E. Lee Delivered in Real Time," *Newport News Shipyard Bulletin* (October 1960), biographical file—Laboon; *Ethan Allen* (SSBN-608), launching program, biographical file—Laboon, ASBNL.

117. Kulcum, "First Polaris," 32. When the Polaris (and later Poseidon) missile submarines began to age and were retired from the fleet, a new class was built with the USS *Ohio* (SSBN-726) as the lead boat. She was commissioned in November 1981.

countries to justify their production of nuclear weapons based on the premise of self-defense against other nations with similar armament, stating that "people live in constant fear lest the storm that every moment threatens should break upon them with dreadful violence."[118] The moral theologian J. E. Dougherty acknowledged that any first strike of nuclear weapons could never be justified. Yet, he believed that both the Soviet Union and the United States "have the moral obligation under natural law to protect their civilian population as much as possible against the dangers of nuclear war." He thus concluded, "If they approach their task at roughly the same measured pace in a spirit not of panic but of prudent planning ... they need not provoke any undue fright or any pre-emptive attack."[119] On the other hand, the theologian Brian Midgley, while suggesting that many Christians "recognize that the possession of nuclear weapons is ... a proximate occasion of sin," stated, "Yet the case against nuclear deterrents of all types remains non-proven." In the end, however, he concluded that the morality of nuclear deterrence was suspect at best.[120]

What was Jake Laboon's opinion on the new missile system as the vanguard of the United States' defense policy of nuclear deterrence? While extant data does not allow for any authoritative answers, there is no indication that he held any serious reservations toward the policy. As a man of integrity and always forthright with his opinions, if Jake had held any serious reservations with this policy and his ability to minister to people serving as "frontline soldiers" of the strategy, he would have registered his concerns with his superiors.

Jake Laboon's pastoral ministry to FBM crews was punctuated by innovation, especially in regard to his work with a lay leaders' program, preceding what Vatican II would advocate concerning the laity by some five years. Realizing it was not feasible to assign a full-time chaplain to a submarine, especially if he was not a watch stander, Laboon concluded, "Right now, the lay leader appears to be the best answer."[121] Jake was instrumental in developing a program whereby lay leaders, members of the crew, would be

---

118. Pope John XXIII, *Pacem in Terris*, 1963, paragraph 110.

119. J. E. Dougherty, "Morality and [the] Strategy of Deterrence," *Catholic World* 194 (March 1962): 343.

120. Brian Midgley, "Nuclear Deterrents: Intention and Scandal," *Blackfriars* 44 (September 1963): 363–64.

121. Owens, "Parish under the Sea," 7.

trained to conduct basic religious services, especially on FBM submarines during their extended deployments.[122] Presenting it as "Do It Yourself Religion," Laboon described the work of the lay leader:

> He's not a substitute for a chaplain, but I guess you could call him that for want of a better word. He is the person who helps remind people of their religious heritage while the chaplain is absent. He does that primarily through lay leader services and providing religious materials.[123]

One journalist of the period described the submarine lay leader's basic responsibilities:

> Though he does no preaching or counseling, he's the vital cog. He organizes and conducts the various services. It is also his job to take the initiative, with proper regard for military channels, to bring priests aboard whenever possible. Sometimes there are Catholic chaplains on sub tenders and other vessels passing nearby.[124]

Jake Laboon's pastoral ministry centered on the crews of FBM submarines, but it was not one-dimensional, as he served the general Catholic population both on base and in the town of Groton. He described his additional duties:

> On the weekends, I help Father [Donald F.] Kelly, Base Chaplain, with confessions and baptisms on Saturdays.... Sundays I usually celebrate two Masses on the base and hear confessions during the third Mass. I find the work very interesting.[125]

Indeed, during his time in New London, Jake baptized twenty-three children at the chapel on the Thames. Utilizing his previous experience at St. Joe Prep, Jake was very effective working with youth, mostly dependents of the officers and sailors he served. This was manifest through his training of altar servers at the base chapel. Additionally, when asked, he was more than willing to assist at Sacred Heart Church in Groton.[126] Those in the congregations he served appreciated Jake and his ministry. One parishioner and family friend,

---

122. LT John Laboon, fitness report, January 13, 1960, Laboon file, NMPR.
123. Clipping, n.d. [1980], PPWL. Laboon's original program over time became the "Laymen's Enrichment and Development (LEAD) Program; See "The Lay Leader in the LEAD Program," religious services file, ASBNL.
124. Owens, "Parish under the Sea," 6.
125. John Laboon, SJ, to John Daly, SJ, August 19, 1959, Laboon file, ASJM.
126. *Catholic Transcript*, May 14, 1959, biographical file—Laboon, ASBNL; military ordinariate records of baptism—John Laboon, Archives Archdiocese of the Military (hereafter AAM), Washington, D.C.

John Donlon, stated, "He projected the goodness of his vocation. Everyone knew he was a priest, first, last, and always."[127]

Jake Laboon's multifaceted outreach and ministry to the New London sub base community was manifested as well in his continuing interest in sports. Always highly competitive, Jake played first base on the staff baseball team and was a starter on the COMSUBLANT basketball team. Although especially during basketball season his duties often did not allow him to attend practice, he played in games and often dominated play.[128] Besides assisting dependents at the base chapel, he coached a youth football league team. At times Jake traveled to Providence College, bringing youngsters from the base with him to attend basketball games. Once he was invited to speak to a group of athletes at the college, where "he impressed everyone at the dinner."[129]

Even with his numerous duties and many activities, Jake never forgot his family and friends. He enjoyed the company of some of his academy classmates, including Ted Snyder, Ralph Blaine, and Jim Stevens. He was a frequent guest at the home of one parishioner at the chapel on the Thames, John Donlon, whose father had met Jake while the latter was a tertian at Auriesville, New York. Donlon, a submarine school instructor and a daily communicant, came to know Jake as a friend through this regular contact.[130] Always in communication with his family in Pittsburgh, Jake requested and received permission from his Jesuit superiors to use war bonds, which he had invested through his father, to help finance the college educations of his nieces and nephews.[131]

In March 1961, after two years as the founding chaplain for the SSBN fleet, Jake Laboon prepared to move to his next assignment. In a fitness report written on the occasion of Jake's detachment from New London, Rear Admiral L. R. Daspit, COMSUBLANT, commented that Laboon's ex-

---

127. John Donlon, interview with the author, September 9, 2011.

128. Ibid.; reminiscences of Admiral Robert Long, transcribed, AUSNA. Admiral Long told a story that one day when playing baseball, one marine, when crossing the first-base bag, intentionally ran into Laboon. Jake was ready to hit the man, but a marine sergeant said, "Now, Father, remember who you are." Long continued, "Jake had a temper. He had very high ideals. So he was the kind of guy that if you needed help, you could count on him. He was intensely loyal to his friends."

129. John Donlon, interview with the author, September 9, 2011; Bishop Francis Roque and Charles Hogan, interview with the author, April 11, 2012.

130. Ed Snyder, e-mail to the author, December 6, 2010; Ralph Blaine, interview with the author, August 17, 2012; John Donlon, interview with the author, September 9, 2011.

131. John Laboon, SJ, to William Maloney, SJ, July 21, 1959, Laboon file, ASJM.

perience and background, both in the academy and during World War II, plus his professional knowledge as a priest, provided him the perfect background to be an effective chaplain. He was much more mature than anyone else of similar rank. He was applauded for taking assignments somewhat outside the role of the chaplain, yet never forgetting his central function. Regardless of the circumstances, Jake always managed to get the job done and done well. Daspit commented on his many fine qualities:

> LT Laboon is an outstanding example of the qualities required in an effective chaplain in the U.S. Navy. He is firm in defending priciple [sic], yet patient and tactful. Although the recipient of nation-wide publicity, he is humble and cooperative. His past experience and pleasant personality enable him easily to establish rapport with those whom he serves. His sole purpose is to serve God and country through his service to the men entrusted to his care.[132]

Jake's leadership skills were also praised by Daspit. He commented, "Whether donning football clothes and lead[ing] the team to victory or ... from the pulpit [he] give[s] evidence of the same vitality in [a] do-as-I-do philosophy."[133] As early as September 1960 Daspit recommended Jake for early promotion:

> He [Laboon] is the type of officer who could command the attention of the Selection Board for accelerated promotion under normal circumstances but with his naval experiences and ecclesiastical training, it is even more apparent that he is qualified to shoulder the rank of his commander USNA classmates. He is recommended for accelerated promotion.[134]

As Laboon left for his new assignment, Daspit concluded, "[He is] the most eminently qualified officer for immediate promotion from below that I know of in the Navy."[135]

Conclusion

Ordained to the priesthood in June 1956, Jake Laboon returned to the navy two years later, inaugurating a career as a chaplain that would gain him great notoriety and respect, from seaman recruits to four-star admirals. Re-

---
132. LT. John Laboon, fitness report, March 21, 1961, Laboon file, NMPR.
133. Ibid.
134. LT John Laboon, fitness report, September 12, 1960, Laboon file, NMPR.
135. LT. John Laboon, fitness report, March 21, 1961, Laboon file, NMPR.

alizing the prize that it possessed in Jake's previous submarine experience, the navy wisely assigned him, after a brief stint of temporary duty, to be the first chaplain assigned to the fledgling SSBN program at New London, Connecticut. His knowledge of the submarine service and greater maturity than his contemporaries, as well as his pastoral gifts and charismatic and gregarious personality, proved a formula for great success in his initial duty station. Comfortable with every aspect of ministry and willing to do whatever was necessary to meet the needs of those he served, Jake Laboon was indeed impressive, a reality that was noted by all with whom he had contact. A natural leader with the proper talent and human characteristics for his role as chaplain, Laboon was sent to serve the "black shoe navy" in the Far East. There he would continue to serve impressively and create a personal reputation that would cast a bright light across the entire U.S. Navy.

Chapter 6

Circuit Rider, Recruit Chaplain, and Alaska Pastor

★ 1961–1966

Navy personnel are basically seafarers, but for the career man, assignments at sea and ashore come with time. So too was the reality for chaplains like Jake Laboon. While Laboon's initial assignment led him to ride several submarines in an effort to better understand the routine and challenges of the men he served, his ministry largely concentrated on service to SSBN crews in port and their families—especially their pastoral and sacramental needs. As his career unfolded during the bulk of the 1960s, Jake Laboon's service ran the gamut. He began as a circuit-rider priest, serving a variety of at-sea commands as a staff chaplain for Commander Service Squadron Three headquartered in Sasebo, Japan. Next he became a recruit chaplain working with the most junior, and in many ways most vulnerable, of navy personnel at Great Lakes Naval Training Center. He ended this period as a local pastor in the wilds of Naval Station Kodiak, Alaska. Laboon brought his vast and ever increasing military experience, his mature and broad outlook, and his pastoral sensitivity to each of his commands. Although a junior officer, he was viewed by his military superiors as a chaplain far ahead of his peers and ready to accept greater responsibilities. The early and mid-1960s would be a time for Jake to broaden his experience, serving outside his country, in America's heartland, and at the far edges of the nation's domestic military presence. As with every endeavor in life, Laboon threw himself wholeheartedly into these new ventures, gaining him the respect and appreciation of thousands of white hats and their officers.

Staff Chaplain, Commander Service Squadron Three: 1961–1963

The first records of Commander Service Squadron Three (COMSERVRON), operating under Commander Service Force Seventh Fleet, are found in November 1944. Captain Thomas Kelly, riding his flagship USS *Doblin* (AD-3), home ported at Holandia, New Guinea, served as Service Squadron Three's commander. A description of the purposes of a service squadron during World War II is helpful:

> A mobile supply base was the logistic counterpart to the airplane carrier. While flat tops projected naval air power within striking distance of the enemy, SERVRONS Four and Ten (and Three) acted as a logistic annex to Pearl Harbor for servicing the fleet at sea. Advanced naval bases were still needed; but it was the mobile base, in conjunction with the fleet carriers, that permitted leap-frogging with seven-hundred-league boots.[1]

Although there are no extant records concerning Service Squadron Three from 1946 to 1950, it may be assumed that the squadron continued its mission as the mobile logistic force of the Seventh Fleet.

During the 1950s Service Squadron Three experienced the dislocation caused by another war, but by the end of the decade it had returned to steady-state operations. During the Korean War, 1950–53, Squadron Three was divided into two sectors: ships were home-ported at Yokosuka, Japan, but service operations were conducted out of Subic Bay, Philippines. The parent staff remained at Sasebo. When the war ended the service division operation was dissolved. By the end of the decade Service Squadron Three consisted of thirty vessels and five thousand men that provided "beans, bolts, and black oil" to the Seventh Fleet.[2] Oilers, ammunition, combat stores, repair, salvage, and fast combat support vessels were the ship types of Service Squadron Three.[3]

---

1. Commander Service Squadron Three to CNO, February 17, 1960, SERVRON Three Establishment in 1959, command history, NHM.
2. Ibid.
3. COMSERVRON Three command history, 1965 Supplement, January 21, 1966, NHM.

Circuit Rider, Recruit Chaplain, and Alaska Pastor: 1961–1966

The military status of the U.S. Navy in the Pacific theater and the political environment at the dawn of the 1960s were dramatically different from the period immediately after World War II. After the war ended the United States basically abandoned the region. General Albert Wedemeyer, who during the war served as chief of staff to the supreme Allied commander in the South East Asia Command, Lord Louis Mountbatten, once stated, "America fought a war like a football game, after which the winner leaves the field and celebrates."[4] Politically the United States sought to protect the status quo by: (1) stabilizing the governments of Japan and newly independent states through financial, economic, and military aid and (2) maintenance of naval and air control of the Pacific so as to be able on short notice to rush to the defense of any state threatened by Communism.[5] Diplomatically the United States believed it could control Communist expansion through two mutual international agreements: the ANZUS (Australia, New Zealand, U.S.) Security Treaty ratified in March 1952 and SEATO (the Southeast Asia Treaty Organization), signed in November 1954. Writing in 1960, retired Admiral Samuel Morison commented:

We are trying to protect and preserve the present status quo in the Western Pacific—namely the independence of the SEATO powers of Japan, of Korea, of Formosa and of the neutralist and SEATO protocol states as well.[6]

This Western Pacific military and political environment greeted Jake Laboon when he arrived in Japan. Detaching from COMSUBLANT, he took a month's leave, reporting in early April 1961 as staff chaplain, Commander Service Squadron Three. He was further assigned to Support Unit Detachment Charlie as a "circuit rider."[7] The "circuit rider" chaplaincy concept was developed shortly after World War II "to provide a more adequate religious ministry,"[8] seeking to serve numerous at-sea commands with far fewer chaplains than were available during the war. Chaplains were literally ferried from one command to another, staying in one place for a limited amount of time. At any one location divine services, counseling, and a re-

---

4. Quoted in Morison, "American Strategy," 37.
5. Ibid., 43.
6. Ibid., 42, 43.
7. LT John Laboon, fitness report, September 29, 1961, Laboon file, NMPR. The term "circuit rider" was initially popularized in American religious history with Methodist ministers such as Francis Asbury, who traveled through a circuit of towns and missions in his efforts to preach the gospel.
8. LT. Stephen Wallace, "The Fleet Religious Support Activity," 1985, folder 1754/8, Box 89, NCA.

ligious presence were provided. On Sundays, especially for Catholic chaplains, arranging transportation between ships was important so that Mass could be celebrated on as many platforms as possible.[9] One senior navy chaplain explained the concept:

> By assigning the chaplain to an appropriate staff, rather than to a specific ship's company, and by moving him around periodically in a "circuit rider" fashion, many small-sized crews could have the benefit of religious services on an occasional, if not a regular weekly basis.[10]

As one of two chaplains (the other was Protestant) assigned to the squadron, Jake Laboon ministered on some thirty ships that provided service activities from both Yokosuka and Sasebo. His general at-sea time was four to six weeks, spending two weeks on board a vessel, but moving from ship to ship, especially on Sundays, to celebrate the sacraments.[11] Contemporaries of Jake's ministry in the squadron remember his strong advocacy for enlisted personnel, including improving their living conditions. Admiral Harry Train, who served with Jake at the climax of his career in Norfolk as executive officer of the submarine *Entemedor,* remembered one incident. Aware of a significant family problem for a sailor on Train's boat, Jake informed *Entemedor's* skipper that the boat would have to leave without the man. Train commented, "He was forceful to do what was best for the sailor."[12]

It did not take long for the influence of Jake Laboon and his ministry to be felt by those in his new command. An evaluation written only five months after his arrival referred to his outstanding performance due in large measure to his vast experience as a line officer and his understanding of procedures. Having been in situations similar to those of the men he served gave him insights rarely seen in a chaplain. His reporting senior, Rear Admiral H. A. Rankin, COMSERVRON Three, wrote, "His superior competence and leadership is [sic] seldom encountered in a chaplain of his rank. He immediately commands confidence and respect from those with whom he works."[13]

9. John Friel, interview with the author, August 2, 2011.
10. CDR Robert Warren, "The Naval Chaplaincy," 56, folder 5750/11, historical articles, box 27, NCA.
11. William Currie, SJ, e-mail to the author, November 17, 2012; *Catholic Review,* July 17, 1981, AABa.
12. Reminiscences of Admiral Harry Train, transcribed, AUSNA; USS *Laboon* commission booklet, PPJL.
13. LT John Laboon, fitness report, September 29, 1961, Laboon file, NMPR.

Circuit Rider, Recruit Chaplain, and Alaska Pastor: 1961–1966

Laboon could lead, but he also sought to teach others similar skills. As he moved from ship to ship in his circuit-rider ministry he taught leadership skills to the enlisted ranks. He brought his personal experience as well as various examples of leadership from literature. These were combined in a program to educate and train enlisted petty officers, providing them with tools to improve their ability to properly lead men in their divisions. This additional and rather unique contribution was favorably noted by his superiors. Speaking of his leadership training, one reporting officer wrote, "SERVPAC commanding officers state without equivocation that his treatment of the subject is the best they have ever witnessed."[14] Another report stressed the efficacy of his program: "His leadership lectures are adapted to the particular problems of each ship and have proven to be highly effective."[15] Thus Jake moved far beyond normal chaplain duties to improve discipline and consequently assist the command personnel to carry out their assigned duties. Jake's personal leadership and his dedication to improving the general leadership ability within the command merited for him once again a recommendation for early promotion.[16]

During 1962, as he continued to circuit-ride between vessels, his command, COMSERVRON Three, was involved with a variety of tasks under the leadership of Rear Admiral William Post, who relieved Rankin on February 15. The squadron provided logistical and material support for two important fleet exercises. Ships of Task Force 73, part of COMSERVRON Three, provided mobile logistic support for the five-day anti-air warfare exercise Strike X "Bandsaw" in January. Between October 10 and 24, the command participated in the amphibious exercise Lone Eagle, meeting the material needs of various ships.[17]

Typhoons, a regular occurrence in the geographic area of the squadron, often brought severe damage to vessels and port facilities. On November 11, 1962, Typhoon Karen struck Guam with sustained winds of between 150 and 180 knots. The squadron provided the bulk of material support for repairs to facilities damaged by the storm[18]

---

14. LT John Laboon, fitness report, February 15, 1962, Laboon file, NMPR.
15. LT John Laboon, fitness report, August 28, 1962, Laboon file, NMPR.
16. Ibid.
17. COMSERVRON Three command history, 1962, January 24, 1963, NHM.
18. Ibid.

Circuit Rider, Recruit Chaplain, and Alaska Pastor: 1961–1966

During the same period Jake continued to impress his superiors with his performance. His suitability for his present assignment, based on his experience as well as personal abilities, was once again noted:

> He expresses himself forcefully and with clarity in conversation, sermons and lectures. These attributes are a special asset in his present assignment, where his work must be accomplished in brief periods in many different Service Force ships.[19]

His presence within the command, both physical and spiritual, was noted in his February 1962 fitness report, which read in part, "His tactful, intelligent, mature, and positive approach in his work calls forth the highest respect and confidence of those under whose cognizance his work is performed."[20] Once again Jake's experience and significant professional knowledge were used to advantage for the betterment of the officers and sailors in the squadron. His new commanding officer, Rear Admiral Post, commented:

> Chaplain Laboon utilizes fully his previous service as an unrestricted line officer. He has a complete working knowledge and understanding of the officers and men with whom he comes in contact on the various SERVRON Three ships.[21]

Additionally, his strong personal example was noted: "His deep spiritual convictions and his military acumen fit him well for his work in the Navy Chaplaincy."[22]

In 1963 the squadron once again was involved with various fleet exercises, now under the command of Rear Admiral Russell Kefauver, who relieved Post on January 25, 1963. The first major event of the year came in February with the introduction of the Pacific Fleet Augmentation Plan, a new procedure to conveniently and efficiently position additional stocks of high-demand general stores and ship's store–type items on provision store ships (*AF*). The new program, it was hoped, would "provide more frequent availability of high usage items while releasing viable space aboard the *AKS* [general stores ship] for greater quantities of fast-moving items."[23] In the spring Squadron Three participated in two specialized exercises, Sea Serpent in April and Operation Glass Door between May 27 and 31. The latter "was designated to test the capabilities of the Seventh Fleet's response to

---

19. LT John Laboon, fitness report, February 15, 1962, Laboon file, NMPR.
20. Ibid.
21. LT John Laboon, fitness report, August 28, 1962, Laboon file, NMPR.
22. Ibid.
23. COMSERVRON Three command history, 1963, January 30, 1964, NHM.

a generated contingency, without prior knowledge or use of existing operations orders or letters of instruction for the particular exercise."[24] From June 10 to June 30 the squadron participated in Exercise Flagpole, a joint United States–Republic of Korea navy and marine exercise. The squadron command history reported, "[The exercise] provided much valuable training and experience in underway replenishment for both UNREP and customer ships."[25] In July Kefauver shifted his flag from USS *Ajax* (AR-6) to USS *Hector* (AR-7), allowing the former to enter Yokosuka for a needed overhaul. Before the end of the year, however, on December 14, the flag shifted back to *Ajax* with her return to service in Sasebo.[26]

Throughout 1963, as the squadron participated in various exercises, Jake Laboon continued to impress in his traveling ministry. In July, Kefauver commented:

Chaplain Laboon has completed his duties as a "circuit rider" during this reporting period in an exemplary manner. He sets an example for Navy chaplains in his purposeful approach, his manly bearing and devotion to his job.[27]

Reporting seniors spoke of his "devotion, moral values, and intelligent insight in the field of counseling and sense of humor combined with a realistic approach as to what our personnel think[, making] him a most effective chaplain."[28] A significant barometer of Laboon's efficacy with the crew was also noted: "I have personally seen enlisted men spot him and ask when he is going to ride their ship during its current employment."[29] Once again Jake's experience was seen as the source of the insight and gifts he demonstrated in ministry. Noting how "he is unanimously liked and respected," a report written in July 1963 commented, "His professional knowledge and background as a former submarine officer make him particularly valuable as a Navy Chaplain."[30] Complimenting him on his "poise and courtesy as well as forcefulness when needed," his detaching fitness report placed things in perspective: "He exhibits the finest sense of devotion to both his priestly and military duties."[31]

24. Ibid.
25. Ibid.
26. Ibid.
27. LT John Laboon, fitness report, July 26, 1963, Laboon file, NMPR.
28. LT John Laboon, fitness report, January 25, 1963, Laboon file, NMPR.
29. Ibid.
30. LT John Laboon, fitness report, July 26, 1963, Laboon file, NMPR.
31. Ibid.

Circuit Rider, Recruit Chaplain, and Alaska Pastor: 1961–1966

As a circuit rider Jake Laboon was privileged to see many ports, including Okinawa, Hong Kong, Taiwan, Vietnam, and Subic Bay, Philippines, but his ministry was centered in the Japanese cities of Sasebo and Yokosuka. While in Yokosuka he celebrated the sacraments at the Chapel of Hope, which was located at the naval station. There he baptized two children in 1963. Most important, however, in his ministry was his work with the common sailor. Admiral Harry Train recounted how one evening, prior to the departure of his boat, USS *Barbel*, he and Jake were enjoying conversation over a beer at the Officers Club. The next morning, at 6 a.m., prior to the submarine's departure, Jake arrived to bless the boat and its crew, an act that was, in Train's mind, unprecedented.[32]

Whenever he was in Yokosuka, Jake always made time to visit the Jesuit community, located at Taura Bay adjacent to the city. The Society's compound was a large piece of land that during World War II had served as a Japanese submarine base. After the war General Douglas MacArthur, U.S. administrator in Japan, sold it to the Jesuits for one dollar with the stipulation that a junior and senior high school be started there. Taura Bay was actually home to two Jesuit communities. One, a group of German Jesuits who had been in Japan since before the war, built a high school on the land in 1949. By 1960 this institution had become one of the most prestigious secondary schools in Japan. The other community was a group of Jesuit scholastics, mainly from Spain, the United States, and Latin America, who were engaged in an intensive two-year Japanese language program. The two Jesuit communities participated in culture wars with each other. Addressing this situation, Father William Currie, SJ, one of the scholastics at the time, commented, "Enter Jake Laboon who with his extraordinarily larger-than-life personality won the respect and admiration of both sides of the cultural divide, enabling him to serve as a great bridge-builder."[33]

Currie, who later served as president of Sophia University in Tokyo, remembers when Jake Laboon visited Taura Bay. He wrote, "When Jake was in town, everybody was happy."[34] During his tour with Squadron Three, Jake twice spent Christmas and Holy Week in Yokosuka. On these occasions he

---

32. William Currie, SJ, e-mail to the author, November 17, 2012; military ordinariate records—baptism, AAM; Reminiscences of Admiral Harry Train, transcribed, AUSNA.
33. William Currie, SJ, e-mail to the author, November 17, 2012.
34. Ibid.

asked the Jesuit scholastics to assist him in his duties aboard various ships. The Jesuit students formed a choir and sang carols at masses and the base hospital. Jake arranged for the scholastics to come to the Officers Club. He organized tours on several ships in port, especially submarines and aircraft carriers such as the *Midway, Lexington, Coral Sea,* and *Kitty Hawk,* giving the students a break from their intense language study. He also provided material things for the Jesuit house, including books and records in English. Expressing gratitude for his "wonderful homilies," Currie described how Laboon was received by his fellow students:

> Jake became a hero to us scholastics just by being Jake, with his wisdom, his humor, his deep spirituality which he carried with a very candid easy-going straight-from-the-shoulder, no-nonsense sort of grace.[35]

The model behavior upon which many of his military superiors had commented was evident to the Jesuit scholastics as well as they observed him operate in his two frames of reference: the military and the Society. Again Currie commented,

> His interaction with all kinds of people—officers, enlisted men, spouses, children, fellow chaplains, both older and younger Jesuits—was a beautiful thing to see and to us a living example of what a very human, very Christ-like priest should be.[36]

Recruit Chaplain—Great Lakes Naval Training Center: 1963–1965

On July 19, 1963, after slightly more than two years as a circuit rider for COMSERVRON Three, Jake Laboon detached and returned to the United States. After enjoying leave with family and friends, he arrived in late August at the Naval Training Center, Great Lakes, Illinois, under the command of Captain Slade Cutter. Having worked with a broad range of peoples, both in age and expertise, Jake was now asked to concentrate his significant gifts on a younger population: new recruits who would soon take their place in various navy commands. Having received a temporary appointment to the rank of lieutenant commander on August 1, a promotion consistent with his

---

35. Ibid. An interesting side note: One of the Jesuit scholastics who assisted Jake Laboon during his visits to Yokosuka was Adolfo Nicolas, today the superior general of the Society of Jesus.
36. Ibid.

time in service and rank, Jake, as with all his endeavors, dove into his new responsibilities with great vigor.[37]

The facility to which Jake was assigned was a central cog in the navy system and, over the course of its history, had gained a very positive reputation. A naval training center on the Great Lakes was first considered in 1902. A tract of 172 acres was obtained on July 1, 1905; with additional appropriations for construction, the facility opened on July 1, 1911, and was officially dedicated on October 28. From these humble beginnings the facility greatly expanded prior to 1917, becoming the primary center for naval training during World War I. Beginning on July 1, 1933, due in large measure to the lack of recruits during the Great Depression, Great Lakes was changed into a maintenance base. However, during World War II it regained its preeminence as the largest naval training facility in the country. The rapid need for trained sailors prompted expansion of the station's facilities; by late September 1942 its capacity was 100,000 men. The post–World War II era saw another demobilization, but not as drastic as after World War I.[38]

The recruit training command to which Jake Laboon reported was established in July 1944. Its mission was

to provide a program which will effect a smooth transition from civilian to Navy life; promote the dignity of the individual, inculcate understanding and appreciation of the fundamental workings of democracy and the Navy's place in democracy; develop a desire for self-improvement and advancement; promote high standards of responsibility, conduct, manners, and morals; provide sufficient knowledge in Naval subjects to enable the recruit to be of early usefulness to the Service; develop observation of Naval customs and traditions and stress pride in self and in the Navy.[39]

Great Lakes had also been the site of the first recruit training school for women, which opened in 1948, but four years later it was shifted to the Naval Training Center (NTC) in Bainbridge, Maryland. Nevertheless, the facility simultaneously expanded to meet the needs of the Korean War.[40]

---

37. LCDR John Laboon, fitness report, June 12, 1964; secretary of the navy to John Laboon, October 17, 1963, Laboon file, NMPR; active-duty chaplains, 9th Naval District, Great Lakes, Ill., March 1, 1965, folder 1301, box 9, NCA; Great Lakes Naval Training Center, 1960–65, Report, January 7, 1964, NHM. Although Jake's fitness reports consistently suggested advanced promotion, his advancement to lieutenant commander was consistent with his peers.

38. Narrative history, enclosure to CO, U.S. Naval Training Center, Great Lakes to CNO, August 25, 1959, Great Lakes NTC, 1902–58, NHM.

39. Ibid.

40. Ibid.

In 1963, when Jake Laboon arrived, NTC Great Lakes was once again in a stage of expansion. In 1961 the station, now home to several commands—Service School Command, U.S. Naval Examining Center, Administrative Command, and Recruit Training Command—celebrated its fiftieth anniversary, noting that since its opening over 2.5 million sailors had been trained at the center. Facilities worth over $100 million provided training for some 60,000 sailors annually. In 1962 significant additions to facilities were made. A new mess hall, costing $2.2 million, a classroom at $1.4 million, and new barracks replacing temporary facilities from World War II at a cost of almost $1.2 million, were built. Additional housing for officers and staff enlisted were constructed.[41] The Cuban Missile Crisis of October 1962 prompted a proud comment on the readiness and efficacy of the facility:

The Naval Training Center's primary mission of providing competent manpower for the fleet assumed added importance during the year when the Navy was called upon to show the nation it was truly ready and responsive.[42]

NTC Great Lakes' readiness was also demonstrated just prior to Jake's arrival when a spinal meningitis outbreak at NTC San Diego forced the facility to close temporarily. Recruits scheduled for training in San Diego were sent to Great Lakes, which absorbed the unexpected six thousand trainees with no significant difficulties.[43]

The chaplain's office at Great Lakes was established in July 1911. In its early days the office served mainly as the coordinating agency for the many religious and social welfare activities at the station. As time passed and the facility grew physically, so too the chaplains' responsibilities became more complex and more concentrated on the individual. In 1959 the chaplain's office described its function:

The Chaplain's primary task still is that of helping young men become better Americans and more accomplished sailors through awareness of their duty to their country and their obligations to God. The Chaplain's methods and techniques may change, but the mission remains static.[44]

---

41. Great Lakes Naval Training Center, 1962–65, reports, January 26, 1962, January 23, 1963, NHM.
42. Great Lakes Naval Training Center, 1962–65, report, January 23, 1963, NHM.
43. Great Lakes Naval Training Center, 1962–65, report, January 7, 1964, NHM.
44. Narrative history, Enclosure to CO, NTC Great Lakes to CNO, May 25, 1959.

Jake reported to his new job as assistant chaplain, Recruit Training Center, wasting no time to enter fully into his ministry. His primary work was with transient recruits engaged in the nine weeks of basic training, generally called "boot camp" in navy parlance. Speaking about working with a younger population, he once stated:

> To be a military chaplain today you have to like kids. When you are talking about the military today you are talking about 18- and 19-year-olds. They're really kids although we put them aboard ship and give them a tremendous amount of responsibility. You need a priest first of all who can deal with teenagers, and lets them know it. Then you do not become overwhelmed by their problems.[45]

As might be expected, many of those Jake encountered at Great Lakes were homesick, but he was more concerned about the caliber of recruits the navy was attracting, especially during the counterculture days of the mid-1960s.[46]

The challenges this new population brought did not dampen in any way the efficacy he had demonstrated with more fleet-savvy sailors in the past. A civilian who observed Jake's ministry at Great Lakes stated, "He put sailors or basically anyone at ease, because he had essentially seen it all." He wanted recruits to know that the chaplain was there for them. Each Sunday Jake celebrated what many described as the "Recruit Mass," attended for the most part by the young sailors in boot camp who heard one "talk kindly for the first and only time all week."[47]

Jake's ministry went beyond the recruit population as he also worked with families of those assigned to the various Great Lakes' commands. He taught religious education (CCD) to dependents of those assigned to the station. One of Jake's students spoke of the impression he made upon the youth: "To see a priest that was so tall was amazing. He was 6'5" and smoked cigars. I was impressed by his size and his casual and friendly nature." As a teacher Jake was able to make direct connections with his students. One commented, "He treated us with respect. He was open about his own experiences; he was a real person." He had the ability to present Catholicism in a way that young people found attractive: "He encouraged us to learn the Faith and to learn to accept the sacraments as a way to grow in faith."[48] Laboon's pastoral sense

---

45. *Catholic Review*, July 17, 1981, AABa.
46. Ibid.
47. Jim Byrnes, interview with the author, April 27, 2011.
48. Ibid.

was clear and manifested itself through his generous spirit of time and presence; he did not "push" the faith upon anyone. One observer commented, "He was my confessor for over a year ... and his kindness combined with his height made an impression on me. I believed what he said."[49]

Laboon's ministry, as with his earlier time in New London, even extended to the local church and geographic region. He arranged for the sacrament of confirmation to be conferred by Cardinal Albert Meyer, archbishop of Chicago. On Sunday, July 26, 1964, Jake appeared on Chicago television, WMBQ, Channel 5, with two other navy chaplains, commanders Glen Power and P. W. Reigner, discussing their work and ministry. As a former great athlete and avid sports enthusiast, he was more than happy to attend, along with some three thousand others, the annual Armed Forces Benefit Football Game, played between the Chicago Bears and the St. Louis Cardinals and Cleveland Browns on successive years at Soldiers Field.[50]

Jake's military superiors were very pleased and praised his highly effective ministry with the Great Lakes community. As in the past, reporting seniors noted his exceptional experience from the academy and World War II as a recipe for success, making him "an extremely effective chaplain." His knowledge of all aspects of navy life, including history, tradition, and customs was reflected in his personal demeanor and military bearing. One report stated, "Because of this he was held in high esteem and respect by all his shipmates, both officers and enlisted."[51] Possibly because of his rank and great experience as a chaplain, Jake was not afraid to promote his views and forcefully push for what he believed was correct and could aid people he served. Again, a reporting senior commented:

At this present assignment in the Recruit Training Command, he has demonstrated outstanding moral courage, force and initiative, especially at conferences with the Commanding Officer, Naval Aptitude Board meetings and Recreation Council meetings. In these meetings he has exhibited a deep concern about matters of morale and he has repeatedly and persuasively offered useful suggestions which are constantly being translated into improved living conditions and recreational facilities.[52]

49. Jim Byrnes, e-mail to author, n.d. [2011].
50. Great Lakes Naval Training Center, 1960–65, report, January 7, 1964, January 6, 1965, NHA; *Great Lakes Bulletin,* July 24, 1964, GLNSL The benefit game was sponsored by the Chicago Newspaper Publishers and the Chicago Bears.
51. LCDR John Laboon, fitness report, June 12, 1964, Laboon file, NMPR.
52. Ibid.

Jake also lobbied strongly for improved worship facilities at the station. His fitness report stated, "As a Roman Catholic priest, he is deeply concerned about the spiritual welfare of his parishioners."[53]

Jake's work with recruits was especially noteworthy. During his tenure he completely revised the basic recruit lecture indoctrination program, making it a much more effective tool for both presenters and those instructed. His reporting senior wrote,

> His ability to correctly evaluate the Recruit Guidance Lecture Program triggered a studied review of the entire program and has resulted in recommendations for its substantial improvement. On his own time he submitted a detailed outline for a new lecture which would add immensely to the total project.[54]

It was Jake's personal charisma, sensitivity, and priestly identity more than his administrative expertise, however, that truly marked his ministry with young sailors. This quality was noted by Captain W. H. McLaughy, commanding officer of Naval Administrative Command, Great Lakes:

> His very manly appearance coupled with a most sympathetic understanding of the frailties of human nature has brought herds of recruits to his office seeking help and guidance. Through his mature appraisal of problems which often proved to be stumbling blocks for the recruits and his personal intercession in their behalf, many men have been saved for service in the Navy who might otherwise have been discharged.[55]

Laboon appealed as well to his peer chaplains and superior officers. He was "extremely well-liked and greatly admired by his fellow chaplains of all faiths" and was "a continuing source of inspiration to his peers and those junior to him in the Chaplain Corps as well as to officers and men with whom he has been associated." His "unwavering loyalty to a higher moral standard" was a splendid example for others."[56]

His two years of dedicated service to the recruit command was recognized in a special way through a letter of commendation presented him by Captain Ira King, commanding officer of NTC Great Lakes. Stating that, to his knowledge, Laboon was the first chaplain ever to receive a letter of commendation at the Great Lakes facility, King spoke of Jake's experience and expertise as "of inestimable value to this command in the furtherance of its

---

53. Ibid.
54. Ibid.
55. LCDR John Laboon, fitness report, April 1, 1965, Laboon file, NMPR.
56. Ibid.

religious and moral guidance programs." Describing his great pleasure in working with Jake and his regret that he would soon detach, but confident that his gifts would continue to be an outstanding asset in his new assignment, he applauded Laboon for his work with the staff and many individuals in developing a "high level of morale and sincerely religious attitude" among all facets of the station. Jake's significant abilities as a counselor were "effective because of his mature and realistic understanding of the individual's needs and desires and selfless persistence in pushing forward to a satisfactory solution every individual's personal problems." King thanked Laboon for going the "extra mile," taking off-duty time to work with recruits in order to develop a beneficial religious and social program for them.[57]

Jake informed his Jesuit superiors about this rare honor and about a feature story on him published in the base newspaper, yet in his always humble manner he gave credit to a higher source. He wrote to his provincial:

> I mentioned this by way of the effectiveness apparently that being a good priest has on these people. You know well enough to realize that these are merely the direct results of *Ad Majorem Dei Gloriam* [to the greater glory of God]. They [the letter and article] mean *nothing* to me personally.[58]

Jake's assistant provincial, Hugh Kennedy, SJ, congratulated Laboon, informing him of the pride of the Society in his good ministry.[59]

Naval Station Kodiak, Alaska: 1965–1966

After nineteen months at NTC Great Lakes, Jake Laboon was on the move again. He informed his provincial, John Daly, SJ, that he was being sent to Kodiak, Alaska, to serve as the Catholic chaplain on base. Additionally, he was given a collateral duty as district chaplain of the 17th Naval District. He also told Daly that, due to the isolated nature of the command, the standard assignment for a priest was one year. When Jake arrived, the new commanding officer at Naval Station Kodiak was Captain Ira M. Powell.[60]

---

57. CAPT Ira M. King to LCDR John Laboon, March 12, 1965, Laboon file, NMPR. King wrote, "Your keen insight and understanding of the spiritual needs of the young and new military man have been demonstrated on countless occasions in your satisfactory solution of the many and varied problems and emergencies that arise each day."
58. John Laboon, SJ, to John Daly, SJ, March 16, 1965, Laboon file, ASJM (emphasis original).
59. Hugh Kennedy, SJ, to John Laboon, SJ, March 19, 1965, Laboon file, ASJM.
60. John Laboon, SJ, to John Daly, SJ, March 16, 1965, Laboon file, NMPR; *Great Lakes Bulletin,*

Jake's transfer to another command and the thought in his mind that a navy career might be in the offing prompted him to investigate augmentation to the regular navy. When Laboon reentered the navy in 1958, he was commissioned in the naval reserve and placed on active duty, but a transfer to regular-duty status was necessary if he was to be a career officer. Captain King at Great Lakes was very supportive of Jake's desire:

> You have indicated to me your sincere desire to devote your professional and spiritual services to the welfare of Navy men as a career in the Chaplain Corps. I heartily endorse your request for augmentation. The benefits accruing to the Navy from this permanent association would be inestimable.[61]

Buoyed by support from the navy, Laboon planned to discuss the matter with Cardinal Francis Spellman, head of the military ordinariate, and his chancellor, Monsignor Joseph Marbach.[62] Jake was not able to speak with Spellman; a rather brief conversation with Marbach did not gain him any insight into the possibility of a regular commission. Instead, he journeyed to Pittsburgh to visit family before leaving for Kodiak.

Despite Marbach's rather lackluster attitude to his request, a few months later Laboon did make application for augmentation, but the initial response from the office of the ordinariate was negative. Marbach explained:

> I hope you will forgive me if I say that we prefer not to endorse a religious for the Regular Navy. This is just a policy of self-protection because, theoretically, the Holy See does not seem to wish religious to stay in for twenty.... I hasten to add, of course, that we certainly *want* you to stay in for twenty years if possible, but to be frank we like to keep this quiet.[63]

March 19, 1965, GLNSL; Naval Station Kodiak Alaska command history, 1965, February 15, 1966, NHM.

61. CAPT Ira M. King to LCDR John Laboon, March 12, 1965, Laboon file, NMPR.

62. John Laboon, SJ, to John Daly, SJ, March 16, 1965, Laboon file, ASJM. Monsignor Joseph Marbach, chancellor of the military ordinariate, had written to Laboon, congratulating him on his letter of commendation: "We are most grateful to you for your complete dedication to the work of the recruits at Great Lakes"; see Joseph Marbach to John Laboon, SJ, March 11, 1965, Laboon file, ASJM.

63. Joseph Marbach to John Laboon, SJ, March 11, 1965, Laboon file, ASJM. "Religious" is a term used by Roman Catholics to describe a sister, brother, or priest in a religious community, such as the Jesuits. The fear was that religious priests like Laboon would be less likely to receive permission from their superiors to stay in the navy for a career, thus the reticence to allow Laboon to transfer to the regular navy from the reserves (emphasis original).

Laboon informed his provincial that his application had been rejected, but he continued to voice a need for his augmentation, suggesting that navy people saw great potential in him for future assignment. Laboon wrote,

> It seems that many Navy Chaplains and the Bureau [of Naval Personnel] are most anxious for me to become Regular Navy, but for selfish reasons too. There was a move afloat to prepare me for the Chief of Chaplains. This is between you, me and the lamp-post though.[64]

He informed Daly that he would do whatever the provincial wished, but for now the navy was a very satisfactory ministry:

> I have no definite plans at all. I would like to stay on because priests are needed so badly.... I know that I am doing effective work within the Navy, and because of this, I am anxious to stay on. As long as I am effective and my superiors wish me to stay in the Navy, then here I stay.[65]

Three months later, however, for reasons that are not extant, the military ordinate reversed itself and endorsed Laboon's request for transfer to the regular navy. Marbach wrote to Rear Admiral J. Floyd Dreith, navy chief of chaplains, informing him that the ecclesiastical approval for Laboon's transfer to the regular navy was received.[66] Laboon informed his provincial, telling him that the endorsement "came as a surprise." He went on to say that he had "heard through the grapevine" that Dreith had talked with the military ordinariate staff about its earlier rejection of his application. Obviously the chief of chaplains was persuasive and successful in his lobbying efforts. When Jake informed his Jesuit superiors, he received hearty congratulations.[67]

The Kodiak, Alaska, naval station to which Jake reported in late April 1965 had only been in existence twenty-five years. Congress authorized construction of a naval station at Kodiak on April 25, 1939. A naval air station was established on June 15, 1941; an auxiliary submarine base was established thirteen months later in July 1942. The latter facility was disestablished in June 1945; the former was dissolved on October 1, 1950. Thus the

---

64. John Laboon, SJ, to John Daly, SJ, March 16, 1965, Laboon file, ASJM. Laboon wrote to Daly, "In the back of the minds of the authorities was to permit me to stay on Active-Duty if and when the time comes after I complete 20 years."
65. Ibid.
66. Joseph Marbach to RADM J. Floyd Dreith, June 15, 1965, Laboon file, ASJM.
67. Hugh Kennedy, SJ, to John Laboon, SJ, July 14, 1965, Laboon file, ASJM.

designation of the facility was changed to naval station at that same time.[68] The station was isolated on Kodiak Island, approximately seven miles from the city of Kodiak. One former navy chaplain who served at this facility described it as "a rough environment."[69] The mission of the naval station was to operate and maintain facilities and provide services and material support for units of the operational forces of the navy.[70]

When Jake Laboon arrived the facility was recovering from a severe earthquake that struck the region on March 27, 1964. Many repairs to various facilities, especially in areas near the ocean, where sea damage was significant, were still underway. Manpower and material shortages had slowed repairs. The Alaska State Department of Aviation lent the naval station several pieces of machinery to assist in repair activities. An annual inspection of Naval Station Kodiak, conducted on October 4–7, 1965, by Commander, Fleet Air Alaska, reported, "U.S. Naval Station, Kodiak was carrying out its mission and assignments in an effective and efficient manner."[71] Later that same year, on December 4, a new $600,000 recreation building called the "Tsunami Center" featuring eight bowling lanes and various hobby shops opened. By July 1966 equipment borrowed from the state had been returned and facilities were in working order.[72]

As senior chaplain at the naval station Laboon had many administrative duties, but for the Catholic community he served as local pastor, a position he had not previously held as chaplain or priest. His collateral duties at the naval station were many and varied, including as chairman of the naval station nursery, advisory board member for the commissioned officers' mess, member of the Moral Standards Council, executive vice president for the Navy Relief Society, and project officer for the Navy Relief and American Red Cross fund drives.[73] His duties as pastor for the Catholic community included being custodian of the Catholic Chapel Fund, moderator of the Altar

---

68. Narrative history, enclosure to CO, U.S. Naval Station, Kodiak, Alaska, to CNO, August 28, 1959, Naval Station Kodiak, 1941–60, NHM.

69. Peter Pilarski, interview with the author, January 14, 2011.

70. Naval Station, Kodiak, Alaska, command history, 1966, May 2, 1967, NHM.

71. Naval Station, Kodiak, Alaska, command history, 1965, February 15, 1966, NHM.

72. Ibid.; Naval Station, Kodiak, Alaska, command history, 1965, February 15, 1966, NHM.

73. It should be noted that some reticence was present in allowing a chaplain to handle funds of any nature, save donations made at regular Sunday Mass or services. Thus, Laboon's collateral duties indicate the respect with which he was held by others, including seniors who assigned him to various duties.

Circuit Rider, Recruit Chaplain, and Alaska Pastor: 1961–1966

and Rosary and Holy Name societies, and adviser to the Teen Club. He was an active counselor, especially due to the isolated nature of the command. In April 1965 his senior officer commented:

> In this relatively isolated location, with its high percentage of unmarried men, or men without their families, he has provided vital counseling services and has, along with his ministry, provided many practical services which have been of immeasurable value to the morale of the command.[74]

He was also applauded for being a "tireless worker" with respect to the numerous supervisory responsibilities he had with various groups, both those directly associated with his role as chaplain and those more generic to the naval station.[75]

His work with youth was particularly noteworthy in various areas, but most prominently in religious education programs. Working with a religious Sister of Providence, Laboon designed the course of instruction for lay people to serve as catechists for youth classes. He revamped the program in the spirit of Vatican II, which concluded its fourth and final session in December 1965.[76] He worked with Protestant chaplains in some joint efforts, including "Vacation Church School" held in June 1966.[77] Laboon combined his skill of working with this population, together with his previous experience, both at Auriesville and in the navy, to provide an excellent program of religious formation for local dependents.

Beyond his normal assigned duties, Jake was a leader in recreational efforts. As in New London, Jake combined ministry with various sports activities. His strong contribution in this area was noted: "He is an outstanding athlete in his own right, and through his organization and participation in athletics, has been able to further foster a feeling of acceptance, belonging, and respect among the personnel of this command."[78]

The approach and special care that Laboon took in his duties as se-

---

74. LCDR John Laboon, fitness report, April 27, 1965, Laboon file, NMPR.
75. Ibid.
76. Naval Station, Kodiak, Alaska, command history, 1966, May 3, 1967, NHM; LCDR John Laboon, fitness report, May 4, 1966, Laboon file, NMPR. The Second Vatican Council (1962–65), the 21st Ecumenical Council of the Roman Catholic Church, was transformative in many ways but especially in encouraging active participation by lay men and women in the day-to-day operations of the church. A much more detailed outline of Vatican II and its significance is provided in chapter 7 of this volume.
77. *Kodiak Bear,* May 20, 1966, Naval Station Kodiak, 1962–66, NHM.
78. LCDR John Laboon, fitness report, April 27, 1965, NMPR.

nior chaplain were observed by his superiors. His ability "to motivate and inspire personnel through [h]is personal knowledge and experience" was especially noteworthy. His ability to integrate spiritual matters into day-to-day life gave special relevance to his activity, especially positively impacting those with whom he associated. He was described as "a dynamic and dedicated officer of great ability and potential."[79]

Jake Laboon's many less significant duties as senior chaplain for the naval station at Kodiak were complemented by his collateral position as chaplain for the 17th Naval District. The command, which included several subordinate agencies, provided command and control supervision for the entire Alaska and Aleutian Islands area.[80] The mission of the district chaplain was "to advise the Commandant in all matters pertaining to religious activities and character education programs, and to supervise and inspect the work of chaplains in the district."[81] As district chaplain Jake supervised three other chaplains, one at Kodiak and two at Adak.

The challenge of administrative oversight of numerous programs and peoples tested the mettle of Laboon. Rear Admiral R. E. Riera, commandant of the 17th Naval District, was impressed with how Jake could so easily and graciously serve as a liaison with other military services and in so doing "enjoy their complete respect." In a repetitive chorus, Riera reported that Jake's previous experience as a line officer provided him with a "keen understanding of the needs of servicemen and their dependents. This is evident in the manner in which he meets such needs." His ability to "completely update and modernize the administrative procedures in his Department" was also praised.[82]

79. Ibid.
80. A History of the Alaska Sea Frontier and 17th Naval District, 1959, Alaska Sea Frontier, 1959, NHM. The subordinate commands for the 17th naval district were: Naval Station Kodiak; Naval Station Adak; U.S. Naval Communication Station Kodiak; U.S. Naval Communication Station Adak; Marine Barracks Kodiak; Marine Barracks Adak; District Public Works Officer; Industrial Manager; Fleet Aircraft Service Squadron; and U.S. Navy Commissary Kodiak.
81. Command History commander, 17th Naval District, enclosure to commandant 17th Naval District to CNO, January, 1960, Alaska Sea Frontier, 1959, NHM. The specific functions of the district chaplain were to: (1) provide naval personnel and their dependents with religious services such as funerals, marriages, baptisms, and counseling; (2) establish and maintain liaison with social, welfare, and religious organizations; (3) assist in recruitment and selection of candidates for appointment as chaplain; (4) provide specialized logistics and professional guidance as necessary; (5) administer naval reserve chaplains' programs; and (6) perform duties of district "on-base" schools officer.
82. LCDR John Laboon, fitness report, March 2, 1966, Laboon file, NMPR.

Jake's *modus operandi*, which always meant going beyond what was normally expected, was also noted by his superiors at COMSEVENTEEN. His interest in building morale and character through sports, community relations, and moral leadership was noteworthy. An evaluation written in May 1966 was illustrative:

> His contributions to this Naval District have not been limited to the religious and spiritual needs of personnel and their families, but have been extended to such areas as sports, recreational programs and projects which have a widely favorable effect on overall morale.[83]

In May 1966, as his one-year tour came to a close and he prepared to detach for his next duty station, Jake received praise for a job well done. He was lauded for his strong personal character and leadership qualities, which were "above reproach." His commanding officer praised his ecumenical efforts: "He has gained a very high degree of respect from personnel of all religious faiths, not only as a chaplain, but as a Naval Officer as well." Describing him as "one of the finest chaplains I have observed during my career," Rear Admiral D. M. White lamented the great loss he would be to his staff.[84] In what was not a normal pattern, Jake was recommended for advanced promotion and for assignment to the naval academy.[85] As he detached, Jake informed his new provincial, Edward Sponga, SJ, of his new duty station and of his official movement to the regular navy.[86]

Conclusion

The early to mid-1960s, a period in American history that saw a rising tide of the nation's involvement in Vietnam and numerous manifestations of social unrest, was a time when Jake Laboon gained significant experience as a navy chaplain in three highly varied assignments. Transferring from the

---

83. LCDR John Laboon, fitness report, May 4, 1966, Laboon file, NMPR.
84. Ibid.
85. Ibid. Actually, Jake had first been recommended for duty at the naval academy in 1961. RADM L. R. Daspit, COMSUBLANT, when speaking of Laboon's education and experience, far ahead of his contemporaries, concluded, "It is a combination which with his personality mark him as ideally suited for assignment as the Naval Academy Chaplain"; see LT John Laboon, fitness report, March 21, 1961, Laboon file, NMPR.
86. John Laboon, SJ, to Edward Sponga, SJ, January 18, 1966, Laboon file, ASJM; LCDR John Laboon, fitness report, April 27, 1966, Laboon file, NMPR.

comfort of the submarine force, with which he was highly familiar, he was sent to serve as a circuit-riding chaplain in Japan. Adaptable to all circumstances, Jake learned the ins and outs of the black-shoe navy. His navy superiors began to take notice when, on his own initiative, he went far beyond the standard duties of providing religious services and counseling, inaugurating a leadership training program for the men of COMSERVRON Three. Transferring from what would be his only sea tour, Jake was sent to the nation's heartland to minister to recruit sailors at the Great Lakes Naval Training Center. While primarily working with young sailors, he also ministered to navy families, especially youth. After two years of service, and thinking about a career in the navy, Jake was once again on the move, this time to the naval station at Kodiak, Alaska, where he served as senior chaplain and local pastor for the Catholic community. Simultaneously, he doubled as district chaplain for the 17th Naval District. Each of these brief assignments brought its challenges, but also opportunities for growth in ministry and advancement through the chaplain corps. In each case Jake Laboon continued to garner plaudits from navy personnel, from the most junior to the most senior. As he began to move into the more senior ranks of the chaplain corps, he stood ready for his next challenge: a return to his alma mater, the U.S. Naval Academy, an assignment he not only relished, but attacked with his usual and always appreciated vigor.

Chapter 7

Return to the Naval Academy
★ 1966–1969

Returning to one's college or university alma mater is a significant event that brings great satisfaction through the many memories of people, events, and trusted friendships that provided the springboard from which one vaults into professional life. Generally one returns to his alma mater for the annual homecoming football game, class reunions, and possibly simply to visit. Few are ever given the privilege to return in a more official capacity as a teacher, administrator, or some other more permanent position. Because of the nature of the institution, the naval academy does provide the opportunity for select military personnel to return as professors or possibly supervisory officers. In the spring of 1966 Jake Laboon was granted the rare privilege to return to the academy, the first graduate to ever serve in the Yard as a chaplain. Laboon's career had already been marked by uniqueness—specifically as his selection as the first chaplain assigned to the SSBN program. Jake's return to the hallowed grounds of his college days allowed him to blossom to his maximum extent. His previous experience as a midshipman and war hero, as well as his continued athleticism and interest in sports, combined with his pastoral sensitivity, allowed him to serve the academy community in ways that touched the lives of hundreds of midshipmen as well as many other personnel assigned to the academy. Overjoyed to once again be in an environment that had fed him in a significant and personal way some twenty-five years earlier, Jake immersed himself in his new assignment.

Return to the Naval Academy: 1966–1969

U.S. Naval Academy—1960s—Background

In April 1966, when Jake Laboon returned to his alma mater after more than twenty years, he experienced a different place. He was greeted by a new superintendent, Rear Admiral Draper Kauffman, who was known as a disciplinarian and a traditionalist with respect to naval tradition.[1] In February 1957 an additional fifty-three acres had been added to the academy yard by filling in Dewey Basin and extending Farragut Field, bringing the grounds to approximately 287 acres. In April 1966, for the first time since 1851, enlisted personnel working in various capacities at the academy moved ashore. Previously enlisted personnel had resided on ships anchored at the academy's waterfront. Now they occupied a new three-story building, Ricketts Hall, adjacent to Halsey Field House and not far from the main gate (Gate 1).[2] While academy traditions endured, there were modifications with respect to the treatment of plebes within the brigade of midshipmen as a result of a December 1966 review of the plebe indoctrination program. It was agreed that midshipmen needed to be involved in the development of a new system that would maintain discipline but eliminate abuses. A midshipmen committee formed for this task "did an extremely commendable job in revising the Plebe Indoctrination Program." Officers and faculty were pleased with the modifications, stating that the new system "will achieve a more harmonious balance between allocation of Plebe time to indoctrination training and academic education."[3]

While some physical changes to the Yard were in evidence, the major transformation to the academy from Jake's time as a midshipman was its academic program. In 1959 the Department of the Navy initiated a major review of the academy's academic programs. The Folsom board, named for its chairman, Dr. Richard Folsom, president of Rensselaer Polytechnic Institute, conducted this review in order to achieve greater flexibility and

---

1. RADM Draper Kauffman, superintendent USNA, report to naval academy alumni, June 1965–June 1968, USNA command history, 1968, NHM. As one example of his more disciplinarian approach, Draper, immediately upon his arrival in 1965, revoked a privilege given only one year earlier to first-class midshipmen to own and operate a vehicle at the academy, beginning on September 1 of their 1/C year.
2. "A History of the U.S. Naval Academy, 1845–1958," 16, enclosure to USNA command history, 1966, NHM.
3. "Naval Academy History 1966," USNA command history, 1966, NHM.

more effective coordination of instruction and facilities. One report read, "The academic reorganization serves to pave the way for changes in the curriculum and provide effective means for administering the new elective and validation programs."[4] Thus midshipmen could "test out" or validate certain courses based on previous training and take free electives. In its 1963 report the board of visitors, commenting on the new academic program that the class of 1963 was the first to complete, stated:

> The validation program coupled with the large numbers of elective courses now available allows each midshipman to advance at a rate commensurate with his educational capacity and also to acquire additional knowledge in the field of his special interest.

The report continued,

> We believe that the new curriculum is providing the graduates of the Naval Academy with a broader educational base and at the same time more effectively preparing them to meet the constantly changing needs of the future in technology and science as applied to weaponry and operations.[5]

One year later, in the fall of 1964, the position of academic dean was created.[6]

Improvements to the academy's academic program continued through the mid-1960s. In the summer of 1966 the secretary of the navy established a twelve-member academic advisory board (AAB) to supplement the board of visitors. Composed of noted educators, leaders of business, the vice chief of naval operations (CNO), and a retired admiral who had served as the superintendent of the naval academy, the AAB first met in November 1966. Two members of the board, Dr. Folsom and Admiral Horatio Rivero, vice CNO, had been part of the 1959 Folsom board that had initiated the academic improvements.[7]

As a result, the class of 1968 was given a new and updated curriculum when its members started class in September 1964. Midshipmen were able to major in any of twenty-three different disciplines, including engineer-

---

4. "Recent Academic Improvement at the Naval Academy," November 1966; "A History of the U.S. Naval Academy, January 1, 1959 to December 31, 1959," n.d. [1960], USNA command history, 1966, NHM.

5. Quoted in "Recent Academic Improvement at the Naval Academy," November 1966, USNA command history, 1966, NHM.

6. "Naval Academy History 1966," USNA command history, 1966, NHM.

7. Ibid.

ing, history, politics and economics, foreign affairs, literature, foreign languages, mathematics, core sciences, and oceanography. The rationale for the program was explained: "The new approach was designed to educate midshipmen better for the complex problems of the modern world."[8] The new program placed greater emphasis on social sciences: the humanities as well as pedagogy. One report read, "The emphasis at the Naval Academy is on faculty members who are excellent teachers in addition to being excellent scholars as evidenced by their records in the profession."[9] The new curriculum for the class of 1968 also reduced the number of semester credits required for graduation, "to allow each student more time in which to study in greater depth than was previously possible," so that midshipmen would develop habits they would use continuously after graduation. Less time devoted to classroom instruction would, it was hoped, translate into more time to outside study.[10] Kauffman realized that this new program, considered by some to be an "academic revolution," created some problems, but he concluded, "The changes were so important and so essential that the problems involved were heavily outweighed by the advantages gained."[11]

Specialized programs for talented midshipmen also became part of the academic scene. In the spring of 1963 the Trident Scholars Program was instituted. Open to 1/C midshipmen in the top 10 percent of their class academically, the program was "an effort to recognize and utilize the capabilities of highly talented students by permitting them to embark upon areas of independent study in undergraduate research."[12] The new program also provided an opportunity for post-baccalaureate education. For example, forty-two members of the class of 1967 were allowed to pursue master-level degree programs immediately after graduation. The new curriculum also generated

---

8. USNA catalog, 1966–67; "Naval Academy History 1966," USNA command history, 1966, NHM.

9. "Recent Academic Improvement at the Naval Academy," November 1966; RADM Draper Kauffman, superintendent USNA, report to the naval academy alumni, June 1965–June 1968, USNA command history, 1968, NHM. One statistic to support this shift in emphasis was the percentage of civilian faculty. In 1945, 19 percent of the faculty were civilians; in 1967, 54 percent were civilians.

10. Ibid.; "The Educational Program of the U.S. Naval Academy," academic year 1966–67, USNA command history, 1966, NHM.

11. RADM Draper Kauffman, superintendent USNA, report to the naval academy alumni, June 1965–June 1968, USNA command history, 1968, NHM.

12. "Recent Academic Improvement at the Naval Academy," November 1966, USNA command history, 1966, NHM.

several Fulbright Scholarship winners, as well as one Rhodes Scholar.[13] The new program was touted in an internal evaluation report:

> Today's Naval Academy has an up-to-date and challenging educational program. This program provides the background required of naval officers in the performance of their very duties as well as support in depth for postgraduate study in a wide-ranging choice of programs.[14]

In late June 1968, when Rear Admiral James Calvert relieved Kauffman as superintendent, a ceremony at which Jake Laboon offered the benediction, there was every reason to believe that the significant academic improvements of the 1960s would continue into the next decade.[15]

Vatican II, the American Church, and the Nation—1960s

Throughout the history of Christianity ecumenical councils have been called for two basic reasons: to root out perceived or acknowledged heresy and to define significant church doctrine or dogma. The first council, held in Nicaea in 325, served both purposes: first, it condemned the theology of the priest Arius, who viewed Christ as a *tertium quid*, one not fully human or divine; second, it formulated the Nicene Creed, which was modified into its present form at Constantinople in 381. Vatican I, the twentieth council, held between 1869 and 1870, defined the dogma of papal infallibility in its document *Pastor Aeternus*. In the interim, eighteen other councils, including the famous gatherings at Constance (1414–17), which ended the Great Western Schism, and at Trent (1545–63), which presented the Catholic response to the Reformation, gave direction, corrected abuses, and defined teachings in the church.

The Second Vatican Council was called by Pope John XXIII in a speech at

---

13. Ibid.; "Naval Academy History 1966," USNA command history, 1966, NHM. Prior to this academic policy change former midshipmen who sought post baccalaureate degrees could only apply after completing a four-year tour of duty, and they would be sent to the Naval Postgraduate School at Monterey, California. The forty-two members of the class of 1967 were slated to pursue master-level programs at such institutions as North Carolina State University, Georgia Institute of Technology, and the Catholic University of America, as well as the Naval Postgraduate School.

14. "The Educational Program of the U.S. Naval Academy," academic year 1966–67, USNA command history, 1966, NHM.

15. Change of command ceremony for superintendent, USNA, June 28, 1968, USNA command history, 1968, NHM.

the Basilica of St. Paul's Outside the Walls on January 25, 1959, the last day of the annual week of prayer for Christian unity. John, who had been elected only in the previous October, was, because of his age—seventy-six—considered an interim pope. Thus, his dramatic announcement came as a great surprise to the entire world, especially the Catholic Church. The pope called for a diocesan synod for Rome, a revision of canon law from the 1917 code and an ecumenical council of the world's bishops. He also stated the council's three principal purposes: to promote ecumenism, to bring the church into the modern world (he used the word *aggiornamento*), and to be pastoral in nature and work.

Preparations for the council began almost immediately when the pope asked over eight hundred theologians, the hierarchy, heads of male religious orders, and the faculties of thirty-seven Catholic universities worldwide to provide suggestions for what the council should address. The church enjoyed a relative oasis of calm in the midst of the secular Cold War upheaval. Thus seemingly free of both heresy and uncertainty about doctrinal matters, it was initially thought that there would be minimal response to the pope's call for action. However, over two thousand individuals and institutions provided ideas for possible study by the council. Cardinal Alfredo Ottaviani, prefect of the Holy Office (today the Congregation for the Doctrine of the Faith), put in charge of organizing the council, was a strong theological conservative who was wary of modernization in any form. He used his influence and position to "pack" the preparatory commissions with only "safe" theologians who would not move the church from the position it had maintained, with barely an inch of movement, since the time of Trent in the mid-sixteenth century. The twelve commissions that were established developed seventy schemas for possible debate by the council fathers, including revelation, moral order, the deposit of faith, family, liturgy, the media, and Christian unity. All the draft documents were neo-scholastic, juridical, and moralistic in tone and content.

The council was formally convoked with the document *Humanae Salutaris* of December 25, 1961. In this document Pope John used the terms "signs of the times" and *"aggiornamento,"* expressions that would prove significant for the future direction of the council's work. The pope's comments reversed the longstanding edict proclaimed at Lateran V (1512–17), which said "men must be changed by religion" to "religion must be changed by men." With the pope leading the way, shortly after the first session of the council opened on October 11, 1962, the bishops voted to move away from the rather staid tone of the preliminary schema, substituting a more open view that would allow the bishops themselves to determine the council's direction. Ottaviani and his conservative forces were thus routed at the outset, setting the tone that would be carried through to the council's conclusion on December 8, 1965.[16]

The four sessions of Vatican II produced sixteen documents, more by far than any previous council, which were divided into three areas of descending significance. Four constitutions, including documents on liturgy, revelation, the church, and the church in the modern world, were the council's crowning achievement. Nine decrees were published, including important treatises on ecumenism and the lay apostolate, and three declarations, including the one document with a distinctively American tone, the Declaration on Religious Liberty, were published. The net effect of these documents was the emergence of a new self-understanding for Roman Catholicism, exemplified most significantly in the rise of collegiality, the increased role of the laity, ecumenical dialogue, and a complete updating of the liturgy,

---

16. Many fine historical sources on Vatican II have been published. A representative sample follows: Robert McAfree Brown, *Observer in Rome: A Protestant Report on the Vatican Council* (Garden City, N.Y.: Doubleday, 1964); Anthony J. Cernera, ed., *Vatican II: The Continuing Agenda* (Fairfield, Conn.: Sacred Heart University Press, 1997); Henri De Lubac, "The Church in Crisis," *Theology Digest* 17 (1969): 312–25; Dennis M. Doyle, *The Church Emerging from Vatican II: A Popular Approach to Contemporary Catholicism* (Mystic, Conn.: Twenty-Third Publications, 1992); Adrian Hastings, ed., *Modern Catholicism: Vatican II and After* (New York: Oxford University Press, 1991); Christopher Hollis, *The Achievements of Vatican II* (New York: Hawthorn, 1967); Rene Latourelle, ed., *Vatican II Assessment and Perspectives Twenty-Five Years After (1962–1987)*, 5 vols. (New York: Paulist Press, 1988); Timothy G. McCarthy, *The Catholic Tradition: Before and After Vatican II 1878–1993* (Chicago: Loyola University Press, 1994); Timothy E. O'Connell, ed., *Vatican II: An American Appraisal* (Wilmington, Del.: Michael Glazier, 1986); John W. O'Malley, "Developments, Reforms, and Two Great Reformations: Towards a Historical Assessment of Vatican II," *Theological Studies* 44 (1983): 373–406; Joseph Ratzinger, *Theological Highlights of Vatican II* (New York: Paulist Press, 1966); Xavier Rynne, *Vatican Council II* (Maryknoll, N.Y.: Orbis, 1999); Edward Schillebeeckx, *The Real Achievement of Vatican II* (New York: Herder and Herder, 1967); Alberic Stacpoole, ed., *Vatican II Revisited by Those Who Were There* (Minneapolis: Winston, 1986); Herbert Vorgrimler, ed., *Commentary on the Documents of Vatican II*, 5 vols. (New York: Herder and Herder, 1969); Massimo Faggioli, "Vatican II: The History and the Narratives," *Theological Studies* 73, no. 4 (December 2012): 749–67; James F. Keenan, "Vatican II and Theological Ethics," *Theological Studies* 74, no. 1 (March 2013): 162–90; Michael Lacey and Francis Oakley, eds., *The Crisis of Authority in Catholic Modernity* (New York: Oxford University Press, 2011); O'Malley, *What Happened at Vatican II* (Cambridge, Mass.: Belknap Press of Harvard University Press, 2008); and Faggioli, *Vatican II: The Battle for Meaning* (New York: Paulist Press, 2012).

including the use of vernacular language. The importance of Vatican II in the history and direction of the church might best be stated in the work of the Jesuit theologian Karl Rahner. In his division of church history into epochs, Rahner provides three: the apostolic era, 30–49, the era of the church, 49–1962, and the era of Vatican II, 1962 to the present.[17]

The Second Vatican Council had significant impact on the American church, raising many issues. Many Catholic intellectuals in the United States offered their ideas on the concerns and questions that were central at the close of the council. The priest sociologist Andrew Greeley proposed three questions central to the American church in the post-conciliar age: (1) Can and ought the church trust the modern world? (2) Can the church accept the basic orientations of American society? (3) Should the church seek evolution or revolution?[18] The Catholic philosopher Daniel Callahan suggested the true issue was orthodoxy: What determines orthodoxy and what degree of orthodoxy is necessary for membership? He wrote, "Orthodoxy is a value in the Church, yet by no means the most important. At times it must give way to the more pressing demand of charity and intellectual investigation."[19] The noted educator Jacqueline Grennan suggested that the question of the post-conciliar American church was authority and responsibility of decision-making.[20]

The heart of the question and the subsequent struggle for control in the American church can be understood best by comparing two opposed views on its approach to society. Leslie Dewart, a professor of philosophy at St. Michael's College, University of Toronto, believed the church had clung far too long to the belief that change is impossible for fear of what might happen. He wrote, "In the person of John XXIII, the Catholic Church now made an active faith in the precisely opposite idea: that the truth of Christianity needs for its health perfection and development the reality of man's individual and cultural growth and consciousness."[21] The Jesuit priest and retreat director Herbert Smith took a completely opposite tact:

There is serious evidence that the invitation to all members of Christ to participate in the search for answers is leading to a "George Gallup attitude" toward truth. Is

17. Karl Rahner, *Theological Investigations*, vol. 20, *Concern for the Church* (London: Darton, Longman, and Todd, 1981), 77–89, especially 82–84.
18. Robert G. Hoyt, ed., *Issues That Divide the Church* (New York: MacMillan, 1967), 8–9.
19. Quoted in Ibid., 3–4.
20. Ibid., 10.
21. Leslie Dewart, "Have We Loved the Past Too Long?" *America* 115 (December 17, 1966): 799.

the search still for truth or only for answers? Is the sense of God being lost amid a secularist anthropocentric Christianity so that the sense of sin is degenerating from awareness of tragic personal offense against God into a concept of more psychological aberration or of misconduct through ignorance—an error as old as Plato? Is the purpose of Vatican II now being undermined by doctrinal self-seeking, secularist evaluators and the promotion of personal idiosyncrasies?[22]

This stark contrast begs another question that was central to the whole debate in the post-conciliar American church: Can varied views of Catholicism coexist? The prominent Catholic journalist Donald J. Thorman expressed the need for ecumenism and dialogue within the church. Without such a discussion, he concluded, "We shall be in danger of hardening our deep-seated differences of opinion into permanent divisions." Realizing the reality of serious differences, yet believing in the need to learn from one another, he presented his approach:

If we seriously intend to build a working unity durable enough to withstand the contemporary pressures of a new-found freedom and an increasing less "Orthodox" and traditional theology, we must begin immediately to initiate our own "ecumenical movement" within the Church. Increasingly there are variant viewpoints within the Church, viewpoints that can be called Catholic or Orthodox, but which represent divergent worldviews and philosophies of life. Before there is open conflict we must begin to develop the wonderful ecumenical habit of tolerant dialogue and mutual self-seeking.[23]

Daniel Callahan was equally forceful in his call for the spirit of greater openness, as he understood the council to teach:

Can we make room for people like this in the Church? The sufferers? The wavering seekers? Those who have hard questions to ask? The experimenters? The alienated? The creative mavericks? Or are we to continue playing the inquisitorial role (now modified, but not abolished), driving these people from our midst? Are we a community of love—of patience, mutual sharing of pain, fellow seekers of truth—or do we prefer to go on allowing the principle of orthodoxy to devour some of our own children? Those who need the Church as much as we do?[24]

The issues generated by Vatican II that became the subject of dialogue and debate in the post—conciliar church brought American Catholicism to

---

22. Herbert F. Smith, "Assent to God after the Council," *America* 116 (February 25, 1967): 284–85.
23. Quoted in Hoyt, *Issues That Divide the Church*, x.
24. Quoted in ibid., 5.

a new self-identity. Leslie Dewart explained that American Catholicism was now socially and historically determined; the concrete concept of faith in the past was now shattered.[25] Social historians Maurice Isserman and Michael Kazin wrote:

> During the 1960s the world of American Catholicism imploded and had to be rebuilt.... The most tradition laden of Western churches suddenly became the site of furious innovation—and of an equally vehement backlash among the defenders of old ways.[26]

The church found itself in a state of confusion, torn between opposing views. The old adage "Scratch one Catholic and they all bleed," no longer seemed to apply. Rather, some were using the term "A church in revolution." Bishop James Shannon, auxiliary in St. Paul, Minnesota, used this expression, stating, "The transformation going on in the Church is so profound that any lesser term is inadequate to describe it."[27] The Catholic scholar Douglas Roche provided this analysis:

> Here, I think, lies the essence of the revolution. The "underground church" as a loose union of liturgical experimenters, no matter how far out, is only a phenomenon. The underlying reality is a change of attitude toward the institution, the altered concept of what it means to be a Catholic.[28]

The most prominent image of American Catholicism in the post-conciliar era was unquestionably a church in the process of adaptation. The priest and canon lawyer Peter Shannon clearly articulated this position:

> The Church is, in the words of Vatican II, a pilgrim Church, always moving, always changing. Thus all Church laws, as such, partake of a provisional non-absolute dimension. The Church of 1967 is not the same as the Church of 1917 because the world of 1967 is not the same as the world of 1917. And the Church, in its law as well as its worship, must adapt itself to the social conditions of the world in which it finds itself at a given point in its pilgrimage. Otherwise the Church cannot possibly transform the world or even relate to the world.[29]

---

25. Dewart, "Have We Loved the Past Too Long?" 800.
26. Maurice Isserman and Michael Kazin, *America Divided: The Civil War of the 1960s* (New York: Oxford University Press, 2000), 248.
27. Quoted in Douglas J. Roche, "Catholic Revolution," *Catholic World* 208 (October 1968): 34.
28. Ibid., 33–34.
29. Peter M. Shannon, "Changing Law in a Changing Church," *America* 116 (February 18, 1967): 249.

The Redemptorist father and prominent writer Francis X. Murphy was highly critical of bishops who did not take the ideas of Vatican II seriously, believing them to have "taken refuge in an intransigent attitude of both suspicion and repression." He summarized a more progressive and clearly dominant American Catholic view in the wake of the council:

> What this [the message of the council] means is that the ideology behind the Church's doctrinal statements is open to reconsideration and possible challenge. It does not mean that the fundamental truths of divine revelation and their derivatives as defined by the popes and Councils or the doctrinal facts embodied in the Church's fundamental conditions are open to question. But it is possible that even these truths and traditions will undergo re-evaluation and restatement.[30]

The Catholic sociologist Thomas O'Dea articulated one of the most balanced views of the state of the post-conciliar American church. He certainly believed Vatican II to be a watershed event where

> the aspirations for renewal and reform represent a second major attempt to bring the Christian religion into a relevant relationship with the evolving modern world characterized by science, technology, the demise of traditional social and political entities, the vast expansion of knowledge, rapid communications, and a new valuation of secular activity.[31]

He believed that the spirit of *aggiornamento* "represent[ed] a great and indeed probably final opportunity for Christianity." Yet Catholicism will only succeed "by preserving its own unity, for only a unified body can provide the setting for genuine dialogue among various tendencies and perspectives which are found in the great historic process."[32]

American Catholicism's ongoing quest for self-identity was a subject addressed by Protestant theologians, as well. The prominent theologian Harvey Cox, in his seminal work, *The Secular City*, spoke in generic terms:

> This is the age of the secular city.... The world looks less and less to religious rules and rituals for its morality or its meanings.... For fewer and fewer does it [religion]

---

30. Francis X. Murphy, "Defection: Protest or Treason?" *America* 116 (February 11, 1967): 198–99. Murphy also stated, "The Council's documents have introduced substantial changes in the explanation of the Church's teaching concerning its very nature. The decrees refashion the whole problematic of *communicatio in sacris* and give a new situational emphasis to Catholic moral thinking about man's nature, not to mention the basic reforms in both doctrinal preaching and ritual practice in the Constitution on the Liturgy."

31. Thomas F. O'Dea, *The Catholic Crisis* (Boston: Beacon, 1968), 3, 5.

32. Ibid., 9.

provide an inclusive and community system of personal and cosmic values and explanations.[33]

Will Herberg was much more direct characterizing American Catholicism in disarray, sapped of its strength. But in contrast to the prevailing message of Catholic resistance to progressivism, Herberg suggested that the culprit was modernity. He wrote,

> What *aggiornamento* has done, what has been taking place in the backwash of Vatican II, is that the morale of the Church has been sapped, the armature of faith has been weakened, the lid has been lifted and the word has gone out from certain elements speaking in the name of the Council that anything goes, that open season has been declared on the Church and on the ancient Church tradition.

Further, Herberg suggested, "Once it [the church] boasted *semper eadem* (always the same); today in the view of the 'progressives,' the appropriate maxim would seem to become 'Everything subject to change without notice.'" He suggested that the church's resistance to pervasive religious liberalism, secularism, and communism were its perennial strengths. However, in 1968 he concluded, "I find all of these points of Catholic strength seriously challenged, imperiled, and in some cases actually eroded within the church, all in the name of Vatican II and the spirit of *aggiornamento*.[34]

Thus, from both Catholic and Protestant viewpoints, post-conciliar American Catholicism found itself in a period of great internal upheaval, confusion, and uncertainty. The historian Philip Gleason, using the word "disintegration" to describe this era in the church, wrote, "The strongest sense I had was of a Church, a religious tradition that was undone, breaking apart, losing its coherence."[35] Symptoms of disintegration included a massive exodus from the priesthood and religious life, the drop-off in vocations, the closing of Catholic schools, a breakdown of respect for ecclesiastical authority, and the sexual revolution. The chaos felt by many American Catholics during this period was accentuated when people recalled the great sense of unity that dominated the church between 1920 and 1960. The disintegrative impact of changes in the post-conciliar church was especially trou-

---

33. Harvey Cox, *The Secular City: Secularization and Urbanization in Theological Perspective* (Toronto: MacMillan, 1965), 3.
34. Will Herberg, "Plight of American Catholicism," *National Review* 20 (August 27, 1968): 852.
35. Philip Gleason, "In Search of Unity: American Catholic Thought, 1920–1960," *Catholic Historical Review* 65 (1979): 186.

blesome to those whose faith had been formed during the comparatively peaceful period between 1920 and 1960.[36]

The fallout from the 1968 publication of *Humanae Vitae*, the Encyclical letter of Pope Paul VI, reinforcing and reiterating the traditional church prohibition against all forms of artificial birth control, also had a devastating effect on the American church.[37] John O'Brien, a professor of theology at the University of Notre Dame, commented on the seriousness of the crisis:

> This document [*Humanae Vitae*] produced a painful crisis of conscience for many churchmen—and a crisis in the Church itself more serious than any since the mighty religious appeal of the 16th century which split Christendom into fragments.

He suggested that people should follow their own enlightened conscience with respect to the birth control issue, "for such a conscience will be to you stronger than a wall of brass and radiant with the luster of God."[38]

As important as it was, the Second Vatican Council was only one episode in an era of dramatically shifting traditions, experienced as a shift in social and cultural values, especially in the United States. Beginning in 1954 with the famous *Brown v. Board of Education* Supreme Court ruling, which reversed the 1896 *Plessy v. Ferguson* decision of "separate but equal" schools and sought to end racial segregation in public education, the American Civil Rights Movement marched forward. With the leadership of Martin Luther King Jr. and his Southern Christian Leadership Conference, as well as the more militant approach of Black Power advocates Malcolm X and Stokely Carmichael, the movement peaked in the sixties, effecting legal

---

36. Ibid., 186–89.

37. Unquestionably the primary example of the breakdown in ecclesiastical authority came in the wake of the 1968 publication of *Humane Vitae*, Pope Paul VI's Encyclical letter, which continued the church's traditional stance against artificial forms of birth control. The negative reaction to the pope's letter was heightened when it was revealed that the majority opinion of the Papal Birth Control Commission, established by John XXIII and continued by Paul VI, recommended some modification in the church's teaching in this area. The priest sociologist Andrew Greeley argues that *Humanae Vitae* was the principal catalyst to upheaval in the American church, manifest most significantly by losses from the priesthood and religious life; see Greeley, "American Catholics—Ten Years Later," *Critic* 33 (January–February 1975): 14–21. For a full history and analysis of the Papal Birth Control Commission and *Humanae Vitae*, see Robert McClory, *Turning Point: The Inside Story of the Papal Birth Control Commission and How Humanae Vitae Changed the Life of Patty Crowley and the Future of the Church* (New York: Crossroad, 1995).

38. John A. O'Brien, "Birth Control and the Catholic Conscience," *Reader's Digest* 94 (January 1969): 112, 115.

change and social transformation.³⁹ Catholic officials, although not totally supportive to African Americans (especially Catholics) in the past, began to take a bolder stand with the black community and its quest for racial justice. Priests and religious marched with Dr. King and other civil rights advocates. Father Theodore Hesburgh, CSC, president of the University of Notre Dame, served as a member of the U.S. Civil Rights Commission beginning in 1957 and acted as its chair from 1969 to 1972.⁴⁰

The 1960s was also a period of great disillusionment for many Americans. Beginning in the late 1950s under President Dwight Eisenhower, American involvement in the war in Vietnam escalated, expanding to other nations of Southeast Asia. Although the United States had been embroiled in several armed conflicts in the twentieth century, including two world wars and Korea, the nation had never found itself engaged in such an unpopular and misunderstood conflict, creating dissension on all fronts and breaking the lives of so many, including President Lyndon Johnson, who prosecuted and escalated the war throughout his tenure in office.⁴¹ The 1960s also wit-

---

39. The volume of material associated with the American Civil Rights Movement is staggering. Some representative significant sources are: Herbert Aptheker, *Anti-Racism in U.S. History: The First Two Hundred Years* (New York: Greenwood, 1992); Joseph Barndt, *Dismantling Racism: The Continuing Challenge to White America* (Minneapolis: Augsburg, 1991); Jack Bloom, *Class, Race, and the Civil Rights Movement* (Bloomington: University of Indiana Press, 1987); Rhoda Lois Blumberg, *Civil Rights: the 1960s Freedom Struggle* (Boston: Twayne, 1984); Kenneth B. Clark, "The Civil Rights Movement: Momentum and Organization," *Daedalus* 95 (Winter 1966): 595–625; John Hope Franklin, *The Color Line: Legacy for the Twenty-First Century* (Columbia: University of Missouri Press, 1993); David J. Garrow, *Protest at Selma: Martin Luther King and the Voting Rights Act of 1965* (New Haven, Conn.: Yale University Press, 1978); Henry Hampton and Steve Fayer (with Sarah Flynn), *Voices of Freedom: An Oral History of the Civil Rights Movement from the 1950s through the 1980s* (New York: Bantam, 1990); Herbert Hill and James E. Jones, *Race in America: The Struggle for Equality* (Madison: University of Wisconsin Press, 1993); Peter B. Levy, ed., *Documentary History of the Modern Civil Rights Movement* (Westport, Conn.: Greenwood, 1992); and Harvard Sitkoff, *The Struggle for Black Equality, 1954–1992* (New York: Hill and Wang, 1993).

40. The most significant failure of the American church toward African Americans was its reticence to allow them to be ordained priests. The full story of this failure is told in Stephen Ochs, *Desegregating the Altar: The Josephites and the Struggle for Black Priests 1871–1960*, (Baton Rouge: Louisiana State University Press, 1990).

41. The literature associated with American involvement in Vietnam is abundant. A few representative books on the subject are: Peter A. Poole, *Eight Presidents and Indochina* (Huntington, N.Y.: R. E. Krieger, 1978); Robert D. Schulzinger, *A Time for War: The United States and Vietnam, 1941–1975* (New York: Oxford University Press, 1997); Allan R. Millett, *A Short History of the Vietnam War* (Bloomington: Indiana University Press, 1978); James W. Mooney and Thomas R. West, eds., *Vietnam: A History and Anthology* (St. James, N.Y.: Brandywine, 1994); Marilyn Blatt Young, *The Vietnam Wars, 1945–1990* (New York: Harper Collins, 1991); Stein Tonnesson, *Vietnam 1946: How*

nessed the assassinations of leading Americans, including President John F. Kennedy in 1963 and, within two months of each other in 1968, Martin Luther King Jr. and Senator Robert Kennedy. Social unrest, the desire of freedom and autonomy that characterized the "counter culture," and a general distrust of traditional structures created an environment of disillusionment.

Naval Academy Chaplain

In April 1966 Jake Laboon exchanged his heavy parka needed for the Alaskan winter for the light sweater of the mid-Atlantic spring when he arrived at the naval academy. He joined a team of five chaplains that also included Captain James Reaves, Commander Mark Sullivan, and lieutenant commanders Roy Popst and Charles Greenwood. While all were subject to Reaves as senior chaplain, Jake was also responsible to Sullivan, who served as the senior Catholic chaplain.[42] Shortly after he arrived, on July 1, he was advanced to the permanent rank of lieutenant commander, although he had been wearing the gold oak leaves symbolic of that rank since August 1963.

It did not take Jake long to settle into his new ministry, for he was quite familiar with the environment from his student days at the academy. He was certainly happy about being in Annapolis, referring to his presence as "a plum assignment," but he was somewhat surprised that he had been selected for this position. He wrote to his provincial, "Although I had known for some time that I was slated for the Academy, nevertheless the orders came as somewhat of a surprise. Since I volunteered for duty in Vietnam, I thought that might get priority."[43] The provincial told Laboon, "I look forward to having you in the area again." He was certain that other Maryland Province Jesuits felt the same.[44] Jake was provided a home in the Yard near Worden Field, the parade ground at the academy. His residence gave him

---

the War Began (Berkeley: University of California Press, 2010); Michael Hunt, ed., *A Vietnam War Reader: A Documentary History from American and Vietnamese Perspectives* (Chapel Hill: University of North Carolina Press, 2010); Herbert Y. Schandler, *America in Vietnam: The War That Couldn't Be Won* (Lanham, Md.: Rowman and Littlefield, 2009); A. J. Langguth, *Our Vietnam: The War, 1954–1975* (New York: Simon and Schuster, 2000).

42. John Laboon, eulogy for Michael Smith, tape recording, 1986, PPJL; USNA catalog, 1966–67, AUSNA; annual register of USNA, 1966–67, USNA annual report 1967, NHM.

43. *Catholic Review*, July 17, 1981, AABa; John Laboon, SJ, to Edward Sponga, SJ, January 18, 1966, Laboon file, ASJM.

44. Edward Sponga, SJ, to John Laboon, SJ, January 22, 1966, Laboon file, ASJM.

the opportunity to offer hospitality to his many friends, who often came to attend sports events.[45] The ease with which he moved into his new work was clearly evident from a fitness report generated only a few months after his arrival: "During the brief period of this report, he has demonstrated warmth, enthusiasm, and dedication."[46]

Laboon's new assignment brought multiple duties and required his presence and participation with various faiths. As an academy chaplain Jake's first responsibility was, of course, to the midshipmen, but chaplains also served staff officers and enlisted sailors, civilian professors and families, and the community at the naval station across the Severn River from the academy.[47] The USNA catalog described the chaplain's role:

> Chaplains are always available for counseling at their offices in the Chapel and at Bancroft Hall. They welcome the opportunity to meet with parents and join them in the hope that the faith of their sons will grow and flourish during their time as Midshipmen at the Naval Academy.[48]

At the time midshipmen were required to attend divine worship services on Sundays. Catholics attended Mass in the academy chapel; Protestants attended a common chapel service or traveled to the church of their choice in the city of Annapolis. Midshipmen of the Jewish and Greek Orthodox traditions attended synagogue or church services in town. Consistent with this policy, the superintendent, Rear Admiral Draper Kauffman, stated, "I hope we never forget the order of priority of our written mission—to develop midshipman *morally* [emphasis Kauffman], mentally and physically."[49] Jake's basic role was that of a pastor, but with extended duties. Working with the chaplain staff, Jake assisted at the sacraments, but he also helped with such projects as the presentation of Handel's "Messiah" and a twelve-part lecture series to 1/C midshipmen on the role of the chaplain in the U.S. Navy. Chaplains also conducted briefings to 4/C midshipmen as part of the revised plebe indoctrination program, assisted with Bible study classes, and

---

45. Joseph Ryan, interview with the author, March 2, 2011; Tom Laboon, interview with the author, February 24, 2011,
46. LCDR John Laboon, fitness report, September 8, 1966, NMPR.
47. Robert Ecker, interview with the author, December 17, 2010.
48. USNA catalog, 1966–67, USNA command history, 1967, NHM.
49. Robert F. McComas, "The Chaplain's Ministry at the Naval Academy," *Navy Chaplain's Bulletin* (Summer 1968): 7 (emphasis Kauffman).

were active with the Naval Academy Christian Association.[50] One of Jake's classmates, Admiral Randy King, then serving as head of engineering at the academy, remembered the chaplains' office as a smooth operation. He commented, "There was a nice exchange of chaplains."[51]

One of Jake Laboon's most prominent ministries at the academy was his work with the Pre-Cana program, the Roman Catholic marriage preparation program. Laboon conducted these classes, generally offered in groups of six to eight couples, at his quarters. Besides the more informal group sessions, Jake met with each couple individually, speaking to them about personal issues or whatever might be relevant to the couple. Many midshipmen spoke of how fulfilling these sessions were, providing practical advice on many issues. Former Senator James Webb (D-Va.) commented, "We were amazed at his frank comments and approach."[52] The efficacy of Laboon's ministry and respect that others held for him was clearly evident:

> He engaged the group; he elicited responses which were not always in keeping with Catholic teachings; he showed all of us (Mids and fiancés) that the Catholic Church was more than stilted ceremony and remote priests. I do not believe that any member of our group left those meetings with anything but the highest regard for Jake and a better understanding of the role of the Church in our lives.[53]

The pastoral way that Jake approached this ministry to engaged couples was refreshing and consistent with the prevailing, more progressive view of Vatican II. The experience drew others to him and prompted people to take a new look at the church.

In addition to his ministry with the Pre-Cana program, Jake was also moderator of the academy's Newman Club, which met twice a month. Jake's experience and numerous friends provided him with contacts to invite well-known guests to speak to club members, including the famous heavyweight boxing champion Rocky Marciano and Bishop Peter Moran of Aberdeen,

---

50. Quarterly report, USNA chaplains' office, October–December, 1967, January 4, 1968, folder 5216/8, box 153, NCA; chapel papers, box 1 (folder 9), correspondence and miscellaneous materials, AUSNA. Bible study was conducted at 0600 on Mondays "with pretty fair attendance"; see McComas, "Chaplain's Ministry," 10.

51. Admiral Randy King, interview with the author, April 7, 2011.

52. Steve and Maureen Phillips, interview with the author, November 17, 2010; John O'Neill, interview with the author, February 21, 2011; Felix Bassi, interview with the author, May 4, 2011; James Webb, interview with the author, October 4, 2010.

53. Ed Sullivan, e-mail to the author, December 2, 2010.

Scotland. In 1967 Jake asked the famous Jesuit theologian John Courtney Murray to speak to the group in September. He felt remiss in making suggestions as to what Murray might use as a topic, but nonetheless suggested "Authority in the Church" in the light of Vatican II.[54] Although Murray was not able to speak, it was clear to Jake that he "cast a huge spiritual shadow" that touched the hearts of many. Speaking of Laboon's association with the club, Dennis Rizzardi, who served as the Newman president for the class of 1968, commented:

> The thing about Father Laboon is the quietness and serenity he possessed. When you are around him you are totally relaxed. He was a man of the world, but somehow you knew you were in the presence of a Saint. He never bragged or talked about himself. He was one of the nicest and kindest people I have ever known. He exuded calmness and spiritual confidence, and those around him could not but be affected.[55]

Other academy groups and many individuals also felt the gentle touch of Father Jake. He worked directly with the Catholic glee club and often traveled with the Catholic Chapel Choir.[56] His preaching was moving and effective. Those who heard him speak described his homilies as down-to-earth. One person commented, "He could relate to midshipmen. He preached more to midshipmen than others at Mass. He was neither afraid to voice his opinions nor to speak about controversial topics. For example, he never shied away from speaking about the War in Vietnam. He took the fighting off the front page and made it real, allowing his congregation to feel the situation and the emotions. He never spoke above people, but rather "spoke in every man's language."[57]

The relationship of mutual respect that Jake Laboon built between himself and the midshipmen was based on his vast experience, pastoral

---

54. John Laboon to John Courtney Murray, March 17, 1967; John Courtney Murray to John Laboon, March 28, 1967; John Laboon to John Courtney Murray, July 21, 1967, John Courtney Murray papers, box 1, folder 134, AGU. It appears that Murray and Laboon were never able to agree on a mutually convenient time.

55. Dennis Rizzardi, e-mail to the author, January 26, 2011. In 1968 there were 140 members of the Catholic choir, under the direction of MUC Joseph McCuen, USN; see McComas, "Chaplain's Ministry," 9.

56. Besides the Newman Club for Catholics, the Naval Academy Christian Association (NACA) was very popular with midshipmen; see McComas, "Chaplain's Ministry," 9.

57. Steve and Maureen Phillips, interview with the author, November 17, 2010; Len Mrozak, interview with the author, August 17, 2011; Bruce Kahn, interview with the author, August 3, 2011.

sensitivity, and warm personality. From the outset, the midshipmen were well aware that he had been "one of their own," a reality that brought him instant respect. Jake had immediate credibility because he understood the academy environment; he knew how to talk to midshipmen, to get to their level, and to understand their concerns, hopes, and desires.[58] His reporting senior commented only months after his arrival, "Chaplain Laboon is particularly well qualified for duty at the Naval Academy. As a Graduate of the Class of 1944, and an experienced submarine officer in combat, he is in a very fine position to establish rapport with the midshipmen."[59] Laboon's commanding physical, yet never intimidating, presence made him noticeable to everyone; midshipmen could identify with him in every way. Additionally, he had experienced the navy during a time of war, which gave him a perspective that added to the magnetic attraction he had upon people. Admiral Mike Mullen, former chairman of the Joint Chiefs of Staff, remembered how he and his naval academy classmates thought of Jake: "He was a very special human being we all revered."[60]

For many of the midshipmen, he was much more than a chaplain. Even as a senior officer he served as a mentor and friend to many students who felt close and connected to him. John O'Neill, a member of the class of 1968, commented:

His stature, height, cigar, ready smile, and friendliness were extraordinarily attractive to us as young men and he became in many respects a role model, as a Catholic man, especially one who was going to be a military officer.

He concluded, "The influence that Laboon had on midshipmen cannot be overestimated."[61]

The magnetism of Jake Laboon's influence on midshipmen attracted Catholics and non-Catholics alike. Former Senator James Webb, a non-Catholic, spoke of how Laboon possessed a rare and special ability to listen to people and respond with ideas and thoughts that were principled but never

---

58. James Webb, interview with the author, October 4, 2010; Kevin Kidd, interview with the author, October 5, 2010.

59. LCDR John Laboon, fitness report, September 8, 1966, NMPR; Steve and Maureen Phillips, interview with the author, November 17, 2010; Len Mrozak, e-mail to the author, February 28, 2011. In agreement with Laboon's reporting senior, Mrozak stated, "Being an Academy grad[uate] himself, it was easy for him to establish rapport with the mids."

60. Mike Mullen to the author, November 23, 2010.

61. John O'Neill, interview with the author, April 26, 2011.

judgmental. Midshipmen listened to him and took to heart what he had to say. Webb concluded, "I never met a man of God that I respected more than Father Laboon."[62] Bill Murray, another non-Catholic member of the class of 1968, wrote, "There was a true admiration and loyalty by all who had contact with Father Laboon during their time at the Academy."[63]

Midshipmen were smitten by Laboon's tough, no-nonsense approach. Their respect for him was not derived from a pandering attitude that praised midshipmen because some had declared them "America's finest," or that he understood the "Mid's life," but rather from a perspective of expectation and high standards. One midshipman commented, "Laboon did not tell you what to think, but challenged you in how to think."[64] He did not allow midshipmen to slack off, but rather always mandated high principles and values. Jake expected midshipmen to act in the role they would soon take, as an officer and a gentleman. One midshipman related a story that characterized his expectations. One Sunday at the end of Mass he asked all midshipmen to stay in the chapel, excusing others. He proceeded to give the Mids a severe tongue-lashing, for he realized that when the congregation was processing up to receive Communion, some midshipmen, sitting in the "Sleepy Hollow" section of the chapel, were "rating" young women, presumably dates of other midshipmen. The midshipman concluded, "He [Laboon] would not put up with nonsense from anybody."[65] Laboon did not refrain from chastising midshipmen from the pulpit. On one occasion, during the semester break, Jake offered a retreat that very few attended. Disappointed in what he perceived to be poor choices, Jake lashed out, stating, "Instead of going on retreat you will be shacking up with your girlfriends." His words shocked many.[66]

The high standards that Laboon set for midshipmen did not in any way negate his strong respect for them. Only two years before his death, when offering a eulogy for Michael Smith, class of 1967 and member of the ill-fated *Challenger* space shuttle disaster, Jake expressed his respect for the

62. James Webb, interview with the author, October 4, 2010.
63. Bill Murray, e-mail to the author, January 23, 2011.
64. John O'Neill, interview with the author, February 26, 2011.
65. James O'Brien, interview with the author, January 11, 2011. "Sleepy Hollow" is a section in the balcony of the naval academy chapel where midshipmen often would doze or sleep during liturgical services, trying to "catch a few winks" lost during the week just ending. Again, Jake's personal experience as a midshipman allowed him to see and analyze a situation, whereas other chaplains might be completely blind to what was happening.
66. Steve and Maureen Phillips, interview with the author, November 17, 2010.

commitment made by them. He told the midshipmen that he came before them "to show my respect for you ... for coming to the Naval Academy, and giving your youth to God and your country." He told them, "You and I know what our dedication means." Combining his understanding of military life and his faith, he offered words of congratulations within the context of the commitment the men and women before him had made:

> The day you raised your right hands, standing with your classmates in front of Bancroft Hall, the day you were sworn in as midshipmen in the United States Navy. That was the moment of truth. That was the moment you died to yourself. You literally gave your life for your country at that moment.[67]

As a member of the chaplain corps, Jake Laboon was assigned to the naval academy to provide religious and related services to midshipmen and the other communities in the Yard, but his accessibility, presence, and personality transcended such limited responsibilities. His constant presence in the Yard at all sorts of functions made him very much a part of the brigade's life. One midshipman opined, "He was always around—in the yard, on the field, and in Bancroft Hall. He was at all events; he was everywhere all the time."[68] Another commented, "He created an emotional environment around him that made us like to be in his presence."[69] One of his fitness reports spoke of how Jake gave "unstintedly [sic] of himself to the Brigade of Midshipmen."[70] Jake would often stroll the Yard, talking with midshipmen about whatever was on their minds. His dedicated ministry of presence to midshipmen, his constant availability, was noticed by his superiors:

> He has been a midshipman and has taken the time to know the midshipman today. His interest in them and dedication to the priesthood has [sic] won him the respect of all.... He is seen everywhere midshipmen are gathered. His total involvement in their life opens up avenues of service by which he is able to help large numbers of them professionally.[71]

Jake's ministry was not pointed to Catholics alone—all benefited from his wisdom. Such openness and broad perspective were noted by his reporting

---

67. John Laboon, eulogy for Michael Smith, 1986, tape recording, PPJL. In 1976 the first women were admitted to all the service academies, including the naval academy.
68. Tom Laboon, interview with the author, February 24, 2011.
69. Jonathan Hine, interview with the author, December 13, 2010.
70. LCDR John Laboon, fitness report, June 6, 1967, Laboon file, NMPR.
71. LCDR John Laboon, fitness report, May 7, 1968, Laboon file, NMPR.

senior: "Ecumenical in spirit and in purpose, he serves the whole Brigade and Academy community. He promotes the kind of unity that is healthy and desirable."[72] Stories of Jake's presence with one group or another circulated through Bancroft Hall as swiftly as some contagion; soon everyone knew of him, even if one did not personally encounter the man.[73]

The personal approach that typified the ministry of Jake Laboon made him, even in his own time, "a living legend."[74] He was described as "a guy's guy," "a man's man," equipped with a personality, interest, and loving concern that allowed him to relate well to midshipmen. His senior chaplain commented, "Chaplain Laboon has a great appeal for midshipmen."[75] Yet it was his approachability that drew people to him. One midshipman captured the thoughts of many when describing a conversation with Jake Laboon: "As a midshipman, you felt you were not speaking with an officer; you were speaking with someone who really cared."[76]

Jake Laboon became well-known within the brigade for his pastoral sensitivity. This was manifest generically through his accessibility and the ability he had to help young people talk through whatever was troubling them. He was known to be a good listener; he did not often offer solutions, but rather helped individuals find the answers they sought by themselves.[77] A sports columnist for the *Annapolis Evening Capital* wrote of Laboon, "Jake could get the midshipmen to talk about problems they might have been having. He understood them. He liked them. He enjoyed working with them. He enjoyed helping them."[78] When tragedy or problems struck for a midshipman or his family, Jake was there to assist. When the brother of one midshipman was killed in Vietnam, Jake tracked down the midshipman and with sensitivity informed him of what had happened. He did everything he could to assist midshipmen who had issues of conduct or problems in the classroom. One midshipman, who admittedly was not a great student, said, "Father Laboon went out of his way to try and keep me out of trouble when I was going down for my third gasp of air." On another occasion, Laboon

72. Ibid.
73. Bill Murray, e-mail to the author, January 23, 2011.
74. Bishop Francis Roque and Charles Hogan, interview with the author, April 11, 2012.
75. CDR John Laboon, fitness report, December 2, 1968, Laboon file, NMPR.
76. Jonathan Hine, interview with the author, December 13, 2010.
77. Ibid.
78. *Annapolis Evening Capital*, August 3, 1988.

went to bat for a 1/C midshipman who had received a second "Class A" offense, interceding for the young man and most likely saving him from being excused from the academy.[79]

Jake Laboon's ministry of presence was also manifested in his active participation with the academy's sports program, both collegiate and intramural. From his earliest days as a midshipman and continuing throughout his career as a chaplain, Jake never lost his fervor for sport. Beyond his chaplain duties he was often found on the practice field, often in gym clothes, assisting with various sports teams. Alan Cameron, Jake's former football teammate from the 1942 season, was athletic director and welcomed Laboon's participation with the athletic programs. During the fall 1966 season Jake served as an assistant coach for the plebe team, working specifically with ends, the position he played as a midshipman. At times he would don pads and coach by direct example. He was never averse to "mixing it up with the mids."[80] Cameron voiced appreciation in a letter to the senior chaplain at the academy: "Subject duty was performed outside of normal working hours and required the presence of LCDR Laboon on weekends. He performed his duty voluntarily and gave freely of his time.... His contribution is deeply appreciated."[81] In addition to football, Jake assisted with plebe basketball and lacrosse.[82] Also, he often served as a chaplain for the varsity football team, traveling with the squad on numerous occasions and serving in the dual roles of chaplain and avid fan.[83] One sports columnist from the local paper commented, "Jake had a soothing way about him. He demonstrated a combination of the best attributes of a coach and priest. That made him unique."[84]

Jake also served as adviser to the activities committee, which, among other things, was responsible for organizing pep rallies before football

---

79. Kevin Kidd, interview with the author, October 5, 2010; Al Costlow, interview with the author, January 10, 2011. Possibly Jake's own difficulties in the classroom gave him more sympathy with those who struggled with academics.

80. Richard Harvey to John Cardinal O'Connor, February 23, 1993, A-99, folder 10, Archives Archdiocese of New York (hereafter AANY), Yonkers, N.Y.; Steve and Maureen Phillips, interview with the author, November 17, 2010.

81. Director of athletics [Alan Cameron] to senior chaplain, USNA, December 12, 1966, enclosure to fitness report of June 6, 1967, Laboon file, NMPR.

82. CDR John Laboon, fitness report, May 3, 1969, NMPR.

83. Terry Murray, interview with the author, October 25, 2010.

84. *Annapolis Evening Capital*, August 3, 1988.

games. Laboon was tasked with approving planned activities at these rallies. Midshipmen of the period especially remember one occasion during the rally prior to the annual Notre Dame game. One midshipman, dressed like the pope and carrying a bedpan, was conveyed into the pep rally "blessing all with holy water from the bedpan." Clearly, Jake was open to a bit of "off-color humor" if it would promote the spirit of the brigade.[85]

Because he was so involved with the total life of the brigade of midshipmen, Jake Laboon's three-year return to his alma mater passed swiftly. Before his assignment ended, however, he was promoted, in January 1968, to commander. With the reassignment of Chaplain Sullivan, Jake became the lead Catholic chaplain, working with Lieutenant Commander Eugene O'Brien.[86] Appreciation for his work at the academy, expressed by both senior officers and the people he served, was abundant. His unusual combination of previous experience and special gifts was noted, but superiors lauded his accomplishments in new areas, as well. It was noted that Jake was "a priest who has kept himself current regarding new developments in church liturgy, theology, and ecumenism." The latter idea, clearly consistent with the teachings of Vatican II, was an area that gained him great appreciation. His detaching fitness report read in part, "Highly ecumenical minded he [Laboon] promoted harmony between those of all faiths and preached at Protestant Chapel services and invited a Protestant Chaplain to preach at the Mass. He is a popular counselor and an effective speaker." It was, however, his general love for midshipmen that characterized his service at the academy. The report concluded, "He [Laboon] is well known and liked by most midshipmen and he has earned their recognition and respect by extreme devotion to his duties and through involvement in their activities and life of the midshipman."[87]

Conclusion

The opportunity to return to the site of his initial contact with the navy and his vocation as a priest and officer was a pleasant and welcomed surprise to Jake Laboon. Arriving in this familiar setting after a year in the Alaskan

85. Al Costlow, interview with the author, January 10, 2011.
86. USNA catalog, 1968–1969, AUSNA.
87. CDR John Laboon, fitness report, May 3, 1969, NMPR.

wilderness, Jake took to the academy like a fish to water. Gaining instant acceptance by all from his former status as both midshipman and war hero, he made his presence known throughout the Yard. Seemingly omnipresent, whether that was in his role as chaplain, through sacramental ministry, counseling, working with various organizations such as the Newman Club, or his presence on the athletic field as a volunteer assistant coach in plebe football and lacrosse or as varsity football chaplain, Jake's physical presence and his dynamic personality brought people to his side. Always going far beyond what might be expected, he continued to gain the respect of all classes with his ability to navigate safely through waters occupied by the most junior or senior personnel. For many midshipmen, Jake Laboon's presence brought a warm and soothing face to both the most joyous and most heart-wrenching of situations. Having gained the recognition, admiration, and respect of all and with his achievement of senior rank, he stood ready to begin a new chapter in his life that would be inaugurated with his return to war.

Chapter 8

War Chaplain—Vietnam
★ 1969–1970

The social unrest that marked the 1960s in the United States was anchored in the nation's participation in an unpopular war in Vietnam. The length of the conflict, manifested most notably in a continually growing military presence in the area, the apparent lack of progress toward a victorious end, and the morality or, some critics would say, immorality of American involvement in the region, combined with the general disarray of the decade, was a recipe for significant unrest in the United States in general and, more specifically, in the military-industrial complex. The war destroyed the political career of President Lyndon Johnson and became a source of increased conflict concerning America's proper course as the 1960s drew to a close. It would be the task of the newly elected president, Richard Nixon, to set United States U.S. policy and chart a course for the nation's eventual disengagement from the war, becoming the second armed conflict the United States had not brought to a successful completion in its two-hundred-year history.[1]

While the historical record shows that Jake Laboon had volunteered as early as 1966 for Vietnam, it was only with the completion of his tour at the naval academy in April 1969 that he received orders to serve with the U.S. Marines as a regimental chaplain. As a result of their interservice connection, the marines in Vietnam were serviced by navy chaplains. The first navy chaplain to actually serve with the Marine Corps was Father J. F. Flem-

---

1. Many historians would suggest the stalemate in Korea (June 1950 to July 1953) was not a successful end where clear victory was attained.

ing, who in 1912 went ashore with marines in a campaign in Nicaragua. Five years later, beginning in 1917, navy chaplains began to serve with marines on a continuous basis.[2]

Jake Laboon brought his indomitable spirit, positive view on life, and his desire to serve those in harm's way. These qualities provided both the motivation and the base from which his ministry would emanate and develop. Having served in the Pacific during World War II, Laboon could well understand the mentality, fears, and apprehensions of the men he served in Vietnam. The war's unpopularity in the minds of many Americans only further motivated Jake to fulfill his commission to serve God and country. He would do so utilizing his many gifts, acting at times heroically, but always keeping in mind his commitment to those to whom he dedicated his life in service.

Vietnam–Background

On September 2, 1945, Vietnam declared its independence from France. In a gesture of support, U.S. warplanes and U.S. Army officers were present in Hanoi when the announcement was made. The historian George Herring has commented:

The prominent role played by Americans at the birth of modern Vietnam appears in retrospect one of history's most bitter ironies. Despite the glowing professions of friendship on September 2, the United States acquiesced in the return of French troops to Vietnam and from 1950 to 1954 actively supported French efforts to suppress Ho's [Ho Chi Minh] revolution, the first phase of a quarter-century American struggle to control the destiny of Vietnam.[3]

America's presence at this event, the same day that the official peace treaty ending the war in the Pacific was signed on the battleship *Missouri* in Tokyo Bay, was not indicative of the basic anti-Communism foreign policy followed by the United States for almost the next fifty years.

The Allied victory in World War II actually set the stage for the Cold War, which pitted the democratic West against the Communist-controlled East. The "Containment Policy" of President Harry Truman was the United States'

---

2. CDR Robert Warren, "The Naval Chaplaincy," folder 5750/11, historical articles, box 27, NCA; Mode, *Grunt Padre*, 62.

3. George C. Herring, *America's Longest War: United States and Vietnam, 1950–1975* (Philadelphia: Temple University Press, 1996), 3.

initial response to the Soviet advance in Europe. In April 1946 the principal architect of this policy, George F. Kennan, then serving as deputy head of the U.S. mission in Moscow, warned that Soviet influence in the world needed to "be contained by the adroit and vigilant application of counterforce at a series of constantly shifting geographical and political points."[4] In accord with this policy, two programs were implemented in Europe: the Truman Doctrine and the Marshall Plan. The Truman Doctrine sought to control the advance of the Soviet Union in the regions of Greece and Turkey by funneling to these nations economic and military aid. The Marshall Plan, officially known as the European Recovery Program (ERP) and named after Secretary of State George Marshall, sought to rebuild European economies by the removal of trade barriers and the modernization of industry.

Although U.S. officials were present when Hanoi declared its independence from France in September 1945, the general manifestation of the "Containment Policy" in Indochina was basically pro-French neutrality. The United States wanted to control any spread of Communism, but believed the responsibility in this region lay with the French. By early 1950, however, American policymakers had embraced the so-called "Domino Theory," the idea that if one nation in Indochina fell to Communism, the other nations in Southeast Asia would soon fall like one domino cascading upon another. Thus, fearful that Vietnam might be the first nation to fall, the United States abandoned neutrality and supported French forces through military and economic aid in its fight against the Vietminh. By the end of 1950 the United States had committed more than $133 million of aid to Indochina.[5]

The Vietnamese revolution against France was in many ways the personal creation of Ho Chi Minh, a highly charismatic patriot who came to prominence as early as 1941 as leader of Vietnam's independence movement. He had joined the Indo-Chinese Communist Party in 1930. The surge of Vietnam's resistance to the French and the alliance forged between Ho Chi Minh and the Soviet Union in 1950 caused U.S. officials concern. Herring comments on the situation: "American officials agreed that Indochina and especially Vietnam was the key to the defense of Southeast Asia."[6] Yet,

4. Kennan telegram, February 22, 1946; see George Washington University, National Security Archive, Cold War Documents, at http://www.gwu.edu/~nsarchiv/coldwar/documents/episode-1/kennan.htm.
5. Herring, *America's Longest War*, 14, 18.
6. Ibid., 5, 13–14.

as France's position weakened and increased aid, including a military presence, was requested from the United States, Washington balked. The end of the Korean War in a stalemate made it clear to many U.S. officials that a land war in Asia would be considerably difficult at best. Therefore, the commitment of ground forces to Vietnam was not seriously considered at the time. NSC Directive 124/2 of June 1952 stated nothing about troops, but suggested the United States should use its "influence to promote political, military, economic and social policies."[7]

The situation in Vietnam came to a climax on May 7, 1954, at Dien Bien Phu. Communist forces had conducted a fifty-five day onslaught of the city, prompting the French to ask the United States to conduct a massive air strike on the region to halt Ho's forces. Congress discussed the idea, but, after Korea, the American people had no stomach for such military action and, therefore, demurred. Without American support the French could not hold out and surrendered. At the ensuing peace treaty negotiations at Geneva, the United States was a reluctant participant. Vietnamese in the north and south agreed to a temporary partition of their country along the 17th parallel to allow regrouping of military forces from each side, to be followed by elections in 1956 that would reunify the nation.[8] Backed by the United States, however, political leaders in South Vietnam, led by Ngo Dinh Diem, blocked the mandated 1956 elections. As the separation between North and South took on a state of permanence, the United States between 1954 and 1961 poured over $1 billion of aid into the region. Yet Diem, a Catholic, was not popular with many in the Buddhist-dominated nation, and Communist forces in the South began to mobilize against him, creating the National Liberation Front (NLF), commonly known as the Viet Cong.[9]

The election of John F. Kennedy in 1961 did not significantly alter American policy in Vietnam. On January 19, 1961, on his last day in office, President Dwight Eisenhower met with Kennedy and their respective cabinets to discuss issues, including Vietnam. Eisenhower was most concerned about Laos, suggesting, using the Domino Theory, that the loss of this nation would precipitate loss of the entire region.[10] When he took office, Kennedy seemed con-

---

7. Quoted in Ibid., 21–23.   8. Ibid., 28–41.
9. Ibid., 43–72.
10. Clark M. Clifford, "A Vietnam Reappraisal: The Personal History of One Man's View and How It Evolved," *Foreign Affairs* 47 (July 1969): 604–5.

cerned about Vietnam, but made no immediate changes. Upon the advice of General Maxwell Taylor, Kennedy introduced U.S. military advisers and increased aid to the nation.[11] Kennedy's rather banal attitude toward Vietnam was not held by all. Clark Clifford, political adviser to four presidents and secretary of defense during the last year of the Johnson administration, held a counter view. After a visit to Vietnam in 1961, he commented, "The loss of South Viet Nam would set in motion a crumbling process that could, as it progressed, have grave consequences for us and for freedom."[12]

Kennedy's assassination on November 22, 1963, brought Lyndon Johnson to the Oval Office, leading to a significant escalation in America's involvement in Vietnam from a limited commitment to open war. Chief among these events was the Tonkin Gulf Resolution, written in response to an attack by North Vietnamese forces on U.S. naval vessels in violation of the Charter of the United Nations and the Southeast Asia Collective Defense Treaty. The resolution, passed by Congress 504–2 on August 7, 1964, stated in part:

> The Congress approves and supports the determination of the President, as Commander-In-Chief, to take all necessary measures to repel any armed attack against the forces of the United States and to prevent further aggression.

The resolution extended this idea beyond Vietnam, authorizing armed force "to assist any member or protocol states of the Southeast Asia Collective Defense Treaty requesting assistance in defense of its freedom."[13] In November Johnson ordered the commencement of air attacks on the North. These attacks, which intensified in February 1965, became the pretext for the introduction of ground troops. Initially two battalions of marines and two battalions of army soldiers were sent. By June 1966 American troop strength in Vietnam had reached 431,000.[14] During this early stage of U.S. involvement, the American people, voicing a patriotic chorus of anti-Communism, were generally supportive of Johnson's policies. However, time, lack of military progress, and especially the mounting number of casualties soon turned public opinion against the war.

---

11. Herring, *America's Longest War*, 73–107.
12. Clifford, "Vietnam Reappraisal," 605.
13. Ibid.; Public Law 88–408, "The Gulf of Tonkin Resolution," U.S. Congress, August 10, 1964; see http://www.cfr.org/united-states/gulf-tonkin-resolution-southeast-asia-resolution-public-law-88-408/p21064.
14. Herring, *America's Longest War*, 108–43.

In early 1968 dissent and calls for a change in American policy increased dramatically after the Tet Offensive. On January 30, 1968, approximately 80,000 North Vietnamese regulars (NVA) simultaneously attacked over one hundred cities and towns throughout South Vietnam. This coordinated attack was wrought against thirty-five of forty-four provincial capitals, thirty-six district towns, and many villages and hamlets. While eventually the onslaught was repulsed, the attack has often been seen by historians as the decisive battle of the war because of its effect on American politics and public attitudes.[15] Indeed, the Tet Offensive led fabled CBS news anchorman Walter Cronkite to proclaim:

> We have been too often disappointed by the optimism of American leaders, both in Vietnam and Washington, to have faith any longer in the silver linings they find in the darkest clouds.... For it seems now more certain than ever that the bloody experience of Vietnam is to end in stalemate. To say that we are mired in stalemate seems the only realistic, yet satisfactory conclusion.[16]

The battle prompted many prominent U.S. officials to agree with Cronkite, voicing with frustration their belief that the war was probably not winnable. Tet placed the NVA in a highly favorable position for a political settlement. On March 31, 1968, in a speech to the nation, President Johnson offered North Vietnam a negotiated peace. To enhance that possibility he announced in the same speech that he would not run for reelection in November. The Paris Peace Talks began on May 10, 1968.[17]

Richard Nixon came to the presidency in January 1969 on a policy of "peace with honor." At a minimum, Nixon demanded, any settlement had to give South Vietnam a chance to survive. On June 8 Nixon met with the president of South Vietnam, Nguyen Van Thieu, on Midway Island. At the end of the conference the two men announced a gradual withdrawal of American forces from Vietnam and a plan of Vietnamization— turning over responsibility to South Vietnamese forces various commands and geographic areas

---

15. Berman, *Zumwalt*, 160–61; J. W. Lewis and J. S. Werner, "The New Stage in Vietnam," *Bulletin of the Atomic Scientists* 25 (January 1969): 21–22.

16. Quoted in Berman, *Zumwalt*, 161.

17. Clifford, "Vietnam Reappraisal," 615; Lewis and Werner, "New Stage in Vietnam," 24. Johnson stated in his speech, "I shall not seek, and will not accept, the nomination of my party for another term as your president." It should also be noted that the surprising strength of Eugene McCarthy in the New Hampshire primary, losing to Johnson by only 7 percent, most likely also was a factor in his decision.

that were now manned by American forces.[18] The plan sounded good on paper, but as editorials in various American magazines stated, South Vietnamese forces simply did not have the manpower or capability to defend their territory, let alone carry the fight to the North.[19] The journalist Maynard Parker believed that the Vietnamization policy was flawed in two significant ways. First, such a plan would still necessitate a force of some 250,000 U.S. troops in the country for years to come. Second, the South Vietnamese Army (ARNV), while improved, could not match the North Vietnamese. Thus he suggested that President Thieu should seek a compromise with the Communists. Such a policy would be risky, but if nothing were done the United States would have to make a deal with Hanoi on its own.[20]

Indeed, 1969, the year Richard Nixon entered the White House and Jake Laboon left the tranquility of the naval academy for the violence and uncertainty of war, was a time when debate about American policy in Vietnam reached a fever pitch, with arguments voiced on both sides. Some suggested the United States needed to continue the fight, based on its previous commitment, the instability of the South Vietnamese armed forces, and the need for strength during the ongoing Paris peace talks. One editorial of the day suggested that an American pullout would embolden the North Vietnamese to strike more frequently and more stridently into the South, placing the entire nation in jeopardy. A. J. Langguth, a journalist for the *New York Times*, wrote:

With more than half a million American troops in Vietnam, the United States cannot walk away. If the United States president began to pull out troops now, he would lessen America's influence in the Paris talks and almost certainly prolong the war. Should the United States withdraw without concluding a peace, forces of Hanoi and the National Liberation Front would win the war, as they would have won four years ago if we had not increased our commitment.[21]

The secretary of defense, Melvin Laird, reported to the American people after a visit to Vietnam, "I regret to report that I see no indication that we can

---

18. Withers M. Moore, Herbert L. Bergsman, and Timothy J. Demy, *Chaplains with U.S. Naval Units in Vietnam, 1954–1975* (Washington, D.C.: History Branch, Office of the Chief of Chaplains, Department of the Navy, 1985), 81.

19. "Can U.S. Get Out of the War Now? Report from Saigon," *U.S. News and World Report* 66 (May 5, 1969): 34.

20. Maynard Parker, "Illusion of Vietnamization," *Newsweek* 74 (September 29, 1969): 33.

21. "Can U.S. Get Out of the War Now?" 34–36; A. J. Langguth, "Vietnam: How Do We Get Out?" *Saturday Evening Post* 242 (February 8, 1969): 19.

presently have a program adequate to bring about a significant reduction to the U.S. military contribution in South Vietnam."[22]

The voices of the "hawks" were more than answered in a resounding chorus by many who viewed American policy in Vietnam as tantamount to insanity. A sense of weariness from more than two decades of armed violence told people, even in Vietnam, that the killing and destruction must cease. The journalist William Pfaff suggested that the success or failure of Nixon's administration would teeter on settling the war promptly. A bad settlement, in his opinion, was better than no settlement of all. He wrote:

> Washington has no reasonable alternative to settlement. The military option has been discredited; no one in Washington can believe that more war of any kind would produce a quick victory; and if there cannot be a quick victory there will have to be a settlement.[23]

Some voices stated that the Nixon policy as it was conceived could not generate a victory in Vietnam. One editorial, published in February 1969, read in part:

> If one is to judge Mr. Nixon by his background, his words or his appointments, then the prospect of peace in Vietnam looks bleak indeed. We have the strength to continue bombing and killing forever—the real question is our faltering will to do so.... For there will be no victory in Vietnam. Only when we realize that unpleasant fact will we be able to make peace.[24]

Dissenters suggested that the United States must drop the illusion that it could achieve its original goal—namely, autonomy for the South Vietnamese people. The perspective that a political compromise would be disastrous paled in the minds of many when paired with the destructive effects of the war. Another editorial spoke of how the United States was "muddl[ing] through this stinking war, knocking off civilization, and pouring forgotten American manhood into the valleys of death."[25] The journalist Maynard Parker summarized the frustration of many:

> The nation wants an end to the war. But the government is moving toward this goal with the same kind of stumbling steps, the same ambivalence that first led it into

---

22. "Laird's Official Report on Vietnam: The Basic Problem Remains; Statement of March 19, 1969," *U.S. News and World Report* 66 (March 31, 1969): 35.
23. William Pfaff, "This Way Out," *Commonweal* 89 (February 14, 1969): 612.
24. "Vietnam: End in Sight?" *Saturday Evening Post* 242, no. 3 (February 8, 1969): 4.
25. "Anachronistic War," *Commonweal* 90 (September 19, 1969): 555–56.

the quagmire; and this erratic route may bring a conclusion no less tragic than the original process of involvement.[26]

Political voices were equally strong that Vietnam was an albatross that weighed down the nation and needed to be removed. Senator George McGovern (D-South Dakota) wrote that U.S. involvement in Vietnam was a "policy of madness— the most tragic diplomatic, military, and moral blunder in our national history."[27] Upon leaving his position as secretary of defense, Clark Clifford suggested, "We cannot realistically expect to achieve anything more through our military force, and the time has come to begin to disengage." He further recommended that it was time to devote more attention and energy to domestic problems and, therefore, to set a chronological limit to U.S. involvement in Vietnam. Clifford expressed the view of many:

> Viet Nam remains unquestionably the transcendent problem that confronts our nation. Though the escalation has ceased, we seem to be no closer to finding our way out of this infinitely complex difficulty. The confidence of the past has become the frustration of the present. Predictions of progress and of military success, made so often by so many, have proved to be illusory as the fighting and the dying continue at a tragic rate. Within our own country, the dialogue quickens and the debate sharpens. There is a growing impatience among our people, and questions regarding the war and our participation in it are being asked with increasing vehemence.[28]

Speaking on the floor of the United States Senate, Frank Church (D-Idaho) suggested, "There is no victory we can win in Vietnam worthy of the name." He suggested that the time has come to end the pretense that achieving an honorable settlement and avoiding a disqualified defeat are possible. He stated, "The truth is that as long as our troops stay in South Vietnam, we shall occupy a hostile country. There is no way that the United States, as a foreign power and a Western one at that, can win a civil war among the Vietnamese."[29] He suggested that few fail to recognize that America's original intervention was an error. He wrote, "Two years ago, our political skies

---

26. Parker, "Illusion of Vietnamization," 32.
27. George McGovern, "Ending the Vietnam War," *Current* 111 (October 1969): 14.
28. Clifford, "Vietnam Reappraisal," 601. Clifford wrote further (603), "Decisions which our nation faces today in Viet Nam should ... be based upon our present view of our obligations as a world power; upon our current concept of our national security; upon our conclusions regarding our commitments as they exist today; upon our fervent desire to contribute to peace throughout the world; and, hopefully, upon our acceptance of the principle of enlightened self-interest."
29. Frank Church, "Vietnam: Disengagement Now," *Vital Speeches* 36 (November 1, 1969): 34.

were still filled with hawks; today scarcely a hawk can be seen on the wing."[30] Analogizing America's participation in Vietnam to the British in the American Revolution, and clearly discrediting the Domino Theory, Church believed that the United States would suffer no long-lasting injury by disengaging from the conflict. He concluded his speech by saying that the primary obligation of the government was not to Vietnam but rather to the American people "to *their* security and well-being." He concluded:

> The fact remains that our presence in Vietnam can be justified—if it can be justified—in terms of *American* interests, correctly defined as the freedom and safety of the American people.... From the standpoint of our interests, we have been fighting an unnecessary war for five long years, making it possibly the most disastrous mistake in the history of American foreign-policy. It can never be vindicated; it can only be liquidated.[31]

Vietnam, the Church, and Chaplains

In January 1968, approximately fifteen months prior to Jake Laboon's arrival in Vietnam, there were 110 navy chaplains serving with marines in country.[32] By 1969, due to the Vietnamization program and at least in theory the desire for less engagement by American troops of the NVA and NLF, newly arrived chaplains, for the most part, spent less time in the field. Nonetheless, they were very busy counseling men with a whole host of psychological difficulties experienced by those in combat. Herbert Bergsma, the historian of the service of navy chaplains in Vietnam, has written:

> Although with the relatively low level of fighting rather few chaplains were sweating out their ministry in combat roles, circumstances arose in the areas of counseling that often caused more sweat and tears than combat, and challenged chaplains to new heights of contributions to their people.[33]

Race relations, drug abuse, and general issues concerning violence were addressed by chaplains.

The almost palpable division that Vietnam created among Americans

---

30. Ibid., 37.
31. Ibid., 35–36 (all emphases original).
32. Herbert Bergsma, *Chaplains with Marines in Vietnam, 1962–1971* (Washington, D.C.: History and Museum Division, Headquarters U.S. Marine Corps, 1985), 155.
33. Ibid., 177.

was also experienced in the church. The American church historian Gerald Fogarty, SJ, has suggested, "The Vietnam War ... marked the beginning of a change in the hierarchy's stance toward American society." Whereas in the past American bishops were, almost to a man, united in their patriotic support for America's wars, Vietnam was different. Many bishops raised questions about the morality of the war; some spoke in favor of selective conscientious objection. Thus, the bishops began to engage a question that in the past had been considered strictly political, but now was seen as an issue of conscience.[34] For example, Cardinal Lawrence Shehan of Baltimore, hinting that Vietnam might not measure up, insisted that any war must be conducted morally or "our cause will be betrayed."[35] While some members of the hierarchy (and certainly priests and religious, as well) questioned the war, others were supportive. In 1966 Cardinal Francis Spellman, head of the military ordinariate, wrote to his fellow bishops and superiors general of religious communities pleading for more priests to be allowed to volunteer for chaplain service. Specifically, he asked each diocese and religious order to allow one additional priest to volunteer. He went so far as to suggest that if sufficient volunteers were not present, the government would consider drafting priests as they did doctors and dentists.[36] Jake probably would have agreed with such a policy, stating years later, "If you don't send Roman Catholic priests into the military, whether it's Army, Navy, Coast Guard or Marines, then what you're really saying is: 'We do not give a damn about Roman Catholics in the military.'"[37]

While division was found in the hierarchy, the prevailing attitude of leading American Catholic theological voices toward the morality of Vietnam was decidedly negative at the time of Jake Laboon's arrival. The Jesuit Robert Springer, while suggesting that the morality of Vietnam must be an individual decision, concluded that Vietnam had been a disaster, especially from an economic perspective. Paulist father John Sheerin, editor of *The Catholic World*, concluded, "My judgment is that the morality of our involvement in Vietnam is very doubtful." The Jesuit moral theologian James

---

34. Fogarty, "Public Patriotism," 47.
35. Lawrence Shehan, "Peace and Patriotism: A Pastoral Letter," *Catholic Mind* 64 (September 1966): 4.
36. Cardinal Francis Spellman to eminences, archbishops, bishops, superiors general, October 4, 1966, military affairs chaplains, 1964–66, Office of General Secretary, NCWC, ACUA.
37. Fragment, *Catholic Review*, July 17, 1981, AABa.

Hanigan sought to find justification for the war analyzing theologies of holy war, pacifism, and just war. He concluded that all were inadequate, stating, "We are seeing in Vietnam today the horrors that occur when man sins by excess. It must end. The present United States involvement in Vietnam in style and in substance must be considered a crime and abomination."[38]

The divisive nature of Vietnam, even within the church, raised debate on the ethical role of the chaplain. While few ever questioned the justification for World War II and therefore chaplain participation, Vietnam was a different story, raising questions about a minister in uniform. An editorial in *Time* raised the question: "Viet Nam is a different kind of war, and clerical critics— including a few ex-chaplains—are beginning to question whether a minister in uniform can really be honest to God while remaining faithful to the Pentagon."[39]

Those suggesting the impossibility of serving both the military and the church found a champion in the Catholic pacifist Gordon Zahn. He suggested that any chaplain who enthusiastically defends the military and wears the uniform cannot be totally dedicated as a representative of religion and its values. He believed a military chaplain was not free to counsel soldiers or sailors who might have a conscientious objection to war. While chaplains addressed such important moral issues as sex, drugs, drinking, and inappropriate personal behavior, they could not address the morality of war. Zahn wrote,

> Stated directly it is to the extent that the chaplain embraces or allows himself to be absorbed by the military ideology and values, the less qualified he will be to provide adequate moral guidance to the man in his charge on issues relating to the nature of a given war, its objectives and its means.... Faced with the broader moral issues concerning the war itself, issues that trouble the world—be [it] conscientious objector and the political deserter, the pastor in uniform is all too likely to take refuge in proclaiming the virtues of military obedience and loyalty to the state.[40]

Zahn proclaimed that the role of the chaplain should be broader, recognizing moral guidance in other areas. He continued,

---

38. Robert Springer, "The Moral Issue in Vietnam," *U.S. Catholic* 34 (October 1968): 7–10; Sheerin, "The Morality of the War in Vietnam," *Catholic World* 202 (March 1966): 330; James Hanigan, "The Theology of War in Vietnam," *Chicago Studies* 7 (Summer 1968): 142.

39. "Honest to God or Faithful to the Pentagon?" *Time* 93 (May 30, 1969): 49.

40. Gordon Zahn, "What Did You Do During the War, Father?" *Commonweal* 90 (May 2, 1969): 196–97.

It is not a matter then, of abolishing the chaplaincy but, rather, one of creating a broader more effective, and truer ministry, one which recognizes and accepts much more of moral guidance function than has been the case until now.[41]

Concluding that chaplains should no longer be commissioned to hold rank in the military, a decision that would eliminate the conflict he perceived, he wrote:

Much as one may honor those pastors in uniform who insist upon sharing the same hardships and dangers experienced by the men placed in their care, there remains a serious threat to their spiritual ministry in those aspects of the chaplaincy which produce too close an identity with the military establishment, its values, and its purposes. If the spiritual ministry must be provided, it should be provided on the churches' terms and not on the terms defined and established by the military.[42]

While Zahn was prominent during the Vietnam era, his voice was not alone but rather represented a general concern for the role of the chaplain. Constitutional concerns have been raised, since the chaplain's role appears to validate U.S. government support for organized religion. Specifically, some suggest that the establishment clause of the First Amendment requires neutrality and non-engagement with respect to government association with religion. The constitutional lawyer Julie Kaplan has written, "Because military involvement with religion implicates grave establishment clause concerns, it is essential that the chaplaincy program be finally tailored to minimize the establishment offense."[43] She does note, however, that while military chaplaincy represents government support for religion, "Several justices have cited the chaplaincy as an example of permissible government accommodation of religion."[44] Gordon Zahn's fear, that an inherent conflict exists between being a military officer while simultaneously promoting the gospel message, was echoed more recently by Tom Cornell, a cofounder of the Catholic Peace Fellowship and *Pax Christi:*

---

41. Ibid., 198.

42. Ibid. The Lutheran pastor (later convert to Catholicism and priest) Richard John Neuhaus, a strong antiwar critic, charged that clerics in the military service expose themselves to "spiritual prostitution." In Neuhaus's view there was an unresolvable contradiction between Christianity's gospel of peace and a minister's participation in the war that a growing number of Americans regarded as immoral; see "Honest to God or Faithful to the Pentagon?" *Time* 93 (May 30, 1969): 49.

43. Julie B. Kaplan, "Military Mirrors on the Wall: Non-establishment and the Military Chaplaincy," *Yale Law Journal* 95, no. 6 (May 1986): 1212.

44. Ibid., 1210–11.

Priests enlist in the military as chaplains with the best of intentions: to serve pastoral needs. But this is not why they are commissioned as officers or what they are paid for. According to their employers, the chaplaincy's purpose is to contribute to the military success of the unit to which the chaplain is attached. This purpose may cause cognitive dissonance for some chaplains. It is not unreasonable to assume that many, however, will resolve their distress in favor of the presuppositions of the officer corps of which they are a part and into which they have been socialized.[45]

While possibly not as vociferous, the voices of those who believed the chaplain's role completely consistent with one's vocation to God challenged Zahn's views. Robert Lutz, a Franciscan priest and army chaplain, rejected the presumption that chaplains had cast aside their moral fiber to serve in the military:

From where I stood I admired the wisdom of chaplains doing a difficult job. In general, I never thought they sold their souls to the military. If they thought they should speak out, they spoke out and let the chips fall where they may.... The chaplain does recognize legitimate military authority, but like a good Christian should *never* exercise military authority himself.[46]

A *Time* editorial maintained that the vast majority of chaplains serving in Vietnam were convinced of the justice of the American cause, even going the extra mile to support the military in untraditional ways, including service in the field.[47] Claude Newby, an army chaplain who served multiple tours in Vietnam, asserted that the chaplain serves soldiers, not the country, not a war:

As a chaplain in Vietnam, I served no war, just or unjust. I served soldiers—heroes—faithful souls who stepped forward when called upon by their country, while others received accolades for refusing to serve. It took a special kind of hero to step forward in the decade of the sixties.[48]

Jake Laboon's view of his role as a chaplain in Vietnam was very much akin to that of Claude Newby, viewing his role as service to marines. He once commented, "By my presence I am neither approving [n]or disapprov-

---

45. Tom Cornell, "The Chaplain's Dilemma: Can Pastors in the Military Serve God and Government?" *America* (November 17, 2008): 14.
46. Robert A. Lutz, "Response to 'What Did You Do during the War, Father?'" *Commonweal* 90 (June 27, 1969): 422 (emphasis original).
47. "Honest to God," 49.
48. Newby, *It Took Heroes*, viii.

ing the U.S. involvement in Vietnam. I am here because these young Marines need me—and that is why."[49] Responding to those who suggested that one's role as a priest is compromised in the military, he stated, "We all have certain reservations as to what the military does, but that does not mean it changes my role as a Catholic priest one bit."[50] Jake's basic political philosophy was in many ways linked to his ministry as chaplain. He expressed his affirmation in the Domino Theory:

No one wants to be in Viet Nam, but like all Americans I was ordered to Viet Nam and I realized that it was there that America must stem the spread of communism. If we lose Viet Nam we open the doors to losing Japan and the Philippines to communism.[51]

During his time in country, Jake wrote to his provincial venting his frustration with his fellow Americans over their attitude toward the war in Vietnam. He could not understand how people could be so callous and unsupportive to those on the front lines doing their duty:

The war is far from over. It seems that everyone back home has the war won except the people out here who are actually engaged in the conflict. It is a very nasty war with little or no support from the people back home. This is what hurts the troops so much. If the people back home really cared, then to get killed or even wounded might be meaningful to these young men, but as it stands now, most Americans would consider them fools for being involved with the NVA [North Vietnamese Army]. Strange, isn't it?[52]

The role of the chaplain in Vietnam was multidimensional, including religious and civic activities, but it was also wrapped into the personal challenge of dealing with war. Although leading seemingly routine and mundane lives, navy chaplains in Vietnam participated in many local activities, supporting not only marines, but local civilians. The distribution of food, clothing, and school supplies to schools, churches, and orphanages was a regular task. Working with local agencies to sponsor parties for infirm and underprivileged children and teaching basic English to leaders in local Vietnamese communities were also common. Chaplains also went with navy doctors as part of a medical care program to visit villages and provide as-

---

49. Clipping, *Church World* 63, no. 36 (February 25, 1993): 3, PPJL.
50. *Catholic Review*, July 17, 1981, AABa.
51. Clipping, *Valley Independent*, May 25, 1966 [*sic;* 1969], PPWL.
52. John Laboon, SJ, to Jim Connor, SJ, August 15, 1969, Laboon file, ASJM.

sistance. Working more directly with marines, chaplains were responsible for delivering lectures to U.S. forces on Vietnamese religious customs, especially Buddhism.[53]

Sensitivity to the specialized situation and the need to find inner strength were basic qualities required for the chaplain to succeed. John Cohill, who served as a regimental chaplain with the Third Marines one year prior to Jake's arrival, wrote of the chaplain's daily work:

Shaking a man's hand, hearing him out after a terrifying experience, holding the head or hand of a wounded or dying man, enabling a man to ventilate his feelings, joking about danger, particularly fear but with a light touch, just being present are as important as the celebration of the Eucharist or a sermon in combat.[54]

The basic test and therefore foundational quality for the chaplain was the need to possess inner strength so as to be strong for the needs of others. Chaplain Cohill wrote:

Even before he sets foot on the Danang airstrip, the Navy Chaplain, heading for the unknowns of combat with the Third Marine Division, senses keenly that his greatest challenge may be himself. But the test will be his own manhood and his grasp of the stuff of eternity—his ability to enable men to understand something of the grace of God in a situation that, on the surface, seems a denial of that very grace.[55]

Importantly, he also realized how the chaplain is enriched by the lives of others. He commented, "Deeply conscious that he [the chaplain] came to comfort, he comes away comforted. He came to cheer others and found [that] his brother chaplains, officers, NCOs and troopers enabled him to feel 'lifted up in heart.'"[56]

The critical role of the navy chaplain in Vietnam was also discussed by John O'Connor, a Vietnam navy chaplain, close friend of Jake Laboon, future chief of chaplains, and later still cardinal archbishop of New York. He admitted that much of the work is routine and would be the same if one were stationed on a ship or a shore installation. Counseling recipients of "Dear John" letters, breaking the news of death or injury at home and arranging for emergency leaves, conducting services, giving religious in-

---

53. Commanding general FMF Pacific to commandant of the Marine Corps, nd. [1969], folder 5216/9, box 150, NCA.
54. John Cohill, "Grace and Gratitude," n.d. [1968], folder 5750/2, box 229, NCA.
55. Ibid.
56. Ibid.

struction, and fighting the inevitable battles of promiscuity, infidelity, and religious indifference—these were the daily routine. Yet Vietnam had several additional challenges. Maintaining a presence close to a field hospital where the wounded, dying, and dead were brought, while at the same time tramping through the hills and villages to meet the spiritual needs of the living, was a significant test. O'Connor also walked the tightrope, expressed by Laboon and others, concerning the moral issue the war had become. In a summary report written upon detaching from his Vietnam assignment, he wrote:

More than a little time is spent in simply talking with men, calming the fearful, reasoning with the skeptical, helping the uncertain understand why they are here. Confused by the sophisticated news analysis, disheartened by letters from ever more confused parents, wives, sweethearts, many men worry more than they admit—or more than they can verbalize about the moral validity of America's position in Vietnam, and of their own role in the war.[57]

In a book written about his experience, O'Connor again addressed the moral question of the war. On the one hand he suggested that a policy of peace at virtually any price, especially if that price is some form of slavery, is far too high, even higher than paying with one's life. He wrote:

Indeed, the truth does not matter if world order is ever to be maintained, if justice is to be effective, and if negotiations are to bear even a semblance of honor. To declare that the war must be concluded at any cost may sound extremely pious. It is, in fact, I think extremely naïve and morally irresponsible.[58]

Praise for those who served as chaplains was also clearly in the mind of O'Connor. From his own perspective he saw Vietnam as "one of the finest opportunities ever given the Navy chaplaincy, and one of the finest tours of duty a Navy chaplain could possibly have."[59] He commended his fellow chaplains for their dedication, even when many challenged their presence in uniform:

Our chaplains keep pushing, driving, sweating, [and] praying. They are acutely conscious that men can starve to death without even feeling hungry. I see no calendars in their tents with days crossed off as though their only mission in life were to rotate

57. John J. O'Connor, "A Point of View in Vietnam," n.d. [1965], folder 5750/2, box 231, NCA.
58. O'Connor, *A Chaplain Looks at Vietnam* (New York: World, 1968), 4, 2.
59. O'Connor, "Point of View."

to the states. I have yet to hear a single chaplain suggest that his tour is fruitless, his time wasted, his duty an inevitable exile he endured for "career planning." Nor do I know a single one of our chaplains who thinks himself a hero. For the most part, he is simply to[o] busy to think of such nonsense at all.[60]

Still, he acknowledged the reality of war and the toll it took on everyone, including chaplains:

> No priest can watch the blood pouring from the wounds of the dying—be they American or Vietnamese of North or South—without anguish in the sense of desperate frustration and futility. The clergy back home, the academicians in their universities, the protesters on their marches are not the only ones who cry out, "Why?"[61]

Regimental Chaplain—Third Marines

After detaching from his post as senior Catholic chaplain at the naval academy in the spring of 1969, Jake, after a brief respite at home in Pittsburgh, continued west for specialized training. One year earlier the navy had initiated a three-week pre-embarkation program at Camp Pendleton Marine Base just north of Oceanside, California. The program, specifically designed for chaplains assigned to Vietnam, included participation in infantry training, a field medical service school, physical fitness and survival skills, and counter-insurgency tactics.[62] Upon completion of the course, Laboon's fitness report read in part, "Throughout the program of training, Commander Laboon was most cooperative and displayed a keen interest in all subject matter."[63] Jake proceeded to the marine barracks at Treasure Island, San Francisco, for transport to Vietnam.[64]

Jake arrived in country on April 9, 1969, accompanied by five other chaplains. Immediately assigned as regimental chaplain for the Third Marine Division, he was one of twenty-six chaplains in the division, with Captain John Zoller as his command chaplain.[65] In many cases the average age of

---

60. Ibid.
61. O'Connor, *Chaplain Looks at Vietnam*, 4.
62. Mode, *Grunt Padre*, 65; LT A. S. Kirk, "Vietnam Report," May 1967–May 1968, folder 5750/2, box 91, NCA.
63. CDR John Laboon, fitness report, April 16, 1969, Laboon file, NMPR.
64. BUPERS order 163209 form, CDR John F. Laboon, January 21, 1969, Laboon file, NMPR.
65. John Laboon to "Hugh [Kennedy]," May 28, 1969, Laboon file, ASJM.

chaplains was just over forty, raising some concern about the arduous conditions and the physical demands of the ministry, but Zoller contended that while physical ability had to be considered, the situation called for experienced people.[66] The distribution of chaplains in country, especially within the Third Marine Division, was another concern, leading to some changes of assignment. Rear Admiral James Kelly, chief of chaplains, informed the Force Chaplain Fleet Marine Force (FMF) Pacific that the Third Marines had too many Catholic chaplains, yet at the same time had insufficient coverage for marines in the northern coastal region. Part of the difficulty lay with the ongoing Vietnamization program and the simultaneous geographic shifting and removal of U.S. forces. As one of his first administrative endeavors, Jake worked with Zoller and his fellow regimental chaplains to correct these imbalances by shifting chaplains to various commands to maximal provision of chaplain services.[67] Shortly after arriving he wrote to a Jesuit friend with his initial impressions: "All goes well here although it is unbelievably hot every day. There have been rocket attacks on this base the past two weeks, but so far no major damage. No lives have been lost which is most important."[68]

Those newly arrived in Vietnam, including chaplains, had to learn some important "do's and don'ts" that were applicable in this foreign land. Some of the important "do's" for new arrivals included: (1) Do identify yourself with the goals and interests of the local people by following their customs, using their language, and understanding their way of life; (2) Do demonstrate to the people your knowledge of their government and your respect for its officials and laws; (3) Do show the Vietnamese soldier that you know and respect his rank and experience; (4) Do remember security, remain alert, and be ready to react with military skills; (5) Do treat prisoners of war according to the Geneva Convention. Some important "don'ts" were also presented: (1) Do not forget where you are and why you are here. Always use restraint and consciously avoid any actions that would discredit our motives and weaken our standing with the Vietnamese people; (2) Do not use unnecessary force; (3) Do not attract attention by loud or rude behavior;

66. John Zoller, "End of Tour Report," n.d. [1969], folder 5750/2, box 235, NCA.
67. RADM James Kelly to CAPT Gerald Saget, Force Chaplain FMF Pacific, August 14, 1969; CAPT Gerald Saget to RADM James Kelly, August 21, 1969, folder 5216/9, box 150, NCA; Senior chaplain U.S. Steel support activity Da Nang to chief of chaplains, July 11, 1960, folder 5216/9, box 147, NCA.
68. John Laboon to "Hugh [Kennedy]," May 28, 1969, Laboon file, ASJM.

(4) Do not separate yourself from the people by an open display of wealth and privilege.[69] Newly arrived chaplains were also given an initial indoctrination lecture. Training and fellowship meetings for all chaplains were held on a weekly basis. Zoller set the tone and presented his expectations to his chaplains:

> It was my desire to develop in each chaplain an increased professional competence and confidence, a deep sense of teamwork and cooperation, a greater imagination and initiative in his work and an awareness of utter and honest openness in all relationships with the Division Chaplain.[70]

One chaplain who served in Vietnam a year prior to Laboon provided some salient counsel for those who would follow him:

> I have a little advice for those who follow after me—stay loose, keep your sense of humor, and if you do not have one, develop one—relate with the men—never take the easy way out when it is tough for others—preach the Gospel—adjust to the operational and tactical situation—do not be a crybaby—if you cannot get wheels, walk or hitch hike.[71]

During Jake Laboon's time in country, the Third Marines were geographically responsible for Quang Tri Province, bounded by the Demilitarized Zone (DMZ) to the north, Thua Thien Province on the south, on the east by the South China Sea and on the west by Laos. The area consisted of flat, somewhat marshy coastal plain that was contiguous with a rolling piedmont section. The western half of the province was rugged mountains covered with thick jungle growth and elephant grass.[72]

As regimental chaplain, Jake's duties were supervisory, pastoral, and administrative. He was responsible for inspecting and supervising three Protestant battalion chaplains serving with him. Jake's task was not one of inspection but rather to assist his fellow chaplains in every possible way with constructive suggestions and to encourage them by recognizing a job well done. In a letter to his provincial, Jake complimented the men with whom he worked: "They are fine men, go about their work, and need little or no help from me." As a senior officer, Jake, along with his other regimental

---

69. General information, U.S. Naval support activity, Da Nang, n.d., folder 5216/9, box 147, NCA.
70. John Zoller, "End of Tour Report," n.d. [1969], folder 5750/2, box 235, NCA.
71. F. W. Cassidy, "Out of This World—One Year," n.d. [1968], folder 5750/2, box 229, NCA.
72. John Zoller, "End of Tour Report," n.d. [1969], folder 5750/2, box 235, NCA.

chaplains, met with Chaplain John Zoller, his division chaplain, regularly in an effort to coordinate their common efforts to serve sailors and marines. Chaplains gathered whenever possible for spiritual enrichment themselves, including retreats often held at the Catholic seminary at Da Nang.[73]

Because of its rather unique environment and war setting, Vietnam created some specific problems that directly impacted Jake Laboon and his fellow chaplains. One significant problem was the prevalence of drugs. Chaplain Zoller admitted, "The ready availability and inexpensive cost of marijuana in Quang Tri Province presented a serious problem."[74] More troubling, however, were the attacks perpetrated by one marine on another. Again Zoller commented, "The appearance of vicious threats and ruthless violence by some of our own personnel against their fellow soldiers and Marines is unprecedented, perplexing and alarming."[75] In seeking answers for such behavior, it was suggested that racism and constant exposure to combat violence were part of the reason. However, there was a general lack of moral character among some of America's combat forces. Zoller described those involved in such actions: "The dearth of any real inner sense of right and wrong within the perpetrator—a lack of moral development, a moral cripple."[76]

Vietnam was also an opportunity for chaplains to minister in highly specialized ways. It was imperative that chaplains understand and appreciate the tensions, frustrations, conditions, and situations of the men they served and with whom they lived. Knowledge in these areas was critical in order to bring their religious ministry to these men. Chaplains were required to be creative and to adapt to the situation they found. Church services might happen in a tent, an underground bunker, or an open hillside. An altar might be ammunition or C-ration boxes. Yet, as one chaplain wrote about such experiences, "The men brought a deep sense of devotion and by their own attitude made of these moments a true and relevant period of worship."[77] Robert Fiol, a Protestant chaplain who served with the Third Marines along with Laboon, beautifully described how he experienced his ministry in Vietnam:

73. Ross Trower, interview with the author, May 14, 2011; Senior chaplain naval support activity, Da Nang to distribution list, August 20, 1969, folder 5750/2, box 235, NCA.
74. John Zoller, "End of Tour Report," n.d. [1969], folder 5750/2, box 235, NCA.
75. Ibid.
76. Ibid.
77. LT A. S. Kirk, report, May 1967–May 1968, folder 5750/2, box 219, NCA.

I shall never forget the many occasions of ministering spiritually to these fine men. To see the Word of God come alive and have life and meaning in their lives under the worst conditions; to know that you have been used in a small way to bring comfort to scared Marines facing death and uncertainty for the first time; to have deep and sound satisfaction that through the Grace of God you may be able to touch lives and see them go forward strengthened spiritually, emotionally, and morally; to read letters from families where comfort and reassurance have been given.... These are the rewards and satisfactions that make all the long months of loneliness, difficulty, sweat, dust, and rain worthwhile because these were months when I was able to observe God at work.[78]

Throughout Jake Laboon's in-country deployment, but especially from late June to late September, the Third Marines were engaged in almost constant combat with the 9th NVA regiment.[79] American forces were engaged in "search and destroy missions," looking to clear enemy forces from specific areas. The NVA forces primarily used hit-and-run tactics on small groups of American soldiers and Marines. In response to this situation, one chaplain wrote:

Chaplains strove to minister to that condition, adapting once again to the shift in combat circumstances. The chaplain had to be greatly mobile and when he arrived at an outpost his ministry had to be more than camaraderie.[80]

As a regimental chaplain it would have been normative for Laboon to spend his day in a "safe area" away from the front lines. However, when he heard that units had sustained casualties, he would "hop a helicopter" to the scene and minister as needed. He once wrote, "I do a lot of flying by Helo to the units in the field. It is difficult to cover most of them because they are on the move so much. We do what we can for them."[81] While in the field he heard confessions, celebrated Mass, and spent hours talking with marines.[82] In

---

78. Robert Fiol to division chaplain, Third Marine Division, n.d [1969], John Robert Fiol personnel file, NCA.
79. CDR John Laboon, fitness report, September 28, 1969, Laboon file, NMPR.
80. Bergsma, *Chaplains with Marines*, 181.
81. John Laboon, SJ, to "Hugh [Kennedy]," May 28, 1969, Laboon file, ASJM; John Toland, interview with the author, November 17, 2010.
82. During his ministry in the field Jake would often use "general absolution" in celebrating the sacrament of penance. The normative way to celebrate the sacrament is individualized confession with reception of penance and absolution. However, in the post-Vatican II revision of sacramental rites, general absolution became a possibility. Rarely used, the concept is that a large group of penitents could be absolved at one time, as it would be an extreme hardship for one priest to hear so many individual confessions. The rite does say, however, that those who receive general ab-

such situations he would stay a day or two, even at times going on all-day patrols. He would preside at memorial services, held if possible in the area where marines had died.[83] One young platoon leader who observed Laboon in the field commented, "His presence meant a lot to everyone."[84]

While obviously inspirational to the men he served, Laboon violated the unwritten policy that asked chaplains not to participate in combat scenarios. The rule was instituted not only for their safety, but for the men on patrol with him. The rationale was clear: to take an extra unarmed man (chaplains do not carry firearms) on patrol endangered the remainder of the squad, which felt responsible for the chaplain's safety, thus placing in possible jeopardy the entire unit.[85] Although basic rules existed, prudence, pastoral necessity, and proper judgment were utilized in all cases, sometimes resulting in a violation. John O'Connor commented on this dilemma during his tour in country:

> In our Vietnam today we can have no "policy" on patrols. We have chaplains whose good sense we can trust. If they consider the specific patrol one they should accompany, if weighing all the values involved they feel their presence essentail [sic] they go on patrol. If not they stay in the CP [Command Post]. We discuss the pros and cons, offer suggestions and very general guidelines, and decide as intelligently and prayerfully as possible. At times we were wrong.[86]

One chaplain serving with Laboon detailed the benefits of ministry in the field: "Our ministry as chaplains is greatly enhanced as we live with them and share their pain, sorrow, frustrations, joys and life."[87]

In 1969, realizing that heavy fighting required chaplains to be more mobile, Fleet Marine Force (FMF) needed a new plan. The commanding general of FMF Pacific informed the commandant of the Marine Corps that in order for chaplains to make their services available to the largest number of men, their presence "in harm's way" might at times be necessary. He wrote, "It is now necessary for the chaplains to accompany their troops, as rapidly

---

solution must at their first opportunity seek out a priest for individual confession; see John Toland, interview with the author, November 17, 2010.

83. Len Mrozak, interview with the author, August 17, 2011.
84. Ibid.
85. Robert Ecker, interview with the author, December 17, 2010.
86. O'Connor, "Point of View in Vietnam," n.d. [1965], folder 5750/2, box 231, NCA.
87. Robert Fiol to division chaplain, Third Marine Division, n.d. [1969], John Robert Fiol personnel file, NCA.

Figure 8-1. Jake Laboon saying Mass in Vietnam, 1969

changing movements [require] in order to minister to the greatest possible number."[88] Thus, utilizing the more open policy, Jake was often found in the field, either at a firebase or possibly on patrol. He wrote to a fellow Jesuit informing him he had been "three weeks in the bush with Marines."[89] Laboon's September fitness report, speaking of the "bright encouragement, example, and cheer" he brings to the troops went on to say, "He went ev-

88. Commanding general FMF Pacific to commandant of the Marine Corps, n.d. [1969], folder 5216/9, box 150, NCA.
89. John Laboon to "Hugh [Kennedy]," May 28, 1969.

erywhere, exposing himself to hostile fire when necessary."[90] Marine General Terry Murray remembers Laboon stating, "Let us go where the Marines are." Murray further commented, "He was at home there as much as he was in the states."[91] On patrol Jake carried a backpack that contained all he needed for Mass plus a change of clothes. One Marine commented, "What made him so special was that he lived the life of the Marine infantryman. He empathized the best way by spending lots of time with us."[92] A member of the naval academy class of 1968, with Laboon in Vietnam, commented, "He was practical in his ministry, handling priesthood in an environment where annihilation was the norm."[93] Jake's bravery in the field was acknowledged in a citation when he was awarded the Legion of Merit:

> During extended combat operations, he completely disregarded his own safety as he moved through areas subject to hostile fire to reach forward elements of his command to provide worship services, religious counsel, and guidance for the myriad problems faced by men in combat.[94]

The danger that Jake encountered, however, never seemed to destroy his easy-going personality and approach to life. Commenting years later about their common Vietnam experience, Cardinal John O'Connor stated, "I never saw Father Jake lose his ease of manner: not in a hole in the ground in Vietnam.... When shells whistled by he calmly puffed on his cigar."[95]

Another significant aspect of Jake's ministry in Vietnam was his service at field hospitals. Triage units filled with wounded and dying, operating rooms working at maximum capacity, and wards that could accommodate no additional patients were the norm.[96] One triage unit in Quang Tri Province was the site of a memorable episode for Jake Laboon and a young marine officer, Second Lieutenant Oliver North, who in 1987 became almost a

---

90. CDR John Laboon, fitness report, September 28, 1969, Laboon file, NMPR.
91. Terry Murray, interview with the author, October 25, 2010. One anecdote illustrates the relative calm Jake demonstrated, even in the field. One day Laboon was on patrol with some marines and they were forced into foxholes due to enemy fire. Seemingly unperturbed by the situation, Jake lit up a cigar. His action gave courage to others; he seemed to be completely at peace. His attitude brought inner peace to the marines around him; see Joe Maloy, interview with the author, January 11, 2011.
92. John Toland, interview with the author, November 17, 2010.
93. John O'Neill, interview with the author, February 26, 2011.
94. Citation—Legion of Merit—John Laboon, n.d. [1970], Laboon file, NMPR.
95. *Catholic New York*, February 25, 1993, PPJL.
96. Bergsma, *Chaplains with Marines*, 181.

household name as a result of the Iran-Contra Affair during the presidency of Ronald Reagan. North describes how Laboon was somewhat responsible for saving his life. In a firefight North was severely wounded when a tank turret struck him, flinging him into the air as one swats a tennis ball. He was flown by helicopter to Quang Tri, along with other marines wounded in the same action. On this particular day the field hospital was overwhelmed with injured and decisions had to be made who was well enough to survive and who was not. As North was receiving initial emergency care, he spotted Father Jake, whom he had known at the naval academy, standing beside him. North writes, "Jake was a legend and a close friend.... I had come to know him well at Annapolis." Laboon wiped the blood from North's face and told him to perk up so that the doctors could see that he had a chance to live. As North recalls the story, Laboon told the attending physician, "Probably ought to take my friend here—he looks pretty good."[97]

The admiration that many had expressed for Laboon in his earlier assignments was manifested in Vietnam, as well. Many spoke of how he never forgot a friend. Former Senator James Webb of Virginia recalled how one day he was waiting for a bus to get to the navy exchange in Da Nang. While waiting, a small local bus holding approximately twenty people drove by. Laboon was holding on to a bar with his feet on the back bumper of the bus. When he spied Webb he jumped from his perch and came over to speak with him, remembering the young marine lieutenant from his days at the academy. The two spent an hour or two in conversation on the spur of the moment. Webb also said that when anything was troubling him he would always seek out Father Jake: "I trusted him and respected him as much or more of any man of God I have known."[98] Monsignor Robert Ecker, who served with Jake during his Vietnam tour, marveled at how troops reacted to him: "Jake was sort of a majestic presence. His spiritual presence, his humble manner, his unassuming style—the troops just loved him."[99] Jake's athletic bearing, especially, made him a very impressive person, but it was his spiritual aura that attracted sailors and marines. Commenting on a me-

---

97. Oliver North, with William Novak, *Under Fire: An American Story* (New York: HarperCollins, 1991), 105; Oliver North and David Roth, *One More Mission: Oliver North Returns to Vietnam* (New York: HarperCollins, 1993), 186–87. RADM Tom Lynch verifies this story; see RADM Thomas Lynch, interview with the author, August 16, 2010.

98. James Webb, interview with the author, October 4, 2010.

99. Robert Ecker, interview with the author, December 17, 2010.

morial service conducted in the field for a unit that had lost sixteen men in two recent firefights, one marine commented, "God spoke through him. He was very comforting and pastoral."[100] One young marine junior officer summarized Jake Laboon's impact on him: "Of my thirteen-month tour in Vietnam, he was the highlight film."[101] Laboon did not see life through rose-colored glasses; rather, he emphasized reality, but always in an optimistic way. One family friend addressed Jake's lifetime positive countenance: "It was not necessarily that everything would be all right, but that you would be able to deal with it."[102]

In keeping with the Vietnamization policy instituted by President Richard Nixon, Third Marines of Quang Tri Province began to turn over their responsibilities to South Vietnamese forces, preparatory to reassignment from Vietnam. Jake wrote to his provincial, "There has been talk about our leaving for Okinawa, in the next few months, but the war is far from over."[103] Not happy about the prospects of leaving Vietnam, Jake sought a transfer to the First Marines, but instead he was assigned to the 12th Marine Regiment, an artillery unit in the Third Marine Division scheduled to move to Okinawa in October. Jake had mixed emotions about his transfer and shared them with his provincial:

I am not happy about the troop removal, but it does mean that a lot of young Marines will be alive when this is over because of the pull-out. That of course makes me happy. I would rather stay here in Vietnam then go to Okinawa, but I have no choice. I have just finished six months in Vietnam which is exactly half of my tour overseas. The first six months have really slipped by rather quickly. None of us look forward to the next six months in Okinawa. Can you imagine battle-hardened troops in a peacetime atmosphere? I cannot![104]

Jake's personal reflections of his time in Vietnam centered on the men he served, but he did describe his experience by the Three Rs: "rain, rats, and rockets."[105] Jake attacked the fear, loneliness, and conflict over conscience that many of his marines experienced by telling them that these emotions must be shared with others. Such an attitude allows one to work

---

100. Len Mrozak, interview with the author, August 17, 2011.
101. John Toland, interview with the author, November 17, 2010.
102. Christopher Kidd, interview with the author, October 4, 2010.
103. John Laboon, SJ, to Jim Connor, SJ, August 15, 1969, Laboon file, ASJM.
104. John Laboon, SJ, to Jim Connor, SJ, October 7, 1969, Laboon file, ASJM.
105. *Catholic Review*, July 17, 1981, AABa.

and live with such uncertainties. He expressed his general philosophy: "My whole approach was to get the Marine to be a good person and meet Christ in his own way. I try to get them to develop a personal relationship with each other and their God."[106] He told his men that they could justify their actions by understanding that they were protecting their own lives and those of the South Vietnamese. Therefore, they were not killers, but defenders of selves and others. Again, reflecting care for others, he summarized his time in country:

My year in Vietnam was a great year but a sad year because of the number of Marines we lost. I remember many times when the Colonel and I would sit down and cry at night because of the tremendous impact of the loss.[107]

He subsequently commented, "It was always very sad. One day you would go up and see these kids and they would get hit and the next day you'd see them come back in body bags."[108]

Third Marine leadership was very pleased with Jake Laboon's work as regimental chaplain. His reporting officer commented, "In 27 years of service, I have never met Father Laboon's equal as a chaplain. He has a warmth and magnetism that draws Marines of all ranks to him. In the span of 21 days, he has the officers and men in this Regiment 'eating out of his hand'... deeply and sincerely interested in people, intellectually curious, tough physically and mentally, yet compassionate and kind, honest and candid, yet acutely aware of men's sensitivities." The report continued, "Dedicated to his work, [Laboon] seizes every opportunity to be with the rifle companies in the field, and seems never to give a thought to his own personal safety." The evaluation concluded by stating that Jake, for the first time in his career, be nominated for accelerated promotion-flag selection.[109]

The movement of Third Marine Division, 12th Regiment to Okinawa prompted a detachment evaluation for Laboon. He was applauded for his supervisory skills in working with battalion chaplains and his direct access to troops and being available at all times. It was also noted that Jake had a

---

106. *Honolulu Advertiser*, n.d. [1972], Laboon personnel file, AUSNA.
107. News clipping, n.d. [1980], PPJM.
108. *Catholic Review*, July 17, 1981, AABa.
109. CDR John Laboon, fitness report, June 1, 1969, Laboon file, NMPR. "Flag rank" in the military refers to the ranks of admiral in the navy and coast guard and general in the army, air force, and marines.

tremendous capacity for getting along with all types of people, thus making him an invaluable resource on all levels. His evaluation concluded, "Perhaps the highest compliment I can give him is to say that I relied and leaned upon him heavily in the discharge of my command responsibilities.... This officer was invaluable to me in this Regiment."[110]

Okinawa

Now as a chaplain for the 12th Regiment, Third Marine Division, Jake moved in late September 1969 to Okinawa, which served as a support facility.[111] While there Laboon worked with two other chaplains, Robert Ecker and John Dolegan, at Camp Hansen. Jake and his colleagues participated in a "ministry of presence" with the marines.[112] As senior Catholic chaplain, Jake was responsible for sacramental ministry. He worked with Ecker to form a popular team that filled the Catholic chapel on Sunday morning, in part because of the excellent music they were able to provide.[113]

Beyond the chapel the "ministry of presence" was manifested in almost daily walks through Kin Village. Laboon and Ecker wanted the marines to know that two navy chaplains represented their parents back home. The two wandered freely among the troops, striking up conversations and making their presence known and felt. About their ministry, Ecker commented, "They [the Marines] knew their father was watching." As always, Jake was active athletically, recreating frequently, especially with those marines he had met only a couple years earlier when they were midshipmen at the naval academy.[114] One junior marine officer spoke of how Jake might have a drink, sample some Kobe beef, and play a bit of poker.[115] Jake's reporting senior wrote, "In addition to the normal duties of a chaplain, he was active in the multitude of programs involving recreation and troop morale."[116]

110. CDR John Laboon, fitness report, September 28, 1969, Laboon file, NMPR.
111. Abstract of service and medical history, n.d., Laboon file, NMPR; Len Mrozak, interview with the author, August 17, 2011.
112. The concept of a "ministry of presence" refers to physically being present with others. Ministry is generally seen to be some overt act, but simply being around people can be a powerful influence.
113. Robert Ecker, interview with the author, December 17, 2010.
114. Ibid.
115. Len Mrozak, interview with the author, August 17, 2011.
116. CDR John Laboon, fitness report, June 4, 1970, Laboon file, NMPR.

While Jake's duties in Okinawa were tame when compared to Vietnam, he continued to make a positive impression on others. His fitness report read, "His dynamic personality and unusual ability to empathize with the troops made him a pillar among the men, one to whom they could look to any need. He devoted long hours to guiding and counseling." Described as a "remarkable priest, "an outstanding officer in all respects," he was viewed as a tremendous asset to the command whose transfer would be a great loss to the regiment.[117] One reporting senior summarized how many felt:

Father Laboon is *everything* the Navy Chaplain should be. Calm and courageous in combat, able to communicate effectively with seniors and subordinates alike, forceful in his personal and spiritual leadership—yet compassionate and understanding in dealing with troubled young Marines. Father Laboon's performance of duty exemplifies the highest standards of the Navy, Marine Corps Team. It is a privilege to have served with him.[118]

Jake Laboon's outstanding service as regimental chaplain in Vietnam was recognized in a formal way. He rated wearing the Republic of Vietnam campaign medal, but it was his reception of the Legion of Merit that truly exemplified the outstanding ministry he had performed. In the citation he was applauded for his tireless work "to enhance the spiritual and moral welfare of his command." It was noted that he "effectively directed programs to ensure continued support for an orphanage sponsored by his unit." His ability to maintain "religious fervor and [a] compassionate spirit contributed significantly to the morale of his command." His ministry "to remote fire specific bases ... where positions frequently came under attack" demonstrated his "exceptional courage."[119]

Conclusion

The 1960s, a decade that saw Jake Laboon journey from the relative comfort and familiarity of the submarine force to the comfort of the naval academy, with intermediate stops as a circuit rider and recruit chaplain and as pastor of a small flock in Kodiak, Alaska, was capped with service to U.S. marines and sailors in Vietnam. The turbulent decade, the counterculture of student

---

117. Ibid.; CDR John Laboon, endorsement to fitness report, April 1, 1970, Laboon file, NMPR.
118. CDR John Laboon, fitness report, February 26, 1970, Laboon file, NMPR. Emphasis original.
119. Citation—Legion of Merit—John Laboon, n.d. [1970], Laboon file, NMPR.

protests, and the violent murders of prominent American figures split the nation. But no event was more divisive than the war in Vietnam. Indeed, as the social historians Maurice Isserman and Michael Kazin have written, "It [the war] also proved the most demoralizing for Americans, plunging the nation into its most bitter civil conflict in the century."[120] As American involvement increased, leading to a drain of economic resources and the loss of thousands of lives, America's rationale for its military presence in Southeast Asia and the morality of the war itself were questioned by great numbers of the nation's citizens. Into this firestorm stepped Jake Laboon. While he supported the basic premises of American involvement in Vietnam, for him the moral rationale for American involvement was secondary to his desire to serve the brave men and women in uniform, few of whom desired to be involved, yet through duty to country and citizenship found themselves in harm's way. With his usual vigor, Jake ministered to U.S. marines and sailors on the front lines as well as in the relative safety of a regimental command post. Admired by all for his desire to be one with the marines he served, Jake's meritorious service was noted. Now a senior chaplain, he was ready and qualified to serve in the positions of greater authority for which he had been trained and recommended throughout his career.

120. Isserman and Kazin, *American Divided*, 67.

Chapter 9

Florida, Hawaii, and New London Again
★ 1970–1976

Having completed more than ten years of service in the chaplain corps and now having achieved senior rank status, Jake Laboon was ready for positions of greater authority. His broad experience, knowledge of the navy and the military life, and the high respect with which he was held by all, from the most junior to the most senior, were his qualifications. Following his well-respected tour in Vietnam, Jake gained his first experience with naval aviation by his assignment as senior Catholic chaplain at the Saufley Field Naval Air Station, Florida. Recall that as a midshipman at the naval academy he had originally considered naval air as his first choice, but realizing the training pipeline was long, and with his desire to enter more rapidly into the fray of World War II, he changed and opted for submarines. His tour at Saufley allowed him the opportunity to experience another branch of the naval service. From there Jake was again sent west, this time to Hawaii for service as assistant fleet chaplain. Gaining more and valued experience, in this case for a future officer-in-charge role, he was once again assigned to New London. As command chaplain for Commander Submarine Force Atlantic Fleet (COMSUBLANT) Jake enjoyed his third career assignment with submarines. Although due to rank and position he seldom was able to minister to "deck plate" sailors, he never lost his desire to do so when the opportunity presented itself—to minister to any and all whom he encountered. A priest before all other titles, Jake Laboon would once again answer the call to ministry.

Florida, Hawaii, and New London Again: 1970–1976

Saufley Field

Saufley Field, located near Pensacola on the Florida panhandle, was a product of the pre-World War II expansion of the U.S. military. In August 1939 the U.S. government took possession of the land, and one year later, on August 26, 1940, Saufley Field was officially commissioned, under the command of Lieutenant Commander George G. Mead, as an auxiliary air field of Naval Air Station Pensacola, the home base for naval aviation training. The field was named for Lieutenant Junior Grade Richard Caswell Saufley, naval aviator no. 14, who was killed in a crash on Santa Rosa Island in 1916 while successfully breaking his own flight endurance record of 8 hours and 43 minutes. Between 1940 and 1960 the basic mission of Saufley was training naval aviators, but in that latter year Training Squadrons One and Five were designated tenant commands, and the base's mission was altered to that of providing support for these two specialized groups.[1] In July 1968 Saufley was designated a naval air station.[2] As part of the navy's larger aviation training facility at Pensacola, Saufley held a specialized mission. While it provided services and material support for the Naval Air Training Command, it also served as a training facility for military personnel given foreign assignments. Its mission statement in part read:

> To serve as an effective instrument of U.S. Foreign-policy, by initiating and continuing action programs which promote positive relations between the command and foreign nations and which assist individual Naval personnel and their families to work effectively, live with dignity and satisfaction and function as positive representatives of the Navy and the United States while overseas.[3]

During Jake Laboon's tenure as senior chaplain, Saufley functioned as a base for support of flight training operations. This included aircraft maintenance and operational training, academic training of flight students, coordination of training schedules, and provision of facilities, especially training aids and equipment, for aircraft squadrons. On February 1, 1972, Training Air Wing Seven was established at Saufley. This new command was to act as a liaison between individual commands at NAS Saufley—namely, Training

---

1. A tenant command is a unit that is located on base but is not part of the chain of command.
2. Command history, NAS Saufley Field, September 3, 1959; command history, NAS Saufley 1970, February 19, 1971, NHM.
3. Command history, NAS Saufley Field, 1972, March 26, 1973, NHM.

Squadron One (VT-1) and Training Squadron Five (VT-5)—and the chief of Naval Air Training. Saufley also maintained a petty officer leadership school to provide navy noncommissioned officers an update and review of the nontechnical responsibilities of their rating.[4]

When Jake Laboon detached from his duties with the Third Marines on April 7 he took some needed and well-deserved leave before reporting to NAS Saufley on May 15, 1970. He replaced Lieutenant Commander Benjamin Walker as the Catholic chaplain, but due to his now senior rank he held the additional position of senior chaplain on station.[5] When he arrived Jake was greeted by the base commanding officer, Captain S. A. Sparks, but in short order Sparks was relieved by Captain Glenn E. Lambert, a classmate of Jake's from the academy. Enjoying a few of the privileges that come with senior rank, Jake settled into a comfortable three-bedroom red brick ranch house located off-base, but near the station.[6]

His quarters allowed him a bit more freedom to relax, but more importantly from his perspective, to offer hospitality to family and to friends, including fellow Jesuits who came to visit. Ever faithful to his family, Jake held the role of dutiful uncle in hosting his nephew John, who was stationed aboard the USS *Saratoga* in Mayport, Florida. The younger Laboon often visited his uncle, providing the opportunity for conversation and the enjoyment of family time. Jake's home, located on an estuary of the Gulf of Mexico, was a perfect setting for swimming, allowing family members to recreate with their still athletically oriented relative. Jake also played host to his brother chaplains, including fellow Jesuit Frank Metzbauer, who like Jake had just detached from Vietnam and was now serving at the Naval Technical Training Center, Corry Station. Jake hosted Metzbauer for a couple of months until the latter obtained his own quarters.[7]

The whirlwind of activity that most assuredly characterized Jake's day-to-day activity as regimental chaplain in Vietnam became somewhat more

---

4. Ibid.; command history, NAS Saufley Field, 1970, February 19, 1971, NHM.

5. Commanding officer, NAS Saufley Field, to CDR John Laboon, May 15, 1970, Laboon file, NMPR; news clipping, n.d. [1970], PPJM. In an interesting historical coincidence, the priest Jake relieved, Benjamin Walker, was from the Diocese of Pittsburgh and an ordination classmate of Laboon's younger brother, Joe.

6. John Laboon, interview with the author, January 31, 2011.

7. Ibid.; Frank Metzbauer, SJ, interview with the author, January 19, 2011; Joe Malloy, interview with the author, January 11, 2011.

routine, but nevertheless busy, in Florida. While Pensacola and Saufley were independent naval air stations, their close proximity and common mission allowed for many activities to be shared. On Memorial Day, then May 30, shortly after his arrival, Jake participated in the annual ceremony where flowers, blessed by the chaplains, were dropped from a T-28 Trojan aircraft into Pensacola Bay in memory of the nation's military dead. A joint vacation bible school, "which had much success in the past two years," was once again offered by the chaplains' offices from both commands.[8] Between August 17 and 21 the chaplains held a professional seminar at Pensacola that was labeled "a success in every respect."[9] The highlight of Jake's first year in Florida was undoubtedly when NAS Saufley was awarded the Naval Air Basic Training Admiral's Cup Efficiency Award for the third consecutive year, "a feat never previously accomplished since the award's inception." The commanding officer, Captain S.A. Sparks, wrote to Laboon congratulating him on his contribution to this award:

I take pleasure in commending you for your high degree of performance which was directly a contributing factor in winning the CNABATRA "E" award during the past fiscal year. I extend my hearty congratulations on a job "Well done."[10]

Having settled in with his new command, Jake, as one who served all personnel, not just Catholics, continued to participate in various events that rounded out his first full year in Florida. February was highlighted by the annual prayer breakfast, which welcomed over two hundred civic leaders in Pensacola as well as senior naval personnel. On Easter Sunday, April 11, Jake attended the annual Protestant Easter sunrise service, held onboard USS *Lexington* (CVT-16) with Captain R. E. Elliott, staff chaplain for the chief of naval training, delivering the sermon. Saufley was the site of an annual air show and public open house, featuring a performance of the Blue Angels precision flying team as well as a demonstration by Navy UDT Seals and public displays of various civilian and military aircraft.[11] A major program to address the growing problem of drug abuse in the navy, a reality Jake

8. Command history, NAS Pensacola, 1970, February 19, 1971, NHM.
9. Staff chaplain chief of naval air training to chief of naval personnel, October 23, 1970, folder 5216/9, box 146, NCA.
10. Commanding officer, NAS Saufley [S.A. Sparks] to CDR John Laboon, October 1, 1970, Laboon file, NMPR.
11. Command history, NAS Saufley Field, 1971, March 19, 1972; chaplains' activities command history, NAS Pensacola, 1971; command history, NAS Saufley Field, 1970, February 19, 1971, NHM.

had clearly seen in Vietnam, received special attention by the chaplains at Saufley and Pensacola. To deal with the problem, programs of prevention and treatment were instituted. One report stated, "Chaplains throughout CNATRA's [Chief Naval Air Training] Command have been taking a more active part in numerous drug abuse programs. A great deal of personal interest and involvement is being demonstrated by the chaplains."[12] In May a one-day training seminar to promote logistical support for various religious programs was held at Pensacola. It was described as "beneficial in every respect."[13] The summer months were highlighted by a visit from Rear Admiral Francis Garrett, navy chief of chaplains, who visited and toured Saufley on August 11. That same month the chaplains' office at Saufley hosted a group of fifty-five teenage campers from Memphis, Tennessee. A letter of appreciation sent to the chief of naval training commended Laboon and his colleagues: "Spiritual enrichment for the boys was provided by NAS Saufley Chaplains through rap sessions and a Sunday church service which included an impressive graduation ceremony."[14] The year ended with the chaplains' office sponsoring the annual NAS Selected School Children's Christmas Party, held for 150 underprivileged children from local Pensacola schools. Children were provided with gifts, including clothing and toys, and treated to cartoons and lunch. The highlight was the arrival of Santa Claus by helicopter. The chaplains' annual report stated, "This party has become a major event for this office and ends the year on a happy and rewarding note."[15]

Jake Laboon's involvement at Saufley continued apace throughout 1972, although his personal participation was limited by his impending transfer to a new command. He helped plan an effort to integrate the religious education programs of Saufley and Pensacola, Protestants and Catholics alike. The report described the effort: "Common goals were identified and efforts made to coordinate the programs as nearly as possible." Significant planning also went into a conference to write a new chaplain's manual. It was held at Pensacola between October 16 and 20 and attended by the chief of chaplains.[16]

---

12. Staff chaplain, chief of naval air training, to chief of naval personnel, August 5, 1971, folder 5216/9, box 146, NCA.
13. Ibid.
14. Chief of naval training to chief of naval air training, September 10, 1970, Laboon file, NMPR.
15. Chaplains' activities, command history, 1971, NAS Pensacola, n.d. [1972], NHM.
16. Chaplains' activities, command history, 1972, NAS Pensacola, n.d. [1973], NHM.

Jake Laboon's ministry with the Saufley Field community was noted for its pastoral sensitivity in effectively providing religious and related services to the people he served. He was applauded for his "outstanding knowledge and devotion to duty as Catholic chaplain of the station [Saufley]." His efficacy in ministering to the Catholic population on base was noted by his reporting senior:

His congregation steadily grows due to his infectious love of God and people, complemented by a keen insight of religion during these modern day pressures and influences. CDR Laboon is most effective in the moral and spiritual welfare of the men and dependents of Saufley.[17]

Laboon's ability as a counselor, which most assuredly had to be sharpened from his recent ministry in a war zone, was also commended. Applauding him for his ability to understand navy families and some of the more unique problems they faced, his reporting officer continued:

Cooperative, always willing to assume added responsibility and assist others, he is exceptionally adept in guiding and counseling personnel with personal, legal, and disciplinary problems and advising the command of any potential problem areas.[18]

He was especially effective in working with couples. An August 1971 report read, "He counsels young married couples including officers, enlisted, and aviation officer candidates who experience difficulties in their marital lives or the rigorous demands of the Flight Training Program."[19] He was also extolled by Rear Admiral J. M. Thomas, chief of naval air training, who succinctly summarized Laboon's leadership:

As senior Catholic chaplain in the Pensacola area, CDR Laboon has been an influential and effective member of the Navy and civilian communities. He is a compassionate, understanding, and sincere chaplain who was dedicated to his religion, fellow man, Navy and country.[20]

As usual, Jake's life and influence could not be defined merely by his work in the chaplain's office alone. He was very active as a member of the Chief of Naval Aviation and Training (CNATRA) Speakers Roster, making various presentations to high schools as well as church, military, and civic

---

17. CDR John Laboon, fitness report, April 15, 1970 [sic; 1971], Laboon file, NMPR.
18. Ibid.
19. CDR John Laboon, fitness report, August 18, 1971, Laboon file, NMPR.
20. CDR John Laboon, fitness report, September 3, 1971, Laboon file, NMPR.

groups. He was described as "an excellent speaker with a vast background of experience which he expertly weaves into his communication with others."[21] Throughout his time in Florida he served as the chaplain for the Knights of Columbus Council in Pensacola.[22] Obviously Jake could not stay away from the athletic field, especially in the generally favorable weather of the Florida panhandle. Besides pickup basketball, he played on the NAS Pensacola softball team.[23] Laboon's overall contribution to the Saufley command was noted in an August 1971 fitness report:

> Father Laboon is a very dedicated Naval Officer, who gives freely of his off-duty time for the benefit of the men and dependents of NAS Saufley. He has participated fully in the sports and social affairs of this command and has enjoyed the respect and admiration of the entire community. His infectious love of God and people, even temperament and fine sense of humor have contributed materially to maintaining morale and contentment among the officers, men and their dependents.[24]

Jake Laboon's generosity of time and spirit had been demonstrated throughout his life, from taking his siblings on rides in the rumble seat of his Model T, to counseling sailors on *Peto*, to numerous manifestations in varied assignments as a navy chaplain. However, in Florida this generosity manifested itself in an additional way through the economic support of those less advantaged. Working with a religious sister from local Catholic charities, Jake began to pay the tuition of some African American students attending Pensacola Catholic High School. He also paid bills, especially medical prescriptions for some indigent people who had been cut off from government assistance.[25] His contribution in this area was noted by his reporting senior:

> In addition to his military duties, he has been very active in community affairs. At his own expense, he has financed [the] living and educational support for several teenage boys in the local community without homes and has provided them with needed guidance and supervision with outstanding results.[26]

---

21. CDR John Laboon, fitness report, April 15, 1970 [*sic;* 1971], Laboon file, NMPR.
22. "CAPT John F. Laboon, Jr., CHC, USN, Biography," PPJM.
23. James O'Brien, e-mail to the author, December 1, 2010; emergency room record, April 4 [1971–1972?], Laboon file, NMPR. The medical record says that while playing softball Jake ran into another player, slightly injuring his shoulder. Obviously his athletic spirit had not dimmed.
24. CDR John Laboon, fitness report, August 18, 1971, Laboon file, NMPR.
25. John Laboon, SJ, to Jim Connor, SJ, August 11, 1972, Laboon file, ASJM.
26. CAPT John Laboon, fitness report, June 15, 1972, Laboon file, ASJM.

Jake's outreach to the disadvantaged reached its apex in January 1972 when a local juvenile court judge asked him (and another navy man, a medical corpsman) to become the legal guardians for two troubled youths. The young men lived with the corpsman in a trailer that Jake helped to rent. In a letter to a fellow Jesuit, Jake explained that the judge in court told the young men, "Father Laboon is the only person in all Pensacola who would take you in and give you a home."[27]

Information concerning Jake's outreach to the poor in the Pensacola area drifted back to his Jesuit superiors, who apparently, at least to some degree, questioned his actions. While there is no extant letter that challenges Laboon, Jake wrote to his provincial, Jim Connor, SJ, with a detailed explanation of his actions. He told Connor that he had financially assisted numerous people during his time in the navy. He defended his deeds:

> I do not think all of the above [description of financially aiding others] would be considered as squandering money. Realizing as I do that the above was done without permission, nevertheless I also thought you would understand and approve. Never once did I consider this contrary to the spirit of the Society and contrary to my vow of poverty. Maybe I was wrong, but at least it was not for me or for my personal gain that this was done. There were people in need, poor people, and if I did not help them, who knows what might have happened to them.[28]

Quite obviously, the charity, compassion, and outreach that Jake demonstrated to sailors and marines were shared with all whom he encountered on the road of life.

The long shadow that Jake's 6'5" frame cast over the community at Saufley, and to some extent Pensacola, was also shared with Ellyson Field, part of the Pensacola naval aviation command triad of training bases. In 1940 the navy purchased farmland sixteen miles northeast of NAS Pensacola for a future auxiliary base. As America's preparations for World War II intensified, it was decided to expand the site, assuming increased flight training needs. Construction on Ellyson Field, named for Theodore G. "Spuds" Ellyson, the navy's first aviator, began on February 26, 1941. The field was dedicated on October 1. During the war the field was the training location

---

27. John Laboon, SJ, to Jim Connor, SJ, August 11, 1972, Laboon file, ASJM. Jake assisted others at different times in his career, such as with school tuition, food, and shelter. He did much good work for many people, but silently, without fanfare or recognition for his generosity.

28. Ibid.

for squadron VN-2A. Between March 1947 and December 1960, Ellyson was deactivated, but on December 3, 1950, Helicopter Training Unit number 1 was established at the base. Thus Ellyson became the center training facility for helicopter pilots. In 1967, due to an increased need for helicopter training to support America's efforts in Vietnam, Ellyson was advanced from being a satellite command of NAS Pensacola to a full-fledged naval auxiliary air station.[29]

Shortly after Jake arrived at Saufley, he was assigned additional duty at Ellyson Field, serving from May 21 to November 1, 1970. He was fortunate that the base chapel had recently been renovated and rededicated in February. During his short tenure, Laboon played host to the navy's senior chaplains, who convened there on June 22, 1970, for a week-long workshop, "Executive Development Sensitivity Seminar." Directed by Dr. Norman M. Paris, professor of psychology at the University of West Florida, the workshop investigated patterns of interpersonal relations. The drug awareness program at Pensacola and Saufley was also promoted at Ellyson Field.[30] The commanding officer at Ellyson, Captain L. W. Metzger, was very impressed with Laboon and grateful for his assistance. He commented that Jake "possesses the qualities needed in a professional chaplain.... Chaplain Laboon has a warm, friendly personality and participates in all functions of the command and tenant activities where his services are needed."[31]

The positive comments he received for his short tenure at Ellyson were duplicated and made more elaborate and specific by his reporting seniors at Saufley. As senior chaplain it was noted that Laboon "provided outstanding ecclesiastical counseling to all Catholic chaplains in the area."[32] In the same light his leadership skills, so critical in his supervisory role, were extolled. Because of his exceptional knowledge of the navy and his warm concern for all with whom he associated, he could establish rapport with all personnel, regardless of rank or church affiliation. He was commended for "his ability and skill in communicating with and inspiring all personnel regardless of age, rank, race or creed."[33] He positively directed the energies of junior per-

29. "History of Ellyson Field," http://www.tailhook.org/Ellyson; command history, 1967, auxiliary landing field/auxiliary air station, Ellyson Field, n.d. [1968], NHM.
30. Command history, Ellyson Field, 1970, February 26, 1971, NHM.
31. CDR John Laboon, fitness report, February 10, 1971, Laboon file, NMPR.
32. CDR John Laboon, fitness report, endorsement, May 17, 1971, Laboon file, NMPR.
33. CAPT John Laboon, fitness report, June 15, 1972, Laboon file, NMPR.

sonnel toward the general goal of the service of others. Jake was especially effective at ferreting out problems and correcting them before a crisis arose. He was commended for "minimizing discipline problems and improving morale."[34] One report read,

> He has this command advised of any potential problem areas and has displayed considerable tact and fairness in his dealings with subordinates, thus showing that he is the most effective leader of minority as well as majority groups.[35]

Laboon's communication skills and the ability to mingle easily with both military and civilian personnel, combined with his experience and general professional capability, prompted his reporting officer, as had many in the past, to suggest promotion in advance of his contemporaries. His detaching fitness report read, "Chaplain Laboon has tremendous potential for assuming positions of high responsibility, and I consider him to be exceptionally well-suited for flag rank. He is strongly recommended for accelerated promotion."[36]

The call by Jake's superiors for his promotion was answered as he began the process to transition to another duty station. On April 7, 1972, he was "frocked" to the rank of captain by his classmate and commanding officer, Glenn Lambert.[37] With his new rank, Jake was ordered to staff duty Commander Service Force Pacific (COMSERVPAC) and additionally as assistant fleet chaplain commander in Chief Pacific Fleet (CINCPACFLT).[38]

COMSERVPAC and Assistant Fleet Chaplain Pacific

Jake Laboon arrived in Hawaii in July 1972 and took up his dual role from his office in the Makalapa hills overlooking Pearl Harbor. As in Florida, his senior rank allowed him to secure an off-base house in Aiea, a bedroom community adjacent to Pearl Harbor. Jake glided into his new assignment

---

34. Ibid.
35. CDR John Laboon, fitness report, August 18, 1971, Laboon file, NMPR.
36. CAPT John Laboon, fitness report, June 15, 1972, Laboon file, NMPR.
37. "News Release," n.d. [1972], John F. Laboon alumni file, AUSNA. The term "frocked" refers to pinning rank on a person who has been approved for promotion and is serving in a billet normally occupied by a person of the advanced rank, yet is not at the time drawing the higher pay of advanced rank. Laboon was the last active-duty member of the class of 1944 to be advanced to the rank of captain.
38. CAPT John Laboon, fitness report, July 21, 1972; PUPERS order 184537 for CDR John Laboon, April 6, 1972, Laboon file, NMPR.

with apparent ease. He wrote to his provincial, "My work goes well. This job is not as exciting as it might sound. I am really running the Fleet Chaplain's office and the many chaplains who belong to the Pacific fleet."[39]

The primary command to which Laboon was assigned, Commander Service Force Pacific, was originally established in December 1922 under the name "Fleet Base Force." Its stated mission was "to defend such fleet bases as may be established."[40] The command was the principal logistic agent of Commander in Chief Pacific Fleet (CINPACFLT), providing material support for Pacific fleet and other forces as assigned. While much of his work dealt with the assignment of chaplains, Laboon believed it was essential that he reacquaint himself with the sea commands, as it had been ten years since he had served as a circuit rider for COMSERVRON Three. Thus, after establishing himself in his new environment and becoming grounded in his dual command post, he decided to take a six-month cruise in the western Pacific from July 1972 to January 1973. Besides getting to know the specifics of his command, his presence was especially noteworthy in his leadership concerning racial issues. While in Subic Bay, Philippines, as noted by reporting seniors, Laboon worked with minority personnel, assisting them to understand their place in the navy's mission and working to alleviate any reasonable grievances.[41] Jake's general attitude of outreach to those on the margins is evident here. All personnel were of equal value; rank, race, or creed had no bearing on his ministry to all he served.

Although technically his secondary role, Jake's position as assistant fleet chaplain required much, if not the majority, of his time. He worked closely with the fleet chaplain, Captain Ross Trower. Their office was at CINPACFLT headquarters at Makalapa, Hawaii. Trower described the office as "full and busy. I would say we followed the pastoral schedule."[42] The two men worked well together. There was constant traffic through various Makalapa offices as people passed the chaplains' office for one reason or another. Often casual meetings led to more serious discussions. Laboon and Trower led group sessions, mostly for non-rated navy enlisted, as a means to open a broader discussion and allow sailors to know that the chaplains' office was there for

39. John Laboon, SJ, to Jim Connor, SJ, August 11, 1972, Laboon file, ASJM.
40. Commander Service Force to CNO, April 20, 1961, Service Force U.S. Pacific Fleet through 1958, NHM.
41. CAPT John Laboon, fitness report, February 3, 1973, Laboon file, NMPR.
42. Ross Trower, interview with the author, May 11, 2011.

them. Commenting on Laboon's effective work with sailors, one reporting senior wrote, "Enlisted personnel are attracted to him as a result of his genuine concern for their total welfare and his honesty with them."[43] Working as a team, Trower and Laboon made it a point to always welcome new chaplains to Hawaii, greeting them at the airport and doing what they could to make the transition smooth. Speaking of their teamwork, Trower commented, "I was very glad to serve with Jake. I had close contact with and great admiration for him."[44]

An important element of Laboon's work as assistant fleet chaplain, like his principal duty with COMSERVPAC, was visits to fleet units. These inspection tours brought him to Korea, Japan, the Philippines, and Guam. He was commended for his efforts to monitor and supervise the most effective utilization of chaplain billets in the fleet, working together with the chief of chaplains "to ensure the highest quality personnel placement" in fleet units. In a time when personnel resources were scarce, he utilized his knowledge of people and his former experience as a circuit rider to direct chaplains in ways to most effectively utilize their time, energy, and ministerial expertise.[45] Admiral B. A. Clancy, CINCPACFLT, described Jake's rapport with his fellow chaplains: "In conferring with chaplains of the Fleet, he has encouraged and inspired them in the performance of their duties."[46] He was also applauded for his attention "to emergency problems providing constructive solutions for them."[47] Additionally, Jake was instrumental in assuring that all ships had trained lay leaders and Catholic Eucharistic ministers.[48]

The ministry of Jake Laboon was administrative, but as a priest it was centered around the sacraments. His outreach was to all, from the deckplate sailor to the four-star admiral. He would often leave his Makalapa office and venture down to the piers to talk with any he might encounter. He would simply walk and strike up conversations. Often he celebrated Mass onboard ships. The care and concern he had always demonstrated, from the time he worked with high school students at St. Joe Prep to his present status as a senior navy chaplain, never wavered. This ability to "cover all bases"

43. CAPT John Laboon, fitness report, February 3, 1973, Laboon file, NMPR.
44. Ibid.
45. CAPT John Laboon, fitness report, October 15, 1975, Laboon file, NMPR.
46. CAPT John Laboon, fitness report, September 29, 1973, Laboon file, NMPR.
47. Ibid.
48. John Friel, interview with the author, August 2, 2011.

was noticed by another senior chaplain: "His ministry focused on the Mass, but he certainly cared for sailors. When he was aboard ship or on the docks, he made a point to talk with sailors."[49]

Jake's ministry as assistant fleet chaplain connected with his recent time in Vietnam through Operation Homecoming. The initial return of prisoners of war (POWs) from Vietnam during February and March 1973 prompted a program of welcome and reintegration to society. Chaplains from all branches of the military came together through this specialized operation, providing a special opportunity for interservice and ecumenical cooperation. Upon arrival in the Philippines, the former prisoners were given extensive debriefings. One theme that chaplains noticed was echoed by most all: "My faith in God, faith in my fellow man, and faith in my country got me through these long years."[50] The navy chaplain team was headed by Trower; Jake Laboon assisted with debriefings at Clark Air Force Base, Philippines. Four chaplains, two Protestants, one Catholic, and one Jewish, were available to the former POWs for daily services and counseling. Commenting on Jake's assistance in these debriefing sessions, one reporting senior commented, "Chaplain Laboon has demonstrated his ability to assume increased responsibilities and carry them out in an effective manner."[51]

Returning to Hawaii, Jake once again donned his administrative cap. Along with the fleet chaplain, he played host to many distinguished religious visitors who passed through the CINCPACFLT Command, including Bishop Prince Taylor of the United Methodist Church, Rt. Rev. Clarence Hobgood, Episcopal bishop of the armed forces, Dr. Robert Harriman, director of the Presbyterian Council for Chaplains and Military Personnel, and Rev. Wayne Heil, Pacific Far East representative for the Church of God. In June 1975 Laboon and Trower hosted a marriage and family counseling seminar attended by fourteen chaplains.[52] Appreciation for Laboon's efforts in his post as assistant fleet chaplain was especially acknowledged in the personal dimension he brought to his work. Commenting that the command was "enhanced by Chaplain Laboon's presence and accomplishments," one senior reporting officer wrote, "Everywhere he is welcomed as

49. Alvin Koeneman, interview with the author, May 16, 2011.
50. Operation Homecoming: "The Navy Chaplain Report," 1973, NCA.
51. CAPT John Laboon, fitness report, October 5, 1973, Laboon file, NMPR.
52. Command history, CINCPACFLT 1975, September 7, 1976, NHM.

a friend and a leader of profound integrity."[53] He was clearly held in great respect and "enjoy[ed] the confidence of a large number of senior officers, who have known him intimately during his years of naval service."[54] A junior chaplain who observed Laboon closely in Hawaii commented, "Jake was the most influential assistant fleet chaplain one could possibly have had."[55]

In a way similar to his prior assignment in Florida, Jake was given an additional assignment during his time on Oahu. Between October 1, 1974, and October 1, 1975, he assisted with Naval Logistics Pacific (NAVLOGPAC). His duties included being a member of the Commander Naval Logistics Pacific Human Relations Council and the Pearl Harbor Dependents Activities Council. His work was noted for "initiating actions and offering constructive comments" at various meetings and serving as one of the most competent and informed members" of the LOGPAC staff.[56] His presence with various Hawaii commands was clearly welcomed and respected:

Captain Laboon has consistently demonstrated top level outstanding performance of duty. His contribution to the NAVLOGPAC staff and the Navy/Marine Corps population of the Makalapa, Hawaii community continued to be unsurpassed.[57]

As a senior chaplain much of Jake's day-to-day activity and work were centered in administrative functions, but he never lost his priority for the pastoral work of the priesthood. His administrative hats with COMSERVPAC, CINCPACFLT, and NAVLOGPAC were complemented by his role as the Catholic pastor for the chapel at Makalapa. This small quonset hut, serving both Catholics and Protestants, had once been the mess for Admiral Nimitz during World War II.[58] Laboon took his responsibilities to the small Catholic community very seriously, serving in every capacity from being a crossing guard outside the chapel to the priest celebrating the Mass. Admiral Charles Heid, whose family attended Mass at the Makalapa chapel, was struck by Jake's sermons, which were "to the point and well spoken."[59] A "valued and respected confessor among personnel attached to this staff,"

53. CAPT John Laboon, fitness report, February 3, 1973, Laboon file, NMPR.
54. CAPT John Laboon, fitness report, September 29, 1973, Laboon file, NMPR.
55. John Friel, interview with the author, August 2, 2011.
56. CAPT John Laboon, fitness reports, February 3, 1973, October 5, 1973, Laboon file, NMPR.
57. CAPT John Laboon, fitness report, October 15, 1975, Laboon file, NMPR.
58. Ross Trower, interview with the author, May 14, 2011.
59. Charles Heid to the author, May 24, 2011.

he was "beloved as a pastor of the Catholic community."[60] Moreover, he was remarkably effective and demonstrated great rapport with the dependents, especially teenagers, of those assigned to Makalapa.[61]

Laboon's pastoral and ministerial ability to reach varied groups was remarkable and contributed greatly to his efficacy as a priest and chaplain. Besides working with youth, as he had done so many times in previous commands, he was active in marriage preparation and retreats. He gave retreats, including days of reflection for chaplains in the various branches of the service. He did the same for enlisted sailors. He was noted for his work in contributing "substantially to [the] high level [of] morale and spiritual motivation in the Catholic communities of NAVLOGPAC throughout the Pacific."[62] One comment in a fitness report characterized his ministry: "In his leadership of the Catholic community at the Makalapa Chapel, Chaplain Laboon enriches the lives of his people by his effective preaching, sound counsel and teaching, and his faithful devotion."[63]

The daily routine at Makalapa and his tasks as pastor for the local Catholic community did not in any way impede Jake from being himself, offering hospitality to family and seeking to build cooperation within the various constituencies of his life. The beauty of the Hawaiian environment, often referred to by tourists as "paradise," allowed Jake to continue his love of sports, as he regularly played tennis at Makalapa.[64] A highlight for Jake and his fellow priest chaplains was their weekly Sunday gatherings for fellowship and dinner. Laboon was a primary organizer of these gatherings. Chaplains met, generally from 4 to 7 p.m. on Sunday afternoon at the quarters of one chaplain. After drinks and conversation they would be off to a restaurant for dinner. Typically these gatherings drew from eight to ten priests from the various army, air force, and navy commands on the island.[65] Always a devoted brother, he entertained family members, especially inviting his three religious sisters for visits.[66] In the summer of 1975 Hollywood again knocked on Jake's door. The popular television show

---

60. CAPT John Laboon, fitness report, October 5, 1973, Laboon file, NMPR.
61. CAPT John Laboon, fitness report, October 15, 1975, Laboon file, NMPR.
62. Ibid.
63. CAPT John Laboon, fitness report, February 3, 1973, Laboon file, NMPR.
64. Alvin Koeneman, interview with the author, May 16, 2011.
65. John Friel, interview with the author, August 2, 2011.
66. Charles Heid to the author, May 24, 2011.

Hawaii Five-O was seeking an "extra" to play a navy chaplain in a scene at a burial service. Who better to fill the order than an athletic-looking 6'5" navy chaplain himself? The episode, "Murder: Eyes Only," originally aired on September 12, 1975.[67]

Moving toward the pinnacle of his navy career, Jake Laboon never ceased to impress his associates, both those whom he served and those who observed him. His ability to move so effortlessly and casually between various communities and with peoples of varied persuasions was "a model for emulation by other chaplains." The respect and admiration with which others held him—seniors, peers, and juniors—was almost palpable.[68] Senior officers marveled at the way people of all stripes and ages sought Jake's presence and counsel. Laboon's generosity of spirit, giving of his time and talent and exercising his skills toward the betterment of others, were deeply appreciated. His contributions were described as "broad and imaginative"; he was never content to simply do what was required, but pushed on beyond where others might stop. Laboon integrated his life as a priest and naval officer better than most of his peers. Indeed, this quality was noted by one reporting senior: "He incorporates in his personal character and in the accomplishments of his functions as a member of the staff both the finest attributes of a clergyman of his church and of a naval officer."[69] In January 1975 Jake attained the rank of permanent captain. Nine months later, in late September, as part of his normal rotation, he was relieved of his duties as assistant fleet chaplain.[70]

New London, Force Chaplain Submarines Atlantic: 1975–1976

In November 1975 Jake Laboon moved to a command he knew well from previous experience. After a month's leave he arrived in New London, Connecticut, on November 6, 1975, and reported to the submarine base in his

67. Clipping, *Pittsburgh Catholic,* September 5, 1975, PPWL. The episode was the first of the eighth season of the popular television program. Jake, dressed in navy dress whites, was shown as the presiding chaplain at a burial service.
68. CAPT John Laboon, fitness report, February 3, 1973, Laboon file, NMPR.
69. Ibid.
70. Endorsement document, n.d. [January 1975], Laboon file, NMPR; command history, CINCPACFLT, 1975, September 7, 1976, NHM.

new capacity as force chaplain Atlantic Submarine Fleet and senior chaplain Naval Submarine Base New London. The base was home to attack submarine squadrons, their operational and administrative offices, and overhaul facilities. It was also the base of operations for off-crew training for twenty-five Fleet Ballistic Missile Submarine (SSBN) crews.[71] He supervised three other chaplains, Commander A. E. Purdham, Lieutenant Commander W. E. Parsons, and Lieutenant Commander J. J. Bevins. His collateral duties included serving as executive vice president for the Navy Relief Society and as a member of the United Way Committee and the Protection of Human Subjects Committee. A home in Gales Ferry, Connecticut, served as his quarters. The house became a gathering place for senior members of the submarine force as well as friends from his former days in the area.[72]

His presence on the East Coast allowed Jake to reconnect with many navy personnel, especially classmates and other academy graduates. In that light, in May 1975, Jake was elected as trustee at large to the naval academy alumni association board. He was welcomed by his former football teammate Bill Busik:

Congratulations on your election and a sincere welcome to the Board of Trustees, U.S. Naval Academy Alumni Association. We are glad to have you aboard and we are looking forward to your active participation in the affairs of the Association.[73]

Jake served on the board for three years, 1975 to 1978, during which he was the chairman of the membership committee. During his tenure the association membership increased, exceeding twenty thousand, and a new program of life membership at graduation was initiated.[74]

As always, Jake wasted no time diving into his new duties. One of his first actions was to invite the new bishop of the Diocese of Norwich, Connecticut, Daniel Reilly, to tour the submarine base and to have lunch with the Catholic chaplains.[75] Bishop Reilly also attended a celebratory bicenten-

---

71. CAPT John Laboon, fitness report, June 26, 1976, Laboon file, NMPR.
72. CAPT John Laboon, fitness report, December 17, 1976, Laboon file, NMPR; Nancy Davis, e-mail to the author, December 3, 2010; command history, Submarine Base New London 1975, March 2, 1976, NHM.
73. W. S. Busik to John Laboon, May 19, 1975, John F. Laboon alumni file, AUSNA.
74. Paul D. Stoop to John F. Laboon, June 1, 1978, John F. Laboon alumni file, AUSNA.
75. Command history, Submarine Base New London, 1975, March 2, 1976; command history, Submarine Base New London, 1976, March 1, 1977, NHM; John Donlon, interview with the author, September 14, 2012.

Florida, Hawaii, and New London Again: 1970–1976

nial picnic in July 1976. Furthermore, Laboon immediately reenergized the lay leader program for both Protestants and Catholics. A course was offered monthly to acquaint lay leaders with approved procedures and resources available for them to fulfill their duties aboard boats in the submarine force. A special workshop on liturgy was also provided to help them prepare and practice proper religious services at sea.[76] Jake sought to integrate the chaplains' office into every phase of the submariner's routine, including the departure and arrival of SSBN crews and the arrival of boats from deployment. He assured that all personnel and their dependents knew who the chaplains were and the assistance they could provide. Jake's ability to organize his office and promote programs offered for the betterment of all was noted by his reporting senior:

> As Department head, Captain Laboon develops sound plans and priorities to achieve the goals he has set and then involves subordinates, supervisors and associates by motivating them to contribute their efforts and ideas. He is a professional organizer who not only accepts responsibility, but actually seeks it out.[77]

Laboon was exceptionally effective because of his comprehensive knowledge of both theory and practice in human relations as well as military leadership skills. Referred to by some as an "iconic figure," Jake was an ideal leader, using his gifts and personality in highly productive ways.[78] Indeed, as one report read, "He has a warm personal style which when coupled with his dynamic leadership, makes him an individual who men and women want to follow."[79]

Laboon's move to the East Coast was probably the catalyst that generated an exchange between him and his provincial, Al Panuska, SJ, on his status in both the navy and the Society. Before leaving Pearl Harbor, in a letter informing the provincial of his transfer to New London, he suggested that this might be his last tour in the navy and asked guidance for his return to the Society:

> In the future I hope to be able to sit down with you and discuss what I might do when my time comes to retire from the Navy. That might be in the not too distant

---

76. Command history, Submarine Base New London, 1975, March 2, 1976.
77. CAPT John Laboon, fitness report, December 17, 1976, Laboon file, NMPR.
78. John Donlon, interview with the author, September 9, 2011.
79. CAPT John Laboon, fitness report, December 17, 1976, Laboon file, NMPR.

future. Do you have any ideas where I might work? Counseling in high school might be the best position for me or perhaps working in one of our parishes.[80]

The provincial responded in a measured way: "Your mission seems so important with the navy that I would encourage continued contact as long as you know that you are being well utilized."[81]

In March 1976 the two men resumed their discussions by addressing the possible profession of the fourth vow by Jake. From the foundation of the Society of Jesus by St. Ignatius Loyola in 1540, the Jesuits have had close association with the pope. The "fourth vow" is a promise of obedience to the Holy Father to serve where he might suggest with respect to the missions. In considering his return to the Society, Jake debated about taking the fourth vow, which was necessary for some positions within the community. Responding to a query from Panuska about it, Jake was open to the possibility, but believed it was not necessary:

> At this stage in life and really any time in my life as a Jesuit I do not feel the need for profession *for me*. I am very happy without the fourth vow, am not embarrassed by the lack thereof, and really do not think anything is being added to me by reasons of profession. If the choice was left to me, I say forget it! My *only* reason for retracting what I said above is this. If by reason of my not being professed, the Society cannot give me a job which requires profession, then I would accept that. I will not request this personally, but will go along with the will of consultors.

He concluded,

> I do not wish to make the decision. If you and the consultors feel that I should have a fourth vow, then I will go along with your wishes. As far as JAKE is concerned, forget it![82]

Eventually he did take the fourth vow.[83]

---

80. John Laboon, SJ, to Al Panuska, SJ, July 8, 1975, Laboon file, ASJM.
81. Joseph (Al) Panuska, SJ, to John Laboon, SJ, July 11, 1975, Laboon file, ASJM.
82. John Laboon, SJ, to Al Panuska, SJ, March 26, 1976, Laboon file, ASJM. All emphases original.
83. No extant data explain why Jake changed his mind and took the fourth vow. It was not needed for the ministry to which he was assigned. Chapter 10 describes Jake's decision on the fourth vow more fully. As a short-course Jesuit, Laboon would not have been considered for the fourth vow when he took final profession after completion of his tertianship in 1958. Certain positions in the Society were reserved for those with the fourth vow. In the wake of Vatican II and the 33rd General Congregation of the Society of Jesus, those who had not taken the fourth vow because of their short-course status were given the opportunity to petition for it, not only to make

Laboon's significant contributions to COMBSUBLANT were praised by his commanding officers. His leadership and ability to touch all classes were especially noted by Rear Admiral S. A. White, COMSUBGRU Two:

> Captain Laboon displays unusual qualities of leadership seldom found in the same human being. His inspiration of confidence in all with whom he comes into contact is remarkable. He instantly gains and retains the total respect and admiration of all: senior officers to seamen, adult to child, military to civilian. He is the ideal combination of all the finest attributes of the religious and naval leader, the perfect meld of the chaplain and the naval officer.[84]

Jake was noted for his "extraordinary enthusiasm, knowledge, and sensitivity in the accomplishment of his primary mission of providing moral and religious programs and guidance to both military personnel and dependents in the New London area."[85] His self-confidence, while reassuring to others, also made him more effective in communicating his ideas in ways that could be received positively. Captain R. D. Rawlins, commanding officer of the New London Submarine Base, commented:

> Captain Laboon possesses the moral courage and deep conviction of his views to honestly express his feelings to seniors, juniors and peers. However, he also possesses the tact and verbal ability to make himself clearly understood without alienating those to whom he is expressing his opinions.[86]

The rapport Laboon held with others served as a bridge between various entities in the command, thus improving communication for the betterment of all. Rear Admiral White wrote, "Captain Laboon is without doubt the finest chaplain I have encountered in over 24 years in the Navy."[87]

Comparisons that were drawn between Jake and his contemporaries almost always referred to his superlative performance and thus the need for advancement in rank. Captain Rawlins commented, "Captain Laboon's competence and performance of duty so far excelled that of his contempo-

---

themselves eligible for the restricted positions, but even more so, for the privilege of demonstrating their willingness to serve at the pope's pleasure.

84. CAPT John Laboon, fitness report, June 26, 1976, Laboon file, NMPR. The report went on: "Whether engaged in pastoral activities (counseling, preaching, providing worship service, instruction or consolation) or instilling the military virtues of pride in the service, morale, self-discipline, and dedicated productivity, Captain Laboon gives fully of his many and marvelous talents. He is a skilled administrator and possesses an all-encompassing knowledge of both his professions."

85. CAPT John Laboon, fitness report, December 17, 1976, Laboon file, NMPR.

86. Ibid.

87. CAPT John Laboon, fitness report, June 26, 1976, Laboon file, NMPR.

Florida, Hawaii, and New London Again: 1970–1976

raries that it is difficult to adequately describe his personal and professional excellence."[88] Jake's suitability for higher responsibility and rank was never more forcefully stated than by Rear Admiral John Barrett, COMSERVPAC, who wrote upon Laboon's transfer to New London:

> Captain Laboon is a tremendously valuable senior/supervising chaplain whose gifted leadership should be fully utilized by the United States Navy. Everything about Chaplain Laboon identifies him as a superlative leader and unusually strong performer whose gifts, accomplishments, and experience marked him as a prime contender for immediate selection to flag rank in our Chaplain Corps. He is most strongly so recommended, as early as possible. We need him as a flag officer in our Navy.[89]

Conclusion

Having completed a short tour in the hectic conditions of the Vietnam War, Jake Laboon returned to the United States, crisscrossing the nation from east to west and back to the east, serving in two new venues and a more familiar one. His initial ambition for naval aviation was realized when he was assigned to Saufley Field Naval Air Station, serving both that community and its neighbors at Pensacola and Ellyson Field. Acting for the first time as senior Catholic chaplain at a command, Laboon, as in all previous assignments, was known for his ability to demonstrate skill as both a priest and naval officer. He was next sent west to serve in a dual role with COMSERVPAC and CINCPACFLT. Working closely with the fleet chaplain Pacific, he organized and made available programs for personnel of all stripes, from the most junior to the most senior. Yet his administrative duties never kept him from his pastoral practice, which endeared him to all. After three years, Jake was once again on the move, but this time to the familiar environs of the submarine force at New London, serving both Submarine Group Two and the base chapel community. Although there only one year, he restored prominence to the chaplains' office as an entity involved with all military matters. Having reached the rank of captain, Jake Laboon was now ready to enter the apex of his career and his opportunity for greater responsibility.

88. CAPT John Laboon, fitness report, December 17, 1976, Laboon file, NMPR.
89. CAPT John Laboon, fitness report, October 15, 1975, Laboon file, NMPR.

Chapter 10

Command Climax—Norfolk

★ 1976–1980

The highly competitive pyramid-shaped journey to the top that characterizes American society is familiar to all. At the wide and abundant space at the base of the pyramid, participants begin the climb to the top. Time, expertise, good fortune, and knowledge of policies and individuals are some of the major factors that determine one's progress. As time passes the number of high-level positions decrease, always remaining less than the number of competitors. For the business person the goal is a position in administration or possibly even the top slot of president or chief executive officer. The military has its own pyramid, and the summit for officers is command.[1]

After nearly twenty years of service as a chaplain, Jake Laboon found himself near the top of the pinnacle. Having reached the rank of navy captain and with experience as the senior Catholic chaplain in Florida, assistant fleet chaplain in Hawaii, and senior chaplain in New London, Jake was ready for top-level responsibilities. He had demonstrated all the qualities, both as naval officer and priest, that marked him as qualified, a reality that had been noted throughout his career by his reporting senior officers. Thus Jake Laboon entered the apex of his military career in the fall of 1976 when

---

1. It is important to understand the differences between line officers and chaplains with respect to command. Chaplains technically do not command. Rather, they may serve, as would Jake Laboon, in positions of significant responsibility for personnel and programs. Line officers, who have authority for nonjudicial punishment under the Uniform Code of Military Justice, can and do hold positions as commanding officers. This technical nuance between the chaplain corps and line officers with respect to command had no bearing on Laboon's qualifications to serve in the top level positions he held in Norfolk.

he reported to Norfolk, Virginia. Over the next four years he would hold two positions of significance: officer-in-charge of the Fleet Religious Support Activity (FRSA), a novel and innovative command that was organized to more effectively utilize chaplain resources; and fleet chaplain Atlantic Fleet. As in all previous assignments, Jake's love for the priesthood and navy would be manifested in varied ways, but especially in his role as an officer-in-charge, through his ability to mentor his fellow chaplains, providing those with lesser skills and experience the tools they needed to succeed as naval officers and ministers to God's people.

Fleet Religious Support Activity (FRSA): 1976–1978

After serving on a permanent basis in nine different commands, Jake Laboon reached the zenith of his career when he was assigned to Norfolk in late 1976. On November 23 he relieved Captain Marlin D. Seiders as officer-in-charge of the Fleet Religious Support Activity (FRSA). It was clear at the change-of-command ceremony that Jake's reputation had gained him recognition. In remarks given by Vice Admiral Howard T. Green, deputy commander U.S. Atlantic Fleet, and Rear Admiral John O'Connor, chief of chaplains, Laboon's many accomplishments were praised.[2] These achievements were evident as well to those he encountered in his new command. The naval aviator Rear Admiral James Flatley commented, "His reputation preceded him. He was recognized by his hero status before I got to say hello."[3] A junior chaplain, Bruce Kahn, spoke of how he knew of Laboon long before he personally met him: "He was a legend. I had heard so much about him."[4] Jake himself was very pleased with his assignment. He wrote to his provincial:

Aside from the Chief of Chaplains, this is probably the biggest and best job a Chaplain in the Navy can have. There will be about 50 chaplains working for me and under my guidance in Norfolk, Charleston, and Mayport.[5]

As with his previous commands in Florida, Hawaii, and New London, Jake resided off-base in a home in Virginia Beach.[6]

The Fleet Religious Support Activity (FRSA) was created in response to

2. Relieving ceremony for OIC, FRSA, November 23, 1976, folder 1754/8, box 89, NCA.
3. James Flatley, interview with the author, March 3, 2011.
4. Bruce Kahn, interview with the author, August 3, 2011.
5. John Laboon, SJ, to Al Panuska, SJ, March 20, 1976, Laboon file, ASJM.
6. Report of medical examination, March 28, 1979, Laboon file, NMPR.

the post-Vietnam draw-down of navy personnel, including chaplains. Decisions by top-level navy personnel in the early 1970s led to a significant reduction in the number of chaplain billets in several commands, yet the religious needs of personnel remained. Therefore, the existing system for providing chaplain coverage needed to be modified and an alternative design for ministry created. On the East Coast the answer to this dilemma was FRSA, a system whereby chaplains were shared by assigning them for periods of time to various commands, especially at sea, basically as circuit riders, a format that Jake Laboon understood well from his days in Japan. One brief history of FRSA described the program and its rationale:

> It [FRSA] was not believed to be the ideal model for ministry, but the way to provide the best kind of religious coverage to the greatest number of personnel in the fleet with a fairly limited number of chaplains.[7]

When FRSA was first proposed, it was rejected by the vice chief of naval operations, Admiral James Holloway. However, Rear Admiral Richard Hutcheson, fleet chaplain Atlantic, was persistent and convinced the chief of chaplains, Rear Admiral Francis Garrett, of the viability of the program. Garrett in turn lobbied Admiral Ralph W. Cousins, CINCLANTFLT, who managed to sell the program to the chief of naval operations (CNO). Hutcheson's contribution was noted: "It was his perseverance and dedication that kept the idea alive."[8]

On March 23, 1974, the CNO authorized FRSA-Atlantic Fleet. The official document read:

> Religious ministries to certain ships have long been provided by circuit-riding chaplains assigned to operational staffs. In recent years, staff reductions, personnel cuts and fleet reorganizations have eroded the effectiveness of the system, leaving some ships with no access to chaplain ministries and others with limited access. To maximize the available chaplain resources and provide the most equitable ministry, the Fleet Religious Support Activity, U.S. Atlantic Fleet (FLTRELSUPPACTLANT) has been established.[9]

FRSA was headquartered at CINCLANTFLT with component offices at Norfolk, Virginia, Charleston, South Carolina, and Mayport, Florida.[10]

---

7. LT Stephen Wallace, "The Fleet Religious Support Activity" (1985), 12, folder 1754/8, box 89, NCA.
8. Ibid., 10–11.
9. CINCLANTFLT instruction 1730.4B, July 3, 1978, folder 1754/8, box 89, NCA.
10. FRSA, command brief, n.d. [1979], folder 1754/8, box 89, NCA.

FRSA had a broad and multifaceted mission: "to provide an in-depth and equitable religious team ministry to Atlantic Fleet ships which do not have chaplain allowances."[11] The FRSA had several specific functions: (1) provide circuit-riding chaplains and religious ministry for all major deployments and fleet exercises in ships not having their own chaplains; (2) provide chaplain services and religious ministry to all ships and submarines without chaplains while in port in New London, Norfolk, Charleston, and Mayport; (3) maintain an effective Protestant, Catholic, and Jewish lay leader training program; (4) provide pastoral counseling and dependent assistance to personnel and their dependents of ships home ported in New London, Norfolk, Charleston, and Mayport that are without chaplains; (5) ensure all ecclesiastical equipment and supplies are available to carry out this mission.[12] The development of team ministry was also critical to the overall function and efficacy of FRSA and was highly encouraged:

> The concept of chaplains functioning together as a team in a spirit of mutual support and collegiality is one which is basic to the ministry provided by chaplains. Team ministry is integral to the design and functioning of the FLTRELSUPPACTLANT.... The Fleet Team Ministry has as its sole purpose the meeting of the religious needs and related human needs of personnel.[13]

At the outset, FRSA was organized with a central command and three component local stations. The founding officer in charge, Captain Eugene S. Swanson, was stationed in Norfolk; local component coordinators were present in Charleston, Norfolk, and Mayport. The Norfolk office had branch locations at the Amphibious Base at the Little Creek Naval Station and the destroyer and submarine piers.[14] Initially there were thirty chaplains (nineteen in Norfolk, six in Charleston, and five in Mayport) and ten enlisted personnel on the staff.[15] By the time Jake Laboon arrived the number of chaplains had risen to thirty-eight, all of whom were assigned for all

---

11. Ibid.
12. FRSA command brief, n.d. [1979] folder 1754/8, box 89, NCA. New London was not a component of the original FRSA schema, but it was added during Laboon's tenure.
13. CINCLANTFLT instruction 1730.4B, July 3, 1978, folder 1754/8, box 89, NCA.
14. Pamphlet FRSA, U.S. Atlantic Fleet, formal establishment, July 9, 1974, folder 1754/8, box 89, NCA. The coordinators in the various local regions were: Charleston—CAPT Donald H. Dillard; Norfolk—CDR Dennis C. Kinlaw; Mayport—CDR Ferdinand Slejzer.
15. CINCLANTFLT instruction 1730.4B, October 30, 1975, folder 1754/8, box 89, NCA; "Relieving Ceremony for OIC Fleet Religious Support Activity," November 23, 1976, PPJL.

major deployments and fleet exercises.[16] Regular monthly meetings among the chaplains in any one component were held to exchange ideas and to update all on better training opportunities. In addition to the active-duty personnel assigned to FRSA, there was also a reserve component with fifty-three chaplains and eighteen enlisted billets.[17]

The circuit-riding ministry, foundational to FRSA, had a basic goal to keep 50 percent of the chaplains at sea, as deployed forces were the highest priority, but local operations were not ignored. Chaplains were busy with counseling and conducting active-duty services aboard ship and in port. The 1978 command history, which provides statistics for the numbers of members and dependents serviced by FRSA, concluded, "Combine these figures with [the fact that] circuit riding chaplains spend 40 percent of their time at sea, it can easily be seen that our chaplains had a very busy year."[18]

FRSA members performed the same duties as any chaplain, but their relationship to the command was tenuous and, therefore, at times difficult. Religious services and counseling comprised the bulk of the day-to-day activity, but Bible studies and training lay leaders were other important aspects of their ministry. In port, FRSA chaplains conducted retreats and marriage preparation and assisted with pre-deployment counseling, especially for wives and families.[19] They themselves were sent to firefighting, damage control, helo safety, and survival school in preparation for their deployments.[20]

Although it was experimental, FRSA received high marks from the various commands it served and the chaplains involved. One type commander commented:

The FLTRELSUPPACTLANT has consistently provided outstanding service to personnel of the Naval Surface Forces, U.S. Atlantic Fleet through assignment of chaplains for long-term deployments and import ministry to personnel through utilization of pier side offices. Key factors in the inport ministry have been the one-on-one counseling, numerous spiritual programs and individual family counseling.[21]

16. "Relieving Ceremony for OIC Fleet Religious Support Activity," n.d. [1979], folder 1754/8, box 89, NCA.
17. FRSA command brief, n.d. [1979], folder 1754/8, box 89, NCA.
18. Atlantic Fleet and FRSA command history, 1978, n.d. [1979], NHM.
19. CINCLANTFLT instruction 1730.4B, October 30, 1975, folder 1754/8, box 89, NCA.
20. OIC FRSA to director of naval history, March 12, 1979, found in FRSA command history 1978, n.d. [1979], NHM.
21. Commander Naval Surface Force U.S. Atlantic Fleet to commander Naval Base Norfolk, September 3, 1975, folder 1754/8, box 89, NCA.

Captain Dennis Kinlaw, Norfolk coordinator, felt proud to be a participant: "For us who are privileged to be a part of this new venture in ministry, it is a time of excitement and anticipation."[22] Chaplain Robert G. Gordon evaluated FRSA as "one of the greatest and boldest experimentations ever undertaken by the Navy Chaplain Corps."[23] One command document read, "In the past five years Fleet Religious Support Activity has grown in the area of responsibility and the number of chaplains assigned. It has progressed from a theoretical experiment to an effective, integral part of ministry to the fleet."[24]

The responsibilities as officer in charge (OIC) that Jake Laboon found upon his arrival in November 1976 were mostly administrative but also involved coordinating the efforts of component locations to achieve the command's assigned mission. Specifically the OIC was responsible to maintain FRSA in a state of readiness to provide a responsive religious team ministry to all units in the Atlantic fleet. Ship schedules and the operations of CINCLANTFLT were to be coordinated to assure proper coverage by chaplains. FRSA was also to provide professional training for chaplains and lay leaders through conferences and other professional programs. The OIC was also mandated to make periodic visits, three times per year if possible, to consult with local coordinators at component commands.[25] The most significant OIC responsibility was the scheduling of chaplains for future deployments, maintaining contact with them while at sea, and receiving reports at the conclusion of a deployment with recommendations for improvement in ministry during future deployments and major exercises. Scheduling generally was done twelve to eighteen months in advance, with individual units advised ninety days prior to deployment of the anticipated number of chaplains to be assigned.[26]

As the officer in charge of FRSA, Jake Laboon, with his vast knowledge of the navy and personal friendships with many significant and high-ranking officers, had the opportunity to better the command and to generally enhance

---

22. CAPT Dennis Kinlaw, "The Fleet Religious Support Activity: A Venture in Team Ministry," folder 1754/8, box 89, NCA.
23. Quoted in LT. Stephen Wallace, "The Fleet Religious Support Activity," folder 1754/8, box 89, NCA.
24. FRSA command brief, n.d. [1979], folder 1754/8, box 89, NCA.
25. FRSA Atlantic instruction 5400.1, n.d. [1976], folder 1754/8, box 91, NCA.
26. FRSA command brief, n.d. [1979], folder 1754/8, box 89, NCA.

the presence of chaplains in the Atlantic fleet. Jake understood authority and rank, and he was able to effectively utilize them for the benefit of the men he served. One FRSA chaplain, commenting years later, stated that Jake's experience and naval academy background made him "ideally suited for his job."[27] Admiral Frank Kelso, a former chief of naval operations, agreed that Jake's friendships with senior officers gave him entrée to personnel that allowed him to get things done. He was able to cut a few corners in order to effectively and efficiently achieve the ends he desired.[28]

Laboon's friendship with Admiral Isaac Kidd, who was serving as commander-in-chief Atlantic Fleet (CINCLANTFLT) when Jake was assigned to FRSA, was especially advantageous for him and his command. Since the time they had met on the football field at the academy, the two men had been great friends, although they had never served together professionally. Laboon in many ways served as Admiral Kidd's personal chaplain, accompanying the admiral on numerous trips and to various meetings. When Kidd went to Washington, especially to testify to some congressional committee, he took Jake with him. Rear Admiral Charles Heid remembers being with Kidd and Laboon on a trip to Kaflavik, Iceland. When the admiral went to Europe, wearing his other command hat, supreme allied commander Atlantic for NATO, Jake once again was at his side.[29] Kidd referred to Jake as "my adviser" or on other occasions as "my Black Angel."[30] In January 1977, when forty-eight American servicemen (twenty-four sailors and twenty-four marines) were killed when a Spanish freighter collided with a liberty boat, Jake went with Isaac Kidd to "Dover Air Force Base to welcome the bodies and render honors."[31]

Admiral Kidd's admiration for Jake Laboon was clear and profound. In signing a citation for Jake's reception of the Meritorious Service Medal, Kidd's relationship to Laboon was obvious:

He not only made some recommendations to the Chief of Chaplains for the maximum utilization of chaplain assets, but also served as a respected adviser to the

27. Edwin Condon, interview with the author, January 19, 2011.
28. Admiral Frank Kelso, interview with the author, April 7, 2011; RDAM Alvin Koeneman, interview with the author, May 16, 2011.
29. Charles Heid, interview with the author, May 24, 2011; Frank Kelso, interview with the author, April 7, 2011.
30. Rosemary, deLellis, and Joan Laboon, interview with the author, August 21, 2010; Joe DeSantis, interview with the author, March 31, 2011.
31. John Laboon, eulogy for Michael Smith, tape recording, n.d. [1986].

Commander-in-Chief U.S. Atlantic Fleet [Kidd] in the areas of religion, morale, and the spiritual growth of personnel within the Atlantic Fleet.[32]

In speaking of Jake, Kidd once stated, "I admired his level of seriousness and dedication for telling it like it is in the fleet. If you did not make a decision that was good, he was all over you like a tent."[33]

Members of Admiral Kidd's family recognized the strong relationship between their father and Jake Laboon. Isaac Kidd III commented,

> There was a strong mutual self-support and self-admiration society between these two giants. From my Dad's perspective, Father Jake was the pillar of the Church itself and from Jake's perspective he always admired my father's military prowess and leadership.[34]

Mary Plummer, one of Kidd's daughters, described the relationship between the two men: "They were the closest of brothers."[35] Christopher Kidd remembers the first-name relationship between them. He could never recall from his childhood anyone junior to his father referring to him by his first name save Jake Laboon. He recalled, "My dad called him Jake and he called my dad Ike. No matter how many stars my dad wore or stripes on Jake's uniform, that was their relationship." He went on to speak of how Jake provided Kidd with counsel in a way no one else could:

> My dad saw in Laboon something that he saw in no one else. It was probably a combination of strength, character, confidence, and guidance, because there were many times over my dad's career when he turned to Laboon because he could not turn to anybody else.[36]

Jake Laboon placed his stamp on FRSA by developing new policies and the inauguration of special projects. He added a component unit at New London to complement the original three. By 1978 FRSA had forty circuit-riding chaplains providing ministry to 336 ships, submarines, and staffs. Component staffs were responsible to provide religious ministry to 178,000 military personnel and their dependents.[37] Policy development was another major part of Jake's ministry. He explained,

---

32. Citation—Meritorious Service Medal, n.d. [1980], Laboon file, NMPR.
33. Clipping, Greensburgh (Pennsylvania) *Tribune*, March 19, 1995, PPWL.
34. Isaac Kidd III, interview with the author, September 22, 2010.
35. Mary Plummer, interview with the author, December 18, 2010.
36. Christopher Kidd, interview with the author, October 4, 2010.
37. FRSA and Atlantic Fleet command history, 1978, n.d. [1977], NHM.

That job involves developing a religious program for the fleet through the chaplains and lay leaders aboard all of our ships. Unfortunately we do not have enough chaplains. I'd like to see one aboard most of the ships because I think it adds a tremendous amount to the morale of the crew.[38]

Assigning chaplains, managing schedules, and assuring denominational balance in those who were deployed was a critical and difficult task, but he achieved his goals quite effectively. Lauding his administrative gifts, a citation noted that Laboon "expertly directed the circuit riding chaplains of the Atlantic Fleet assigned to deploy ships, increased their numbers and made frequent visits to detachments to bolster the effectiveness of these chaplains."[39] Sending the chaplain with the necessary gifts for a particular command was anything but an easy task, but Jake had a special flair to know how and where to assign his men.[40] An additional element to his special touch was his ever-willing attitude to minister to personnel aboard ships in port. He never passed up an opportunity to assist those on vessels in port, whether it was celebration of Mass or another need.

Jake had a special relationship with his chaplains that was manifested in varied ways. Not only did he regularly visit his component sites, but also called coordinator meetings at Norfolk to discuss future plans for religious coverage of ships and ways to improve the ministry provided with limited personnel. He discussed with the coordinators his future objectives and asked their input for how to meet them.[41] On a more personal level, working with individual chaplains, he visited ships in port and often spoke with commanding officers, educating them as to how chaplains can be best utilized.[42] He was not afraid to stand up for a chaplain he thought might have been maligned.[43] As he had done in Hawaii, Jake also regularly organized gatherings for navy priests for common fellowship. Usually held once per week, Jake entertained at his house, generally offering his guests his specialty—chili.

38. News clipping, n.d [1980], PPWL.
39. Citation—Meritorious Service Medal, n.d. [1980], Laboon file, NMPR.
40. Admiral Jim Flatley, interview with the author, March 3, 2011.
41. OIC of FRSA to director of naval history, March 12, 1979, enclosure to command history, FRSA 1978, NHM.
42. Admiral Jim Flatley, interview with the author, March 3, 2011.
43. Several chaplains spoke in interviews of how Laboon would intercede for them, especially when conflicts arose between them and ship commanders; Barry Black, interview with the author, October 25, 2010; Bruce Kahn, interview with the author, August 3, 2011.

These gatherings were much appreciated. As one chaplain commented, "He had a great sense of the camaraderie of the priesthood."[44]

During Laboon's tenure as OIC, FRSA initiated several new projects. In March 1978 the chief of chaplains, John O'Connor, assigned Laboon to undertake a study to create metrics to measure the efficacy of FRSA and its work. O'Connor wrote,

> In view of the ongoing requirement to articulate and quantify both the need for and the impact of the ministry of circuit riding chaplains aboard ships, it is requested that you undertake a study to determine standards which can be used to measure and describe the ministry of Fleet Religious Support Activity chaplains aboard ships in the Atlantic Fleet.[45]

O'Connor told Laboon to develop a plan of assessment to include such things as the number of ships served, the number that should be served, the number of sailors without "reasonable" access to a chaplain, the impact of the chaplain aboard ship, and the length of time a chaplain should be aboard to be effective in ministry.[46] On April 27–28, chaplains from the four FRSA components and the special projects officer from O'Connor's office, Alvin Koeneman, met in Charleston, South Carolina, to inaugurate this study. Basically the team was asked, "Is religious ministry being provided by FRSA chaplains under the present structure to personnel aboard ships in the Atlantic Fleet?" A related question was, "Is the FRSA model the best way to provide that ministry?"[47]

FRSA was called to provide various services for fleet exercises and personnel training. In May 1978 a heavy strain was placed on FRSA personnel to support Exercise Solid Shield 78, conducted off the coast of North Carolina. In July the annual deployment—UNITAS—to South America was conducted, requiring additional chaplains. One month later, Northern Wedding, the North Atlantic Fleet exercise, also needed FRSA support.[48] Moreover, fleet support was also asked in the inauguration of a special project, the Division Officer Interview Training Program. Conducted by FRSA

---

44. Edwin Condon, interview with the author, January 19, 2011.
45. Chief of chaplains to OIC FRSA, March 7, 1978, folder 1754/8, box 91, NCA.
46. Ibid.
47. Alvin Koeneman, chief of chaplains, June 13, 1978, folder 1754/8, box 8, NCA.
48. OIC FRSA to director of naval history, May 12, 1979, enclosure to FRSA command history, 1978, NHM.

chaplains, this program was established to aid division officers with basic interview skills to assist in their supervision of enlisted personnel.[49] A third project for FRSA in 1978 was another request from the chief of chaplains to study the need for and effectiveness of circuit riding ministry. The study was to seek data in two areas: (1) What is the extent and quantity of ministry being done by circuit riders, both at sea and ashore? (2) How effective does the fleet perceive circuit riding to be as a method for providing ministry to ships without chaplains assigned as ship's company?[50]

In addition to the special projects at sea, FRSA, under the leadership of Jake Laboon, inaugurated several programs for fleet units ashore. The Fleet Retreat Center at Fort Storey, Virginia, was used for various activities, including days of recollection for chaplains, family enrichment for dependents, training sessions for lay leaders and church school teachers, and seminars that addressed concerns of military life. The facility was available to all U.S. Atlantic Fleet personnel, including marines and coast guard. The religious social center "That Place," a unit adjunct to the Fleet Retreat Center, was a coffeehouse ministry designed to be an informal "living room away from home." It was designed to attract young sailors for activities such as Bible study, various music programs, prayer sessions, movies, overnight retreats, and even parties for the underprivileged. "That Place" was described as providing "constructive, wholesome programs [that] have attracted numerous personnel from ships at the Naval Station piers."[51] FRSA also sponsored the Marriage Training and Family Life Enrichment Program, which sought: (1) to provide naval personnel and their families the opportunity for personal growth through educational training dealing with family and marriage and (2) to give participants the skills to strengthen their interpersonal family relationships.[52] Jake secured a new facility for counseling of sailors and/or their families with the complaint, "The existing austere facilities and crowded conditions do not approach the minimum requirements

49. LT Stephen Wallace, "Fleet Religious Support Activity," 1985, 27, folder 1754/8, box 89, NCA.

50. OIC FRSA to distribution, June 13, 1978, folder 1754/8, box 89, NCA.

51. LT Stephen Wallace, "Fleet Religious Support Activity," 1985, 26–27, folder 1754/8, box 89, NCA; relieving ceremony for OIC Fleet Religious Support Activity, November 23, 1976, PPJL; commander Naval Surface Force U.S. Atlantic Fleet to commander Naval Base Norfolk, September 3, 1975, folder 1754/8, box 91, NCA.

52. LT Stephen Wallace, "Fleet Religious Support Activity," 1985, 26–27, folder 1754/8, box 89, NCA.

for this purpose."⁵³ Another highly significant FRSA program was RALLY (Recovery of Attitude Loyalty Lifestyle to Yourself), an overnight retreat at the FRSA Retreat Center. Specifically designed for sailors who are struggling with self-identity, authority, intimacy, and commitment, the program helped sailors work out their frustrations by taking time to stop on the road of life, to look at where one was, to listen to others so that one could consciously participate in determining the future. One report described the efficacy of RALLY: "We are not certain that the retreats can be measured in terms of loss/gain, win/lose, but we are convinced that they have impact on the participants in terms of assuming responsibility for their decisions."⁵⁴

While his administrative assistance to various programs was significant, the greatest contribution Jake Laboon made as OIC of FRSA was his ability to mentor junior chaplains. He went out of his way to befriend and assist the newly arrived. James Kirstein, a retired navy chaplain who first met Jake at Norfolk when the former had just been inducted in the navy, illustrates this point:

His pastoral concern seemed to be for the welfare of the new chaplain.... In his presence I seemed to forget that he was a seasoned leader and I a neophyte. [He was] a very easy man with whom to talk. He became an example for me in many ways.⁵⁵

From the most junior to the most senior, chaplains realize that the corps is a patriarchy, and it was evident to all in Norfolk that Jake was indeed its father. Kirstein commented, "This [mentoring] role seemed to fall naturally to him and he was extremely efficient in it."⁵⁶ Jake believed it was his task to bring his experience and knowledge to this task. Several who served with him in Norfolk spoke of his ability to do so. One former chaplain described how Jake's past knowledge and experience were attractive: "He seemed to know everything there was to know about the Navy from a line view and from a chaplain view."⁵⁷ Another chaplain echoed the same sentiments: "He brought a wealth of experience for us."⁵⁸ The present chaplain of the United States Senate and former chief of chaplains, Barry Black, commented, "You

53. John Laboon to CO U.S. Naval Base Norfolk, January 28, 1977, folder 1754/8, box 89, NCA.
54. FRSA RALLY, n.d. [1978], folder 1754/8, box 89, NCA.
55. James Kirstein, e-mail to the author, August 11, 2011.
56. Ibid.
57. Bruce Kahn, interview with the author, August 3, 2011.
58. Joseph Capper, interview with the author, October 1, 2012.

could ask him any question and he would provide from the vast reservoir of his experience very wise counsel."[59]

Jake Laboon was a great advocate for his chaplains. He gave them the feeling that he was one with them; he mobilized people to work toward common shared objectives. Jake was always seeking ways to enable and empower his chaplains to maximize their skills and possibilities.[60] He used the power and authority he possessed to assist his chaplains, being especially strident if he felt one was being maligned or inappropriately treated, especially by senior personnel. Black credits Laboon with saving his career as a junior officer when the former got into a disagreement with his command chaplain.[61]

Laboon empowered junior chaplains and challenged them to reach their full potential. Black referred to Laboon as a "servant leader. He did not have a strategic plan that he would force on you. He did a lot of listening to learn what chaplains felt needed to be done."[62] Thus he would provide options; he left it to the chaplain to make the choice, especially when facing challenges. Understanding that these young chaplains needed to learn leadership, Laboon forced them to make decisions. Possessive of significant humility himself, Jake treated those he supervised with great respect. Yet, taking his role as leader and mentor quite seriously, he could not stomach any chaplain who appeared proud or self-centered. He was critical in a positive way by using the old military adage, "Praise in public; reprove in private." Still, there were times when Jake could be "terrifyingly acerbic in taking apart another chaplain who seemed too pompous." One chaplain commented, "For a fellow who was normally soft-spoken and low-key, he could quickly come alive with incisive, colorful and loquacious language."[63]

Association with Jake Laboon was for many young chaplains in FRSA

59. Barry Black, interview with the author, October 25, 2010.
60. Ibid.
61. Ibid. Black tells the story that when he was a junior chaplain at Norfolk he had a heated discussion with his command chaplain over Black's almost constant deployment while other chaplains seldom if ever went to sea. Black wanted to know why. The discussion led the command chaplain to write a poor evaluation of Black, although all his previous fitness reports were superlative. Black went to Laboon and explained the situation. He told Black that he could override the report of the command chaplain or, if Black allowed him, he could handle the situation in his own way. Black agreed to allow Jake to correct the situation as he saw fit, which he did.
62. Ibid.
63. James Kirstein, e-mail to the author, August 11, 2011.

their ticket for future success. Many young chaplains who served under Jake in Norfolk commented that a favorable recommendation received from him launched their future careers. Because of the respect that senior commanders held for Jake and his opinions, if one received a praiseworthy fitness report from Father Jake, the future was bright. Again, Barry Black commented, "If Laboon said you had a future, it magically happened." Speaking about his own career and his aforementioned encounter with Laboon, he commented, "Such supremely kind words, from such a stellar source, meant I was on my way."[64]

The admiration and respect that characterized Jake Laboon's attitude toward his fellow chaplains was equally, if not more, reciprocated by all he encountered. He was held in high regard because of the example he set; he brought smiles to the faces of all. Retired navy chaplain Monsignor Robert Ecker, who eulogized Jake at his funeral, commented:

He had touched their hearts, their spirits, because of his modeling how all of us should be, modest in our manner, humble in our way of conducting ourselves, committed in our approach to ministry, and sensitive to other people.[65]

Others felt comfortable around Jake. Barry Black commented, "He was a pastor and a shepherd. You never thought of him as a line officer."[66] Jake had total credibility; all were aware of his past experiences. Chaplains saw him as a "giant."[67] One retired chaplain commented, "Father Jake was for me the epitome of what a naval officer and chaplain ought to be."[68]

The experimental nature of FRSA as a novel way of providing chaplain services to the Atlantic Fleet required an assessment. Although when Jake arrived the program had been in operation a little over two years, nonetheless, even during his tenure FRSA remained in a state of development and flux. Nonetheless, several significant strengths were found in the evaluation. First was the development of team ministry. Ships had access to a chaplain assigned from a team of chaplains. Second, through scheduling, FRSA chaplains had a more uniform and equitable distribution of at-sea

64. Barry C. Black, *From the Hood to the Hill: A Story of Overcoming* (Nashville, Tenn.: Thomas Nelson, 2006), 103.
65. Robert Ecker, interview with the author, December 19, 2010.
66. Barry Black, interview with the author, October 25, 2010.
67. Peter Pilarski, interview with the author, January 14, 2011.
68. David Atwater, interview with the author, September 26, 2012.

deployments. A third important strength was that FRSA provided a great environment and training ground for new chaplains. One retired chaplain noted, "It allowed a new chaplain to concentrate on ministry rather than spending so much time on collateral duties."[69] FRSA's assessment also manifested some significant weaknesses. First, chaplains had no identification with a particular ship. This was noted by one chaplain:

The fact that we were not working long-term with most of our crews [meant that] we had no idea how to anticipate and prepare for a specific crew's religious needs, what the size of our program might be, or how to prepare logistically.[70]

Another problem that became evident was that for many chaplains it was "survival of the fittest." One retired chaplain explained his experience:

Only strong personalities survived. A chaplain who needed constant encouragement, approval or support—or who had problems with self-confidence and initiative—was of little or no value. It was a much lonelier and more tentative existence than being part of a squadron or a single ship. A weak, mean or otherwise incompetent chaplain OIC could wreak havoc and ruin careers.[71]

Thus, overall, FRSA was viewed as a tremendous training ground but one that demanded strong, self-reliant chaplains who were motivated and already possessed a sense of what to do. While ministry was somewhat truncated and at times less than ideal, it was better than no ministry at all for the many at-sea forces who without FRSA would have received no chaplain services.[72]

Laboon's two years as OIC of FRSA were times of personal growth and accomplishment.. Jake had faithfully served as a chaplain in the navy for nearly twenty years, rising through the ranks to a very senior position, but he never forgot that he was a Jesuit, and thus, when the opportunity arose, he returned to his roots. The issue at hand was his profession of the fourth vow. Because Jake had taken the short course at Woodstock, he was not initially eligible to take the fourth vow. While those vows professed by any member of the Society in the novitiate are perpetual, they are nonethe-

---

69. LT Stephen Wallace, "Fleet Religious Support Activity," 1985, 28–30, folder 1754/8, box 89, NCA; J. D. Atwater, "Personal Reflection," personal papers of J. David Atwater (hereafter PPJDA).

70. J. D. Atwater, "Personal Reflection," PPJDA. Atwater further commented, "We were able to do little more than counsel and hold services. When you're a 'visitor,' COs do not usually develop a high trust factor that enables them to value your input on sensitive issues."

71. Ibid.

72. Ibid.

less simple.⁷³ Thus, the final act of membership is one's final profession of vows. Jake took solemn vows as a spiritual coadjutor on August 15, 1959, approximately a year after his completion of tertianship at Auriesville, New York.⁷⁴ The invitation to profess the fourth vow came in 1977. Recall that one year earlier, Jake and his provincial had dialogued about this issue, but nothing had been concluded. Finally, in August 1977, after spending one year as OIC at FRSA, Jake did profess the fourth vow.⁷⁵ This special event in his life was held at Manresa Retreat House, across the Severn River from his beloved alma mater, the naval academy. With his family and close friends in attendance, including former students from St. Joe Prep and many navy friends, both chaplains and laity, Jake proudly recommitted himself to Christ through the Society of Jesus. He wrote in gratitude to his family for their support of his vocation. He lamented the fact that over the years his trips to Pittsburgh were brief, and thus quality family time had been limited. Hence, he was most grateful for this special time. In gratitude to God and family he wrote:

Each of us ought to thank God daily for one another and for all the many blessings He has sent to us as a family. God has been so good to us that it sometimes makes me wonder what we did to deserve His graces and Hid [sic] love. I guess we can truly say, "Lord I am not worthy."⁷⁶

The beauty and exhilaration that were certainly evident in Jake's profession of final vows was duplicated through his relationship with the family of Admiral Isaac Kidd. While the relationship between these two men, which extended to members of the Kidd family, had been ongoing throughout their careers, their bond became closer through their common service at Norfolk in the mid- to late 1970s. In March 1978 Jake experienced some urology problems leading to prostate surgery.⁷⁷ During his recovery he stayed with the Kidd family. One son referred to him as the "house chap-

---

73. For Jesuits the vows professed at the end of the canonical year are perpetual, but only some years later, after establishing oneself in the Society and in ministry, is a member of the community invited to take the fourth vow, to go where directed by the Holy Father. Thus the vows professed during the novitiate are referred to as simple.

74. John Laboon, SJ, to William Maloney, SJ, July 21, 1959, Laboon file, ASJM.

75. It is not clear from extant data why Laboon changed his mind from a year earlier and accepted the invitation to profess the fourth vow.

76. John Laboon to "Dear Family," August 25, 1977, PPJM.

77. A clinical record, narrative summary, March 16, 1978; active duty in-patient disposition, n.d. [March 1978], Laboon file, NMPR.

lain," because he celebrated Mass in the home.[78] For everyone in the Kidd family, however, he was much more. A bigger-than-life person in many ways, Jake was seen as a member of the family. His period of recovery in the Kidd home was only one manifestation of a longstanding and ongoing relationship between Jake and the family. He often stopped by the house simply to say hello. If a member of the family was in need of his presence, he was there. Jake celebrated the funeral mass for Admiral Kidd's mother; he was present with members of the family one Easter Sunday at St. Patrick's Cathedral in New York when the admiral was received into the Catholic Church, including the sacraments of First Communion and Confirmation. There is much evidence from the recollections of the Kidd family that Jake was instrumental in the admiral's conversion.[79]

On June 9, 1978, after serving slightly less than two years as officer-in-charge of the Fleet Religious Support Activity, Jake was transferred to the staff CINCLANTFLT. He continued to serve at FRSA for three months and wore two hats, FRSA OIC and his new one, fleet chaplain Atlantic. Jake had reached the pinnacle of his career. On September 11, Captain C. E. LeMasters relieved him as OIC at FRSA. The highlight of the ceremony was when Admiral Kidd, CINCLANTFLT, presented Jake with the Meritorious Service Medal.[80] Over two hundred invited guests, plus many chaplains and enlisted personnel from the four components of FRSA, celebrated Jake's achievements. The citation for Jake's award, signed by Isaac Kidd, summarized the significant work he had accomplished at FRSA:

From November 1976 to September 1978 ... Captain Laboon displayed superb leadership and professional competence in developing and directing progressive religious programs for military personnel assigned to the Atlantic Fleet and for their dependents. He expressly directed the circuit-riding chaplains of the Atlantic Fleet

78. Isaac Kidd III, interview with the author, September 22, 2010.
79. Kevin Kidd, interview with the author, August 5, 2010; Isaac Kidd III, interview with the author, September 22, 2010; Christopher Kidd, interview with the author, October 4, 2010; Mary Plummer, interview with the author, December 18, 2010. Two stories help illustrate the relationship between Jake and the Kidd family. Isaac Kidd considered Jake Laboon his brother. When Kidd's mother, Inez Gilmore Kidd, died the admiral depended totally on Jake to get him through the event, almost collapsing in the priest's arms from emotion. On another occasion, when Christopher Kidd was in Bethesda Naval Hospital, Jake came to visit. The young man's parents were in Europe, where Admiral Kidd was serving. Jake visited, according to Christopher Kidd himself, "Because Ike Kidd's son was in the hospital and was alone."
80. Atlantic Fleet FRSA command history, 1978, n.d. [1979]; OIC FRSA to director of naval history, March 12, 1979, NHM.

assigned to deployed ships, increased their numbers, and made frequent visits to detachments to bolster the effectiveness of these chaplains. His emphasis on providing religious lay leaders for every ship in the Atlantic Fleet ... result[ed] in positive improvements in the religious welfare of personnel. He not only made some recommendations to the Chief of Chaplains for the maximum utilization of chaplain's assets but also served as a respected adviser to the Commander-in-Chief U.S. Atlantic Fleet in the areas of religion, morale, and the spiritual growth of personnel within the Atlantic Fleet.[81]

Fleet Chaplain Atlantic

Jake Laboon entered the twilight of his military career in September 1978 when he was assigned as fleet chaplain Atlantic. While on one level it was natural for him to move from one high-level position to another, the influence of Isaac Kidd in his selection cannot be discounted. Members of the Kidd family and senior naval personnel who knew both men have suggested that Kidd asked Laboon to take the position and through his influence was able to secure the assignment for him.[82]

For Jake Laboon the position of fleet chaplain Atlantic presented new and interesting challenges and responsibilities, but also significant opportunities. Again, he wore two hats. First, he was chaplain to the CINCLANTFLT staff and their families, including Admiral Kidd (and later his successor Admiral Harry Train). His pastoral responsibility included daily Mass at a chapel across the street from the staff offices.[83] His broader role, of course, was ultimate responsibility for chaplain ministries in the Atlantic Fleet. The opportunities that senior rank and position gave him made the new role most attractive. His superior knowledge of people and his vast experience gave him the opportunity to speak up in order to effect positive change, when many contemporaries would be hesitant to speak. Admiral Harry Train, who relieved Isaac Kidd as CINCLANTFLT only a few months after Laboon assumed the fleet chaplain position, commented that Jake forcefully gave his opinion on issues of all natures, but when superiors made decisions he carried them out completely and without question. He commented on Jake's efficacy in his new role:

81. Citation—Meritorious Service Medal, n.d. [September 1978], NMPR.
82. Christopher Kidd, interview with the author, October 4, 2010; Charles Heid to the author, May 24, 2011.
83. James Flatley, interview with the author, March 3, 2011.

He was a very authoritative figure and played that role of being the Atlantic Fleet chaplain not only in the pastoral way, but also in a leadership way. He had more leadership in his little finger than most chaplains could dream of, having been a submarine officer in World War II and a Jesuit.[84]

Train also commented on how Jake used his relationships with senior personnel and his position to effectively address any and all issues that came his way. He wrote, "Jake was an exceptional leader.... He did not bring me problems. He solved them."[85]

It took little time for Jake to parlay his experience and position into constructive ways to promote religious activity in the Atlantic Fleet. His recent work at FRSA and his past experience as a circuit-riding chaplain convinced him that this more creative utilization of chaplain resources was beneficial. He asked for and received a higher quota of forty-two chaplains to work for FRSA.[86] On several occasions Laboon worked with individual chaplains, interceding if necessary to assure that they were treated fairly. He taught by example, helping junior chaplains find the proper ropes by following his lead.[87] One important program that Jake instituted was regular "chat sessions" that he held with all his chaplains. Speaking for approximately an hour to some twenty-five to thirty chaplains at any one time, Jake provided general information necessary for the command, but the true measure of these sessions was the opportunity to provide useful guidance as well as answer questions. Typical questions that came from chaplains included length of deployments, information about the schedule, queries on priorities on ministry, and how to handle the special needs and problems of families whose loved one was deployed. Barry Black, who attended many of

---

84. Reminiscences of Admiral Harry Train, transcribed, AUSNA. On another occasion, Train spoke of his great admiration for the Society of Jesus: "My admiration and respect for Jesuits was enormous. They represented one of the most profound influences on my life. Jesuits are very prone to offer their opinions on many things. Few, however, have the experience to back up those opinions as did Jake"; see Admiral Harry Train, interview with the author, January 19, 2011.

85. Harry Train to the author, July 23, 2010.

86. Citation—Meritorious Service Medal, n.d. [September 1978], NMPR; Bruce Kahn, interview with the author, August 3, 2011; RADM Frank Kelso, interview with the author, April 7, 2011.

87. Joseph Capper, interview with the author, October 1, 2012. Laboon taught Capper an important lesson in leadership by taking care of a disagreement between the latter and his commanding officer. Jake was able to diffuse the situation, but did so without Capper thinking that he was victorious over his commanding officer. This incident taught the young chaplain about forms of leadership and the proper way of handling such cases. Capper used the experience as a lesson for how to act in a similar way later in his career.

these sessions, commented, "All [chaplains] got to know him personally. He reached out to everyone."[88]

The lay leader program, which Laboon had pioneered from his first days as chaplain, expanded during his time as fleet chaplain. Very conscious of the need for proper training, he worked with his successor at FRSA to set up quarterly training sessions for lay leaders in all four component locations—Norfolk, Charleston, Mayport, and New London.[89] According to Train, Jake succeeded: "His emphasis on providing religious lay leaders for every ship in the Atlantic Fleet and/or training sessions to increase proficiency resulted in positive improvements in the religious welfare of personnel."[90]

Jake was also instrumental, together with John O'Connor, chief of chaplains, in the institution of a new enlisted rate specifically designed to assist chaplains in their duties. While the proposal was new, there was a recommendation as early as the last quarter of the nineteenth century that chaplains be assisted by qualified enlisted support. In November 1879 a committee requested "each ship to which a chaplain is attached be allowed a schoolmaster, who shall be competent to play an organ and lead ordinary singing."[91] In February 1942 the navy established a Specialist "W" [Welfare] emergency rating to provide, in part, assistants for chaplains during World War II.[92] In April 1948 the Specialist "W" was merged with the PN (personnelman) into personnel specialist (PS) in October 2005. During the 1950s some attempts were made, at the request of the chief of chaplains, to establish a specific rate to assist chaplains, but all efforts were rejected. In January 1965 a specialized yeoman rate, YN-2525, was approved, but seven years later there were only forty-six in the entire navy, only eleven of whom were giving direct support to chaplains. Finally, in April 1977, the Rating and Review Board recommended the "establishment of a general rating that will permit trained enlisted personnel to share in a professional manner in the support of the free exercise of religion in the naval service." Finally, in February 1978, the secretary of the navy approved the new rating.[93]

---

88. Barry Black, interview with the author, August 25, 2010.
89. FRSA command brief, n.d. [1979], folder 1754/8, box 89, NCA.
90. Citation—Meritorious Service Medal, n.d. [September 1978], NMPR.
91. Randy Cash, "Religious Program Specialist Rating Historical Review," n.d., NCA.
92. A second rate, "Specialist C" was also created after the war. This was similar to "Specialist W," but more identifiable as an assistant to a chaplain with the letter "C."
93. Ibid.

The establishment of the religious program specialist (RP) rating and the positive element it added to the chaplain corps had to be weighed against the disappointment created from the disestablishment of FRSA. On July 7, 1980, upon the recommendation of a navy research committee, CINCLANTFLT ordered the disestablishment of FRSA. Three specific reasons were given for this recommendation: (1) There was no similar organization in the Pacific; (2) The administrative burden on a separate activity and subordinate detachments was unnecessary; (3) There was no evidence that FRSA made more chaplains available.[94] Additionally, CINCLANTFLT and other type commanders wanted more direct involvement with staffing chaplain billets.[95] The problems were verified by one chaplain who served with FRSA: "The programs at times were efficacious, but the dearth of chaplains made the program fairly weak. There was not a minimum number of chaplains to get the job done. I do not think FRSA was able to do enough."[96] As one could imagine, Jake strongly voiced his opposition to the disestablishment order. However, FRSA was officially disestablished on August 31, 1981, almost one full year after Jake's official retirement.[97]

Retirement from the Navy

In May 1979, after serving as chief of chaplains since July 1975, John O'Connor retired from the navy to become auxiliary bishop of the military ordinariate. O'Connor's political savvy and drive had allowed him to accomplish what many felt was impossible, completing at least three major tasks: (1) establishment of the aforementioned RP rating; (2) expansion of the chaplain corps by approximately two hundred to three hundred chaplains at a time when the navy was in a period of personnel contraction; (3) movement of the office of the chief of chaplains from the supervision of the Bureau of Naval Personnel to the chief of naval operations. A brilliant and driven man, O'Connor indeed completed some significant projects. One chaplain of the period commented, "J. J. O'Connor as a matter of course did the impossible. He was that brilliant and that politically savvy. He was in many ways the most significant

---

94. LT Stephen Wallace, "Fleet Religious Support Activity," 1985, 32, folder 1754/8, box 89, NCA.
95. OIC FRSA to CIC U.S. Atlantic Fleet, November 28, 1980, folder 1754/8, box 90, NCA.
96. Bruce Kahn, interview with the author, August 3, 2011.
97. LT Stephen Wallace, "Fleet Religious Support Activity," 1985, 33, folder 1754/8, box 89; CINCLANTFLT to All Atlantic Fleet, September 1981, folder 1754/8, box 89, NCA.

Chief of Chaplains of all time."[98] Upon his retirement, O'Connor was replaced by Rear Admiral Ross Trower, who had served as Jake's boss in Hawaii approximately five years earlier.

Many people at the time and possibly even more over the ensuing years have asked why Jake Laboon was never promoted to rear admiral and selected as chief of chaplains. On a few occasions during his career, reporting seniors recommended that he be promoted to flag rank. As early as October 1973, Rear Admiral Parker B. Armstrong, COMSERVPAC, wrote," In every way he is 'head-and-shoulders' above his contemporaries in the Chaplain Corps and is, therefore, recommended for immediate selection to flag rank."[99] Two different reporting seniors in 1976 made similar recommendations. Rear Admiral S. A. White, COMSUBRON 2 (New London) wrote, "From every viewpoint, Captain Laboon has all the requisites for flag rank. The Navy is fortunate, indeed to have him. I wholeheartedly recommend his immediate promotion to Rear Admiral."[100] A contemporary, friend, and future CNO, Admiral Frank Kelso, opined, "Jake had the personality and prescience to be an admiral."[101] Despite his excellent evaluations and, in the minds of many, his eminent qualifications to be chief of chaplains, Jake was not selected. Earlier in his career, beginning at Great Lakes NTC, and once again in 1972, Jake reported to his provincial that there was a move on to appoint him chief of chaplains, "depending on my age, [and] the selection of a Catholic."[102]

Almost all who knew Jake were disappointed at his failure to achieve flag rank. This was certainly true in the mind of Admiral Train when writing Jake's final fitness report: "We in the Navy erred grievously when we allowed this national asset [Laboon] to slip through our fingers by not selecting him for flag rank.... By not selecting him for flag rank we failed our trust to the American sailor."[103] Chaplains who served with Jake, especially in his last duty station, were equally surprised and disheartened. One commented, "He was expected, because of his good reputation, to become the Chief of Chaplains." Another stated, "Jake Laboon was for most people the

---

98. Bruce Kahn, interview with the author, August 3, 2011.
99. CAPT John Laboon, fitness report, October 5, 1973, Laboon file, NMPR.
100. CAPT John Laboon, fitness report, June 26, 1976, Laboon file, NMPR.
101. Admiral Frank Kelso, interview with the author, April 7, 2011.
102. John Laboon, SJ, to Jim Connor, SJ, August 11, 1972, Laboon file, ASJM.
103. Capt John Laboon, fitness report, n.d. [October 1980], PPJM.

hands-on favorite to be the Chief of Chaplains."[104] His failure to be selected was, it seems, a great blow to Jake personally. Admiral Train said Laboon was "greatly disappointed; he was quite hurt."[105] Jake's brother, Father Joe Laboon, and one senior Catholic chaplain both claimed that Laboon's failure to achieve flag rank and be selected as chief of chaplains led directly to his retirement.[106]

There are various opinions concerning Jake's failure to achieve the navy chaplain corps' top position. The most common is that Jake was in the wrong place at the wrong time. Several chaplains pointed to the chaplain corps' unwritten tradition that dictated the position of chief would rotate between a Protestant and a Catholic. Therefore, coming on the heels of Admiral O'Connor, a Catholic, it would have been impossible for Jake to be selected.[107] O'Connor himself alluded to this reality when writing a letter of recommendation for Laboon:

But for a peculiarity of organizational circumstances, Father Laboon would undoubtedly have been selected to be a Rear Admiral in the U.S. Navy, and even the enthusiastic choice of Catholic and Protestant chaplains alike for that rank and for assignment as Chief or Deputy Chief of Chaplains.[108]

Timing was also the explanation of another chaplain but in a slightly different way. Bruce Kahn suggested that Jake's best chance came when a Catholic was slated to replace Rear Admiral Francis Garrett, but O'Connor rather than Laboon was selected.[109]

104. Peter Pilarski, interview with the author, January 14, 2011; Bruce Kahn, interview with the author, August 3, 2011.

105. Admiral Harry Train, interview with the author, January 19, 2011.

106. Joseph Laboon, interview with the author, August 19, 2010; Joseph O'Donnell, CSC, interview with the author, October 8, 2010.

107. Joseph O'Donnell, CSC, interview with the author, October 8, 2010; John Donlon, interview with the author, September 9, 2011. It is important to note that there has never been a policy in the chaplain corps for a rotation between Protestants and Catholics as chief. Similarly, there has never been a policy, sometimes referred to as "the threes," that designates chaplains as (1) Liturgical Protestants, (2) Evangelicals, and (3) Roman Catholics. Some chaplains suggest that assignments have been made in the chaplain corps to maintain a balance in these three groups, assuring, in theory, that religious services would be available to the widest possible population. While these policies have never been officially sanctioned, many chaplains suggest that in practice this has been a reality; see Randy Cash, interview with the author, July 1, 2013.

108. Letter of recommendation, Jesuit School of Theology at Berkeley (JSTB), student application, June 6, 1980, Laboon file, ASJM.

109. Bruce Kahn, interview with the author, August 3, 2011.

A second explanation proposed for Jake's failure to be appointed as chief was that he and O'Connor were "not on the best terms." Admiral Train suggested that O'Connor derailed Jake's possible advancement based on rivalry between the two men.[110] However, there is much to refute Train's theory. Bishop Francis Roque, who served as an auxiliary in the military ordinariate, characterized the relationship between O'Connor and Laboon as "friendly rivals."[111] O'Connor was present at Jake's retirement from the navy, spoke at his funeral, and was the principal speaker at the launching of the USS *Laboon* (DDG-58). On several occasions he wrote to people extolling the accomplishments of Jake. One example provides an illustration: "Jake, as you well know, was a great man and priest. All the accolades combined could never equal the praise due him."[112]

Jake Laboon retired from the navy in October 1980, some ten months after the selection of Ross Trower as chief of chaplains. In February he wrote to the secretary of the navy: "Having completed 27 years of active service, I request transfer to the retirement list to be effective on the first day of November 1980."[113] Jake had first broached the subject of retirement with his Jesuit superiors during his service in Hawaii. In March 1976, he again wrote, "I am ready to retire any time you have something better for me to do." But he went on to say that at the time he believed the province could not match his present challenge.[114] Reactions to Jake's decision to retire yielded a cascade of accolades extolling his accomplishments. His boss, Admiral Train, CINCLANTFLT, wrote: "I have known Chaplain Laboon for many years. His service to his Navy and his country is immeasurable. He will be sorely missed by those privileged to benefit from his ministry."[115] He also lauded Laboon for his significant contributions to the command:

Jake Laboon has been invaluable in his contributions to the difficult task of providing sensitive leadership to the fleet. He has provided important insights to the problems, trials, tribulations, and needs of the men and women in uniform. He has provided constructive feedback on and criticism of policies and decisions affecting

---

110. Admiral Harry Train, interview with the author, January 19, 2011.
111. Bishop Francis Roque and Charles Hogan, interview with the author, April 11, 2012.
112. Cardinal John O'Connor to William Graham, SJ, March 30, 1993, A99, folder 10, AANY.
113. John Laboon to secretary of the navy, February 21, 1980, Laboon file, NMPR. Jake actually had twenty-five years of service: 1943 to 1946 and 1958 to 1980.
114. John Laboon, SJ, to Al Panuska, SJ, March 26 1976, ASJM.
115. CINCLANTFLT to secretary of the navy, March 4, 1980, Laboon file, NMPR.

the fleet. He has wisely led the Chaplains of the Atlantic Fleet in their spiritual activity; and he has served as the spiritual adviser of the headquarters personnel of this staff.[116]

Jake's naval academy football teammate, Bill Busik wrote:

We [Busik and wife] want you to know how proud we are to be your friends. Of the many teammates I was honored to be associated with at the Naval Academy, you have stood out as one of those very special people whose career in the Navy touched all of us. The Navy will miss you, but will bask in the rich legacy you've given it.[117]

Reaction from the military ordinariate was equally laudatory. Joseph T. Ryan, coadjutor archbishop of the military vicariate, wrote to the Jesuit provincial:

Father Laboon has provided priestly ministry to untold numbers of Navy personnel. In all circumstances he proved himself to be a dedicated, talented and faithful priest. His devotion to duty and to the souls entrusted to his care has been an inspiration to all.[118]

Cardinal Terence Cooke, head of the military ordinariate, was equally complimentary:

I was sorry to learn about your plans for retirement ... because all of us will miss you so much. You have been a tower of strength to us and your faithful loving pastoral service to the members of the Navy family is a source of great inspiration.[119]

Laboon told his provincial that Cooke once said, "Jake Laboon is the best in the Navy."[120]

The official retirement ceremony was held on October 31, 1980. This celebration of Jake Laboon's naval career began appropriately with a Mass of thanksgiving, at which Jake presided with his brother Joe and his friends Bob Ecker and John O'Connor as concelebrants. Bishop O'Connor gave the homily.[121] Speaking to O'Connor, Jake sentimentally commented, "John, I guess I love this outfit as much as anybody. When I cut myself shaving, I

---

116. Fitness report. n.d. [October 1980], PPJM.
117. William Busik to John Laboon, October 20, 1980, John F. Laboon alumni file, AUSNA.
118. Joseph T. Ryan to Joseph Whelan, SJ, September 19, 1980, Laboon file, ASJM.
119. Cardinal Terence Cooke to John Laboon, SJ, May 23, 1980, Laboon file, ASJM.
120. John Laboon, SJ, to Joseph Whelan, SJ, June 13, 1980, Laboon file, ASJM.
121. Rosemary, deLellis, and Joan Laboon, interview with the author, August 4, 2010; Joseph Laboon, interview with the author, August 19, 2010; Form DD 214, discharge papers, n.d. [November 1980], Laboon file, NMPR.

Figure 10-1. Jake Laboon (right) and Admiral Harry Train, Laboon retirement ceremony, October 31, 1980

bleed blue and gold."[122] The ceremony, attended by all of Jake's immediate family, including his father, was conducted with the appropriate military precision that characterized his career. Appropriately, Train wrote in Jake's final fitness report of the impact he had made during his career:

> He is the rare combination of an inspirational spiritual leader, role model and down to earth philosopher which only appears once in our lifetime.... While no member of the Armed Forces of the United States is indispensable, Jake Laboon comes close to fulfilling that description. No one or nothing will fill the void in the Navy Chaplain Corps that will be created when he leaves. Nothing will fill the void on the waterfront when he leaves.

Train concluded his remarks, "Jake Laboon will be missed by all."[123]

In a fitting gesture to mark the end of a brilliant naval career, Jake Laboon was once again, as in Vietnam, awarded the Legion of Merit. He was commended for his "exemplary foresight and resourcefulness" in his ability to expand religious services to the Atlantic Fleet, especially by increasing the number of circuit-riding chaplains and his work to inaugurate the religious program specialist rating. He was also applauded for his "compassionate demeanor and impressive devotion to duty.... His limitless wisdom, understanding of people, and successful ministerial service made his sound advice and counsel of immeasurable value to the Fleet Commander."[124]

Appreciation for Jake's service also came from his religious community. Writing on behalf of the Maryland Province, Joseph Whelan, SJ, told Jake that he was mindful of the many emotions, including sadness, that were probably present in his thinking at such a time in life. He told him that his reputation in the province was sound and that he was held in high respect. He wrote:

> I hope you know how proud the Society, and specifically the Maryland province, is of what you have been and are—a truly tall presence—very much out there where thousands and thousands of people could see—of what a Jesuit priest ought to be. Your reputation has gone far and wide, and I guess you know that. I express the gratitude of many of your brothers in thanking you for doing us so proud in this most important ministry, over so many, many years.[125]

---

122. Clipping, "The Legacy of Father Jake," *Soundings*, n.d. [October 1994], PPJL.
123. CAPT John Laboon, fitness report, n.d. [November 1980], PPJM.
124. Citation—Legion of Merit, n.d. [1980], Laboon file, NMPR.
125. Joseph Whelan, SJ, to John Laboon, SJ, August 20, 1980, Laboon file, ASJM.

Figure 10-2. Jake Laboon, retirement photo, October 1980

Command Climax—Norfolk: 1976–1980

Jake Laboon's decision to retire from the navy inaugurated a process of transition back to full-time ministry with the Jesuits. As early as 1972 he began looking toward the future and retirement. He wrote to his provincial, "When I am through with the Navy, I do plan to come back to the Society and look for a job." At that time he made some suggestions: "Maybe my work will be with wayward teenagers. I have been thinking about it. Another possibility is working in the Pensacola area either with the colleges or as a parochial assistant." Still, he was open to possibilities, stating that he wanted to be helpful, in any way he could, to assist the work of the Maryland Province.[126] At the time he submitted his resignation he was once again in touch with his provincial about his future. Perceptive enough to understand his own needs, Jake suggested that Manresa Retreat House might be an ideal way to transition from the navy back to the Society. He wrote to the provincial:

If you are looking for a priest-in-residence, and one who will work out of the house, you may consider me. I mention this fact to you because going to Manresa just might be easier for me than say going to a formal house right away. I think you know what I mean. In this way, I would not be completely cut off from the Navy, nor would I be trying to keep one foot in and one foot out. I am definitely ready to give my next few years of ministry to the Province of Maryland.[127]

While offering counseling as an alternative assignment, he remained completely open to the needs of the province. The provincial informed Jake that Manresa was in the midst of ministerial review and, thus, he was not certain if it would be available.[128]

On April 2 the two men met and discussed his options. It was decided that after a couple of months of relaxation he would enter the sabbatical program at the Jesuit School of Theology at Berkeley, in January 1981. Upon completion of this program of renewal in June, Jake would take a new assignment, with three different apostolates as possibilities: parish work, high school teaching, and counseling or province development.[129] In June Jake requested, until the sabbatical began, to be assigned to Holy Trinity Parish in Georgetown, where the pastor, Jim English, SJ, was a former student at St. Joe Prep.[130]

---

126. John Laboon, SJ, to Jim Connor, SJ, August 11, 1972, Laboon file, ASJM.
127. John Laboon, SJ, to Joseph Whelan, SJ, February 21, 1980, Laboon file, ASJM.
128. Joseph Whelan, SJ, to John Laboon, SJ, February 25, 1980, Laboon file, ASJM.
129. Memorandum, Father Joseph Whelan to Father William Waters, April 10, 1980, Laboon file, ASJM.
130. John Laboon, SJ, to Joseph Whelan, SJ, June 13, 1980, Laboon file, ASJM.

Conclusion

In September 1958, two years after his ordination and completion of his required tertainship, Jake Laboon reentered the navy, an institution that he loved and for which he often claimed he would bleed blue and gold. For the next twenty-two years he crisscrossed the nation and served overseas as he climbed the pyramid of military success, finally reaching the apex of his career in two different but related Norfolk sites. As officer in charge of the Fleet Religious Support Activity (FRSA), an innovative program established only two years earlier to more effectively utilize the reduced number of chaplains, Jake Laboon used his knowledge of the navy, his friendships and associations with high-ranking officers, and his administrative and pastoral skills to advance the work of the chaplain corps at sea and on land. Praised by junior chaplains for mentoring them and supporting their fledgling efforts at ministry, Jake carried out the work of his first command in fine fashion. In November 1978 he moved "across the street" to the staff of CINCLANTFLT to work with Admiral Isaac Kidd, a longtime friend and compatriot, as fleet chaplain Atlantic. In this twilight assignment of his career, Jake continued to serve chaplains, aiding them to bring the message and peace of God to hundreds of ships, numerous shore commands, and thousands of sailors and marines. Apparently frustrated at his being passed over for flag rank and consideration as the next navy chief of chaplains, Jake retired on October 31, 1980. His navy days had been completed, but a new chapter in his life was ready to unfold, as he returned to the Society of Jesus.

Chapter 11

Jesuit Retreat Master and Pastor
★ 1981–1988

In November 1980, Jake Laboon found it necessary to take off the uniform and all the trappings required or implied therein and dress himself in clerical attire alone. Certainly he had always been a priest, but the roles of navy chaplain and of a Jesuit serving a civilian population were vastly different, requiring significant adjustment of methods and ways of thinking. For many, especially those in religious life who experience a significant transition from one ministry or way of life to a vastly different one, a sabbatical is often helpful to ease the accommodation process. Jake was excited about the many possibilities afforded him by the Society, yet he hoped and believed that a couple months of "retooling," especially academically, and the idea of once again living in community would indeed help him to better adjust. Thus, after consultation with his superiors, Jake went west to the Jesuit School of Theology at Berkeley prior to engaging a full-time ministry sponsored by the Jesuits. As with each endeavor in his life, Jake not only took advantage of every opportunity afforded by the sabbatical, but made every effort to prepare himself to minister as well as possible.

Berkeley Sabbatical

After twenty-two years of service in the chaplain corps, reintegration into the life of a Jesuit priest living in a community setting would take time. Almost five years before he actually retired Jake had expressed his openness to work where he was most needed. He wrote,

I do not [have] ambition [for] any position of authority in the Province.... I want to go where I can influence souls for Christ to help in any apostolate where my talents might be needed. I am not afraid of work. [I] want to keep working in some capacity, and plan to contribute within or without the Province where I might find a willing priest needed.[1]

His immediate path had been determined, but precisely what he would do and where he would go after his sabbatical was uncertain. He was very grateful for the provincial's support and welcome, but openly expressed his belief that some in the province did not appreciate his work in the navy. He wrote,

Thanks again for the letter. It lifts my spirits to know that you have appreciated my work in the Navy. I got the impression from time to time that the same impression is not universal in the Province, nor do I think that it should be that way. There are so many of ours who are ignorant/uninformed is a better word of the works of other Jesuits.[2]

The reintegration process was further complicated by the perception from some members of the province that he was an outsider. This attitude, which was over-exaggerated, was generated, of course, because he had been away from community life for so long—basically, his entire priesthood. Writing to his provincial a few months prior to his discharge from the navy, he expressed confidence in his abilities: "I feel very secure in knowing what I can do and what I cannot do." Yet in the same letter he lamented the fact that many in the Society had no idea what he had done for the past twenty-plus years: "Since my release for the Navy in 1958 hardly anyone in the Maryland Province knows what I have done or my accomplishments." This lack of appreciation from the community was to be expected; he was not physically present and had never worked in a Jesuit apostolate. Yet important voices from his navy career spoke of his close connection with his religious community. Ross Trower commented, "Jake was a very faithful member of the Society."[3] Isaac Kidd III stated, "He was a Jesuit first and foremost and though the Navy was a close second, it was always a very definite second."[4] In his funeral homily for Jake, William Graham, SJ, stated, "He was a Jesuit priest and very proud of the fact."[5]

1. John Laboon, SJ, to Al Panuska, SJ, March 26, 1976, Laboon file, ASJM.
2. John Laboon, SJ, to Joseph Whelan, SJ, September 5, 1980, Laboon file, ASJM.
3. Ross Trower, interview with the author, May 11, 2011.
4. Isaac Kidd III, interview with the author, May 22, 2010.
5. John Laboon, funeral audiotape, August 4, 1988.

Jake's love for the Society was recognized by those who knew him well. His sisters remembered Jake often saying, "I am a Jesuit priest on loan to the Navy."[6] One New York Province Jesuit commented, "Although I never had occasion to meet Jake, I have always been impressed by the affection and respect he was accorded by his Jesuit contemporaries. He was deeply admired by all."[7] His novitiate classmate, William Dawson, SJ, stated, "I cannot say as I have ever had a friend like Jake. Our relationship was intangible, but it was real."[8]

In January 1981, after a short period of rest and a couple of months in residence at Holy Trinity Parish in Georgetown, Jake Laboon headed west for his sabbatical semester. He explained his move to friends: "The Jesuits have a very powerful and wonderful school of theology at the University of California's campus and I am going there for an update during the winter and spring semesters."[9] Upon his arrival he entered the School of Applied Theology (SAT). The program was described in the Jesuit School of Theology at Berkeley (JSTB) course catalog:

The professional school is designed to develop mature men and women—lay, priests, ministers, brothers, sisters—as more effective and confident Christian leaders. Contemporary theology and ministerial skills are stressed in this development. The program has been designed to meet the needs of pastors and parish clergy, diocesan and parish directors and coordinators, religious education and CCD directors, chaplains, campus ministry, crisis ministers, deacons, and all those ministering to groups and people in need.[10]

John O'Connor had recommended him for the program: "Father Laboon is intellectually and emotionally qualified for the most demanding graduate program.... He is as fine a priest, person and friend as I have ever known, a credit to the Jesuits and a man of extraordinary competency."[11]

Jake's Berkeley experience was positive and negative. After living on his own for more than twenty years, he resided during his sabbatical in a Jesuit house just north of the University of California Berkeley campus. This opportunity helped him to reenter a community setting in an environment that included students as well as ordained Jesuits. The program, while aca-

6. Rosemary, deLellis, and Joan Laboon, interview with the author, August 4, 2010.
7. Joseph P. Parkes, SJ, to Cardinal John O'Connor, March 17, 1993, A-99, folder 10, AANY.
8. William Dawson, SJ, interview with the author, August 20, 2010.
9. News clipping, n.d. [1980], PPWL.
10. Erin Louthen, e-mail to the author, November 30, 2012.
11. JSTB student application, June 6, 1980, Laboon file, ASJM.

demically oriented, still allowed plenty of time for the celebration of community life. Jake took several courses during his semester, including The Gospel of John, New Horizons in Christology, Sin, Law, and Grace, Jesuit Spirituality, and Paul's Letter to the Romans. No grades were assigned; the purpose was simply to learn in an academic but non-evaluative environment.[12] While Jake enjoyed the classes and the opportunity to mingle with a wide variety of his Jesuit brothers, he did find Berkeley's highly progressive environment with respect to people and theology to be quite challenging.[13]

Manresa-on-Severn

While the Society of the Divine Word (SVD) was involved with laymen's retreats as early as 1906, the movement began in a more formal way on July 9, 1909, when Jesuit father Terrence Sheady gathered a group of eighteen men at Fordham College for a priest retreat. This initial assembly led directly to the foundation on September 8, 1911, of the Layman's League for Retreats and Social Studies headquartered at Mt. Manresa on Staten Island, the first house dedicated exclusively to lay retreats.[14] Sheady's contribution was noted by one prominent scholar: "The [lay retreat] movement is forever indebted to him [Sheady] for his masterly contribution to its development."[15]

Development of the lay retreat movement started slowly but picked up steam toward the end of the 1920s and was in high gear by the 1930s. The first national meeting of the Layman's League for Retreats and Social Studies was held in Philadelphia in 1928. Under the patronage of Cardinal Denis Dougherty, fifty-one delegates, representing fifteen retreat centers and thirty dioceses, were in attendance. At the conference the title "The Laymen's Retreat Movement" was adopted. One year later, on December 20, 1929, the movement received a major boost when Pope Pius XI issued *Mens Nostra*, which gave strong approval for the lay retreat movement. The association found a great friend and supporter in Archbishop John McNicholas, OP,

---

12. Erin Louthen, e-mail to the author, November 30, 2012; Joseph Ryan, interview with the author, March 2, 2011.

13. John Donlon, interview with the author September 14, 2012.

14. J. R. Stack, "Who Was the Father of Laymen's Retreats in the United States?" *Records of the American Catholic Historical Society of Philadelphia* 41 (March 1930): 71–73; William I. Lonergan, *Laymen's Retreats Explained* (New York: America Press, 1930), 94; William J. Kerby, "Lay Retreat Movement," *American Ecclesiastical Review* 92 (June 1935): 586.

15. Kerby, "Lay Retreat Movement," 586.

of Cincinnati.¹⁶ McNicholas saw the retreat movement as the key for building a lay apostolate in the United States. Seeking to support the advocacy of the Holy Father, McNicholas believed that the lay retreat movement would be the inspiration for a new chapter in American Catholic spirituality. He further assumed that the laity could be more "Catholic minded" through participation in such retreats. In a 1930 letter he called for expansion of this ministry:

> The retreat work seems to me quite as important as the mission work and under some aspects even more important. It would mean very much to the great interests of religion in the United States if in every religious order and congregation and every one of the larger dioceses especially, there was a band of priests set aside for lay retreat work.¹⁷

In 1931 the National Conference of Catholic Men (NCCM) also praised the new endeavor:

> We hail with joy the growing interest in laymen's retreats amongst our Catholic people throughout the country, and we heartily endorse and encourage all efforts on the part of our membership to promote this timely and worthy movement.¹⁸

That same year the Benedictine archabbott Alfred Koch told a laymen's retreat conference:

> The retreat movement is not only useful, but necessary, not only necessary but imperative if the doctrine of Jesus Christ must serve as a bulwark against the onslaughts of our materialistic age.¹⁹

Four years later, in February 1935, the apostolic delegate to the United States, Archbishop Amleto Cicognani, provided the connection between the lay retreat movement and Catholic Action, the work of bishops supported by the efforts of the laity:

> Your apostolate, under the direction of the bishops and according to their instructions, merits all praise, encouragement, and support. It is inspired by a sense of real charity towards our neighbor and towards human society; it is one of the choicest activities of Catholic Action and prepares soldiers of Christ for Catholic Action—

---

16. Ibid., 587; Lonergan, *Laymen's Retreats Explained*, 94, 100.
17. Quoted in Kerby, "Lay Retreat Movement," 595.
18. "Laymen's Retreats: Resolutions Adopted by the National Council of Catholic Men," *NCWC Bulletin* 13 (November 1931): 15.
19. Alfred Koch, "Why the Retreat Movement Must Go On," *Catholic Mind* 29 (August 22, 1931): 398.

which by the way, cannot exist, much less be efficient, unless it is based on solid spiritual principles. This apostolate is indeed a generous response to the appeal of our Holy Father.[20]

In the 1930s the lay retreat movement continued to grow, establishing many permanent houses as well as developing a more sophisticated theology and rationale. By 1935 there were twenty-two permanent retreat houses and forty seasonal houses operating in the United States. Sixteen different religious communities were active in this ministry.[21] Physical development of infrastructure was indicative of how the movement had captured the imagination of Catholics in the United States. The theologian William Kerby wrote, "The lay retreat movement is thoroughly representative of Catholic spirituality.... It presents itself as an instrument for spiritual development and an idealism that is the finest flower of faith."[22] Advocates saw the movement as a sacred force to counter forces that threatened religion. The retreat could become a system of higher learning to train the mind, strengthen the will, subdue the passions, and perfect the image of the Creator in one's heart. The result would be a large and strong force of Catholic men with tools to combat the world. Referring to what the lay retreat movement provides, Archabbott Koch wrote:

[It] give[s] us an army of noble-minded laymen who inspire others by their example and conduct and thereby bring men into closer intimacy with their Creator.... [It] give[s] us Catholic men who pass through the world not seeking what they can get out of it, but see what they can put into it.... The interests of Christ and His Church cannot be safely guarded by us unless we are willing to exert ourselves.[23]

The lay retreat movement came to the Archdiocese of Baltimore shortly after Terrence Sheady's initial foundation on Staten Island. In 1914 the first

---

20. "Apostolic Delegate Urges Spread of the Retreat Movement," *Catholic Action* 17 (February 1935): 3. Catholic action was first defined in 1922 by Pope Pius XI in his encyclical *Ubi Arcano* as the work of the laity in support of the work of the bishops.

21. Kerby, "Lay Retreat Movement," 587.

22. Ibid., 589.

23. Koch, "Why the Retreat Movement Must Go On," 401–2. Koch commented on the absolute need for the laity to be major players in the work of the church: "To renew all things in Christ, to hasten the coming out of Christ's Kingdom over the entire Earth, must be the dream and ambition of every Catholic who considers himself worthy of his Master. To believe that the laity are not called to participate actively in the great mission of the Church to convert the world and to seek and to reconquer lost ground, to protect his own, is almost a perversion of the noble term Catholic."

laymen's retreat in the Archdiocese was held at Georgetown University, when eighteen men gathered for a weekend. As these retreats continued and became popular, Georgetown could no longer handle the need, and in 1921 the retreat program was moved to Mt. St. Mary's College in Emmitsburg, Maryland. Shortly thereafter, Archbishop Michael Curley of Baltimore engaged Father Joseph A. McEneany, SJ, president of Loyola College, to secure a location for a permanent retreat house. Eventually the provincial charged Eugene McDonnell, SJ, with responsibility for the project. McDonnell met with representatives of the W.B. and Annapolis Railroad, leading to the purchase in 1925 of a six-acre triangular lot on the north side of the Severn River. Later fifteen additional acres were added at a total cost of $12,640.[24] Construction on Manresa began in March 1926. At the same time the League of Laymen's Retreats was incorporated, along with the "Trustees of Manresa on the Severn," which was approved by the State Tax Commission of Maryland on April 27, 1926.[25]

Manresa hosted its first retreat in August 1926. The event was initially scheduled for August 6, but because "the plasterers were blocking the front door," it was moved to August 13. The new retreat house hosted fifty-two men from Baltimore. Two weeks later, the first group from Washington, fifty-one men, led by the president of Georgetown University, Charles Lyons, SJ, came. Before the end of the year a total of 354 men had made retreats at Manresa.[26] The first student retreats were held in May and June 1927. In 1931, through the generous benefaction of a Baltimorian, a new chapel was built and eventually consecrated on March 13 by Bishop John D. McNamara.[27] From the outset Archbishop Curley was very pleased and took great interest in the retreat movement, promoting its ministry at the many functions he attended.

During its first half-century of operation, Manresa grew steadily, especially during the administrations of Richard Lloyd, SJ (1935–51) and Thomas Brew, SJ (1951–64). In order to meet the need, a new wing with private rooms, a dining room, and an enlarged chapel were constructed in 1955. The addition did not fully meet the need, and Loyola Retreat House in Faulkner,

---

24. League of Laymen's Retreats—Golden Jubilee (1914–64), booklet, 47, Manresa Papers, ASJM.
25. Ibid., 48.
26. Ibid., 48–49.
27. Ibid. The first students to make retreats at Manresa were a group of forty-five from Calvert Hall on May 31, 1927, and thirty men from St. Joseph's College in Philadelphia on June 6, 1927. Mr. Thomas McHugh gave $10,000 as a gift to Fr. Eugene McDonnell for the construction of the chapel.

Figure 11-1. Manresa Retreat House, Annapolis, Md.

Maryland, was built and opened in October 1958. In 1956, an Ignatian year, Manresa held fifty-nine retreats and welcomed 4,295 retreatants.[28]

During the 1960s, and especially after the conclusion of Vatican II, retreatant numbers began to decline, so Vincent Beaty, SJ, the director at Manresa between 1964 and 1966, introduced retreats for married couples.[29] Beatty's successor, Eugene Linehan, SJ, continued the more open policy, with retreats open to families as well as men and married couples. In the spirit of Vatican II, he stated, "Whatever the community need is, we want to answer it. We're moving out of the Catholic ghetto and into the mainstream now."[30] During the directorship of Henry Haske, SJ, 1972 to 1975, Manresa began to offer the Ignatian Spiritual Exercises, but this did not prove economically viable.[31] The house offered directed retreats for men and women religious, men, women, married couples, charismatics, deacons, and groups

28. Ibid., 89; *Manresa* 21, no. 4 (April 1956), Manresa file, AABa.
29. Manresa-on-Severn, 1926–95, Manresa Retreat House file, ASJM.
30. *Baltimore Sun*, September 2, 1968, Manresa file, AABa.
31. Known by Jesuits as "the long retreat," the Spiritual Exercises of St. Ignatius Loyola are mandated at the outset of formation for all Jesuits. Many others, however, laymen and -women as well as religious and priests, have participated in the exercises.

from Alcoholics Anonymous. Still, Manresa experienced a downturn in the number of retreats, creating an operating debt of $45,000 and prompting a serious review of the viability of the ministry. In 1977 the Manresa Project, a three-year period of evaluation of the ministry's viability, was inaugurated. The retreat house continued to operate while physical repairs were made to the plant. In 1980 the Maryland Province made a firm commitment to continue the work at Manresa-on-Severn and to make needed renovations and improvements.[32]

After completing his sabbatical semester in Berkeley, Jake returned east to take up his assignment as the minister (basically house manager) at Manresa-on-Severn. He worked under Joseph Lerch, SJ, the director. As Jake had suggested in his earlier dialogue with the provincial, Manresa was a good fit for his skills as well as a fine location to assist his transition from the navy to civilian life. With the naval academy visible from his bedroom window, Jake was very content with his ministry, engaging its challenges with great vigor. As minister he was responsible for carrying out the recommendations of the Manresa Project for the needed renovations and improvements at the retreat house.[33] Over the next couple of years he supervised the renovation, which included heating and air-conditioning systems, repainting and rewiring the house, and redesigning the chapel.[34] Rear Admiral James Flatley recalls visiting Jake at Manresa. He commented, "He was always in his carpenter's apron with at least two or three tools hanging from it."[35] Laboon's supervisory work was noted by one academy classmate:

By the time Fr. Laboon left Manresa to become pastor at Woodstock, the retreat center was once again a flourishing operation, conducting renewal programs for upwards of 8,000 people annually.[36]

Despite the physical renovation, Manresa continued to operate at a deficit, leading eventually to its closing in 1995.[37]

---

32. Manresa-on-Severn, 1926–95, Manresa Retreat House file, ASJM; *Catholic Review*, August 26, 1977, Manresea file, AABa.

33. *Catholic Review*, July 17, 1981, AABa; Rosemary, deLellis, and Joan Laboon, interview with the author, August 4, 2010; John Donlon, interview with the author, September 9, 2011.

34. "A Project in Memory of Father John F. (Jake) Laboon, SJ, n.d. [1989], Manresa file, ASJM.

35. James Flatley, interview with the author, March 3, 2011.

36. W. Scott Prothero to "Fellow Shipmates," July 10, 1989, PPJM. Prothero's boast of eight thousand retreatants was, unfortunately, a major over-exaggeration.

37. Manresa-on-Severn, 1926–95, Manresa Retreat House file, ASJM. Despite the renovations,

Jake Laboon's ministry at Manresa as house manager did not prevent him from actively engaging other aspects of the center's life. He very much desired to make Manresa more attractive to navy personnel. Therefore, he targeted as prospective retreatants his many military friends, in addition to Catholics in the Baltimore and Washington metropolitan regions. To this end, and to enhance his own spirituality, Jake participated in many retreats, especially those for confirmation classes. Jake teamed with a Jesuit scholastic to give his first confirmation retreat, a great success that was repeated several times. The pair called themselves the Jake and Harry Show.[38] Jake was also an active participant in various workshops on prayer, including a six-day retreat format on various prayer forms.[39]

Prayer was indeed an integral part of Jake's life at Manresa. One member of Isaac Kidd's family commented, "He [Laboon] came across as very spiritual. He was devoted to the Blessed Mother."[40] On several occasions Jake had expressed his spirituality to his family. In a generic letter sent to his family to welcome in the new year of 1975, he wrote:

> God loves us so much that every day can be a day of death and rebirth, of resurrection after failure, of new beginnings in love. There is one catch. If we can be confident on New Years that God has forgiven us and is giving us the chance to start all over again, then there is an obligation for us to forgive others and to give them a chance to start over again in our love just as we begin anew in God's love, but then that's always the catch, isn't it? If God loves us, he expects us to love others.[41]

Jake's busy schedule at Manresa did not preempt his consistent desire to move beyond his immediate ministerial duties. While at the retreat house he was a regular weekend assistant at parishes in the region, especially Our Lady of the Fields. One parishioner commented on his preaching, "He 'wowed' everyone, because he was thoroughly knowledgeable about his subject and his delivery was absolutely fabulous because he spoke to you individually."[42] He

---

Manresa still did not have the facilities or the grounds available at other more modern retreat houses. On May 31, 1995, the Ewing Health Services of Salisbury of Maryland purchased the house and property for use as an assisted living facility, which it remains today.

38. John Laboon, funeral Mass, audiotape, August 4, 1988; Steve and Maureen Phillips, interview with the author, November 17, 2010.

39. *Catholic Review*, June 12, 1981, Manresa file, AABa.

40. Mary Plummer, interview with the author, December 18, 2010.

41. John Laboon, SJ, to "Dear Family," December 31, 1974, PPJM.

42. Steve and Maureen Phillips, interview with the author, November 17, 2010; Neil Werthmann, interview with the author, November 12, 2010.

was sacramentally present, witnessing marriages at the chapel at the naval academy and baptizing two of Isaac Kidd's granddaughters.[43]

Laboon also maintained a high presence level across the river at the naval academy; his navy blood was simply too thick to ignore the opportunity to return to his alma mater and assist there. His love for the navy and his desire to aid midshipmen drew him to the Yard in both formal and informal ways. Father Edwin Condon, who served as a Catholic chaplain at the academy between 1978 and 1982, remembers that Jake was often invited to speak at "Mess Night," an evening that included dinner and conversation with some well-known guests.[44] He regularly attended various events, especially sports.[45] Jake's major contribution was his service as an assistant coach, under Harry Deeds, for the 150-pound football team. Taking his job seriously, he came to practice every day, working especially with linemen. Jake sought to instill athletic expertise and more importantly a desire to always give 110 percent and never give up.[46]

Jake's time at Manresa was also marked by some important personal joys, including time with friends and naval academy classmates. While he was at Manresa, Jake had numerous opportunities to foster old friendships. Former Senator James Webb, who knew Laboon both as a midshipman and a young marine officer in Vietnam, often stopped by seeking the sage advice of his priest friend. Jake associated socially with Barry Black, who had been so impressed with Jake when they served together in Norfolk and who was now a chaplain at the naval academy. On his days off, Jake periodically played golf at Chartwell. He also took the opportunity to enjoy the hospitality of parishioners at Our Lady of the Fields.[47] Jake's proximity to the naval

---

43. Military ordinariate records, nd., AAM; Isaac Kidd III, interview with the author, September 22, 2010.

44. Edwin Condon, interview with the author, January 19, 2011.

45. David Church, interview with the author, September 23, 2012. Church served as an assistant athletic director at Navy during Laboon's tenure at Manresa. He remembered one time watching a Navy baseball game when a certain "fan" seemed to be "riding the umpire" quite vociferously. The "fan" in question was Jake. He told Church, "You have to keep them honest."

46. Ibid.; Felix Bassi, interview with the author, May 4, 2011. Bassi recalled an incident when he, another assistant coach, and Jake traveled to Pottstown, Pennsylvania, when the 150s were invited to play Army in the local "Anthracite Bowl." The Navy team defeated Army earlier in the season and gained, therefore, the coveted N* indicative of a victory over Army. However, in this "extra" game Navy was completely overwhelmed by the Cadets. Laboon was disappointed because he believed the team had given up. It was impossible for him to consider the idea that midshipmen would give up in such a contest.

47. James Webb, interview with the author, October 4, 2010; Barry Black, interview with the

academy also gave him more access to alumni events, especially with his class of 1944.[48]

Jake's time at Manresa was also an important opportunity to reengage his family. His proximity to Pittsburgh allowed more regular family contact. In June 1981, shortly after his return from Berkeley, he went home to Pittsburgh to celebrate his twenty-fifth anniversary of priesthood. The family gathered for a Mass at St. Bernard's, followed by a reception at the family home. Similarly, Jake hosted his family at Manresa to celebrate the twenty-fifth anniversary of ordination of his brother Joe. Jake was especially grateful for all the support they had provided him throughout the years, even though there was much physical separation. The close connection he felt for his family was illustrated in a note he wrote to his youngest sister, Joan, whom he nicknamed "Fannie":

Perhaps I will not have an opportunity to purchase a birthday card for you today. However, I want you to know that this card contains all the love and affection which another card might say. HAPPY BIRTHDAY to you! I wish you the best of health, love, affection, respect and God's Grace which you richly deserve. May God continue to bless you in your work and in your life. We are all very proud of your contribution to God, to the church, to your students and faculty, and to your country. Also included is the fact that you also make a great contribution to the family. May you continue to work and love people as in the past.[49]

In late fall 1984, Jake was transferred to St. Alphonsus Rodriguez Parish in Woodstock, Maryland, a rural community some twenty miles west of Baltimore. The provincial wrote to Jake expressing his gratitude for his ministry at the retreat house: "I want to thank you on behalf of the Province for all you have done at Manresa. Thank you for your dedication to the work of conducting retreats and running the house there."[50]

St. Alphonsus Rodriguez Parish

In October 1869, when the College of the Sacred Heart, later the Jesuit theologate at Woodstock, was opened, Catholics in the area began to worship

---

author, October 25, 2010; Neil Werthmann, e-mail to the author, November 12, 2010; Steve and Maureen Phillips, interview with the author, November 17, 2010.
  48. Robert Harvey, interview with the author, July 5, 2012.
  49. John Laboon to Joan Laboon, March 15, 1977, PPJL.
  50. James Devereaux, SJ, to John Laboon, SJ, October 15, 1984, Devereux papers, ASJM.

in the basement chapel, called Holy Ghost Parish, with Benedict Sestini, SJ, serving as pastor. Prior to this people in the Woodstock region were served by priests who resided in Frederick, Maryland; the nearest Catholic church was some twenty miles distant at Doughoregan, the home of Charles Carroll, the only Catholic signer of the Declaration of Independence, located in Howard County. For the next twenty years the seminary chapel served both the Jesuit scholastics and Catholics in the local region. Baptisms, marriages, and funerals were celebrated as in any other parish.[51]

On May 31, 1885, the cornerstone to a new and more permanent church, called the Church of the Holy Ghost, was laid and blessed by Archbishop (later Cardinal) James Gibbons of Baltimore. The church was completed in 1889, and on April 30 the first Mass was celebrated by Salvatore Brandi, SJ, pastor of the new parish. The church was dedicated by Cardinal Gibbons under the patronage of a newly canonized Jesuit saint, Alphonsus Rodriguez.[52]

The parish continued to operate independently until the mid-1920s, when a school was added to the church. In the fall of 1924, George Wall, SJ, was able, with the assistance of a loan from Archbishop Curley, to purchase a building and eight acres of land for the school called Little Flower, which opened on September 25, 1925. The facility was staffed by three Sisters of Mercy from Mt. Saint Agnes in Baltimore. Enrollment increased sufficiently, creating a need for a larger building. With an additional gift of $1,500 from Curley, Herbert Parker, SJ, erected a new building, a two-story cinderblock school that opened on October 21, 1926.[53] Between 1936 and 1946 Little Flower was closed due to economic problems. The school reopened in 1946 under the direction of Gerald Horigan, SJ, and continued until 1969, when, once again due to declining enrollment and economic problems, the school was forced to close.[54]

---

51. "Stewards for the Lord," history and heritage of St. Alphonsus Rodriguez Church, St. Alphonsus Rodriguez Church records (hereafter SACR), Woodstock, Md.; St. Alphonsus History—100 Years, St. Alphonsus papers; St. Alphonsus Rodriguez photo collection, parish histories, AABa.

52. "St. Alphonsus History—100 Years." St. Alphonsus Rodriguez was born on July 25, 1533. He was unlettered, married, and had three children. By the time he was forty his wife and all his children had died. He asked for admittance to the Jesuits. After a series of rejections he was finally admitted as a lay brother. His ministry for forty-six years was as doorkeeper for Monteson College in Palma on the island of Mallorca. He died in 1617 at the age of eighty-four. He was beatified in 1825 and canonized on September 6, 1888, together with St. Peter Claver, by Pope Leo XIII.

53. "A Brief History of St. Alphonsus Rodriguez Parish," St. Alphonsus papers, AABa.

54. Ibid.; "St. Alphonsus History—100 Years," St. Alphonsus papers, AABa.

Tragedy hit the parish on July 3, 1968, when a lightning strike and an ensuing fire burned the church to the ground. Parishioners were once again forced to worship at the chapel of Woodstock College. Eventually, a new church was constructed, with the first three masses celebrated on Christmas Eve 1971. The church, under the leadership of a new pastor, Francis Diamond, SJ, was actually dedicated on January 23, 1972. By the time Jake Laboon arrived in 1984 a new rectory had been built, opening just the previous year.[55]

On September 10, 1984, Robert Pasquet, SJ, representing the Maryland Province of the Society of Jesus, came to St. Alphonsus to consult with parishioners and then recommend Jake as pastor to the Clergy Personnel Board and the archbishop.[56] In November, with the consultation completed and the approval of Archbishop William Borders, the provincial, James Devereaux, SJ, then assigned him to the parish. He wrote, "Your availability for this new apostolic work is a genuine source of joy for me. Your rich pastoral background will certainly be helpful as you begin your parish duties at Saint Alphonsus."[57] Jake was happy at Manresa, but as an obedient religious "he went without question when asked to take over the parish."[58] In another light, however, Jake saw the assignment as coming home. He had begun his religious training (save the novitiate) at Woodstock; now he was returning in a different capacity to the same location. The parish was relatively small, 235 families.[59]

Jake arrived at the parish in early November. His name first appears in sacramental records conducting a baptism on November 13. His formal installation was held at 10:00 a.m. on November 25, 1984. Working with his parochial vicar, William Wehrle, SJ, Jake wasted no time in getting to know the parishioners and the works of the parish. His first formal letter to the parish came in the form of a Christmas message:

We the people of Saint Alphonsus Parish celebrate the birthday of Christ. Emmanuel, God is with us, once again comes into our lives and into our world to bring

---

55. Ibid.
56. *St. Alphonsus Rodriguez Bulletin*, September 8–9, 1984, SACR.
57. James Devereaux, SJ, to John Laboon, SJ, October 15, 1984, Devereux papers, ASJM.
58. Joe Maloy, interview with the author, January 11, 2011.
59. Clipping, *Catholic Review*, October 23, 1985, St. Alphonsus Rodriguez file, ASJM. Although the parish population was relatively small, nonetheless there were four scheduled weekend masses, one on Saturday evening at 7:00 p.m. and three on Sunday morning, at 8:00 and 10:00 a.m. and 12:00 noon.

peace, joy and love. We indeed benefit from the marvelous gift of God—His only begotten Son. Our Brother, Jesus Christ, became one of us. We welcome Him into our human family. As we celebrate this great event with hearts full of love and gratitude, may all of us grow in love for Him and for one another. May we experience peace on earth and in our community.[60]

Although in the wilds of Kodiak, Alaska, Jake had in some ways been a pastor, Woodstock gave him the authority and freedom to truly be a pastor to a typical congregation. Parishioners remember Jake as one who turned the parish around in many positive ways. His personal touch, high energy level, and willingness to get involved were very attractive to the people at St. Alphonsus. Under his leadership, church attendance, and thereby collections, rose. He attracted people to the parish through his personality, and people were more willing to give. Jake, who did not believe in begging, was content with what people were willing to share. One parishioner said that Laboon's approach "seemed to change our whole attitude."[61] Laboon was able to transform the parish from being one that received financial assistance to one that could provide for others. A typical example was found in Jake's appeal to his parishioners to assist some four hundred families from St. Gregory the Great Parish in Ellicott City. In February 1985, when a home fire took the lives of three children and left their parents destitute, Jake once again called upon the generosity of his parishioners. A collection netted $304.12 for the family, who were members of the local Baptist church.[62]

Jake folded his vast experience from the navy into a parish environment, allowing him to get things done where others could not even begin. His knowledge of people and how to "work the system" were invaluable tools, even for a pastor of a small rural parish. One day a parishioner came to Laboon seeking his assistance with government red tape. The man told Jake that he could not get his father, a World War I veteran, into a veterans' hospital. Within two weeks after having spoken with Jake, the man in question was admitted into the VA system.[63] On another occasion a person, who was greatly worried about what people thought of him, came seeking Jake's

60. *St. Alphonsus Parish Bulletin*, December 22–23, 1984, SACR.
61. St. Alphonsus Rodriguez joint parishioner interview, May 20, 2011.
62. *St. Alphonsus Parish Bulletins*, November 30–December 1, 1985, February 9–10, and February 16–17, 1985, SACR.
63. St. Alphonsus Rodriguez joint parishioner interview, May 20, 2011. Jake spoke with his brother, Joe, who at the time was working as a chaplain in a VA hospital in New Orleans.

advice. In describing his own past experience, he basically told the man that what others thought was irrelevant; he must do what he thought was best. Jake had a special ability to get parishioners involved in every aspect of parish life. His method of leadership drew people into the fold; people wanted to get involved and generally never left.[64]

It did not take long at all for Jake to place his mark on the parish; people knew he was in charge. At first his influence was rather subtle, but nonetheless present. Shortly after he arrived he noticed that artificial flowers were being used in the church. When he told the woman in charge of this ministry that he wanted real flowers, she said she could not help him any longer. He responded, "Well, we are going to miss you."[65] Jake's hand was clearly present in the preparation of the parish weekly bulletin. On one occasion he thanked those who had been involved in the erection of a basketball hoop in the church parking lot. The bulletin read, "*All hands* are welcome to come out and to try your luck with basketball."[66] The navy metaphor was unmistakable. He was clearly popular with the younger set, as he witnessed in his small parish nineteen marriages between July 1985 and June 1988.[67]

The magnetism and charismatic nature of his personality, so evident during his time in the navy, was also manifested as pastor at St. Alphonsus. Parishioners commented on how he liked people and they liked him; the mutuality of respect was evident in every way, uniting the community. One parishioner stated, "He was a very lovable great gentleman. He was a friend to everybody. He drew people into that church like flies to honey."[68] His warm heart, vibrancy in all action, and dedication to his people were trademarks that solidified his bond with the parishioners. His former navy colleague, Barry Black, stated, "Father Laboon was the quintessential pastor."[69] The positive impact that Jake made in such short order upon the parishioners at St. Alphonsus was recognized by his provincial: "Congratulations, Jake, for all you are doing to beautify the church, and the interior lives of its worshipers. I know that they appreciate all you are doing for them and the example you give as a great Jesuit priest."[70]

64. Ibid.
65. Ibid.
66. *St. Alphonsus Parish Bulletin*, March 30–31, 1985, SACR. Emphasis original.
67. Sacramental records—marriage, SACR.
68. St. Alphonsus Rodriguez joint parishioner interview, May 20, 2011.
69. Barry Black, interview with the author, October 25, 2010.
70. James Devereaux, SJ, to John Laboon, SJ, January 9, 1987, Devereux papers, ASJM.

A significant element of Jake's attraction to his parishioners was his preaching. As with his days as chaplain at the naval academy, Jake continued to prepare and deliver homilies that were directly to the point and powerfully preached. He did not speak long; it was not necessary. Rather, he directed his comments in a way to find relevance in the daily lives of those to whom he was speaking. Issues and images from current events were common in the homilies he preached. One parishioner jokingly commented, "We had not even read the Sunday morning paper and he was describing events therein in his sermon."[71] Jake spoke directly to the people, moving down from the sanctuary and pulpit to the level of the congregation. This method led one person to say, "I felt he was talking to me."[72] Many spoke about the quality and attractiveness of his voice; a typical comment was, "He had an amazing voice that was so distinctive. You really liked to listen to him."[73] Always totally prepared and preaching without notes, one man claimed, "He was the best I ever heard."[74]

The power and efficacious nature of Jake's preaching manifested itself in one small controversy during his time at St. Alphonsus. In 1986 the American people became aware of a covert operation of the U.S. government that gained the infamous title "The Iran-Contra Affair."[75] One central figure in the administration of President Ronald Reagan who found himself on the hot seat testifying before Congress was Lieutenant Colonel Oliver North, the same marine whom Jake Laboon had befriended at the naval academy during his days as a chaplain and whose life he had saved in Vietnam. In the

71. Charles Heid, interview with the author, May 24, 2011; St. Alphonsus Rodriguez joint parishioner interview, May 20, 2011.
72. St. Alphonsus Rodriguez joint parishioner interview, May 20, 2011.
73. Steve and Maureen Phillips, interview with the author, November 17, 2010.
74. Neil Werthmann, interview with the author, November 12, 2010.
75. The Iran-Contra affair was a political scandal that came to light in November 1986. During the second term of Ronald Reagan, U.S. government officials facilitated the sale of arms to Iran, although that nation was under an arms embargo. It was hoped that the sale would lead to the release of American hostages and enable U.S. intelligence agencies to fund the Contras in Nicaragua, operating against the government of Daniel Ortega. The Boland Amendment, however, had outlawed funding for the Contras. For information on this scandal, see Daniel Pipes, "Breaking the Iran/Contra Story," *Orbis* 31, no. 1 (Spring 1987): 135–39; Robert Williams, "Presidential Power and the Abuse of Office: The Case of the Iran-Contra Affair," *Corruption and Reform* 3, no. 2 (1988): 171–83; Peter Kornbluh, "The Iran-Contra Scandal: A Postmortem," *World Policy Journal* 5, no. 1 (Winter 1987–88): 129–50; Jonathan Marshall, Peter D. Scott, and Jane Hunter, *The Iran-Contra Connection: Secret Teams and Covert Operations in the Reagan Era* (Boston: South End Press, 1987); Lawrence E. Walsh, *Firewall: The Iran-Contra Conspiracy and Cover-Up* (New York: Norton, 1997).

summer of 1987 Jake supported North from the pulpit, indicating to parishioners that they could write letters in defense of his character and placing North's address in the weekly bulletin. Laboon's action received a rebuke from the archbishop, who told him to stop raising the issue from the pulpit and to apologize for bringing the affair into his homilies. Obedient, as he had always been, Jake did precisely what he was told to do.[76]

Jake's preaching and his pastoral style reveal much about his theological perspective. Throughout his navy career, wherein he served the vast majority of his priesthood, Jake made comments and followed certain ideas that when evaluated indicate that he had both traditional and progressive theological ideas. Twenty years earlier, while serving as a recruit chaplain at NTC Great Lakes, Jake spoke of motivation as central to behavior. He suggested that one cannot be judged simply on external actions, "since a man can do good things for a bad motive." He continued, "The true value of our lives depends on the motives which prompt us to act. These in turn depend on what we believe." He further argued that the good life must be motivated by the word of God. He wrote, "Before acting the next time, stop to ask yourself why you are doing such and so. If your actions are motivated by the Word of God, faith, then you are in truth living a 'good life.'"[77] For Jake Laboon true faith was absolutely essential for life; faith gives inner meaning to all we do. He concluded, demonstrating a more traditional approach to theology:

We cannot pick and choose what pleases us, or which we find convenient or which is merely popular, or even what is comfortably familiar. We must submit to the Word of God totally as He manifested Himself to us.[78]

Several people who knew Jake Laboon consider his basic theological perspective as traditional. A fellow Jesuit navy chaplain, Frank Metzbauer, SJ, claimed, "He had not really processed what happened at Vatican II. He was wedded to the traditions in which he was brought up." John Donlon, who had close association with Jake over a number of years, agrees with Metzbauer's analysis, but with more of a nuance. Describing Jake's theology as "most traditional," he suggested Laboon agreed with Vatican II, save the

---

76. *St. Alphonsus Parish Bulletin,* July 18–19, 1987, SACR; St. Alphonsus Rodriguez joint parishioner interview, May 20, 2011.
77. *Great Lakes Bulletin,* March 13, 1964, GLNSL.
78. Ibid.

ideas that led some to soften church teaching. Donlon put it this way: "He was Council of Trent raised and Vatican II infused."[79] Former Chief of Naval Operations Admiral Frank Kelso understood Laboon to be "theologically conservative."[80]

On the other hand, Ross Trower, who observed Jake closely when they worked together as fleet and assistant fleet chaplains respectively in Hawaii, characterized Laboon as "a forward-looking man." He recalled attending a chaplains' workshop in Washington, D.C., held at a Benedictine monastery. Jake celebrated Mass and, at the time for Communion, he left the consecrated bread and wine on the altar and asked attendees to commune themselves. Trower commented, "It was kind of a shock to people." He provided his overall thought on Jake's theology:

> He would try something he thought was appropriate and certainly within the rules of the Church, but he was not a man who would do things whimsically or impulsively. He thought about things very carefully.[81]

Recall, as well, how Jake was ahead of his time when inaugurating the lay leader program during his assignment with SSBN crews in New London.

One theological area in the actions and teaching of Jake Laboon that is not in dispute is his high priority for justice. He once listed eight specific virtues to be found in the just person: piety, deference, obedience, gratitude, vengeance, truth, friendliness, and liberality.[82] Laboon claimed that every person was bound by the common bond of human dignity to contribute to the reign of justice among all peoples. Jake Laboon's belief in the centrality of justice in human relationships was made evident when he wrote:

> Justice in a man makes him give to everyone else what is due to him. It is not enough that a person has the virtue of justice; a person is obliged to put this habit to work by doing acts of justice. He must actually render to each one whatever is his.[83]

Jake's gifts for administration and preaching and his vast experience in the navy were invaluable tools for his role as pastor, but the reality of the

---

79. John Donlon, interview with the author, September 14, 2012.
80. Frank Kelso, interview with the author, April 7, 2011.
81. Ross Trower, interview with the author, May 14, 2011.
82. *Great Lakes Bulletin*, March 13, 1964, GLNSL. What he meant by vengeance was inflicting punishment on one because of evil done. He defined liberality as the use of a person's riches for the good of others.
83. *Great Lakes Bulletin*, March 19, 1965, GLNSL.

day-to-day routine of parochial life surrounded him almost from the outset. Just prior to his arrival a new rectory opened, with an added wing for offices and a small chapel for daily Mass. The "traffic" of people was a new reality that required adjustment for Jake. Only one year after his arrival he was required to modify the Mass schedule as, due to lack of priests, the provincial determined that St. Alphonsus would be only a one-priest parish. Open to the ideas of others, he asked parishioners for input as to what the new Mass schedule would be.[84]

The parish routine was highlighted by many annual events. A St. Patrick's Day dance welcomed each spring. In addition to the Easter Triduum services, St. Alphonsus hosted an annual Seder meal as outreach to the local Jewish community.[85] Each summer the parish celebrated two important community events, the parish picnic and a fundraising festival. The latter occasions were true joys for Jake Laboon, as he had the opportunity as pastor to celebrate the lives of a large number of his parishioners in an environment that was completely consistent with his gregarious personality.[86]

Jake's special interest in youth, evident from the days of his tertianship at Auriesville, his work with navy recruits at Great Lakes, and even his desire to serve students at a Jesuit high school after his discharge from the navy, was also evident in his time at Woodstock. Ever the athlete, Jake installed a basketball hoop and court in the parish parking lot. Even now, in his early sixties, he took on all challengers in one-on one or other pick-up games. During the summer months he participated in weekly softball games played on the parish grounds. Moreover, Jake often traveled with the youth group and groups of altar servers on various outings. The vitality of young people and his own personality produced a synergistic effect of joy on all. During his tenure the parish sponsored a contest to send two teenagers with a youth group to Rome.[87]

---

84. "St. Alphonsus History—100 Years," St. Alphonsus Papers, AABa; *St. Alphonsus Parish Bulletins*, November 30–December 1, 1985, January 4–5, 1986, SACR.

85. The Roman Catholic Easter Triduum celebrates the paschal mystery, the passion, death, and resurrection of Jesus Christ. Celebrations on Holy Thursday and Good Friday and the Easter Vigil commemorate these central events in the life of Jesus and represent the high point of Roman Catholic liturgy in the liturgical Church year.

86. *St. Alphonsus Parish Bulletins*, March 21–22, 1987, March 2–3, 1985, May 16–17, 1987, May 11–12, 1985.

87. St. Alphonsus Rodriguez joint parishioner interview, May 20, 2011; *St. Alphonsus Parish Bulletin*, January 17–18, 1987. Youth who entered the contest for the trip to Rome were asked to

Faith formation was another vital ongoing activity at the parish, serving youth as well as adults. As was his *modus operandi*, Jake consulted his parishioners concerning issues and topics that should be addressed in his adult education program. Various speakers, including Jesuits and other experts in various areas, were invited to address diverse issues, both in a lecture format and discussion sessions. Religious education classes were provided for youth, leading to the celebration of First Communion and Confirmation. Additionally, a summer Bible school program for children preschool to grade four was held in July 1988.[88]

The general routine and annual events at the parish were punctuated by some major additions to the parish that even today mark Jake Laboon's time as pastor. In November 1985 Jake once again went to his parishioners with an idea—installation of a carillon in the church. He wrote in the parish bulletin, "If you think it ought to be a parish project, please let me know. What do you think?"[89] The parishioners were excited about this addition to the church, and the carillon was installed in 1986. The heat and humidity of a Maryland summer prompted Jake to air-condition the church, a project he completed just prior to his death.[90]

Jake was assigned to St. Alphonsus just prior to the parish's centenary, and plans for a grand celebration began almost from the time he arrived. The planned celebration was to be spread over the course of 1985. The centennial slogan adopted for the parish was "100 Years to the Greater Glory of God." The first event was celebration of solemn benediction and a talk by the Maryland Province provincial, James Devereaux, SJ, on January 6, 1985. Many Jesuits were present for the provincial's talk at 3:00 p.m., followed by a grand centennial dinner. The parish bulletin stated:

In recounting the history of Saint Alphonsus Parish over the past one hundred years, many of us were reminded of the faithful who have gone before us, both clergy and laity who served the parish with distinction.[91]

The principal event of the centenary celebration was held on October 27. A concelebrated Mass was held at 10:00 a.m., with Archbishop William Borders

---

submit an essay of 250 words or more on a topic: "Why I Want to Go to Rome." In addition to evaluation of essays, interviews were conducted.

88. *St. Alphonsus Parish Bulletins*, January 12–13, 1985, May 14–15, 1988, SACR.
89. Ibid., November 2–3, 1985.
90. Rosemary, deLellis, and Joan Laboon, interview with the author, August 4, 2010.
91. *St. Alphonsus Parish Bulletin*, January 12–13, 1985, SACR.

as the principal celebrant, assisted by the provincial, James Devereaux, SJ, and Jake Laboon. Then a festive dinner was held at the Turf Valley Country Club.[92]

Installation of the carillon and air-conditioning and the celebration of the parish's centenary were important events that marked Jake's time at St. Alphonsus, but his true mark was installation of a series of ornate stained-class windows. Two of the windows were rescued from the chapel at Woodstock College. Through the efforts of two of his brother Jesuits, Jim English and Jerry Coll, these stained-glass images of St. Ignatius at Manresa and St. Alphonsus Rodriguez were installed in the church, Ignatius above the altar and Alphonsus in the choir loft. Archbishop Borders dedicated the windows on October 27, 1985, as part of the parish's centenary celebration.[93] One year later, on Easter 1986, a new stained-glass image of the Blessed Virgin Mary, located in the sanctuary, was dedicated.[94]

The second half and major portion of the stained-class window project was announced in June 1986. The plan was to install ten windows, five on each side of the church, to honor Jesuit saints. He informed his provincial about the project, telling him that his rationale was to honor the Jesuits who had studied at Woodstock. Additionally, he asked for financial assistance, concluding, "Please give the project some thought. If you are able to assist financially you will note that the many Jesuits who studied here are not forgotten."[95] Initially Jake thought that the windows, at $10,000 each, might be installed over a ten-year period, but the initial reaction of the parishioners to his proposal astounded him. He wrote in the bulletin:

Since the proposal to stain-glass the church, presented to you last Sunday, three windows have already been taken. There is a very good possibility that two more windows will be purchased by the end of the summer.... The response has been so dramatic to this project that I am writing to tell you about the GOOD NEWS![96]

The highly positive response to the project prompted Jake to believe that five of the windows could actually be installed by Christmas, financed by interested parties.[97]

92. Ibid., August 17–18, 1985; clipping, *Catholic Review*, August 23, 1985, St. Alphonsus file, ASJM.
93. Clipping, *Catholic Review*, October 23, 1985; information sheet, St. Alphonsus Church, n.d. [1985], St. Alphonsus file, ASJM; *St. Alphonsus Parish Bulletin*, August 10–11, 1985, SACR.
94. St. Alphonsus Rodriguez joint parishioner interview, May 20, 2011.
95. Ibid., *St. Alphonsus Parish Bulletin*, June 7–8, 1986, SACR; John Laboon, SJ, to James Devereaux, SJ, Devereaux papers, ASJM.
96. *St. Alphonsus Parish Bulletin*, June 7–8, 1986, SACR.
97. Ibid.

The initial success in selling the project prompted Laboon to write to Archbishop Borders asking his permission to proceed. In the first week of August he wrote, "In my wildest dreams, I thought perhaps it would be possible to install one [window] per year. In June I mentioned the project to the parishioners. By last Saturday, I had all 10 windows purchased."[98] He informed Borders that the Gibbons Company would do the work; the money for each window will be collected privately from individual donors. The archbishop responded with great enthusiasm:

> I can only congratulate you on securing donors for the design and construction of stained-glass windows for the other 10 windows in the church. Your plans sound good, and since you have the money already promised, I certainly am pleased to grant my approval of the project. You may feel free to go ahead with the contract.[99]

One of the ten, dedicated to the Sacred Heart of Jesus, was purchased by Jake in honor of his family. The provincial gave permission for Laboon to take $10,000 of his navy patrimony for the window.[100] The dedication Mass for the new stained-glass windows at St. Alphonsus was celebrated on November 1, 1987. Bishop William C. Newman, vicar of the Eastern Region (Baltimore) was the principal celebrant, with James Devereaux and Jake Laboon as concelebrants.[101]

Final Days and Death

The normal aches and pains that come with age assuredly appeared here and there for Jake Laboon, but beyond that, despite his active life, athletic physique, and positive attitude, he could not avert a major health crisis. In January 1988 he informed his friend and former student from St. Joe Prep, Dr. Joseph DeSantis, that he was having difficulty swallowing solids. At the suggestion of DeSantis Jake received a full physical examination and was diagnosed with esophageal cancer. The best medical advice he received was to

---

98. John Laboon, SJ, to William Borders, August 6, 1986, Borders papers, AABa.
99. William Borders to John Laboon, SJ, August 26, 1986, Borders papers, AABa.
100. James Devereaux SJ, to John Laboon, SJ, January 9, 1987, Devereux papers, ASJM.
101. John Laboon, SJ, to James Devereaux, SJ, September 16, 1987, Devereux papers, ASJM; Mass program, November 1, 1987, SACR. The ten windows honored the Sacred Heart of Jesus and Immaculate Heart of Mary and eight Jesuits: St. Francis Xavier, St. Robert Bellarmine, St. Aloysius Gonzaga, St. John Berchmans, St. Stanislaus Kostka, the Martyrs of England and Wales, the Martyrs of North America, and the Martyrs of Japan; see John Laboon, SJ, to William Borders, August 6, 1986, Borders papers, AABa, and *St. Alphonsus Parish Bulletin*, June 28–29, 1986, SACR.

Jesuit Retreat Master and Pastor: 1981–1988

Figure 11-2. Jake Laboon with his brother, Father Joe, and Sisters deLellis, Rosemary, and Joan at St. Alphonsus parish, Woodstock, Md., c. 1987

have surgery, which was performed at Walter Reed Army Hospital in Washington, D.C, but his situation had already progressed beyond what medical science could resolve.[102]

The next few months were difficult. Initially Jake spent several days in the hospital; while there he was visited by a number of friends, including his brother Jesuits, family, and many navy associates.[103] He requested that he be returned to St. Alphonsus as opposed to a Jesuit infirmary. His condition, as painful as it was, did not impede him from doing whatever he could in his ministry. His three siblings, Sisters of Mercy deLellis, Rosemary, and Joan, spent much time in the ensuing months serving as his primary caretakers. Word of Jake's condition spread rapidly.[104] In late May 1988 he wrote to his naval academy classmates with an update on his status:

102. Dr. Joseph DeSantis, interview with the author, March 31, 2011; Joseph Laboon, interview with the author, August 19, 2010.
103. Rosemary, deLellis, and Joan Laboon, interview with the author, August 4, 2010; Joseph Laboon, interview with the author, August 4, 2010; William Dawson, SJ, interview with the author, October 28, 2010; Alvin Koeneman, interview with the author, May 16, 2011.
104. Rosemary, deLellis, and Joan Laboon, interview with the author, August 4, 2010.

Jesuit Retreat Master and Pastor: 1981–1988

Next week I am scheduled for a checkup at Walter Reed. So far, I have not been undergoing and [*sic;* any] treatment. The doctors want to wait until the cancer reappears, and then I [will] undergo radiation treatment. So far, I have been doing fairly well. My digestive system is not back to normal yet. My weight loss is a concern of mine, but the doctors assure me that my weight will come back. If I could get some strength back I would feel better. Right now, I am active in the parish again, but not restored to full duty. Hopefully it will come in time.[105]

Jake continued his ministry as pastor at St. Alphonsus, but it was clear that he would need assistance. Throughout 1988, Jesuits were sent by the provincial to assist. Jake performed his last baptism on June 12. During the early summer he entertained many visitors, including members of the Isaac Kidd family. He often prayed with his family and celebrated Mass in his room whenever he had strength. While he appreciated the outpouring of love by others, it troubled him that he was a worry for them. Isaac Kidd's wife, Angelique, referring to the love given him by so many, commented, "This care grieved him that he felt himself such a burden. It was his mental suffering and not physical pain that troubled him."[106]

Jake continued to receive visitors and the ministrations of his loving family and friends, but they knew that the end was near. The reality of the situation generated discussions concerning where Jake was to be buried. Admiral Kidd and other senior navy personnel wanted him to be buried below the naval academy chapel, but Jake rejected the idea, choosing to rest for eternity with his Jesuit brothers at Woodstock.[107]

On August 1, 1988, at 1:00 p.m., surrounded by his family, Jake Laboon died.[108] While tributes would come from far and wide over the next days and weeks, a few immediate testimonials spoke of the breadth of his influence. Upon hearing of Jake's death, the pastor of Granite Presbyterian Church in Woodstock wrote, "Fr. Laboon enhanced the life of our community and we are grateful. He gave spiritual sustenance to many people. We are glad he lived and ministered among us."[109] Jake's naval academy football teammate, Bill Busik, spoke for many: "Jake inspired us all. He excelled academically

---

105. Jake Laboon to "Classmates and Lovely Spouses," May 30, 1988, PPJM.
106. John Donlon, interview with the author, September 9, 2011; Mary Plummer, interview with the author, December 18, 2010; Angelique Kidd to the author, n.d. [2010].
107. *Baltimore Sun*, August 5, 1988, SACR; John Laboon, interview with the author, January 31, 2011.
108. Death notice—John Laboon, August 3, 1988, Laboon file, ASJM.
109. Sherman Roddy to John Keenan, SJ, August 5, 1988, PPJM.

and in athletics.... Everyone who knew Jake held the highest respect for him."[110] One tribute synthesized what he meant to the navy:

Father Jake left behind countless service members and their families whose lives he had touched with his compassion and understanding. His courage and genuine concern for all his shipmates was then, is now [sic], and will forever remain an extraordinary example for young sailors and marines everywhere.[111]

The wake and funeral of Jake Laboon transformed Woodstock almost overnight into a spot of national prominence. Having decided before his death that his services would be held at St. Alphonsus, Jake was waked on August 2. Thursday, August 4, 1988, was a hot but dry summer day in Eastern Maryland. His brother, Joe, celebrated the Mass of Christian burial for Jake. The homily was given by a fellow Jesuit, William Graham, and a eulogy by his friend and fellow navy chaplain Robert Ecker. Additional comments at the end of Mass were made by Cardinal John O'Connor of New York, Jake's friend and navy contemporary.[112]

The funeral Mass was attended by many prominent people as well as many rank-and-file parishioners at St. Alphonsus, all of whom were touched by Jake. Some of the dignitaries attending were: chief of naval operations, Admiral Carlisle A. H. Trost; the commandant of the Marine Corps, General Alfred M. Gray Jr.; the secretary of the navy, James Webb; commander in chief Atlantic Fleet, Admiral Frank Kelso; former astronaut, General William Anders, USAF; former Vietnam POW and U.S. senator, Rear Admiral Jeremiah Denton; and Laboon's longtime friend, Admiral Isaac Kidd. The church was well represented by Archbishop William Borders, three of his auxiliary bishops, and many Jesuits.[113] Dignitaries may have abounded, but Jake Laboon was a pastor, and the people of his small parish were there. The *Baltimore Sun* reported:

---

110. Donald T. Fritz, "The Original All-American Hero," clipping, September 1990, PPJL.
111. "Laboon Legacy," http://goodjesuitbadjesuit.blogspot.com; accessed around March 5, 2013.
112. Mass program, n.d. [August 4, 1988], John F. Laboon alumni file, AUSNA. The readings for the Mass were: Wisdom 3:1–9; Revelation 14:13; and John 14:1–6. Typical with funerals of many navy and former navy personnel, the navy hymn, "Eternal Father," was sung after Communion.
113. List of pallbearers; *Baltimore Sun*, August 5, 1988, PPJL. The list of honorary pallbearers included: General William Anders, (NASA astronaut); Captain Bo Coppege (USNA director of athletics); Senator Jeremiah Denton; Captain Burt Findley, (shipmate on the *Peto*); General Alfred Gray, USMC; Jack Johnson (St. Joe Prep); Admiral Frank Kelso; Admiral Thomas Kilkline (president U.S. Armed Forces Retired Officers Association); Chester M. Lee (director NASA Apollo program); and Admiral Wesley McDonald (NATO Supreme Allied Maritime Commander-in-Chief).

Hundreds of ordinary parishioners also came to express their love for Father Laboon, who by all accounts was an extraordinary man who lived an extraordinary life bolstered by an extraordinary ability to deal with people.[114]

Those who spoke at the funeral outlined Jake's life of total dedication and service to others through adherence and fidelity to his three loves, described by William Graham, SJ, in his homily, as Pittsburgh (meaning his family), the navy, and the Society of Jesus. He commented, "It's hard to believe that one man could have three strong loyalties and through it all remain true to them all." He described Jake's strength as found in mind and heart more than in physical prowess. Graham believed Jake's years in the navy were "filled with happiness because he was in service to people and in the service of the one he loved the most."[115] Speaking more spontaneously in his eulogy, Robert Ecker described Jake as a man of "almost unbelievable authenticity." In that light he presented Jake's challenge to the world:

He would never be satisfied to allow us to be any less than we could be. He encouraged us to seek fellowship. He encouraged leaders to lead and use their authority responsibly. He was only causing the potential God placed in each one of us to be realized.

Speaking to a church filled with ranking members of church and state, Ecker nonetheless concluded, "In this chapel today there is nobody who is not a giant, and yet can any one of us stand next to Jake Laboon?"[116] At the conclusion of the Mass, Cardinal John O'Connor, former chief of chaplains and longtime friend of Jake Laboon, was pressed to make some comments. Appropriately, he concluded, "If a man was a man for all seasons, it was Father Laboon."

Following the funeral Mass, Jake's body was taken down a narrow country road to the small Jesuit cemetery that lies outside the former Woodstock Seminary. There he was laid to rest among his Jesuit brothers, including, among others, his former teacher John Courtney Murray. Admiral Isaac Kidd, who had been almost uncontrollable in his grief throughout the services, fittingly commented about his great friend, "He was a bridge throughout his career—from astronauts, to youngsters in Marine and Navy uniforms, to statesmen."[117]

114. *Baltimore Sun*, n.d. [August 1988], John F. Laboon, alumni file, AUSNA.
115. John Laboon, funeral audiotape, August 4, 1988.
116. Ibid.
117. *Baltimore Sun*, August 5, 1988, PPJL.

Conclusion

In November 1980, after twenty-two years of dedicated service as a chaplain in the U.S. Navy, Jake Laboon returned to the Society of Jesus. After a semester to "retool" and reintegrate himself into a pattern of life to which he had dedicated himself so long ago, but had not directly experienced because of his ministry in the navy, Jake was sent in a very real way back home to Annapolis as minister of Manresa-on-Severn. With the naval academy visible to him from his window, Jake served the Jesuit community by supervising the renovation of the entire retreat facility. Additionally, and probably more importantly in his mind, he exercised his pastoral gifts as retreat master and assistant in local parishes. Jake enjoyed his ministry and certainly the environment, but ever an obedient religious, he agreed when asked to be pastor of St. Alphonsus Rodriguez, a small parish in Woodstock, Maryland. As his final stop in ministry and life, Jake returned to the principal site of his religious formation. As his positions of command in the latter days of his navy career allowed him the freedom to plan and make policy, so his final days as pastor gave him the opportunity to direct the small parish and its faithful flock in new ways. He immediately placed his own mark on the parish, both by his democratic and cooperative way of making decisions and his physical improvements of the facilities, including the installation of ten ornate stained-glass windows that honored various Jesuit saints. Still a relatively young man and in full vigor, Jake was struck with cancer, a disease that has no bounds with respect to age. When he died only several months after his original diagnosis, he was honored with the presence of many prominent people of church and state at his funeral. Buried in humility with his Jesuit brothers in a small cemetery near the former Woodstock College, his life would continue through his legacy, both physical and inspirational, that continues today.

Epilogue

Jake Laboon—The Legacy

All men and women must one day succumb to the reality of physical death, but for the privileged few a significant legacy remains. Funerals are times when eulogies and various words of remembrance are uttered by family and friends, but with time and the fading of memories what was said and the sentiments behind them are lost. By most standards today, Jake Laboon died before his time. Not even seventy years old and one who always kept himself in good physical condition, his rather rapid journey to death's door and his passage through it on August 1, 1988, was certainly a shock to many. Yet Jake, like many of the great men and women of history, because of the way he lived, the people he influenced, and the good that he did, is privileged to have a more significant legacy than most. Jake's naval experience gave him the advantage to meet and associate with many who at the time or later in their lives held positions of power and authority. In a tribute to the significant work he did and the many significant accomplishments of his military career, those men and women of prominence who benefited from his ministry used their influence to assure that the legacy of Jake Laboon, war hero, Jesuit priest, and navy chaplain would continue to live in the memories of many.

The Person

People who encountered Father Jake remembered their first impressions, for, indeed, he was a striking figure. At 6′5″ and with an athletic physique that he always maintained, Jake Laboon was, as described by many, "bigger than life," both physically and in the things he accomplished.[1] You simply could not miss him. People who first met him noticed not just his physical size and warm smile, but often the cigar in his mouth and, if they met him in his office, the beret on his head. One chaplain commented, "He smoked cigars constantly and carried 're-loads' (as he called them) in a brown paper bag."[2] One woman who worked with Father Jake when he was a chaplain at the naval academy remembered, "We could always tell when he was coming up to the office ... , because you could smell the cigars ahead of time."[3] Jake liked a good meal and took his bourbon straight up, but always in moderation. Described by many as a "stunning man," he was supremely confident and an imposing yet gentle presence wherever he went.[4] He wore an inviting smile and a gentle manner, even though he was a giant of a man, physically and by reputation. He placed people at ease; they felt instantly accepted by him.[5] Jake was a good conversationalist and, as a daily paper reader, was knowledgeable and comfortable in all discussions. As one longtime friend said, "He always had an answer. Father [Laboon] could fit into any conversation."[6]

Jake Laboon possessed a personality that matched his corporal nature, enhancing his attractiveness to all. Few people ever had as many friends as Jake. His friendliness toward others, manifested in the way he took interest in what people said and the activities of their lives, drew people to him like a magnet. Friendly, outgoing, inviting, and considerate were words used to describe his personality. He had a special ability to make a person feel that he was a friend for life, even on a first encounter.[7] His charismatic personality was so outgoing that people related to him from the moment they met him. He was gregarious and possessed a certain charisma that is rarely seen. He loved people and spent hours talking and engaging those around him.

1. William Leahy, interview with the author, October 14, 2010.
2. James Kirsten, e-mail to the author, August 11, 2011.
3. Clipping, *Soundings*, October 5, 1994, PPWL; Bruce Kahn, interview with the author, August 3, 2011.
4. John O'Neill, interview with the author, February 26, 2011; William Leahy, interview with the author, October 14, 2010; Christopher Kidd, interview with the author, October 4, 2010.
5. Robert Ecker, interview with the author, December 17, 2010; John Donlon, interview with the author, September 9, 2011.
6. Thomas Lynch, interview with the author, August 16, 2010; Charles Heid, interview with the author, May 24, 2011.
7. James Kirsten, e-mail to the author, August 11, 2011; Neil Werthmann, interview with the author, November 12, 2010.

As the former chief of naval operations, Admiral Frank Kelso, commented, "He [Laboon] was fun to be around."[8] A good pianist, Jake could be the life of the party at social events.[9] He easily won the hearts of people he engaged. One fellow navy chaplain spoke of how the various pieces of his personality "fit together in a corporate that was so engaging and colorful and personable that people were drawn to him."[10]

Humility also characterized the personality of Jake Laboon. He never spoke of himself or his accomplishments, but rather listened intently and responded to those with whom he was speaking. He was not one of great ego; on the contrary, he knew who he was. Jake had no particular plan based on his own ideas, but rather was open to others. One marine who encountered Jake in Vietnam stated:

> He was one of those people you know who never had another agenda. He was real; he wasn't out to impress anybody. He was just who he was. He never wore his ego on his shoulder. You knew he would go anywhere for you or with you.[11]

He never asked anything of others, but with a generous spirit gave of who he was to others. Robert Ecker stated, "Jake's humility was the cause of his effectiveness on all levels and with all people. His humility in turn prompted all those present to be there for him."[12]

Jake's humble nature, following the lead of the Lord, helped him to be constantly positive in his relationships with people; those he encountered were always first in his mind. Those who met Father Jake felt a sense of energy that stayed with them; he left a portion of himself with others. His positive nature and great self-confidence rubbed off on people, helping them to feel good about themselves simply because of who they were, not what they or others wanted them to be. One fellow chaplain put it this way: "With Jake you felt hugged, nourished, nurtured, and instructed all at the same time."[13] Another chaplain stated, "He wrapped around people. He made them feel good."[14] Jake Laboon had the intangible ability to make you

---

8. John Donlon, interview with the author, September 9, 2011; Frank Kelso, interview with the author, April 7, 2011.
9. Neil Werthmann, interview with the author, November 12, 2010.
10. Bruce Kahn, interview with the author, August 3, 2011.
11. John Toland, interview with the author, November 17, 2010.
12. Robert Ecker, interview with the author, December 17, 2010.
13. Bruce Kahn, interview with the author, August 3, 2011.
14. Robert Ecker, interview with the author, December 17, 2010.

feel good about yourself; he was someone others wanted to be around. His welcoming manner, expressed through a broad smile and a big handshake, marked the way he approached people.[15] Jake was never a person to hold a grudge, but rather always looked for the positive in others. He realized that all humans are imperfect, including him, and, therefore, he always sought to find the "Golden Nugget" of good inside each person. His positive nature made it very easy for others to trust him completely.[16]

Possibly not so obvious, but nevertheless observed by many, was Jake's quick wit and sense of humor. He often came across to people as quiet, sort of a "gentle giant" of a personality, but he was a jovial person and laughed a lot. As with his openness and humility, his sense of humor put people at ease and allowed him to speak to all ranks of people on many different levels. Jake often had a joke that he shared with others.[17]

The jovial, open, and humble personality that drew people to Jake, making them feel comfortable and important, did not mean in any way that he was a pushover who could be manipulated by others. The contrary is more the reality. Many people who knew him well spoke about his ability to be a great communicator and, in the proper situation, a great storyteller, but he also, as the expression goes, "called a spade a spade."[18] Father Jake spoke his mind. Bill Leahy, the son of his naval academy roommate, commented, "He was direct, loud, and had strong feelings. He was not afraid to communicate his ideas."[19] Admiral Frank Kelso stated, "If you knew Jake Laboon you knew he was not reticent to say what he thought."[20] He always spoke with superiors respectfully, but they knew where he stood, even if it was directly opposed to what others thought. At times he could be very critical, especially if, in his mind, a person was arrogant or irresponsible. He could be acerbic, slinging one-line comments from the back row of an auditorium.

15. James Flatley, interview with the author, March 3, 2011; Tom Lynch, interview with the author, August 16, 2010.
16. Frank Kelso, interview with the author, April 7, 2011; Robert Ecker, interview with the author, December 17, 2010.
17. Mary Plummer, interview with the author, December 18, 2010; Steve and Maureen Phillips, interview with the author, November 17, 2010; Tom Lynch, interview with the author, August 16, 2010.
18. Barry Black, interview with the author, August 25, 2010; Neil Werthmann, interview with the author, November 12, 2010.
19. William Leahy, interview with the author, August 14, 2010.
20. Frank Kelso, interview with the author, April 7, 2011.

Again, as Kelso has stated, "He was not a pushover."²¹ Jake had high standards of moral behavior and did not tolerate failures in this realm. He was content in his own skin and wanted others to follow his lead. As Barry Black commented, "He was happy to be who he was. He was an extremely ethically congruent individual."²²

The Personal Legacy

Jake Laboon was a Jesuit priest dedicated to his religious community, but his fame and therefore his legacy are based upon his time in the navy—especially his twenty-two years as a chaplain. Evidence to support his love for and dedication to the navy is echoed by many, both military and church figures. Hugh Kennedy, SJ, stated, "He was completely dedicated to the Navy."²³ In his funeral homily for Jake, William Graham, SJ, stated, "His love for the Navy was deep and very reverent and was filled with incidents that were very affectionately remembered."²⁴ Cardinal O'Connor said, "I never saw Father Jake not in love with the United States Navy, a romance that was to endure until his death."²⁵ Jake perceived the navy as the focal point for his life; it became his adoptive family. He once stated, "I know the Navy is not a democracy. It's built on a hierarchy. I look upon the Navy as my family. I like regimentation. I thought it was made for me."²⁶ As an obedient religious and a "good sailor," Jake saw duty as central to his life. Yet he was certainly not afraid to voice his opinion, especially for someone who had been wronged. His friend Cardinal John O'Connor once stated,

Father Jake never hesitated to tell the highest-ranking naval authorities if ever he believed they might be on the wrong course, particularly if he thought their actions might be morally irresponsible or damaging to the naval service and its people. But his criticisms were always couched in the language of understanding and love. He could speak with authority because his own moral behavior was impeccable, and because he served the Navy with such integrity and self-sacrifice in war and peace.²⁷

---

21. Ibid.
22. Barry Black, interview with the author, October 25, 2010.
23. *Catholic Review*, January 17, 1990, PPJL.
24. John Laboon, SJ, funeral audiotape, August 4, 1988.
25. *Catholic Review*, February 25, 1993, AABa.
26. *Honolulu Advertiser*, n.d., Laboon file, AUSNA.
27. *Catholic New York*, February 25, 1993, PPJL.

Epilogue: Jake Laboon—The Legacy

Jake was well respected. One newspaper article commented, "His courage, compassion, and understanding touched the lives of many service members and their families."[28] Years after his death, one family friend wrote to one of Jake's siblings, "Your brother, Father John, was an exceptional naval officer, who was so well thought of highly and respected by all who knew him."[29] Vice Admiral Philip Beshany described Jake as "the most beloved chaplain I know and the most popular."[30] Admiral Kelso described the depth of Jake's humanity as well as his talent: "I found Jake to be a wonderful companion, a dedicated chaplain for the Catholic Church as well as the Navy."[31] Rear Admiral Alvin Koeneman, a former chief of chaplains who worked closely with Jake in Norfolk, described him as "the prototypical chaplain."[32]

Accolades of a personal nature attributed to Jake were complemented by the many awards he received from his military service. Besides reaching the rank of navy captain on July 1, 1972, he earned thirteen decorations for valor and for exceptional and dedicated service. He was awarded the Silver Star, the nation's third-highest military decoration, for his daring and heroic rescue of the downed American aviator off the Japanese coast in late July 1945. He was also twice awarded the Legion of Merit, one with combat "V" for his service in Vietnam. Additionally, through his combat service on *Peto* during World War II and his service in Southeast Asia, he was awarded several additional awards, including the Submarine Combat Insignia and Vietnam Service Medal.[33]

The dedication that Jake Laboon demonstrated to the navy and the way people experienced him represent only a portion of his personal legacy. Equally important in his memory is the genuine concern he had for all navy and marine personnel and his equitable treatment of those he encountered. One comment typified how Jake touched the lives of so many:

Father Jake left behind countless service members and their families whose lives he touched with his compassion and understanding. His courage and genuine interest and concern for his shipmates was then, is now and will forever remain an extraordinary example for young sailors and Marines everywhere.[34]

28. Clipping, "Navy Ship to Be Named for Jesuit," n.d. [1991], Laboon file, ASJM.
29. William Castleberry to Joan Laboon, RSM, January 18, 2008, PPJL.
30. Reminiscences of VADM Philip Beshany, USN, AUSNA.
31. Admiral Frank Kelso, interview with the author, April 7, 2011.
32. Clipping, n.d. [1980], personal papers of Neil Werthmann (hereafter PPNW).
33. General information sheet, John Francis Laboon Jr., NMPR.
34. "Let Freedom Ring," special edition, 2004, PPRL.

Jake respected all; rank seemed to have no bearing whatsoever in dealing with people, especially when speaking with them. Barry Black commented, "I never had the feeling that he had any concern or even awareness of rank."[35] Cardinal O'Connor stated, "Father Jake was a man who treated a seaman as respectfully as he treated an Admiral.... Everyone was sacred in his eyes—a person of priceless worth.[36] Rear Admiral Koeneman commented on Jake's concern for the religious character of sailors: "I remember his concern for the spiritual quality of life for the sailor.... He never lost his compassion or concern for the deck-plate sailor, the sailor who is the heart and soul of the Navy."[37] One of his nephews characterized Jake as the "champion of the 'white hats.'"[38]

Jake Laboon's dedication to all he encountered, but especially enlisted sailors, was unfortunately not, it seems, universal. While Jake's respect for all never wavered, he did, it seems, have reservations with respect to women in the navy, especially their service aboard ships. His friends related stories about his fear associated with women on ships; but Laboon's position was actually much more nuanced. He explained:

You have to put a community of women aboard ship. If you do not put enough women on ship and they are not able to form a community then they are harassed all the time. As long as you have a large enough community then you can hack it.

He continued, "There are women on non-combat in ships in the fleet now and they're ok."[39]

The recognition and consequent legacy that Jake Laboon left behind as a naval officer cannot be divorced from the fact that he was a priest. People were attracted to him because of his priestly qualities. Fellow chaplains, other people he encountered, and family described him as "a real honest-to-God priest," "a man's man and a priest's priest."[40] His fellow chaplains,

---

35. Barry Black, interview with the author, August 25, 2010.
36. USS *Laboon* commissioning booklet, n.d. [1995], PPJL.
37. *Catholic Review*, January 17, 1990, AABa.
38. Joe Malloy, interview with the author, January 11, 2011.
39. *Catholic Review*, July 17, 1981, AABa. Dr. Joe DeSantis relates a story told him by a retired navy chaplain. The priest said he was attending a meeting where many navy chaplains were gathered. At the meeting a woman representative told the chaplains of the plans to place women aboard U.S. Navy ships. Jake is said to have walked up the aisle and, pointing his finger at the woman, said, "You will ruin the United States Navy"; Joseph DeSantis, interview with the author, March 31, 2011. Ross Trower verifies Jake's attitude toward women aboard ships; Ross Trower, interview with the author, May 14, 2011.
40. Clipping, "Bath Iron Works Launches Aegis Destroyer," n.d. [1993], Laboon file, ASJM; John Friel, interview with the author, August 2, 2011.

including many non-Catholics, spoke of his obedience to the church and to his religious vows. Rear Admiral Trower stated, "He was definitely a priest. There was no question in my mind that he was a priest. He was there to serve Christ and the people with whom he came in contact."[41] People commented on how faith was the guiding light that Jake Laboon followed. One of his nephews commented, "He had such a love for God; there was never anything cavalier about what he did."[42] Similarly, James Webb commented, "He had a true sense of serenity in his faith. It informed everything he did. He was clearly a man of God."[43]

Two illustrative stories paint a picture of the legacy of faith and priesthood that Jake Laboon left to the world. A woman civilian worker at the naval academy chaplains' office spoke of Jake's intense reflective powers. He once told her, "If I am facing the window with my Navy baseball cap on, I am talking with God. I will talk to you when I am done."[44] A nephew recalled a conversation he had with Uncle Jake when he visited him in Florida. Laboon told his nephew that if the Lord would take him in three minutes that would be fine, but he [Laboon] would continue with their conversation. The event demonstrated Jake's intense faith; there was no fear of God. Laboon told his nephew, "Death is not an end, but only the beginning of an eternal life with God."[45]

Jake Laboon's pragmatic view of life and faith is another aspect of his priestly legacy. During the first years after Vatican II, many American Catholics experienced their base of faith shifting; the plethora of liturgical innovations as well as a generally more open and progressive perspective on church teachings caused confusion for many. This situation left some a bit pessimistic about the future. Jake, on the other hand, saw the glass half-full, proclaiming a positive message as he observed the post-council church:

I do not think it's a revolution at all. Sure, we've lost a lot of priests and many of the sisters, but I think this is just indicative of the times. There's a lot of unrest among young people, and the Church is a natural target. When things return to normal, I think the Church will be in an even stronger position than before.[46]

41. Ross Trower, interview with the author, May 14, 2011.
42. John Laboon, interview with the author, January 31, 2011.
43. James Webb, interview with the author, October 4, 2010.
44. *Soundings*, October 5, 1994, PPWL.
45. John Laboon, interview with the author, January 31, 2011.
46. Clipping, n.d. [1970], PPJM.

Epilogue: Jake Laboon—The Legacy

Friendship was one of the Jake's many recognized gifts. As a friend he had a special gift of listening; he was very much attuned to the person with whom he was speaking. Many who encountered him commented, "He really focused on the person; he listened. He was not distracted by what was going on about him. There was always a sense that he cared about what people were saying."[47] Similarly, many have described a conversation with Jake as unique. One woman shared her experience:

People remembered him years after a slight encounter because he had the ability to make every individual encounter memorable. When you were with him, you were the only one he was interested in, and he was true and sincere.[48]

His brother Joe stated, "When you spoke with Jake you felt like the most important person in the world."[49]

Generosity of spirit, trust, and respect were other dimensions of his friendship. One person used a metaphor: "He could step over the garden fence [reference to the problem at hand] and immediately find his way into your heart and you knew to trust him."[50] His breadth of experience helped him in dealing with situations, but always in a measured way with a sense of warmth, openness, and generosity.[51] Jake's respect for others was clear to those whom he met. He always remembered people's names and by his actions and words demonstrated respect for the individual.[52]

The various manifestations of friendship that Jake Laboon demonstrated were part of a general presence among people that was real, powerful, and long-lasting. Jake's physical prowess, the many significant accomplishments of his life, and his ebullient and charismatic personality made heads turn. One retired navy chaplain commented, "He was a powerful presence with great credibility."[53] His friend Monsignor Robert Ecker recalled an

---

47. John Laboon, funeral audiotape; Steve and Maureen Phillips, interview with the author, November 17, 2010.

48. Nancy Davis, e-mail to author, December 3, 2010.

49. Joseph Laboon, interview with the author, August 19, 2010. One member of the naval academy class of 1968, who encountered Jake in Vietnam, as well, stated, "He [Laboon] was always a friend to all, and made you think you were a lifelong friend, even though you may have just met him"; Len Mrozak, e-mail to author, February 28, 2011.

50. Christopher Kidd, interview with the author, October 4, 2010.

51. Angelique Kidd to the author, n.d. [2010]; Admiral Harry Train to the author, July 23, 2010.

52. William Graham, SJ, to Cardinal John O'Connor, March 23, 1993, O'Connor papers, A-99, box 10, AANY.

53. Edwin Condon, interview with the author, January 19, 2011.

incident at an annual chaplain corps celebration at the Washington Navy Yard. As the master of ceremonies was speaking, Jake entered the room and received spontaneous applause. Ecker commented, "He was so well-known and appreciated that he had become legendary."[54] He concluded, "He was such a giant of a person in regard to his humility and presence and his spirituality."[55]

Jake Laboon's personal legacy as naval officer, chaplain, priest, and friend can be summarized by speaking of how he carried himself and how he was received by others. He was revered and loved by others for whom he was more than the gifts he possessed. In many ways his life was given to others for their betterment. One assessment of Jake's life captured much of his legacy:

Because of his widespread and varied assignments and his genuine interest and concern for his shipmates and their families, Father Laboon was the most widely known and respected chaplain among the officers, sailors and marines of the Navy-Marine Corps Team.[56]

On the occasion of Jake's death, Joe Goss, a sports columnist for the *Annapolis Evening Capital,* summarized his personal legacy in this way:

He was the kind of man who was good for religion. Jake did not preach it. He lived it. He got respect by giving respect. He made people of all religions feel comfortable in his presence. He never held himself above anyone.[57]

The Physical Legacy

Prior to 1989 only six vessels in the history of the U.S. Navy had been named after a chaplain. The first, USS *Livermore* (DD-429), was named for Chaplain Samuel Livermore, who distinguished himself aboard the USS *Chesapeake* in a battle fought in the War of 1812 on June 1, 1813. The *Livermore* was commissioned in 1940 and decommissioned sixteen years later. The other five vessels were the USS *O'Callahan* (FF-1051), USS *Kirkpatrick* (DE-318), USS *Rentz* (FFG-46), USS *Schmidt* (DE-676), and most recently USS *Capodanno* (FF-1093), named after Vincent Capodanno, the Maryknoll priest whose

---

54. Robert Ecker, interview with the author, December 17, 2010.
55. Ibid.
56. Citation summary, n.d. [1993], PPJM.
57. *Annapolis Evening Capital,* August 3, 1988.

Epilogue: Jake Laboon—The Legacy

heroic death in Vietnam gained him the Congressional Medal of Honor.[58]

On May 9, 1989, the secretary of the navy, William Ball, announced the decision to name a vessel after Jake Laboon. The official notice spoke of Jake's heroism during World War II and his long career as a navy chaplain. Ball concluded, "His courage, compassion, and understanding touched the lives of many service members and their families."[59] Positive reactions to this rare honor abounded. Jake's brother Joe commented, "He was a guy who had great love for his family, his home and his Church. He loved the Navy and the Navy, of course, is returning his love with this great honor."[60] Michael McCormack, OP, director of communications for the Archdiocese of the Military Services, was elated about the decision: "It is always an honor to have a ship named after one of our Navy chaplains. To honor an individual such as Father Laboon is appropriate."[61] Cardinal O'Connor was also pleased: "For many years it was my privilege to serve with Father John Laboon. I believe that the designation of the new guided missile destroyer in his name is certainly merited."[62]

It seems that a few highly influential navy and government officials were responsible for this honor. Laboon family members and Secretary Ball acknowledged the influence of Admiral Kidd, whose disappointment that Jake was never promoted to admiral and appointed chief of chaplains prompted him to find an appropriate way to show appreciation for his great contribution to the navy. Others recognized the influence of Admiral Train.[63] One retired chaplain, Rabbi Bruce Kahn, attributed the naming to ranking officers in general: "There is a ship named for Jake Laboon; his relationships with people, especially Navy brass, [but acting] as a loving human and great pastor brought this about."[64] The personal involvement of Secretary Ball was also evident. In a letter to Ball, one Laboon family member stated, "I

---

58. Mode, *Grunt Padre*, 162; Randy Cash, e-mail to the author, January 23, 2013.

59. William Ball, SecNav notice 5030, May 9, 1989, NCA. Ball's father was a navy chaplain with the Seabees during World War II. He desired to name a ship after a chaplain if possible; see William Ball, interview with the author, March 19, 2013.

60. Clipping, *Pittsburgh Post-Gazette*, n.d. [May 1989], PPJM.

61. Clipping, n.d. [1990], SACR.

62. Cardinal John O'Connor to Sean O'Keefe [secretary of the navy], January 29, 1993, O'Connor papers, A-99, folder 10, AANY.

63. Rosemary, deLellis, and Joan Laboon, interview with the author, August 4, 2010; John Donlon, interview with the author, September 9, 2011, William Ball, interview with the author, March 19, 2013.

64. Bruce Kahn, interview with the author, August 3, 2011.

Epilogue: Jake Laboon—The Legacy

understand from Admiral Kidd that while you were Secretary the Navy you directed that one of the Arleigh Burke guided missile destroyers be named for our brother, Captain John Francis Laboon, Jr."[65]

USS *Laboon* (DDG-58) was the eighth Arleigh Burke–class guided-missile destroyer. The first vessel of this class, USS *Arleigh Burke* (DDG-51), named after the famous World War II naval officer and former CNO (1955–61) was launched at Bath Iron Works on September 16, 1989.[66] The *Laboon*'s purpose was described: "The mission of *Laboon* is to be prepared to conduct prompt, sustained combat operations at sea, in support of national policy."[67] The ship displaces 8,315 tons fully loaded and is 505 feet in length with a beam of 66 feet. Its maximum speed is 30+ knots on four gas turbines that generate 100,000 horsepower. *Laboon* carries the Aegis weapon system, one 5"/54-caliber gun, Standard, Tomahawk, and Harpoon missiles, ship-launched torpedoes, and a close-in air-defense weapons system. The ship carries a crew of 320 men and women.[68] The ship has the nickname "Fearless Fifty-Eight," gained from its motto: "USS *Laboon* meets all challenges, milestones, and obstacles 'WITHOUT FEAR.'"[69] The ship's crest symbolizes some of the great events of Jake Laboon's life:

> The life preserver symbolizes Chaplain Laboon's heroic rescue of a downed fighter pilot from the sea while under enemy fire. The preserver's straps are red reflecting courage and sacrifice and denote his service with the Marines in Vietnam. The star commemorates the Chaplain's Silver Star award and also represents his five successful submarine combat patrols. The wreath of laurel is emblematic of honor and accomplishment.[70]

The ship's coat of arms is also highly symbolic for the vessel's namesake, describing his heroism, loyalty, and devotion to duty. The shield, colored in navy blue and gold, represents the sea, highlighting Jake's dedicated naval service. The white background signifies integrity and purity of purpose.

---

65. Sr. Joan Laboon to William Ball, April 29, 1992, PPJM. William Ball never met Jake, but was very impressed with his contribution to the navy.
66. "Arleigh Burke: A Remarkable Ship," essay, n.d., PPJM. During World War II Burke was the commander of Destroyer Squadron 23. He was known as "31-Knot Burke" for his relentless high-speed pursuit of the Japanese. The essay states, "Burke raised destroyer tactics in the Pacific to new levels of sea warfare."
67. USS *Laboon*, information sheet, n.d. Laboon file, ASJM.
68. Ibid; *Navy Chaplain*, July 14, 1995, Laboon file, ASJM.
69. USS *Laboon*, information sheet, n.d., Laboon file, ASJM.
70. USS *Laboon*, commissioning booklet, PPJL.

Epilogue: Jake Laboon—The Legacy

The quartered shield suggests a cross reflecting the mission of a chaplain. The upright trident symbolizes sea prowess and highlights *Laboon*'s three primary attack threats: submarine, anti-surface, and anti-air warfare. The bottom spike of the Triton, pointing to the ocean depths, also represents Jake's service as a submariner, both as a line officer and a chaplain.[71] In *Laboon*'s mast five coins are embedded: a 1944 half-dollar, representing the naval academy class of 1944, a 1958 nickel, representing the year Jake returned to the navy, a 1921 penny, representing the year Laboon was born, a 1943 penny, representing the year Jake graduated (accelerated) from the naval academy, and a 1945 penny, representing the year he was awarded the Silver Star. The total coinage, 58 cents, represents the hull number of the ship.[72]

Laboon was launched on a bitterly cold day, February 20, 1993, at Bath Iron Works, Maine. Jake's family, navy personnel of all stripes, and many dignitaries, as well as a contingent of former students from St. Joe Prep, were in attendance. In his invocation on that day, Joseph Laboon prayed:

As Father Jake was a channel of your peace during his earthly life, may this ship which bears his name be a symbol of might, freedom and democracy that America stands for and may its strength be a sign of peace to all the world.[73]

Several people spoke at the launching ceremony, including Rear Admiral George Huchting, AEGIS program manager; Admiral Frank Kelso, CNO and acting secretary of the navy; Tom Andrews, U.S. Congressman, Maine; and George Mitchell and William Cohen, U.S. senators from Maine.[74]

The principal speaker at the event was Cardinal John O'Connor, who had been invited by Sean O'Keefe during his brief stint as secretary of the navy.[75] In his remarks O'Connor spoke of how Jake captured the imagination of the navy and the church by the way he treated people:

Father Jake was a man among men, a priest.... Father Jake was both Mr. Navy and Mr. Church, who treated a seaman as respectfully as he treated an admiral. He saw

---

71. USS *Laboon*, information sheet, n.d., Laboon file, ASJM.
72. Mast ceremony for DDG-58, USS *Laboon*, PPJM.
73. Invocation, Joseph Laboon, on the occasion of the launching of USS *Laboon*, February 20, 1993, PPJL.
74. USS *Laboon*, launching program booklet, February 20, 1993, O'Connor papers, box A-99, folder 10, AANY.
75. John O'Connor to Sean O'Keefe, January 29, 1993, O'Connor papers, box A-99, folder 10, AANY. O'Keefe was secretary of the navy from October 2, 1992 to January 20, 1993.

Epilogue: Jake Laboon—The Legacy

Figure E-1. USS *Laboon* under way

in every human person the image and likeness of God, and treated everyone accordingly with quiet dignity.... Father Jake fought relentlessly for improved living conditions for white hats and their families, below decks and ashore. Yet he never ignored the rights or needs of officers or their families either. Everyone—everyone—man and woman—was sacred in his eyes, a person of priceless worth.[76]

The cardinal also expressed Jake's dedication to the navy as an institution, to which he dedicated his ministry as a priest: "I never saw Father Jake not in love with the United States Navy, a romance that was to endure until his death. They wept profoundly at his Funeral Mass because they knew how much he loved them, and they loved him unabashedly in return."[77]

The launching ceremony was disrupted by the actions of a group of peace activists, members of Pax Christi.[78] Some two dozen protesters demonstrated outside Bath Iron Works during the ceremony, but one woman managed to get to the podium while O'Connor was speaking, challenging the idea that a warship would be named after a priest. The woman was ushered away in quick order, but her protest was answered later by Agnes Laboon, Jake's sister-in-law, who stated, "He [Laboon] was a man of peace who entered the profession of warriors to keep the peace."[79]

76. *Catholic New York*, February 25, 1993, O'Connor papers, box A-99, folder 10, AANY
77. Ibid.
78. Pax Christi (The Peace of Christ) is a Roman Catholic–based activist group that was especially prominent in the late 1960s and early 1970s in its opposition to the Vietnam War and nuclear weapons.
79. Rosemary, deLellis, and Joan Laboon, interview with the author, August 4, 2010; "Pro-

Epilogue: Jake Laboon—The Legacy

The ceremonial christening of *Laboon* was graciously performed by his three religious siblings, deLellis, Rosemary, and Joan. One year earlier, in March 1992, the secretary of the navy, H. Lawrence Garrett, had invited Jake's sisters to christen the vessel. When breaking the bottle of champagne over the bow, the women, invoking the motto of the Society of Jesus, said, "We launch this ship the *Laboon* for the greater honor and glory of God."[80] Writing after the ceremony, Commander Douglas McDonald, *Laboon*'s first commanding officer, spoke on behalf of the ship's crew: "From everything I have heard about Father Jake, he was a great Naval officer and a man of peace, and I cannot think of a more fitting tribute than using his name for this magnificent ship whose strength and mission will be to ensure world peace!"[81]

During the next two years *Laboon* was made ready for fleet operation. She successfully completed her sea trials and then transited to Norfolk, Virginia, her home port, arriving from Bath Iron Works in early March 1995. *Laboon* was commissioned on Saturday, March 18, at Norfolk Naval Station, pier number 12. As with the launching, Jake's brother, Joe, prayed the invocation. Remarks were made by Commander in Chief Atlantic Fleet Admiral William J. Flanagan; the principal speaker was Senator Rick Santorum (R-Pennsylvania). At the voice command of Jake's three religious siblings, *Laboon*, with all the navy's tradition and protocol, was manned. In gratitude Joan Laboon wrote to a navy representative:

> For the members of Jake's family we will always remember with great excitement the moment when sailors brought the ship to life. I am happy that the Navy has seen fit to preserve so much tradition and protocol; money can't pay for a heritage such as we have.[82]

USS *Laboon* (DDG-58) had joined the fleet.[83]

Unquestionably the commissioning of USS *Laboon* was the greatest physical legacy awarded to Jake, but his service to God and country were remembered and memorialized in other concrete ways. Almost immediately

---

test Launches the *Laboon*," clipping, n.d. [February 1993], PPJM; "BIW Launches Aegis Destroyer," clipping, n.d. [February 1993], Laboon file, ASJM.

80. Rosemary, deLellis, and Joan Laboon, interview with the author, August 4, 2010; John Friel, interview with the author, August 2, 2011.

81. D. D. McDonald to Joseph Laboon, February 28, 1993, PPJM.

82. Joan Laboon, RSM, to LCDR Scott Anderson, March 23, 1995, PPJL.

83. *Navy Chaplain*, July 14, 1995, Laboon file, ASJM; USS *Laboon*, commissioning videotape, PPJL.

Epilogue: Jake Laboon—The Legacy

after his death a committee formed to preserve the memory of Jake Laboon at Manresa-on-Severn. When Laboon came to Manresa, he was assigned as minister with the task of renovating the house. He completed the task except for the chapel. As a testimony to his memory, several of Jake's naval academy classmates and other friends formed the Laboon Memorial Committee to raise money for renovation of the Manresa Chapel and its rededication in the name of Jake Laboon. The committee set its goal at $200,000 for the project. Letters were sent to five thousand people, including members of the *Peto* crew, and many navy and church friends and associates. The renovation was completed at a cost of $201,000, 75 percent of which was raised from donations.[84] The chapel was rededicated on October 1, 1989, with a Mass celebrated by Jake's brother Joe. The homily was given by William Graham, SJ, of the Manresa staff, who had preached at Laboon's funeral. Laboon family members as well as friends were present for the event.[85]

The memory of Father Jake was also kept alive at Central High School in Pittsburgh. Before his death Jake established a scholarship to help boys who might need economic assistance to attend the school. His death prompted the inauguration of an annual "Reverend John F. Laboon Award," granted to a graduating senior for outstanding service to campus ministry.[86]

The U.S. Naval Academy, which had been so influential in Jake's life, also remembered one of its distinguished alumni. In December 1993 the noted motion picture *Schindler's List*, chronicling the efforts of German industrialist Oskar Schindler in saving the lives of many Jews in Poland during World War II, hit American theaters. After viewing the film, two naval academy chaplains, Father John Friel and Rabbi Robert Feinberg, believed that all midshipmen should see the film because of its moral message. This was especially important as efforts to regain the moral high ground were ongoing after a cheating scandal in the electrical engineering department was revealed in the early spring of 1994. The two chaplains "felt that there

---

84. Rev. John F. Laboon, SJ, memorial update, October 1, 1989; W. Scott Porthero to "Fellow Shpmates," July 10, 1989, PPJM; Frank Andrews and Joseph Currie to Neil Werthmann, May 22, 1990, PPNW.

85. Program—Re-Dedication of the Chapel of St. Ignatius Loyola—Manresa in Memory of Fr. John Laboon, SJ, October 1, 1989 PPJM.

86. Rosemary, deLellis, and Joan Laboon, interview with the author, August 4, 2010; "The Quadrangle," newsletter for alumni and friends of Central Catholic High School, Pittsburgh, Pennsylvania, Spring 1993, PPJM.

was a synergy" between the contributions of Steven Spielberg, the film's producer and director, and Jake Laboon in always seeking the moral high ground. On May 4, 1994, Spielberg was given the "John Francis Laboon Award for Distinguished Service to Humanity."[87]

There was still one more significant honor, again from his beloved naval academy, to solidify the legacy of Father Jake. In August 1993 the Jesuits made the decision to close Manresa-on-Severn, which would mean the loss of the newly renovated chapel. A drive was initiated to transfer the memorial plaque and other mementos across the river to the academy. Spearheaded by Jake's academy roommate, Bill Leahy, an agreement was forged to move the memorial from Manresa to the academy. The Jesuits agreed to pay for the move and renovation of a section of Mitscher Hall to create the "Laboon Ministry Center."[88] The center was "structured to support innovative ministerial programs for the Brigade of Midshipmen extending to those of all creeds."[89] The Laboon Ministry Center was dedicated on July 17, 1994. At the dedication a plaque from the USNA class of 1944 was unveiled. Additionally, the senior chaplain at the academy, Father John Friel, spoke of an incident that in his mind captured the essence of Jake Laboon. He recalled that some twenty years earlier, when serving as a junior chaplain in Hawaii, he encountered Father Jake walking the piers at the Naval Station Pearl Harbor. Jake, dressed in the tropical white long uniform of the day, asked Friel to hear his confession. Immediately, Jake knelt down on the pier, heedless of the dirt or what others might think or say, and proceeded to confess his sins to a junior chaplain. It was clear to Friel that Jake was so in love with God that he was blind to how people might react to such a scene.[90]

Conclusion

John Francis Laboon Jr., Jack to his family, but Jake to the rest of the world, was a giant of a man not just physically, but equally and more importantly,

---

87. John Friel, e-mail to the author, September 11, 2012; Jennifer Bryan, e-mail to the author, March 20, 2012; Program, USNA, May 4, 1994, PPJM. Spielberg's reception of the "Laboon Award" was the only time it was presented.

88. *Shipmate* 59, no. 1 (January–February 1196): 17. The Jesuits were able to pay for the move and renovation from some of the proceeds from the sale of Manresa and its property.

89. Frank Andrews and Terrence Toland, SJ, to "Friends of Father John F. Laboon," July 25, 1993.

90. John Friel, interview with the author, January 31, 2011.

in all the significant dimensions of life. Raised in a large family of nine children where faith, commitment, duty, and hard work were taught daily, he was a man who answered the call, accepting various commissions in life. His first call was to the navy, through the naval academy and his heroic service aboard USS *Peto* in the Western Pacific during World War II. Hearing a second call, an invitation from God to follow a different path, he responded by joining the Society of Jesus and was ordained in 1956. Two years later he once again responded to a third commission, this time to service of nation and God as a navy chaplain. Over a distinguished career of twenty-two years, Jake Laboon traveled widely and served many different navy communities, including his beloved alma mater and, in Vietnam, the U.S. Marines. After completing two tours in Norfolk, Virginia, in positions of significant responsibility, he retired on October 31, 1980. However, Jake's service to God's people was far from over. On the contrary, he returned to the Jesuits, serving in retreat ministry and as a pastor. The qualities that had made him so renowned in the navy were also evident in these latter years, only in different ways. When he finally succumbed to cancer at the age of sixty-seven, his legacy, born through a life of service to God and country, began in earnest.

The life and accomplishments of Jake Laboon were always grounded within the context of his rock-solid faith in God. He realized that what he did was not for him, but rather as the signature motto of the Jesuit proclaims, "For the greater glory and honor of God." The beauty and the power of his life, the contributions he made, and the base upon which he operated can be summarized by a prayer attributed to St. Ignatius of Loyola that he articulated when giving a eulogy for Michael Smith, naval academy class of 1967, one of the astronauts killed in the *Challenger* disaster of January 28, 1986: "Dearest Lord, teach me to be generous, teach me to serve thee as thou deservest, to give and not to count the cost, to fight and not to heed the wounds, to toil and not to seek for rest, to labor and not to ask for any reward, save that of knowing I am doing your will."[91] Fittingly, one fellow Jesuit speaking of the influence of Jake Laboon put it this way: "A tremendously big hearted generous man and a real priest—when comes another JFL? When indeed."[92]

---

91. John Laboon, SJ, eulogy for Michael Smith, n.d. [1986], audiotape.
92. William Currie, SJ, e-mail to the author, November 17, 2012.

Bibliography

Alden, John D. *The Fleet Submarine in the U.S. Navy.* Annapolis, Md.: Naval Institute Press, 1979.

Alden, John D., and Craig R. McDowell. *United States and Allied Submarine Successes in the Pacific and Far East During World War II.* Jefferson, N.C.: McFarland, 2009.

Alexander, June. "Staying Together: Chain Migration and Patterns of Slovak Settlement in Pittsburgh Prior to World War I." *Journal of American Ethnic History* 1, no. 1 (Fall 1981): 56–83.

———. *The Immigrant Church and Community: Pittsburgh's Slovak Catholics and Lutherans, 1880–1915.* Pittsburgh, Pa.: University of Pittsburgh Press, 1987.

Allitt, Patrick. "American Catholics and the New Conservatism of the 1950s." *U.S. Catholic Historian* 7, no. 1 (Winter 1988): 15–37.

"Anachronistic War." *Commonweal* 90 (September 19, 1969): 555–56.

Anderson, Lars. *The All Americans.* New York: St. Martin's Press, 2004.

"Apostolic Delegate Urges Spread of the Retreat Movement." *Catholic Action* 17 (February 1935): 3–4.

Auel, Carl A. "A Chaplain's Ministry in Vietnam." *Navy Chaplains' Bulletin* (Summer 1970): 1–7.

Baldwin, Hansen. W. "We Dive at Dawn." *New York Times Magazine* (February 14, 1943): 14–15, 39.

———. "New Battleship: The A-Submarine." *New York Times Magazine* (March 16, 1958): 13, 100–1.

———. "Nuclear Navy." *New York Times Magazine* (August 24, 1958): 8–9.

Baldwin, Leland D. *Pittsburgh: The Story of a City.* Pittsburgh, Pa.: University of Pittsburgh Press, 1937.

Bauman, John F., and Edward K. Muller. *Before Renaissance: Planning in Pittsburgh, 1889–1943.* Pittsburgh, Pa.: University of Pittsburgh Press, 2006.

Baute, Paschal. "What Did You Do during the War, Father?" *Commonweal* 90 (May 23, 1969): 275, 303.

Bergman, Jules. "William Raborn's Multi-Billion-Dollar Gamble." *Readers' Digest* 78 (February 1961): 181–82, 184.

Bergsma, Herbert. *Chaplains with Marines in Vietnam, 1962–1971.* Washington, D.C.: History and Museum Division, Headquarters U.S. Marine Corps, 1985.

Bibliography

Berman, Larry. *Zumwalt: The Life and Times of Admiral Elmo Russell "Bud" Zumwalt, Jr.* New York: HarperCollins, 2012.

Betten, Neil. "Charles Owen Rice: Pittsburgh Labor Priest, 1936–1940." *Pennsylvania Magazine of History and Biography* 94, no. 4 (October 1970): 518–30.

"Bishops Statement on the War." *Commonweal* 37 (November 27, 1942): 131.

Black, Barry C. *From the Hood to the Hill: A Story of Overcoming*. Nashville, Tenn.: Thomas Nelson, 2006.

Blair, Clay, Jr. *Silent Victory: The U.S. Submarine War against Japan*. Annapolis, Md.: Naval Institute Press, 1975.

Blanshard, Paul. *American Freedom and Catholic Power*. Boston: Beacon Press, 1949.

Bodnar, John, Roger Simon, and Michael P. Weber. *Lives of Their Own: Blacks, Italians, and Poles in Pittsburgh, 1900–1960*. Urbana: University of Illinois Press, 1982.

Braeman, John, Robert H. Bremmer, and David Brody. *The New Deal: The State and Local Levels*. Columbus: Ohio State University Press, 1975.

Brodie, Bernard. "War at Sea: Changing Techniques and Unchanging Fundamentals." *Virginia Quarterly Review* 19, no. 1 (January 1943): 1–19.

——. "New Tactics in Naval Warfare." *Foreign Affairs* 24, no. 2 (January 1946): 210–23.

Brokaw, Tom. *The Greatest Generation*. New York: Random House, 1998.

Burgoyne, Arthur G. *The Homestead Strike of 1892*. Pittsburgh: University of Pittsburgh Press, 1979.

"Can U.S. Get Out of the War Now? Report from Saigon." *U.S. News and World Report* 66 (May 5, 1969): 34–36.

Cascino, Joseph. "From Sanctuary to Involvement: A History of the Catholic Parish in the Northeast." In *The American Catholic Parish: A History from 1850 to the Present*, edited by Jay P. Dolan, 1:7–116, New York: Paulist Press, 1987.

Catholic Historical Society of Western Pennsylvania. *Catholic Pittsburgh's One Hundred Years*. Chicago, Ill.: Loyola University Press, 1943.

"Catholic President?" *Newsweek* 53 (January 12, 1959): 29–30.

"Catholics in Public Office: Discussion." *Commonweal* 65 (January 4, 1957): 348–50.

"Catholics in Public Office: Discussion." *Commonweal* 65 (February 8, 1957): 489–90.

Church, Frank. "Vietnam: Disengagement Now." *Vital Speeches* 36 (November 1, 1969): 34–39.

Clancy, Kathleen. "Retreat." *Catholic World* 134 (March 1932): 671–75.

Clary, Jack. "Ballfield to Battlefield." *Naval History* 18, no. 5 (October 2004): 35–38.

Clifford, Clark M. "A Vietnam Reappraisal: The Personal History of One Man's View and How It Evolved." *Foreign Affairs* 47 (July 1969): 601–22.

Cogley, John. "Anyone Listening?" *Commonweal* 67 (February 7, 1958): 185.

Connor, Charles P. *John Cardinal O'Connor: Culture and Life*. Staten Island, N.Y.: Alba House, 2011.

Conrad, Thomas M. "Vietnam: Are There Any Lessons?" *Commonweal* 90 (April 4, 1969): 78–80.

Contosta, David R. *St. Joseph's: Philadelphia's Jesuit University 150 Years*. Philadelphia: St. Joseph's University Press, 2000.
Cornell, Tom. "The Chaplain's Dilemma: Can Pastors in the Military Serve God and Government?" *America* (November 17, 2008): 12–14
Couvares, Frances G. *The Remaking of Pittsburgh: Class and Culture in an Industrializing City, 1877–1919*. Albany, N.Y.: SUNY Press, 1984.
Cox, Harvey. *The Secular City: Secularization and Urbanization in Theological Perspective*. Toronto: MacMillan, 1965.
Cronin, John F. "Clergymen and the Conflict in Vietnam." *Catholic Mind* 65 (April 1967): 7–9.
Cross, Robert D. *The Emergence of Liberal Catholicism in America*. Cambridge, Mass.: Harvard University Press, 1967.
Curran, Francis X. "Vocations Keep Climbing." *America* 96 (February 9, 1957): 521–23.
Darden, Joe T. "The Effect of World War I on Black Occupational and Residential Segregation: The Case of Pittsburgh." *Journal of Black Studies* 18, no. 3 (March 1988): 297–312.
"Deadly Teeter-Totter: The George Washington." *Newsweek* 55 (January 11, 1960): 55.
"Deep Deterrence." *Time* 73 (June 15, 1959): 28.
Denopewolff, Richard F. "Our New Missile-Firing Submarines." *Science Digest* 47 (April 1960): 35–39.
Dewart, Leslie. "Have We Loved the Past Too Long?" *America* 115 (December 17, 1966): 798–802.
Dougherty, J. E. "Morality and [the] Strategy of Deterrence." *Catholic World* 194 (March 1962): 337–44.
Dower, John W. *War without Mercy: Race and Power in the Pacific*. New York: Pantheon, 1986.
Doyle, Thomas P. "Ministry to the Military: Valid or Not?" *Priest* 43 (November 1987): 43–49.
Drury, Clifford. *The History of the Chaplain Corps, United States Navy*. 9 Vols. Washington, D.C.: Bureau of Naval Personnel, 1984.
Dunigan, Vincent. "The Military Chaplain." *Priest* 28 (May 1972): 50–58.
Eliot, George F. "The Submarine War." *Foreign Affairs* 21 (April 1943): 385–400.
Ellis, John Tracy. "American Catholics and the Intellectual Life." *Thought* 30, no. 118 (Autumn 1955): 351–88.
"Era of Good Feeling?" Summary of Address. *Time* 71 (June 2, 1958): 66–67.
"Euphoria Polaris." *Nation* 191 (August 6, 1960): 62–63.
Faggioli, Massimo. *Vatican II: The Battle for Meaning*. New York: Paulist Press, 2012.
Ferguson, M. P. "The RP Rating: An Interpretive Historical Sketch." *Navy Chaplain* 2, no. 6 (1988): 3–10.
Field, John. "West to Japan: U.S. Sub Sinks 70,000 Tons of Shipping." *Life* 14 (March 15, 1942): 84–86.

Bibliography

———. "Submarine Trip to Japanese Waters: Interview with Lieutenant Commander W. A. Saunders." *Life* 12 (June 29, 1942): 14, 16.

Fogarty, Gerald P. "Public Patriotism and Private Politics: The Tradition of American Catholicism." *U.S. Catholic Historian* 4, no. 1 (1984): 1–48.

"Fourth Polaris Submarine Joins Atlantic Fleet: USS Theodore Roosevelt." *Missiles and Rockets* 8 (March 6, 1961): 16–17.

Fuchs, Lawrence H. "A Catholic as President?" *America* 99 (September 13, 1958): 620–23.

Gilroy, William F. R., and Timothy J. Demy. *A Brief Chronology of the Chaplain Corps of the United States Navy.* Washington, D.C.: Bureau of Naval Personnel, 1983.

Gleason, Philip. "In Search of Unity: American Catholic Thought, 1920–1960." *Catholic Historical Review* 65 (1979): 185–205.

Glenn, Francis A. *Shepherds of Faith, 1843–1993: A Brief History of the Bishops of the Catholic Diocese of Pittsburgh.* Pittsburgh: Catholic Diocese of Pittsburgh, 1993.

Goldman, E. O. *Sunken Treaties: Naval Arms Control between the Wars.* University Park: Pennsylvania State University Press, 1994.

Golway, Terry. *Full of Grace: An Oral Biography of John Cardinal O'Connor.* New York: Simon and Schuster, 2001.

Greeley, Andrew. "American Catholics—Ten Years Later." *Critic* 33 (January–February 1975): 14–21.

Gormley, James J. *A History of St. Joseph's Preparatory School 125 Years, 1851–1976.* Philadelphia: St. Joseph's Preparatory, 1976.

Graham, Robert A. "Our Constitution and the Church." *America* 97 (July 6, 1957): 381–83.

"Great Polaris Breakthrough." *Life* 49 (August 1, 1960): 23–25.

Greenwald, Maurine W., and Margo Anderson, eds. *Pittsburgh Surveyed: Social Science and Social Reform in the Early Twentieth Century.* Pittsburgh: University of Pittsburgh Press, 1996.

Gurian, Waldemar, and M. A. Fitzsimmons, eds. *The Catholic Church in World Affairs.* Notre Dame, Ind.: University of Notre Dame Press, 1954.

Hanigan, James. "The Theology of War in Vietnam." *Chicago Studies* 7 (Summer 1968): 127–42.

Hastings, Adrian, ed. *Modern Catholiicsm: Vatican II and After.* New York: Oxford University Press, 1991.

Hays, Samuel P., ed. *City at the Point: Essays on the Social History of Pittsburgh.* Pittsburgh: University of Pittsburgh Press, 1989.

Heineman, Kenneth J. "A Catholic New Deal: Religion and Labor in 1930s Pittsburgh." *Pennsylvania Magazine of History and Biography* 118, no. 4 (October 1994): 363–94.

———. *A Catholic New Deal: Religion and Reform in Depression Pittsburgh.* University Park: Pennsylvania State University Press, 1999.

Hentoff, Nat. *John Cardinal O'Connor: At the Storm of a Changing American Catholic Church.* New York: Scribner, 1988.
Herberg, Will. *Protestant—Catholic—Jew: An Essay in American Religious Sociology.* Garden City, N.Y.: Doubleday, 1955.
———. "Plight of American Catholicism." *National Review* 20 (August 27, 1968): 852–53.
Herring, George C. *America's Longest War: The United States and Vietnam, 1950–1975.* Philadelphia: Temple University Press, 1996.
Hessler. W. H. "Navy's Submersible Missile-Launching Base: Polaris." *Reporter* 18 (June 12, 1958): 14–16.
Hogan James J. "Another Look at the FBM Subs." *Navy Chaplain Bulletin* (Winter 1962–63): 7–10, 13.
"Honest to God or Faithful to the Pentagon?" *Time* 93 (May 30, 1969): 49.
Hopkins, Samuel W., Jr. *A Chaplain Remembers Vietnam.* Kansas City, Mo.: Truman Publishers, 2002.
Hoyt, Robert G., ed. *Issues That Divide the Church.* New York: Macmillan, 1967.
Huber, Raphael. *Our Bishops Speak.* Milwaukee: Bruce, 1952.
Isserman, Maurice, and Michael Kazin. *America Divided: The Civil War of the 1960s.* New York: Oxford University Press, 2000.
"Is the Church Committed?" *America* 98 (October 19, 1957): 64.
Johnson, Gerald W. "The Muckraking Era." In Lorent, *Pittsburgh: The Story of an American City*, 261–320. 1964.
Johnson, James D. *Combat Chaplain: A Thirty-Year Vietnam Battle.* Denton: University of North Texas Press, 2001.
Johnson, Raymond. *Postmark: Mekong Delta.* Westwood, N.J.: Revell, 1968.
Joyce, Edward. "The Roots of the Diocese." In Catholic Historical Society of Western Pennsylvania, *Catholic Pittsburgh's One Hundred Years.* 1943.
Kaplan, Julie B. "Military Mirrors on the Wall: Non-establishment and the Military Chaplaincy." *Yale Law Journal* 95, no. 6 (May 1986): 1210–36.
Kelly, James. "The Ministry in Vietnam." *Navy Chaplain Bulletin* 19, no. 2 (Summer 1967): 4–5.
Kelly, Timothy. "Suburbanization and the Decline of Catholic Public Ritual in Pittsburgh." *Journal of Social History* 28, no. 2 (Winter 1994): 311–30.
———. "Pittsburgh Catholicism," *U.S. Catholic Historian* 18, no. 4 (Fall 2006): 64, 66.
———. *The Transformation of American Catholicism: The Pittsburgh Laity and the Second Vatican Council, 1950–1972.* Notre Dame, Ind.: University of Notre Dame Press, 2009.
Kennedy, David M., ed. *World War II Companion.* New York: Simon and Schuster, 2007.
Kerby, William J. "Lay Retreat Movement." *American Ecclesiastical Review* 92 (June 1935): 586–98.

Bibliography

Kimmett, Larry, and Margaret Regis. *U.S. Submarines in World War II: An Illustrated History*. Seattle: Navigator, 1996.

Kintner, E. E. "Admiral Rickover's Gamble." *Atlantic* 203 (January 1959): 31–35.

Klein, Philip. *A Social Study of Pittsburgh: Community Problems and Social Services of Allegheny County*. New York: Columbia University Press, 1938.

Knochel, Mary Ann. *Roman Catholic Diocese of Pittsburgh*. Charleston, S.C.: Arcadia, 2007.

Koch, Alfred. "Why the Retreat Movement Must Go On." *Catholic Mind* 29 (August 22, 1931): 398–403.

Kulcum, Edward H. "First Polaris Launched from Submarine." *Aviation Week and Space Technology* 73 (July 25, 1960): 32–33.

"Laird's Official Report on Vietnam: The Basic Problem Remains; Statement of March 19, 1969." *U.S. News and World Report* 66 (March 31, 1969): 35.

Langguth, A. J. "Vietnam: How Do We Get Out?" *Saturday Evening Post* 242 (February 8, 1969): 19–21, 48–49.

Latourelle, Rene, ed. *Vatican II Assessment and Perspectives Twenty-Five Years After (1962–1987)*. 3 vols. New York: Paulist Press, 1988.

Lautenschlager, Karl. "The Submarine in Naval Warfare, 1901–2001." *International Security* 11, no. 3 (Winter 1986–87): 94–140.

"Laymen's Retreats: Resolution Adopted by the National Council of Catholic Men." *NCWC Bulletin Review* 13 (November 1931): 15.

"Laymen's Role." Editorial. *Commonweal* 66 (June 28, 1957): 315–16.

Leonard, Guy. "Submarine Chaplain." *Navy Chaplain Bulletin* (Spring 1960): 4.

Lewis, J. W., and J. S. Werner. "The New Stage in Vietnam." *Bulletin of the Atomic Scientists* 25 (January 1969): 21–26.

Lonergan, William I. *Laymen's Retreats Explained*. New York: American Press, 1930.

Lorant, Stefan, ed. *Pittsburgh: The Story of an American City*. Garden City, N.Y.: Doubleday, 1964.

Lubove, Roy. *Twentieth-Century Pittsburgh: Government, Business, and Environmental Change*. New York: Wiley, 1969.

———. *Twentieth-Century Pittsburgh*. 2 vols. Pittsburgh: University of Pittsburgh Press, 1994–96.

Lutz, Robert A. "Response to 'What Did You Do during the War, Father?'" *Commonweal* 90 (June 27, 1969): 403, 422.

Maritain, Jacques. "Just War: Criteria for a Just War as They Apply to the Present Conflict." *Commonweal* 31 (October 22, 1939): 199–200.

Martin, Pete. "Tokyo Bound: Life on an American Submarine; Part I." *Saturday Evening Post* 216 (July 3, 1943): 9–11, 36, 38, 41–42.

Maynard, Theodore. "Lurking Suspicion of Catholicism." *Catholic World* 180 (February 1955): 327–33.

McAvoy, Thomas T. "Catholics and the American Way." *Ave Maria* 53 (May 3, 1941): 551–53.

———. "American Catholics and the Second World War." *Review of Politics* 6 (April 1944): 131–50.

———. "American Catholic Tradition." *Ave Maria* 66 (July 12, 1947): 46–49.

———. "The Philosophers and American Catholic Education." *Catholic Historical Review* 48 (November 1949): 579–85.

———. "The Catholic Church in the United States." In *The Catholic Church in World Affairs,* edited by Waldemar Gurian and M. A. Fitzsimmons, 358–78. Notre Dame, Ind.: University of Notre Dame Press, 1954.

———. "Catholicism and the American Way of Life: Symposium." *America* 98 (November 9, 1957): 162–63.

———. *The Great Crisis in American Catholic History, 1895–1900.* Chicago: Henry Regnery, 1957.

McCarthy, Timothy G. *The Catholic Tradition: Before and After Vatican II 1878–1993.* Chicago: Loyola University Press, 1994.

McClory, Robert. *Turning Point: The Inside Story of the Papal Birth Control Commission and How Humanae Vitae Changed the Life of Patty Crowley and the Future of the Church.* New York: Crossroad, 1995.

McComas, Robert F. "The Chaplain's Ministry at the Naval Academy." *Navy Chaplain's Bulletin* (Summer 1968): 7–10, 13.

McDaniel, J. T. "Fire in the Torpedo Room." *Naval History* 25, no. 4 (August 2011): 46–50.

McDonald, Craig R. *The USS Puffer in World War II: A History of the Submarine and Its Wartime Crew.* Jefferson, N.C.: McFarland, 2008.

McGovern, George. "Ending the Vietnam War." *Current* 111 (October 1969): 13–18.

Menges, Richard M. "Lay Leaders: A Problem." *Catholic World* 185 (July 1957): 280–84.

Michno, Gregory F. *USS Panpanito: Killer Angel.* Norman: University of Oklahoma Press, 2000.

Midgley, Brian. "Nuclear Deterrents: Intention and Scandal." *Blackfriars* 44 (September 1963): 363–72.

Miller, Helen H. "Catholic for President?" *New Republic* 137 (November 18, 1957): 10–13.

———. "Catholic for President?" *New Republic* 137 (November 25, 1957): 10–13.

———. "Catholic for President?" *New Republic* 137 (December 2, 1957): 10–12.

Mode, Daniel L. *The Grunt Padre: The Service and Sacrifice of Father Vincent Robert Capodanno, Vietnam, 1966–67.* Oak Lawn, Ill.: C. M. J. Marian, 2000.

Moody, John N. "Catholic Liberal—Conservative Debate: With Editorial Comment." *Commonweal* 67 (February 14, 1958): 499, 503–7.

Moore, Withers M., Herbert L. Bergsman, and Timothy J. Demy. *Chaplains with U.S. Naval Units in Vietnam, 1954–1975.* Washington, D.C.: History Branch, Office of the Chief of Chaplains, Department of the Navy, 1985.

Bibliography

Morison, Samuel E. "American Strategy in the Pacific Ocean." *Oregon Historical Quarterly* 62, no. 1 (March 1961): 4–56.

Moskin, J. Robert. "Sixty Days Out of This World." *Look* 22 (December 23, 1958): 22–26.

Murphy, Francis X. "Defection: Protest or Treason?" *America* 116 (February 11, 1967): 198–99.

Murphy, John L. "The American Catholic." *Catholic World* 182 (February 1956): 331–35.

Murray, John Courtney. "Special Catholic Challenges." *Life* 39–40 (December 26, 1955): 144–46.

Neal, Arthur. *National Trauma and Collective Memory: Extraordinary Events in the American Century.* Armonk, N.Y.: M. E. Sharpe, 1998.

Neuhaus, Richard John. "The War, the Churches, and Civil Religion." *Annals of the American Academy of Political and Social Science* 387 (January 1970): 128–40.

Newby, Claude D. *It Took Heroes: One Chaplain's Story and Tribute to Combat Veterans and Those Who Waited for Them.* Bountiful, Utah: Tribute Enterprises, 2000.

"New Weapons System." *Time* 71 (March 3, 1958): 14–15.

"New Weapon That Will Stop Russia? Interview with H. G. Rickover." *U.S. News and World Report* 44 (March 21, 1958): 68–72.

North, Oliver L. *Under Fire: An American Story.* With William Novak. New York: HarperCollins, 1991.

North, Oliver L., and David Roth. *One More Mission: Oliver North Returns to Vietnam.* New York: HarperCollins, 1993.

O'Brien, Edwin F. "The Role of Military Chaplains." *Origins* 37, no. 20 (October 25, 2007): 317–20.

O'Brien, John A. "Birth Control and the Catholic Conscience." *Readers' Digest* 94 (January 1969): 111–15.

Ochs, Stephen. *Desegregating the Altar: The Josephites and the Struggle for Black Priests 1871–1960.* Baton Rouge: Louisiana State University Press, 1990.

O'Connor, John J. *A Chaplain Looks at Vietnam.* New York: World, 1968.

O'Dea, Thomas F. *American Catholic Dilemma.* New York: Sheed and Ward, 1958.

———. *The Catholic Crisis.* Boston: Beacon, 1968.

O'Donnell, Joseph F. "Clergy in the Military—Vietnam and After: One Chaplain's Reflection." In *The Sword of the Lord: Military Chaplains from the First to the Twenty-First Century,* edited by Doris Bergen, 215–32. Notre Dame, Ind.: University of Notre Dame Press, 2004.

O'Malley, John W. "Developments, Reforms, and Two Great Reformations: Towards a Historical Assessment of Vatican II." *Theological Studies* 44 (1983): 373–406.

———. *Tradition and Transition: Historical Perspectives on Vatican II.* Lima, Ohio: Academic renewal Press, 2002.

———. *What Happened at Vatican II.* Cambridge, Mass.: Belknap Press of Harvard University, 2008.

Ong, Walter J. *Frontiers in American Catholicism: Essays on Ideology and Culture.* New York: Macmillan, 1957.

———. *American Catholic Crossroads: Religious-Secular Encounters in the Modern World.* New York: Macmillan, 1959.

Osborne, John. "Vietnam: The President's Failing Hope." *New Republic* 161 (September 27, 1969): 17–19.

Owens, Joseph A. "Parish under the Sea." *Columbia* (November 1960): 4, 6–7.

Parker, Maynard. "Illusion of Vietnamization." *Newsweek* 74 (September 29, 1969): 32–33.

Pearson, R. "Some of My best Friends." *Commonweal* 65 (February 15, 1957): 571.

Penna, Anthony N. "Changing Images of Twentieth-Century Pittsburgh." *Pennsylvania History* 43, no. 1 (January 1976): 48–63.

Pfaff, William. "The Way Out." *Commonweal* 89 (February 14, 1969): 611–12.

"Polaris: New Star of Peace?" *America* 103 (August 13, 1960): 530–31.

"Polaris: The Big Undersea Deterrent." *Newsweek* 51 (April 4, 1958): 35–36.

"Polaris Development Testing Accelerated." *Aviation Weekly* 70 (January 19, 1958): 32–33.

"Polaris Fleet Missile Stressed as Inexpensive Deterrent Weapon." *Aviation Weekly* 68 (March 17, 1958): 24.

"Polaris Goes to Work." *Time* 76 (November 28, 1960): 21.

"Polaris Sub Project Triumphantly Beats Its Schedule." *Business Week* 1613 (July 30, 1960): 32–33.

Polmar, Norman. *The American Submarine.* Annapolis, Md.: Nautical and Aviation, 1983.

———. *The Death of the USS Thresher: The Story behind History's Deadliest Submarine Disaster.* Guilford, Conn.: Lyons Press, 2004.

Powers, Richard Gid. *Not without Honor: The History of American Anticommunism.* New York: Free Press, 1995.

Prados, John. *Vietnam: The History of an Unwinable War, 1945–1975.* Lawrence: University Press of Kansas, 2009.

Raborn, William F. "Polaris Submarine." *Vital Speeches* 24 (May 1, 1958): 428–31.

Rahner, Karl. *Theological Investigations.* Vol. 20, *Concern for the Church.* London: Darton, Longman, and Todd, 1981.

Ratzinger, Joseph. *Theological Highlights of Vatican II.* New York: Paulist Press, 1966.

Reeves, James. "The Diocese under Bishop Boyle." In *Catholic Pittsburgh's One Hundred Years.* Catholic Historical Society of Western Pennsylvania, 1943.

"Religion: Underwater Parish." *Time* 73, no. 18 (May 4, 1959): 41.

Rickover, Hyman G. "Another Kind of Satellite: U.S. Missile Firing Submarines." *U.S. News and World Report* 43 (October 25, 1957): 60–62.

Robinson, Walton L. "Down-Under Ships of the Navy: Submarine Force of Unprecedented Striking Power." *Scientific American* 167 (November 1942): 196–98.

Roche, Douglas J. "Catholic Revolution." *Catholic World* 208 (October 1968): 33–36.

Roscoe, Theodore. *United States Submarine Operations in World War II*. Annapolis, Md.: U.S. Naval Institute Press, 1954.

Rynne, Xavier (Francis Murphy). *Vatican Council II*. Maryknoll, N.Y.: Orbis Books, 1979.

Sayre, Elizabeth E. "Submarine from Corregidor." *Atlantic Monthly* 170 (September 1942): 40–46.

Scharleman, Martin. "Why Military Chaplains?" *Priest* 26 (March 1970): 70–72.

Schuyler, Joseph B. "Status of American Catholicism." *America* 93 (May 14, 1955): 196.

Scogna, Kathy Miller. *A House of Bread: The Jesuits Celebrate 70 Years in Wernersville, Pennsylvania*. Wernersville, Pa.: Kathy M. Scogna, 2000.

"Seamen of the Deep: Training for Sub Duty Speeded." *Newsweek* 18 (October 6, 1941): 30–31.

Seim, Jim E. "Duty in Vietnam." *Navy Chaplains Bulletin* 18, no. 2 (Summer 1966): 11.

Seymor, B. A. "Retreat Movement in the United States." *NCWC Bulletin Review* 12 (February 1930): 13–15.

Shannon, David A. *Between the Wars: America 1919–1941*. Boston: Houghton Mifflin, 1965.

Shannon, Peter M. "Changing Law in a Changing Church." *America* 116 (February 18, 1967): 248–50.

Sheerin, John B. "Protestant-Catholic Cold War." *Catholic World* 182 (December 1955): 161–65.

———. "Has the Catholic Church Arrived?" *Catholic World* 184 (February 1957): 324–25.

———. "American Bishops and Protestant Fears: How Soon a Catholic America?" *Catholic World* 187 (August 1958): 321–24.

———. "The Morality of the War in Vietnam." *Catholic World* 202 (March 1966): 326–30.

Shehan, Lawrence. "Peace and Patriotism: A Pastoral Letter." *Catholic Mind* 64 (September 1966): 1–5.

"Sixty Days." *Newsweek* 52 (October 13, 1958): 30–31.

Slawson, Douglas. *The Foundation and First Decade of the National Catholic Welfare Council*. Washington, D.C.: The Catholic University of America Press, 1995.

———. *The Department of Education Battle, 1918–1932: Public Schools, Catholic Schools and Social Order*. Notre Dame, Ind.: University of Notre Dame Press, 2005.

Smith, Herbert F. "Ascent to God after the Council." *America* 116 (February 25, 1967): 283–85.

"Sociology and American Catholicism." *America* 93 (April 30, 1955): 118.

Sonder, Frederic Jr. "Navy's Terrible New Weapon." *Readers' Digest* 74 (March 1959): 54–58.

Spittler, John J. "A Just Ship: Letter to the Editor." *Seapower* 36, no. 7 (July 1993): 7.

Springer, Robert. "The Moral Issue in Vietnam." *U.S. Catholic* 34 (October 1968): 7–12.
Stacpoole, Alberic, ed. *Vatican II Revisited by Those Who Were There.* Minneapolis: Winston Press, 1986.
Stack, Joseph R. "Who Was the Father of the Laymen's Retreats in the United States?" *Records of the American Catholic Historical Society of Philadelphia* 41 (March 1930): 68–78.
Stave, Bruce M. *The New Deal and the Last Hurrah: Pittsburgh Machine Politics.* Pittsburgh, Pa.: University of Pittsburgh Press, 1970.
Steinfels, Peter. "President's Speech." *Commonweal* 91 (November 21, 1969): 242.
Stevens, Sylvester K. "The Hearth of a Nation." In *Pittsburgh: The Story of an American City*, edited by Stefan Lorant, 177–206. Garden City, N.Y.: Doubleday, 1964.
Sturma, Michael. "Atrocities, Conscience, and Unrestricted Warfare: U.S. Submarines During the Second World War." *War in History* 16, no. 4 (2009): 447–68.
———. "U.S. Submarine Patrol Reports during World War II: Historical Evidence and Literary Flair." *Journal of Military History* 74, no. 2 (April 2010): 475–90.
"The Submarine Barb." *America History Illustrated* 1, no. (7 (November 1966): 44–51.
"Submarine School Trains Men for Toughest Service." *Life* 12 (March 30, 1942): 93–101.
"Subs in Pacific." *Newsweek* 194 (January 5, 1942): 16
Swauger, John. "Pittsburgh's Residential Pattern in 1815." *Annals of the Association of American Geographers* 68, no. 2 (June 1978): 265–77.
Tarr, Joel A. ed. "Infrastructure and City—Building in the Nineteenth and Twentieth Centuries." In *City at the Point: Essays on the Social History of Pittsburgh.* Edited by Samuel Hays, 213–63. Pittsburgh: University of Pittsburgh Press, 1989.
———. *Devastation and Renewal: An Environmental History of Pittsburgh and Its Region.* Pittsburgh: University of Pittsburgh Press, 2003.
Timberg, Robert. *The Nightingale's Song.* New York: Simon and Schuster, 1995.
"Togetherness for 60 Days." *Time* 72 (October 20, 1958): 23.
Tozer, E. "World's Biggest Sub." *Popular Science* 173 (July 1958): 88–91.
Trott, Harlan. "Morale: The U-Boat's Vital Rivet." *Christian Science Monitor*, Weekly Magazine Section (February 21, 1942): 3.
United States Submarine Losses World War II. Naval History Division. Washington: D.C.: U.S. Government Printing Office, 1963.
"U.S. Catholics Climb Economic Scale." *Christian Century* 75 (July 2, 1958): 773.
"U.S.S. Barb." *American History Illustrated* 1, no. 7 (1966): 44–51.
U.S. Submarine Losses in World War II. Washington, D.C.: U.S. Government Printing Office, 1946.
"U.S. Submarines at Work. *Life* 14 (February 8, 1943): 26–27.
Van der Vat, Dan. "Vietnam: End in Sight?" *Saturday Evening Post* 242, no. 3 (February 8, 1969): 4.

———. *The Pacific Campaign World War II: The U.S.–Japanese Naval War, 1941–1945*. New York: Simon and Schuster, 1991.

———. *Stealth at Sea: The History of the Submarine*. London: Weidenfeld and Nicolson, 1994).

Wade, Richard C. *The Urban Frontier: The Rise of Western Cities, 1790–1830*. Cambridge, Mass.: Harvard University Press, 1959.

Wagner, Henry T. "The Catholic Chapel Program of Continuing Christian Development." *Navy Chaplain* (November 1977): 11, 15.

Walsh, Victor A. "'A Fanatic Heart': The Cause of Irish-American Nationalism in Pittsburgh during the Gilded Age." *Journal of Social History* 15, no. 2 (Winter 1981): 187–204.

Warren, Robert H. "The Naval Chaplaincy: Bringing Men to God and God to Men." *U.S. Naval Institute Proceedings* (August 1969): 55–60.

———. "Fleet Retreat Center, U.S. Atlantic Fleet." *Navy Chaplain Bulletin* (Fall 1975): 14–15.

Wheeler, Keith. *War under the Pacific*. Chicago: Time-Life, 1980.

Whitlock, Flint, and Ron Smith. *The Depths of Courage: American Submarines at War with Japan, 1941–1945*. New York: Berkley Caliber, 2007.

Wright, John J. "Catholics and Anti-Intellectualism." *Commonweal* 63 (December 16, 1955): 275–78.

Young, Marilyn Blatt. *The Vietnam Wars 1945–1990*. New York: HarperCollins, 1991.

Zahn, Gordon C. "Catholic Separatism and Anti-Catholic Tensions." *America* 96 (October 27, 1956): 94–98.

———. "What Did You Do during the War, Father?" *Commonweal* 90 (May 2, 1969): 195–99.

———. "The Military Chaplaincy and Conscientious Objection." *America* 168, no. 17 (May 15, 1993): 5–7.

Zaplotnik, John L. "The Very Rev. John Ev. Mosetizh Vicar General of Pittsburgh, PA: A Biographical Sketch." *Catholic Historical Review* 3, no. 2 (July 1917): 202–9.

Index

ACTU. *See* Association of Catholic Trade Unionists
Aircraft Carrier Task Group *50.1,* 89
ALCOA. *See* Aluminum Corporation of America
Allegheny County Commission, 32
Allegheny County Emergency Association, 31
Allegheny County Sanitary Authority, 50
Aluminum Corporation of America, 19
American Freedom and Catholic Power (Blanshard), 100n2, 119
Anders, William, 315
Andrews, Tom, 330
Annapolis Evening Capital, 47, 52–54, 56, 59–60, 204, 327
anti-Catholicism in America, 23, 100, 119–23. *See also* Catholicism
Armstrong, Joseph, 32
Armstrong, Parker B., 281
ARNV. *See* South Vietnamese Army
Association of Catholic Trade Unionists, 26–27
Athletic Journal, 53
Attack Task Group 17.13, 83
Auriesville, N.Y., 126–28, 140, 309
Australia, operations from, 71–72, 74–76

Bacon, Elijah, 66–67
Balch, William, 131
Ball, William, 328
Ballinger, Francis, 103
Baltimore Sun, 315–16
Bancroft, George, 41
Barrett, John, 259

Bauman, John F., 30
Benedict XV, Pope, 133
Bertelli, Angelo, 55, 58
Beshany, Philip, 323
Bettencourt, E. A., 88–89
Black, Barry, 271–73, 278–79, 300, 305, 322, 324
Blaik, Earl "Red," 56
Blaine, Ralph, 158
Blanchard, Felix "Doc," 56
Blanshard, Paul, 100n2, 119–20
Blume, Robert, 28n70, 106
Bonney, Carroll T., 75
Booze, Bob, 59, 61
Borders, William, Archbishop, 303, 310–12, 315
Boyle, Hugh, 24–26, 29, 33
Bozell, L. Brent, 121, 125
Brady, Genevieve, 104
Brady, Honora, 27
Brady, Nicholas, 104
Brandi, Salvatore, 302
Brew, Thomas, 296
Brown, Wilson, 43
Brown v. Board of Education, 195
Bryson, Thomas H., 29
Buchanan, Franklin, 41–42
Buckley, William, 125
Burke, Arleigh, 145, 329n66
Busik, Bill, 43n24, 53, 55, 255, 284, 314–15

Caldwell, Hugh, 82, 84–87, 89–90, 92, 94–95
Callahan, Daniel, 190–91
Calvert, James, 187
Cameron, Alan, 57–58, 205

349

Index

Campbell, John, 11
Canevin, John, Bishop, 22–24, 25, 28
Capodanno, Vincent, 327–28
Carmichael, Stokely, 195
Carnegie, Andrew, 14, 19
Carnegie Institute of Technology, 32, 37–39
Carroll, Charles, 302
Carroll, John, Bishop, 121
Catholic Action, 294–95
Catholicism: on communism, 125; early ecumenical councils, 187; in early 20th century Pittsburgh, 20–27; and immigrants, 15–16, 21–22; intellectual pursuit and, 123–25; labor priests, 25–27; in 1950s, 116–26; role of laity, 126; theological divide in America and, 121–22. *See also* Vatican II
Catholic Radical Alliance, 26
Catholic World, The, 119, 218
Central Catholic High School, Pittsburgh, 2, 33–35, 38, 40, 106, 333
Chadwick, Walter, 43, 61n87, 66
Challenger space shuttle, 202–3, 335
Chaplain Corps, 5–6, 130, 131
Charities and the Commons, 17–18
Charities Publication Committee of New York, 18
Chauvenet, William, 41
Chetwood, D. B., 103
Chief Naval Air Training Command, 243–45
Christian Brothers, 33
Church, Frank, 216–17
Cicognani, Amleto, Archbishop, 294–95
CINCLANTFLT. *See* Commander in Chief Atlantic Fleet
CINCPACFLT. *See* Commander in Chief Pacific Fleet
CIO. *See* Congress of Industrial Organizations
circuit rider chaplaincy, 163–64
Civil Rights Movement, 195–96
Clancy, B. A., 250
Clark, Clifford M., 212, 216
Clark, John S., 127
Clark, T. B., 141
CNATRA. *See* Chief Naval Air Training Command

Cogley, John, 124
Cohen, William, 330
Cohill, John, 223
Cold War, 125, 143, 145, 209–10
Commander in Chief Atlantic Fleet, 262, 265–66, 276, 277, 280, 283, 289
Commander in Chief Pacific Fleet, 248, 250–52, 259
Commander Service Force Pacific, 248–50, 252, 259, 281
Commander Service Squadron Three, 161–69, 182, 249
Commander Submarine Force Atlantic Fleet, 143–44, 158–59, 163, 239, 254–59
Commander Submarine Force Pacific Fleet, 67, 74–75, 87, 89–90, 95
Commons, John R., 17
Commonweal, 69
COMSERVPAC. *See* Commander Service Force Pacific
COMSERVRON. *See* Commander Service Squadron Three
COMSEVENTEEN. *See* 17th Naval District
COMSUBLANT. *See* Commander Submarine Force Atlantic Fleet
COMSUBPAC. *See* Commander Submarine Force Pacific Fleet
Condon, Edwin, 300
Congress of Industrial Organizations, 26
Connor, Jim, 246
Cooke, Terence, Cardinal, 284
Cooper, Charles, 87–88
Coordinated Submarine Attack Group, 83–84
Cornell, Tom, 220–21
Corrigan, Michael, 121
Cousins, Ralph W., 262
Couvares, Frances, 15
Cox, Harvey, 193–94
Cox, James, 31–32
Curley, Michael, Archbishop, 296, 302
Currie, William, 168–69
Cutter, Slade, 169

Daspit, L. R., 158–59, 181n85
Davis, Glenn, 56
Dawson, William, 105, 111, 292

350

Index

Deeds, Harry, 300
Delano, Frank, 113
Denton, Jeremiah, 315
DeSantis, Joseph, 57n74, 312–13
Devereaux, James, 303, 310–12
Devine, Edward T., 17
Dewart, Leslie, 190, 192
Diamond, Francis, 303
Dickman, Paul W. J., 50
Didusch, Joseph, 104
Diem, Ngo Dinh, 211
Dien Bien Phu, 211
Dietz, Peter, 26
Dolegan, John, 236
Domino Theory, 210–11, 217, 222
Donlon, John, 158, 307–8
Donnelly, W. F., 92, 93n107, 98, 140
Doolittle, Jimmy, 70
Dougherty, Denis, Cardinal, 104, 293
Dougherty, J. E., 156
Downes, W. M., 82
Draemal, Milo, 43, 98
Dreith, J. Floyd, 177
drug abuse programs, 242–43, 247
Duffey, John, Bishop, 31
Dunwiddie, Robert, 10
Dykers, Thomas, 140

Ecker, Robert, Monsignor, 4, 233, 236, 273, 284, 315–16, 320, 326–27
Edwards, R. S., 143
Egan, Michael, Bishop, 21
Eisenhower, Dwight D., 196, 211
Eliot, George F., 96
Eller, Ernest, 96
Elliott, R. E., 242
Ellis, John Tracy, 123–24
Ellyson, Theodore G. "Spuds," 246
English, H. D. W., 18
English, Jim, SJ, 288, 311
European Recovery Program (ERP), 210

Falconio, Diomede, Archbishop, 21
Feinberg, Robert, Rabbi, 333–34
Fichter, Joseph, 121
Fife, James, 78, 83
Findley, Burt, 102

Fiol, Robert, 228–29, 230
First Catholic Slovak Union, 22
Fisher, J. Harding, 104
Flanagan, William J., 332
Flatley, James, 261, 298
Fleet Ballistic Missile Submarine program, 3, 143–59, 160, 161, 255–56, 308
Fleet Marine Force, 226, 230
Fleet Religious Support Activity: assessment of, 273–74; disestablishment of, 280; history of, 261–62; mission of, 263; organization of, 263–65; projects at, 269–70
Fleming, J. F., 208–9
FMF. *See* Fleet Marine Force
Folsom, Richard, 184–85
Foreign Affairs, 96
Fort Duquesne, 10, 21
Fort King George, 10
Fort Pitt, 10
Fort Severn, 41
Friel, John, 333–34
Froude, Bill, 53
FRSA. *See* Fleet Religious Support Activity

Galbraith, John Kenneth, 30
Gannon, Robert, 151
Garnett, Philip, 144
Garrett, Francis, 243, 262, 282
Garrett, H. Lawrence, 332
Gibbons, Edmund, Bishop, 127
Gibbons, James, Cardinal, 122, 302
Glazier, Willard, 13
Gleason, Philip, 194
Glenn, John, 140–41
Gordon, Andy, 112
Gordon, Robert G., 265
Goss, Joe, 327
Graham, William, 34, 291, 315–16, 322, 333
Gray, Alfred M., 315
Great Crash, The (Galbraith), 30
Great Depression, 2, 7, 26, 29–31, 33, 170
Great Lakes Naval Training Center. *See* Naval Station Great Lakes
Greeley, Andrew, 190, 195n37
Green, Howard T., 261
Greenwald, Maurine, 18
Greenwood, Charles, 197

Index

Grennan, Jacqueline, 190
Griffiths, James, 134
Guam, operations from, 67, 86–88, 91–92, 95
Gulf Oil, 19
Guthrie, George, 18

Haas, Francis, 26
Halsey, William "Bull," 72
Hanigan, James, 218–19
Harp, Edward, Jr., 130
Harriman, Robert, 251
Hart, Jeffrey, 121
Harvey, John, 141
Haske, Henry, 297
Hawaii, 248–54. *See also* Pearl Harbor attack
Hayes, Patrick J., 133
Heid, Charles, 252, 266
Heil, Wayne, 251
Hensler, Carl, 26
Herberg, Will, 118, 194
Herring, George C., 209–11
Hesburgh, Theodore, 196
Hines, Howard, 31
Hobgood, Clarence, 251
Ho Chi Minh, 209–10
Holloway, James, 262
Holy Ghost Parish, 301–2
Holy Name Society, 25, 178
Homestead Strike of *1892*, 14
Horigan, Gerald, 302
Huchting, George, 330
Humanae Salutaris, 188–89
Humanae Vitae, 195
Hutcheson, Richard, 262

Ignatian Spiritual Exercises, 297
Involdstad, Orlando, Jr., 137
Iran-Contra Affair, 306–6
Ireland, John, Archbishop, 23

Jesuits. *See* Society of Jesus
Jesuit School of Theology, 288, 290, 292
Johnson, Lyndon B., 196, 208, 212–13
John XXIII, Pope, 155–56, 187–88

Jones, John Paul, 40, 131
just war, morality of, 69, 218

Kahn, Bruce, Rabbi, 5, 261, 282, 328
Kaplan, Julie B., 220
Kauffman, Draper, 184, 186–87, 198
Kefauver, Russell, 166–67
Kelley, Florence, 17
Kellogg, Paul, 17
Kelly, Donald F., 157
Kelly, James, 226
Kelly, Thomas, 162
Kelso, Frank, 266, 281, 308, 315, 320–23, 330
Kennan, George F., 210
Kennedy, Hugh, 175, 322
Kennedy, John F., 100, 125, 197, 211–12
Kennedy, Robert, 197
Kenrick, Francis, 21
Keough, Francis P., Archbishop, 116
Kerby, William J., 295
Kidd, Angelique, 314
Kidd, Christopher, 267, 276n79
Kidd, Isaac, Jr., 48, 148n78, 266–67, 275–76, 289, 314–16, 328–29
Kidd, Isaac, III, 267, 291
King, Ernest, 72
King, Ira, 174–76
King, Martin Luther, Jr., 195–97
King, Randy, 44, 199
Kinlaw, Dennis, 265
Kirk, Russell, 121
Kirkpatrick, Thomas, 48n40
Kirstein, James, 271
Knox, Frank, 45n29, 62
Koch, Alfred, 294–95
Koeneman, Alvin, 269, 323–24
Korean War, 134, 137, 162–63, 170, 211

Laboon, Agnes, 331
Laboon, Catherine. *See* Reilly, Catherine
Laboon, Claire, 27
Laboon, Joan (Sister Joan), 27, 50, 313, 331
Laboon, Joe, 27, 284, 301, 313f, 315, 326, 328, 332–33
Laboon, John (nephew), 241
Laboon, John F. (father), 27, 32–33, 50, 60

Index

Laboon, John Francis, Jr. (Jake): academics and, 36–49, 51, 106–7, 110–12, 114–16; in Alaska, 175–81; as athlete, 2, 34, 47–59, 59–61, 112–13, 205, 245, 253; Berkeley sabbatical, 290–93; at Carnegie Institute of Technology, 32, 37–39; Central Catholic High School and, 2, 33–35, 38, 40, 106, 333; at Chaplain School, 137–43; as circuit rider, 162–69; CNATRA and, 243–45; command of LSM-25, 98; death and funeral, 1–2, 314–16; drug abuse program advocacy, 242–43, 247; as Fleet Ballistic Missile Submarine chaplain, 149–60; as Fleet chaplain Atlantic, 277–80; in Florida, 240–48; and fourth vow, 257, 274–75; as FRSA officer-in-charge, 261–77; graduation and commissioning, 61–62; Great Depression and, 2, 7, 29–33; in Hawaii, 248–54; high school education, 33–35; illnesses, 82, 275–76, 312–14; Isaac Kidd Jr. friendship, 48, 148n78, 266–67, 275–76, 289, 314–16, 328–29; in Japan as staff chaplain, 162–69; at Jesuit School of Theology, 288, 290, 292; juniorate, 107–8; Laboon Ministry Center, 6, 334; lay leader's program and, 156–57; Manresa-on-Severn and, 4, 49, 288, 298–301, 317, 333–34; military honors awarded to, 98, 232, 237, 266–67, 276–77, 286, 323, 330; military promotions, 98, 130, 169–70, 197, 206, 254, 323; military vocation, 130–31; on morality of war, 94, 156; at Naval Submarine School, 2, 65–67; as Naval Training Center chaplain, 3–4, 80, 161, 169–75, 182, 281, 307; in Navy Chaplain Corps, 3, 5–6, 131–37, 265, 281; in New London, 254–59; novitiate, 104–7; in Okinawa as chaplain, 236–37; ordination, 116, 117f; at Patuxent River Naval Air Station, 140–43; Pearl Harbor and, 2, 74, 79–80, 82–83, 88, 95, 97, 99; personal legacy, 322–27; personal qualities, 4, 48–50, 139, 152–53, 157–59, 164–69, 173–75, 318–22; physical legacy, 327–34; Plebe year, 43, 45–49, 51; Polaris Family Center and, 150–53; Pre-Cana program and, 199; as recruit chaplain, 169–75; regency year, 111–14; religious vocation, 101–4; rescue of W. F. Donnelly, 92, 93n107, 98, 140; retirement from navy, 4, 280–88, 285f, 287f; return to navy after ordination, 129–31; return to peace after World War II, 75–97; "Rip" Miller and, 37–39, 52–53, 55, 57; as 17th Naval District chaplain, 175, 180, 182; in *The Silent Service*, 140; Silver Star awarded to, 2, 97–98, 99, 140, 323, 329–30; at St. Alphonsus Rodriguez Parish, 4, 303–12, 314–15; St. Bernard parish and, 28–29, 116, 301–12; submarine training, 64–67; on *To Tell the Truth*, 141; tertianship, 126–28, 140, 309; 25th anniversary of ordination, 301; as U.S. Naval Academy chaplain, 183, 197–206; as U.S. Naval Academy student, 2, 40–62; USS *Peto* and, 81f, 82–95; on Vatican II, 307–8, 325; as Vietnam war chaplain, 200, 208–9, 225–36, 231f; at Woodstock College, 108–16; Youngster year of, 49, 51; youth and family of, 27–35, 117f, 313f

Laboon, Katherine (Kay), 27, 39

Laboon, Mary Jane, 27, 313, 331

Laboon, Patrice (Sister deLellis), 27, 50, 313

Laboon, Rosemary (Sister Rosemary), 27, 50, 313, 331

Laboon, Tom, 27

Laboon Ministry Center, 6, 334

labor priests, 25–27, 31–32

Laird, Melvin, 214–15

Lambert, Glenn E., 241, 248

Lanning, Richard, 148

Larson, Emery "Swede," 51–54, 56–57

Larson, W. J., Commander, 37–40

lay leader's program, 156–57

Layman's League for Retreats and Social Studies, 293

lay retreat movement, 293–98

League of Laymen's Retreats, 296

Leahy, Bill, 101, 334

Leahy, Bill, Jr., 321

Legion of Merit, 232, 237, 286, 323

LeMasters, C. E., 276

Leonard, Guy, 149–50, 151n99

353

Index

Leo XIII, Pope, 25n56, 122
Lerch, Joseph, 298
Lewis, John L., 26
Linehan, Eugene, 297
Livermore, Samuel, 327
Lloyd, Richard, 296
Lockwood, Charles, 74–75, 87, 89
London Naval Treaty of *1930*, 68
Long, Robert, 65, 158n128
Loyola Retreat House, Md., 296–97
LSM-*25*, 98
Lucey, Robert, Archbishop, 31
Lutz, Robert A., 221
Lyons, Charles, 296

MacArthur, Douglas, 71–72, 168
Malcolm X, 195
Maloney, William, 140
Manitowoc Shipping Company, 75, 99
Manresa-on-Severn, 4, 49, 293–301, 297f, 317, 333–34
Manresa Project, 298
Marbach, Joseph, 176–77
Maritain, Jacques, 69
Marshall, Adam, 132
Marshall, George C., 135
Marshall Plan, 210
McArdle, Joseph, 37
McCarthy, Joseph, 125
McDonald, Douglas, 332
McDonnell, Eugene, 296
McEneany, Joseph A., 296
McEvoy, John, 105–6
McGovern, George, 216
McLaughy, W. H., 174
McNamara, John D., Bishop, 296
McNicholas, John P., Archbishop, 293–94
McQuaid, Bernard, 121
Mead, George G., 240
Mechan, Daniel F., 137
Mellon, Andrew, 19
Mellon, Richard Beatty, 31
Menges, Richard M., 126
Mens Nostra, 293
Meritorious Service Award, 266–67, 276–77
Metzbauer, Frank, 241, 307

Mexican War of *1846*, 132
Meyer, Cardinal Albert, 173
Middleton, J. R., Jr., 88
Midgley, Brian, 156
Midway, Battle of, 72
Midway Island, 72, 82–83, 90, 213
Militia for Christ, 26
Miller, Edgar E. "Rip," 37–39, 52–53, 55, 57
Mitchell, George, 330
Molesworth, Keith, 57
Montgomery, Alice B., 17
Montgomery, George "Monty," 60–61
Montgomery, Melvin, 53
Moody, John, 122
Mooney, Archbishop Edward, 69
Moore, William H. "Dinty," 59–60
Morison, Samuel, 72, 147, 163
Mountbatten, Lord Louis, 163
Muller, Edward, 30
Mullins, Thomas, 137
Murray, John Courtney, 114, 124, 200, 316
Murray, Philip, 26

NAAS Ellyson Field, 246–48, 259
NAS Pensacola, 240, 242–47
NAS Saufley Field, 240–48
National Catholic Welfare Conference, 24–26, 69
National Conference of Catholic Men, 294
National Labor Board, 26
National Liberation Front (Viet Cong), 211, 217
Naval Logistics Pacific, 252–53
Naval Station Great Lakes, 3–4, 80, 161, 169–75, 182, 281, 307
Naval Station Kodiak, 175–81
Naval Submarine School, New London, 65–67
NAVLOGPAC. *See* Naval Logistics Pacific
NAVSTA Great Lakes. *See* Naval Station Great Lakes
Navy Chaplain Corps, 131–37, 265
NCWC. *See* National Catholic Welfare Conference
Neal, Arthur, 73
Nelson, William, 75–76, 79

Newby, Claude D., 137, 221
Newman, William C., Bishop, 312
Newman Club, 2, 50, 199–200, 207
New York Charity Organization Society, 17
New York Times, 214
Ngo Dinh Diem. *See* Diem, Ngo Dinh
Nguyen Van Thieu. *See* Thieu, Nguyen Van
Niles Register, 11
Nimitz, Chester, 44, 72, 96, 133–34
Nixon, Richard M., 208, 213–15, 234
NLF. *See* National Liberation Front
North, Oliver, 232–33, 306–7
North Vietnamese Army, 212–14, 217, 229
Nugent, David, 103
NVA. *See* North Vietnamese Army

O'Brien, Eugene, 206
O'Brien, John, 195
O'Brien, William Francis X., 21
O'Callahan, Joseph, 134
Ochenrider, Gordon "Bud," 59n80, 60–61
O'Connor, John, Cardinal, 5–6, 8, 223–25, 230, 232, 261, 269, 279–80, 284–85, 292, 315–16, 322, 324, 328, 330–31
O'Connor, Michael, Bishop, 21
O'Dea, Thomas F., 124, 193
O'Donnell, Joseph, 136
O'Keefe, Sean, 330
Olds, Robin, 59
Olmstead, Frederick Law, Jr., 18
Osborne, James, 154
O'Toole, George Barry, 26
Ottaviani, Alfredo, 188–89
Our Lady of the Fields Parish, 299–300

Pacem in Terris, 155–56
Pacific Theater, 78f, 165–67
Padcock, George, 45
Palmer, Bud, 60
Panuska, Al, 256–57
Paresce, Angelo, 108
Paris, Norman M., 247
Paris Peace Talks, 213
Parker, Herbert, 302
Parker, Maynard, 214–16
Parks, Charles, 132

Parsons, W. E., 255
Pasquet, Robert, 303
Patuxent River Naval Air Station, 141–42
Pax Christi, 220, 331
Pearl Harbor attack, 67–68, 73
Penna, Anthony, 13–14
Pfaff, William, 215
Phelan, Richard, Bishop, 22
Pittsburgh: anti-Catholicism, 23; Catholicism, 15–16, 20–27; flood, 32; flu pandemic of *1918*, 20; historical overview, 10–20; Holy Name Society, 25, 178; immigration and, 12, 14–16, 21–22; as industrial center, 11–12; labor priests in, 26–27; organized labor in, 14–15; physical geography and, 9–10, 17, 22; Pittsburgh Forward program, 20; Pittsburgh Survey, 17–18; political corruption in, 19; population growth, 11; religion in, 15–16, 20–22; social problems, 14, 17–18
Pittsburgh, Diocese of, 21
Pittsburgh Survey, 17–19
Pius XI, Pope, 25, 293
Plan Orange, 67
Plessy v. Ferguson, 195
Plozay, Casey, 53
Plummer, Mary, 267
Polaris Family Center, 150–53
Polaris program, 145–47
Popst, Roy, 197
Porter, David, 42
Post, William, 165–66
Powell, Ira M., 175
Power, Glen, 173
Pownall, Charles, 89
Progress, 18, 20
Purdham, A. E., 255

Quadragesimo Anno, 25

Raborn, William Francis "Red," 145, 147, 153–54
Rahner, Karl, 190
Rankin, H. A., 164–65
Rawlins, R. D., 258–59
Reaves, James, 197

Index

recruit chaplain, Laboon as, 169–75
Recruit Training Command, Great Lakes NTC, 171–73
Reigner, Paul W., 138, 173
Reilly, Catherine, 27, 29, 50
Reilly, Daniel, 255–56
Reilly, John, 27
Republic of Vietnam campaign medal, 237
Rerum Novarum, 25
Rey, Anthony, 132
Rice, Charles Owen, 26
Ricker, Richard W., 137
Rickover, Hyman G., 144, 146–47
Riera, R. E., 180
Rivero, Horatio, 185
Rixey, George, 133
Roberts, Peter, 17
Roche, Douglas, 192
Rodriguez, Alphonsus, St., 302
Russell, G. L., 86
Russell Sage Foundation, 17–18
Ryan, John, 26
Ryan, Joseph T., 284

Sacred Heart Church, Groton, Conn., 157
St. Alphonsus Rodriguez Parish, Md., 4, 301–12, 313f, 314–15
St. Bernard Parish, Mt. Lebanon, Pa., 28–29, 33, 116, 301
St. Isaac Jogues, 104, 127
St. Joseph's Preparatory School, Philadelphia, 111–14
St. Mary's Parish, Annapolis, 2
St. Patrick's Cathedral, New York, 276
St. Patrick's Church, Pittsburgh, 21, 32
St. Paul of the Cross Monastery, Pittsburgh, 23
St. Paul the Apostle, Pittsburgh, 21, 31
Santorum, Rick, 332
Saufley, Richard Caswell, 240
Scaffe, R. C., 57
Schindler's List (movie), 333–34
Schlichte, George, 49
Sciosa, Frank, 81, 88
The Secular City (Cox), 193
Seiders, Marlin D., 261

Sestini, Benedict, 302
17th Naval District, 175, 180, 182
Shannon, James, Bishop, 192
Shannon, Peter M., 192
Shea, C. R., 57
Shea, John Gilmary, 127
Sheady, Terrence, 293, 295
Sheen, Fulton, Bishop, 152
Sheerin, John B., 119–20, 126, 218
Shehan, Lawrence, Cardinal, 218
Shelton, Donipham, 49
Shiel, Bernard, Bishop, 31
Shrine of the North American Martyrs, Auriesville, N.Y., 126–27
Siegfried, Carl, 53
Siegfried, Clyde, 60–61
The Silent Service (movie), 140
Silver Star, 2, 97–98, 99, 140, 323, 330
Simon, Roger, 12
Sisters of Mercy, 50, 104, 302, 313
Sisters of St. Joseph, 28–29
Slovak Catholic Federation, 22
Smith, Herbert, 190–91
Smith, Ignatius, 152
Smith, Michael, 202–3, 335
Snyder, Marvin E., 138
Snyder, Ted, 158
Sobran, Joseph, 121
Society of Jesus: Laboon's novitiate and juniorate, 104–8; Laboon's ordination of, 116; Taura Bay, Japan, 168–69; theology and philosophy, 108–16. *See also* Wernersville, Pa.; Woodstock College
Somers affair, 41
Southeast Asia Collective Defense Treaty, 212
South Vietnamese Army, 213–15, 234–35
Sparks, S. A., 241–42
Spellman, Francis, Cardinal, 120, 133, 176, 218
Spencer, Philip, 41
Spielberg, Steven, 334
Sponga, Edward, 181
Springer, Robert, 218
SSBN. *See* Fleet Ballistic Missile Submarine program
Stark, Harold, 67–69, 93
Steel Town, USA. *See* Pittsburgh

Steffens, Lincoln, 13
Sterling, Yates, Jr., 143
Stevens, Jim, 158
Strassle, Ray, 60–61
Sturma, Michael, 68–70, 93
Submarine Combat Insignia, 323
submarines: malfunctioning torpedoes, 73–74, 80, 86; strategic use in Pacific Theater, 67–75, 96–97. *See also* Fleet Ballistic Missile Submarine program; *and vessels by name*
Suhard, Emmanuel, Cardinal, 126
Sullivan, Mark, 197, 206
Support Unit Detachment Charlie, 163
Swanson, Eugene S., 263
Swartz, Ray, 57
Swauger, John, 11

Taylor, Maxwell, 212
Taylor, Prince, 251
Taylor, Zachary, 132
Tet Offensive, 7, 213
Thieu, Nguyen Van, 213–14
Third Marine Division, 223, 225–37
Third Plenary Council of Baltimore (*1884*), 69
Thomas, J. M., 244
Thomas, William, 50, 62
Thorman, Donald J., 191
Time, 219, 221
Tojo, Hideki, 97
Tonkin Gulf Resolution, 212
torpedoes, malfunctioning of, 73–74, 80, 86
Train, Harry, 164, 168, 277–79, 281–83, 285f, 286, 328
Training Air Wing Seven, 240–41
Training Squadron Five (VT-*5*), 240–41
Training Squadron One (VT-*1*), 240–41
Trost, Carlisle A. H., 315
Trower, Ross, 139, 148, 249–51, 281, 283, 291, 308, 325
Truman, Harry, 209–10
Truman Doctrine, 210

Underwood, G. W., 84, 86
Upshur, Abel P., 40

U.S. Civil Rights Commission, 196
U.S. Naval Academy: AAU accreditation of, 43; academic program changes at, 184–87; accelerated training program at, 43–44; Bancroft Hall, 42–44, 46, 198, 203–4; beginnings of, 40–42; Folsom board of, 184–85; football season *1940*, 47–48; football season *1941*, 52–56; football season *1942*, 56–59; John Francis Laboon Award for Distinguished Service to Humanity, 334; Laboon as chaplain, 183, 197–206; Laboon Ministry Center, 6, 334; lacrosse season *1942*, 59–61; in *1960*s, 184–87; Pearl Harbor and, 45, 56; physical expansion, 44–45; Plebe Indoctrination Program, 184, 198; Pre-Cana program, 199; Trident Scholars Program, 186
USS *Ajax* (AR-6), 167
USS *Arizona* (BB-*39*), 48, 56n68
USS *Arleigh Burke* (DDG-*51*), 329
USS *Bushnell* (AS-*15*), 74–75
USS *Capodanno* (FF-*1093*), 327
USS *Ethan Allen* (SSBN-*608*), 155
USS *Fulton* (AS-*11*), 72n28, 76
USS *George Washington* (SSBN-*598*), 145, 149–51, 153–54, 155f
USS *Laboon* (DDG-*58*), 6, 8, 283, 329–32, 331f
USS *Lexington* (CVT-*16*), 92, 169, 242
USS *Livermore* (DD-*429*), 327
USS *Nautilus* (SSN-*571*), 143–44
USS *O'Callahan* (FF-*1051*), 327
USS *Ozark* (LSV-*2*), 143
USS *Patrick Henry* (SSBN-*599*), 145, 149–51, 154–55
USS *Perch* (SS-*313*), 80, 82, 95
USS *Peto* (SS-*265*): decommissioning, 97–99; description, 75–76; launching, 77f; lifeguard duty, 89–95; patrols, first five, 76–79; patrols, second five, 80–95; Pearl Harbor and, 79–80, 82–83, 88, 95, 97, 99
USS *Robert E. Lee* (SSBN-*601*), 154
USS *Saratoga* (CV-*60*), 241
USS *Seawolf* (SSN-*575*), 143–44, 148
USS *Shad* (SS-*235*), 83, 88–89
USS *Skate* (SSN-*578*), 89–90, 143–44, 151

Index

USS *Skipjack* (SSN-585), 144
U.S. Steel, 14n17, 19, 31
USS *Thresher* (SSN-593), 88–89, 141
USS *Triton* (SSRN-586), 145, 151
USS *Tullibee* (SSN-597), 145
USS *Tunny* (SSN-282), 145
USS *Will Rogers* (SSBN-659), 155

van Leunen, Paul, 79, 82
Vatican II: call to by John XXIII, 187–88; documents of, 189–90; *Humanae Salutaris*, 188–89; impact on American Catholicism, 190–97, 297–98, 325; in 1960s, 187–97; purposes, 188; sessions, 189–90. *See also* Catholicism
Viet Cong. *See* National Liberation Front
Vietnam Service Medal, 323
Vietnam War: background, 209–17; Catholic church and chaplains in, 217–25; chaplain duties, 226–27; effects in U.S., 196, 208–9; France and, 209–11; Laboon and, 200, 225–36; Legion of Merit, 232, 237, 323; Lyndon Johnson and, 196, 208, 212–13; National Liberation Front, 211, 217; North Vietnamese Army, 212–14, 217, 229; Operation Homecoming, 251; Quang Tri Province, 227–28, 232–34; South Vietnamese Army, 213–15, 234–35; Tet Offensive, 7, 213

Wade, Richard C., 11–12
Walker, Benjamin, 241
Walsh, Michael, 81, 88
Warder, F. B., 144
Washington, George, 10
Washington Conference of 1922, 67–68
Webb, James, 199, 201–2, 233, 300, 315, 325

Weber, Michael P., 12
Wedemeyer, Albert, 163
Wehrle, William, 303
Weigel, Gustave, 114, 120
Welsh, William E., 105
Wernersville, Pa., Jesuit facility, 11, 104–5, 107
Western Mission Society, 20
Westinghouse, George, 19, 144
Westinghouse Electric and Manufacturing Company, 19, 144
Wheeler, Ferdinand, 110
Whelan, Joseph, 286
Whelchel, J. E., 52, 56–57
White, D. M., 181
White, S. A., 258, 281
Wilcoe, Bob, 57
Wilkinson, Eugene, 144
Wilson, John W., 47
wolf-packing, 83–84
Woods, Robert, 17
Woods, W. P., 141
Woodstock College, Md.: beginnings, 108–9; building at, 109f; educational studies, 110–11, 114–16, 126; religious formation, 109–10
Works Progress Administration (WPA), 31–33
Wright, John, Cardinal, 124–25

Young, Merle N., 138
Young, S. M., 45

Zahn, Gordon C., 119, 219–21
Zoller, John, 225–28
Zumwalt, Elmo, 49

www.ingramcontent.com/pod-product-compliance
Lightning Source LLC
Chambersburg PA
CBHW031404290426
44110CB00011B/252